CLARK PUBLIC LIBRARY

3 9502 00135 8449

OFFICIALLY
DISCARDED

CLARK PUBLIC LIBRARY

956.7044   Livingston, Gary,
Liv   1942-

            Fallujah, with
            honor.

D1496145

CLARK PUBLIC LIBRARY
303 WESTFIELD AVENUE
CLARK, NJ 07066
732 – 388 – 5999

Fallujah, With Honor

First Battalion, Eighth Marine's Role in Operation Phantom Fury

Gary Livingston

Caisson Press

956.7044
LIV
10-29-07 UT

Fallujah, With Honor
First Battalion, Eighth Marine's Role in Operation Phantom Fury

Caisson Press / December 2005
Second Edition/July 2007

Book Jacket Design by Amber Dail

Cover Photo taken by Marine Corporal Chaverii
FRONT : Left, kneeling and facing left is Lance Corporal Agustin Garcia
Left, standing is Lance Corporal Michael Pristavec
Right, foreground with green backpack is Lance Corporal Jeremy Castellucci
Right, behind Castellucci is Corporal Justin Best
BACK: left, Lance Corporal AJ Parsons
Middle, Corporal Jake Jarvis
Right, Lance Corporal Hector Orrantia

No part of this book may be reproduced or transmitted in any form or by any means, electronic or mechanical, including photocopying, recording, or by any information storage and retrieval system, without the written permission of the publisher, except where permitted by law.

Library of Congress Catalog number: 2005909542
ISBN: hardcover 192872406X

Manufactured in the United States of America

Clark Public Library - Clark, N.J.

ALSO BY GARY LIVINGSTON

An Nasiriyah, The Fight for the Bridges
Tears of Ice, The Littlest Soldiers
Cradled In Glory, The Georgia Military Institute
Among the Best Men the South Could Boast, The Fall of Fort McAllister
Fields of Gray, The Battle of Griswoldville

OTHER BOOKS FROM CAISSON PRESS

I Am My Brother's Keeper, Journal of a Gunny in Iraq
Written by Gunnery Sergeant Jason K. Doran, USMC (Ret)

When Johnny Doesn't Come Marching Home, A Mother's Story of
the Price for Freedom
Written by Rhonda Winfield

This book is dedicated to all those who fought in the Battle for Fallujah.

TABLE OF CONTENTS

"The Conventional army loses if it does not win. The Guerilla wins if he does not lose."
Henry Kissinger

Acknowledgements

I would like to thank all of the Marines who took the time to share their experiences of the Battle of Fallujah. This book is a patchwork of their stories and objective experiences in Fallujah. I wish I could have interviewed every Marine in the battalion for I know they all shared in the fight and have accounts of the action. I personally interviewed ninety-one Marines. Sixty Marines were interviewed at Battalion 1/8's Headquarters and barracks on Camp Lejeune and the remainder were interviewed by phone.

I appreciate the assistance given me by the Camp Lejeune Public Affairs Office, especially Second Lieutenant Barry Edwards who led me to the right Marines I needed to see in order to write *Fallujah, With Honor*.

I would especially like to thank Lieutenant Colonel Gary Brandl who gave me five hours of his time from his busy schedule to describe the battle and the role of 1/8. He allowed me access to his officers, noncoms and the enlisted Marines to gather the information for this book.

A special thanks to Captain Read Omohundro who gave me his accounts of the battle, shared his company report of the battle and most of the photos used in this book. Captain Steven Kahn for his help in coordinating the interviews with other Marines and spending time interviewing with me and answering my many questions on the battalion and battle. My thanks to the *Cajun*, Captain Theodore Bethea II, for sharing his story, company report as well as his pictures of Fallujah. Also, thanks to First Lieutenant Paul Steketee who provided the battalion's yearbook of service in Iraq and videos of the Marines in the city for my use in this book. And Staff Sergeant Corey Lohr for sharing his personal letters home to his wife describing his time in Fallujah. Second Marine Division Combat Camera members, Corporal Trevor Gift, Corporal Cheverri and Staff Sergeant Knauth took most of the photos used.

Over the six months of gathering accounts of the battle, I was on base so often I began to feel that I had become an honorary Battalion 1/8 Marine. I have talked to many Marines but the Esprit that I found for the battalion and the Corps among those officers, noncoms and young Marines was unmatched.

I would like to thank my wife Terry for her help. I would also like to thank Lynn Khanna from Camp Lejeune's Marine Corps Association for urging me to write this book. I would like to acknowledge Karen Fredrickson, the unofficial 1/8 historian, for her assistance in acquiring other interviews and editing help for the second edition of this book. Also thanks to former Lieutenant John Harrold USN for additional editing. My heartfelt thanks to the parents of the fallen Marines for sharing their memories and letters of their sons.

I saved my last thanks for all those young eighteen to twenty-two year old Marines who do what is ask of them time and time again. Where does the Marine Corps find such fine young men who are willing to give their all for the defense of our country? We owe them so much. This book is for and about them, and the sacrifices they make.

Foreword

On October 23, 1983, United States Marines were stationed in Beirut, Lebanon as part of a peacekeeping force and headquartered in a large compound building at the Beirut International Airport. Part of the force that was quartered in the compound were Marines from 1st Battalion, 8th Regiment, from Camp Lejeune, North Carolina.

Battalion 1/8 was first activated in 1940. The unit had participated in five major World War II campaigns and was deployed to Lebanon in 1958. It wouldn't be the last time they would be called on to assist that nation. Battalion 1/8 also participated in the Cuban Missile Crisis and the intervention in the Dominican Republic. In 1983 they joined the multinational peacekeeping force and went back to Lebanon.

On October 23, at 0622, while most of the Marines were still in their bunks, a large yellow Mercedes delivery truck, not unlike many other trucks that came and went around the barracks daily, slowly entered the international airport. The truck turned on an access road that led straight to the Marine barracks and circled menacingly around the parking lot. The driver suddenly turned the truck towards the Marine compound and raced forward. It easily crashed through a chain link and barbed wire fence and roared between two sentry posts, manned by Marines with unloaded weapons. The truck continued racing toward the front door of the building some 450 feet away. The yellow truck picked up speed as it buried itself into the main lobby of the Marine barracks.

The driver then detonated explosives with the power equal to more than 12,000 pounds of TNT. The violent explosion immediately crumbled the four-story building, crushing service members who were stationed there to help keep peace in a nation torn by a brutal religious civil war. In seconds the building had been transformed into a pile of rubble. It was the bloodiest day in the Corps' history since World War II, when Marines had fought to take bloody Iwo Jima. Two hundred and twenty Marines from the 1st Battalion, 8th Regiment lost their lives along with eighteen Navy personnel and three Army soldiers who were also staying at the compound. Sixty other Americans in the building were injured in the violent explosion. This became one of the darkest hours in Marine Corps history.

Actual preparations for the bombing had begun in September of 1983. Iran played a central role and operational coordination was conducted from the Iranian Embassy in Damascus, Syria. Syria was responsible for the technical aspects of the attack and the Palestine Liberation Organization was in charge of operational security. The truck used in the attack on the Marine compound had come from an assembly plant in Iran. Syria eventually gave the final go-ahead for the bombing attack.

The explosion that ripped through the Marines' barracks was determined by FBI forensic investigators to be, at the time, "the single largest non-nuclear explosion on earth since World War II." The bomb composition used in this devastating attack would later be the same as that used in the bombing of the World Trade Center in New York City in February 1993.

Battalion 1/8 would return to the Middle East seven years later for Operations Desert Shield and Desert Storm. In March 2003 they arrived in Mosul, Iraq, where they fought in various combat operations as part of Operation Iraqi Freedom. In June of 2004 they returned again to Iraq to the base at Al Asad. Al Asad is the air hub for all of western Iraq. But Fallujah would eventually be Battalion 1/8's calling in that country.

One of the young Marines at the barracks was a young Second Lieutenant David Hough a member of Bravo Company, 1/8. Hough would be one of the lucky ones to survive the deadly blast in 1983.

Fallujah
Setting the Stage

The ancient city of Fallujah, known as the city of mosques, is located in volatile Al Anbar Province. It lays claim to one hundred and thirty mosques evenly spread throughout the city. The city is situated forty miles northwest of Iraq's capital, Baghdad, in the area recently known as the Sunni Triangle. The 300,000 residents of Fallujah, mostly Sunni, strongly supported the brutal dictatorship of Saddam Hussein while he was in power. Many members of Hussein's Ba'ath Party had come from the city of mosques.

Fallujah is located at the edge of a desert and sprawls two and one-half miles across the flat landscape from west to east and about the same distance north to south. To the west of Fallujah lies the Euphrates River. Two key bridges cross over the meandering waterway that flows to the south. The most southern bridge brings Highway 10 into the city. It is a paved, modern, six-lane highway with a raised median strip. Highway 10 bisects the city from west to east, and along this thoroughfare lies most of the commercial businesses. The industrial area is located in the eastern part of the city and the nicer neighborhoods are located in the southern section.

The city is laid out in a fairly random pattern, even for Iraqi standards. Zoning distinguishing between residential, business, and industrial is almost nonexistent. Walls and courtyards generally line the narrow streets. The houses are densely packed in blocks that touch, or almost touch, the adjacent houses to the sides and rear. The houses are mostly made of brick or cinder block and covered with a thick layer of mortar. Most of the windows in the homes are barred and covered with some sort of blinds or curtains. Almost all of the homes have an enclosed courtyard for privacy. Upon entry into the courtyard, there is usually an outhouse since most homes have no sanitary sewer system. The rooftops of the houses overlook the courtyards and alleyways. The exterior doors of the homes are sturdy, made of metal and wood, some with metal grates covering the door. Quite a few of the homes have two or three entrances leading into them from the adjacent street or alleyways.

During the first Gulf War, the city was hard hit by the Coalition air forces. Laser-guided bombs destroyed a key bridge, and many civilians were killed in the air strikes.

Fallujah was actually one of the country's more peaceful places during Operation Iraqi Freedom in 2003 and the period immediately after the war ended, but things soon changed for the worse for the Coalition.

In April 2003, schools were beginning to open again in many parts of Iraq. It was mostly due to the initiative of parents and teachers in local communities, many of whom worked unpaid for several months while the nation tried to pull itself together. A school in Fallujah was being used as an Army barracks, and a delegation of locals went to have a word with the U.S. Army whose Area of Operation included the city. They complained that the U.S. Army was ignoring them because they were Sunnis.

The citizens went to the streets to demonstrate. On April 28, 2003, the city became enraged when fifteen demonstrating civilians were killed by U.S. troops who said they were defending themselves from attack. Afterward, conditions in the city grew steadily worse as the locals perceived the Americans as their enemy.

Coming and going between Fallujah and Syria, Jordan or Saudi Arabia is not much of a problem if you are not being too conspicuous. The city is also located very close to Baghdad where there are numerous soft targets for terrorists.

Insurgents began filtering into the city with piles of cash, strange accents, and a militant vision of Islam that was at once foreign and fearsome to Fallujah's residents after nearly thirty years of Saddam Hussein's secular regime. The foreigners came from Saudi Arabia, Jordan, Iran, and several countries in North Africa. The Arab fighters told the wary residents of Fallujah that God favors believers who give up their homes and travel to defend Islam. They quoted from the *Qu'ran,*

Islam's holy book, "God has preferred the strivers above the sedentary with a great reward. Whoever emigrates in the cause of God will find in the earth many a refuge, wide and spacious."

The Arab visitors portrayed themselves as the Mujahideen, the storied emigrants who journeyed with the Prophet Muhammad to the Holy City of Medina, Saudi Arabia. The tribes of Fallujah were cast as the Ansar, the helpers who offered the prophet's people refuge and loyalty.

Out of custom and necessity, tribal locals offered their Arab guests sanctuary, and in return they were promised help in keeping American forces out of their city. This trust given to the foreign fighters would eventually prove a grave mistake for the people of Fallujah. Their promises of protection would be left unfulfilled. But mainly the foreign fighters were well armed, much better armed than the locals.

Between November 2003 and January 2004 insurgents brought down three U.S. helicopters killing twenty-five servicemen in the Fallujah area. By March 2004, the insurgents and foreign fighters had a vise-like grip on the city of mosques. The terrorists began controlling the city with checkpoints and roadblocks on the highways leading to and from the commandeered town. The city had become the insurgents' own little fiefdom.

The rebels began imposing a Taliban-like interpretation of Islamic law in the city. Suspects accused of drinking alcohol or refusing to grow beards were flogged publicly. Women who failed to cover their hair or remove their makeup were subjected to public humiliation. Anyone accused of spying for the Americans was summarily executed on the spot. These acts began to alienate the citizens of Fallujah from the foreign fighters who they had thought were their allies.

On March 29, 2004, on another hot sunny day in Iraq, a Blackwater USA security team was traveling in two vehicles escorting a food supply truck for the U.S. military air base located in Habbaniyah, near Fallujah. Blackwater USA was a contract firm, based out of North Carolina, providing security training and defense service for the military. The four security members were Scott Helvenston, Jerry Zovko, Michael Teague and Wesley Batalona. They were riding in two non-armored sport utility vehicles along Highway 10 through the center of Fallujah. All four well-armed contractors had served in the U.S. military before being employed by Blackwater.

The contractors had decided on a short cut that brought them right through the heart of Fallujah, but they hadn't informed the Marines of their intended route. As the small convoy traveled along Highway 10 they began to get bogged down in the local traffic. The contractors were traveling straight into an ambush that had been hurriedly set up by Iraqi and foreign insurgents. Fallujah residents were considered by many of their Iraqi countrymen as being an unruly and unsavory group. Many of the city's citizens stood around and watched as the terrorists set up their deadly ambush.

When the Blackwater security team slowed their vehicles down at an intersection, the foreign fighters sprang their bloody ambush. Insurgents attacked them with rounds of RPGs and AK-47 fire from open windows and rooftops in the surrounding shops. The contractors' two vehicles were both hit simultaneously. Machine gun fire traced patterns on the windows and doors of the white SUVs. The perpetrators of the brutal ambush jumped in a vehicle and sped away before the U.S. military entered the city to investigate. This is what the residents of the city had waited for; men and young boys began to gather around the two smoking vehicles.

The wounded contractors survived the initial attack, but they were shaken and stunned from the sudden violent explosions. When they tried to get their bearings and return fire, an Iraqi mob overwhelmed them and brutally dragged them from their vehicles. Cheering and screaming, the mob finished off the wounded contractors. The four security men were mutilated, stoned, burned, and beaten with iron pipes by the irate mob.

An Iraqi citizen of Fallujah gave a chilling description of how the wounded men were dragged from their car begging for their lives. "They had gasoline splashed on them and were set alight," he said.

Two of the burned bodies were hung from a bridge in the city. The Iraqi mob found some white paint and wrote in Arabic, *Fallujah-Graveyard of the Americans,* on one of the bridge's trestles. Conveniently, a reporter from a foreign television network was on hand to film the gruesome murders, and the pictures were broadcast defiantly around the globe. The entire world saw that Fallujah was spinning dangerously out of control and Iraq could soon follow.

Several rebel sources confirmed that the most hunted man in Iraq, al Zarqawi, had settled in Fallujah. On September 11, 2004, an audio recording that was posted on the Internet by al Zarqawi boasted that Muslim holy warriors had humiliated the Americans through "the brotherhood of jihad, both Muhajireen and Ansar."

The Marines were finally sent in to lay siege to the out of control city and eventually subdue it. Heavy fighting raged off and on around the periphery of the city for over a month. The fighting between Marines and enemy forces was fierce at times. Close-in air support was called in as the Marines entered the city.

A Marine from El Paso, Texas, Corporal Howard Lee Hampton, Jr. recalled the bitter fighting in March and April of 2004, "I remember going into the city in the amtrac and hearing bullets hit off the sides. Once we got in the city, we had hundreds and hundreds of people trying to kill us. We survived in Fallujah because everyone put the Marine next to him ahead of himself. Everyone did so much more than they had to."

One day of fighting in Fallujah, April 26, 2004, saw more top medal nominations than any other day in all of March and April of that year. The Marines felt they were within three or four days of beating back the insurgents and quelling the uprising, when they were suddenly pulled out by U.S. government civilian authorities who believed the operation was only alienating Iraqis.

On April 30, 2004, a former Baathist, Major General Muhammad Latif stepped forward and proposed organizing a Fallujah Brigade to take over and police the city. The American government, not wanting to commit troops to an urban fight, quickly agreed. A cease-fire was brokered and a stalemate was created—the insurgents controlled Fallujah and the Marines controlled the surrounding countryside.

Al Zarqawi loyalists had won favor from some of the citizens of Fallujah during the Marine pullback after the March and April offensive. The foreign fighters took credit for the outcome, and recruited even more outsiders. "When the Marines stepped back in April, the foreigners grew stronger so they persuaded their friends to come and help them hold the victory," said thirty-two-year-old Fallujah resident, Ali Jarallah. The insurgents also began to run weapons around the Marines' blockade and into the volatile city.

Maybe the American civilian leaders should have heeded General George Patton's advice, "Once you've decided, don't delay. A good plan violently executed now is better than a perfect plan next week. Don't let the sons-a-bitches stand still long enough to dig a foxhole." The insurgents now had time to regroup, dig in and prepare for the next Marine onslaught that they knew was sure to come. Would the delay cause more U.S. casualties and how many more would lose their lives when they would eventually have to take the out of control city again?

Major General Muhammad Latif was given a green light by the U.S. to organize a force of 1,100 men to help police the city. The Fallujah Brigade was hurriedly equipped, armed and trained and salaried by the United States government. Hundreds of AK-47s were brought in and handed over to Latif's men. They were to patrol the tumultuous city alongside Iraqi Police and Iraqi National Guardsmen. They were to bring law and order back to the city and quell the insurgent uprising that was taking place. Many of the Fallujah Brigade members were former Saddam loyalists, and among them, many had been involved in the previous month's defense of Fallujah against the Marines. It was as if the U.S. was putting wolves in sheep's clothing, to watch the flock.

Meanwhile, after taking over the city, brigade members began integrating themselves among the various Mujahideen resistance fighters and still collecting paychecks from the U.S. military. To top it all off, the U.S. had helped arm their future enemies. An enemy they would have to eventually militarily deal with.

A wave of foreign hostage-takings, many ending with gruesome beheadings broadcast for the entire world to see, began to become a common occurrence in Fallujah. Al Zarqawi stepped forward to claim responsibility for massive bombings that spilled the blood of hundreds of innocent Iraqis. Fallujah's citizens began to draw distinctions between their homegrown fighters, who favored military and police targets, and the foreigners. The center of the Iraqi insurgency was now centered on Fallujah and it was attracting hard-core foreign fighters who weren't afraid to fight and to die.

A young Fallujah resident, Hudaifa, turned against the insurgents in the city when he witnessed a Yemeni fighter whipping an Iraqi in the public square. He recalled his humiliation. "An outsider beating an Iraqi in his own town? It's such a shame for us," he said. Although the Iraqis in Fallujah were turning from the foreign terrorists, it didn't necessarily mean that they were turning toward the U.S. and Iraq's U.S. backed interim government.

Outside the city the Marines chafed at the sniper fire and at the gall of the insurgents who boasted to the world's media that all they wanted was for the Marines to come in and try and get them. In early September, the boil of Fallujah came to a head when Marines slugged it out with members of their supposed ally, the Fallujah Brigade, which left four members of the brigade dead on the streets of the city.

The Fallujah Brigade lasted only four and one-half months. After the brigade was disbanded in September, Major General Latif showed whose side he was really on when he said, "They leave us no option but to join the resistance." Latif made no mention of his alliance with the U.S. or the Iraqi Interim government who was paying his salary and arming and paying his men. The loaded AK-47s would now be used against U.S. forces if they dared to come in to Fallujah.

The U.S. had no option but to go back to the drawing board and devise a plan that would pacify the city and that plan would definitely include the U.S. Marines. When the U.S. military began planning to retake Fallujah, they dubbed the plan, *Operation Dawn*.

Hearing of these plans spurred the local tribes and Iraqi fighters to immediately step forward and try to negotiate with the U.S. backed Iraqi government. In several of these meetings Iraqi rebels, negotiators, and residents of Fallujah, insisted that it was the foreign fighters who eventually scotched a peaceful settlement in Fallujah, not them.

American military officials believed that many of the attacks carried out by the insurgents elsewhere in Iraq were planned, trained, and outfitted in Fallujah. By retaking the city they hoped to turn the tide against the terrorists in Iraq. November 1, 2004 was the first day of voter registration and the day for candidates to sign up to be in the January 30, 2005 Iraqi election. It would be the first election in Iraq since the fall of Saddam. Fallujah had to be cleared out in time for this first step in Iraq's move toward democracy. Fallujah had become the major flashpoint in a nation of flashpoints and now it was time to call in the Marines.

Operation al-Fajr (Dawn)
Operation Phantom Fury

Operation Dawn, so named to signal a new day for Fallujah residents, was intended to suppress the insurgents and wrest control of the rebellious, dusty, sprawling city forty miles northwest of Baghdad, from the insurgents. Originally, the U.S. Department of Defense had named the attack of Fallujah, *Operation Phantom Fury*, but the Iraqi Defense Minister renamed it, *al Fajr*, Arabic for dawn. The Marines would remember it and continue to refer to the attack on the city as, *Operation Phantom Fury*.

The oncoming storm that was about to break over Fallujah had the complete approval of the interim Iraqi Prime Minister, Iyad Allawi. In a televised news conference to his nation and to the world, Allawi said, "We are determined to clear Fallujah of the terrorists. Today I have reached the conclusion that the terrorists and armed groups don't want a peaceful settlement." Allawi threatened military action unless al Zarqawi was handed over to his interim government. Obviously, Allawi had blamed much of Iraq's mayhem on al Zarqawi and other foreigners, minimizing the homegrown opposition to his interim government.

Prior to launching the operation against Fallujah, Interim Prime Minister Allawi declared a state of emergency across Iraq, excluding the quieter Kurdish area to the north. In Fallujah, a round-the-clock curfew was imposed and residents were warned not to carry weapons. Some of the residents trying to re-enter the city were turned away by the tight cordon now in place by the U.S. military.

As the military noose continued to tighten around the city, Lieutenant General Thomas Metz, the commander of U.S. forces in Iraq, told reporters, "I personally believe some of the senior leaders probably have fled (Fallujah.)" So even before the attack on the city, it was feared that al Zarqawi had already escaped.

From the outset of trouble in Fallujah, U.S. military planners were hesitant about committing their forces to the city. They tried reasoning with the populace before bending over backwards and supporting the Fallujah Brigade. Neither gambit had worked and now with the upcoming Iraqi elections growing ever closer, their only option was to use military force—to commit American ground forces to take an urban city. It would be urban warfare at its worst. Mogadishu, Somalia had not only emboldened America's enemies to take refuge in urban environments, but it was also affecting the way the military planned its own operations.

The insurgents watched TV and read newspapers. They knew the U.S. military abhorred urban warfare and that the U.S. had cut and run in Somalia after suffering casualties in an urban fight. The insurgents knew that America was reluctant to commit forces to secure contested cities. They counted on the U.S. not fighting them in urban centers. Because of this, the cities became a magnet to the insurgents, especially the foreign fighters. The rebels naturally went to the urban areas and dared the Americans to join them in a fight to the death.

The realization that Marines and Soldiers were going to have to go door-to-door in Fallujah finally dawned on the Bush administration and the military planners. The U.S. military would have to show their mettle in an urban fight to the death. They would have to show the insurgents that they would meet them head-on and destroy them in Fallujah. The Marines who had suffered casualties in the April fighting outside the city were champing at the bit to settle old scores with the taunting insurgents of Fallujah. Now they would get their chance. Would the dire predictions about urban warfare in Iraq prove groundless, or would the U.S. suffer Hue, Vietnam size casualties taking Fallujah?

Looking at a photomap of the sprawling Fallujah area, the U.S. military planners could see the warren den of houses in the two and one-half square mile city. Each house was capable of harboring snipers that could tie up a battalion for days. They estimated that the city held upwards of 3,000 insurgents. The military planners knew it would be a hard nut to crack. Fallujah had 1,000 city blocks, and according to intelligence reports many contained weapon caches and ammunition storehouses. They had information about factories that were turning out bombs and explosive devices for roadside attacks against their troops elsewhere in Iraq. The military planners had heard of torture chambers being run in the city where beheadings were taking place. They knew they could take the city, but they wanted it with a minimum amount of military and civilian casualties.

The streets were mostly narrow and generally lined with the walls of the houses and courtyards. As the Marine and Army squads were fighting house to house, the walls of the courtyards and buildings channeled them into the kill zones of the streets and alleyways. It would be a three-dimensional fight—front/back, up, and down. They would have to fight down streets, into houses, room to room, floor to floor all the way up to the rooftop. Some houses would have underground tunnels or bunkers. It would be a brutal fight to the finish.

The military planners knew the enemy had grown smarter over the last year. They also knew their main purpose was to kill as many Marines and Soldiers as they could before fading away.

These were the two insurgent groups:

The *martyrs'* main purpose was to kill as many Marines and Soldiers as possible before they, themselves were killed. They were the die-hards, the more dangerous of the two groups of fighters. They expected to die. All of the foreign-born Arab fighters were martyrs, as were some of the die-hard Iraqis.

The *guerillas* wanted to kill as many Marines as they could and fade away to fight again, elsewhere in the city.

Both of the groups, guerillas and martyrs, employed the same weapons: small arms, grenades, rocket propelled grenade launchers (RPGs) and mortars.

D-Day was set for November 7, 2004, 1900 hours (7:00 p.m. Baghdad time). The operation would use six battalions of Marines and Army Soldiers, plus elements of the newly formed Iraqi Army, along with Navy SEALs, Army Rangers and Marine Recon (Reconnaissance) units. Totaling fifteen thousand Marines, Navy, Air Force and Soldiers in all. Each battalion would utilize Iraqi translators during the battle. Marine tank, air and artillery units were also on hand for support.

Shortly before the attack, Task Force Fallujah was cobbled together with three Regimental Combat Teams (RCT). Each RCT had a Light Armored Reconnaissance (LAR) Battalion, two Marine Rifle Battalions reinforced, and one Army Mechanized Infantry Battalion. RCT-1 consisted of 3rd LAR, 3rd Battalion, 5th Marines (Battalion 3/5), 3rd Battalion, 1st Marines (Battalion 3/1) and 2nd Battalion, 7th Cavalry

(Battalion 2/7). RCT-7 was slightly less weighted but still a formidable fighting force. It consisted of 1st Battalion, 8th Marines (Battalion 1/8), 1st Battalion, 3rd Marines (Battalion 1/3), and the 2nd Battalion, 2nd Cavalry (2/2). Marine Battery C, 1/12, would support Battalion 1/8.

The first prerequisite for an urban battle is to seal the city from the outside. Cutting a swath around Fallujah was the job of an Army brigade known as the Black Jack Brigade. The plan called for the Marine dominated RCTs to assault the city while the Black Jack Brigade sealed the city and kept the enemy from re-supplying and bringing in reinforcements. The six-battalion attack would be a sledgehammer blow that would come from the north and drive south through the city.

There would be liberal Rules of Engagement (ROE) for the Marines and Soldiers fighting in the city. Military age males trying to leave the city would be captured or turned back.

The Marines and Soldiers expected a ruthless fight with a brutal enemy. They had been drilled repeatedly on Rules Of Engagement that require strict separation of fighters from civilians.

Before Operation Dawn began, the first fight was to try and get the civilians of Fallujah to leave their homes and flee the city. Coalition Psy Ops (Psychological Operations) forces used loudspeakers, as well as leaflets dropped from planes, to warn civilians of the impending battle for the city and urged residents to evacuate. Coalition forces waited for most of Fallujah's civilian population to leave their city.

The fighting that followed would be some of the fiercest urban warfare fought in American history. It would be compared to the fighting in Hue during the Vietnam conflict. The 30 and 40-year-old men would bravely lead their charges into combat, but the battle would come down, as it always does, to those 18 and 19-year-old Marines and Soldiers who led their fire teams into the inferno known as the Battle of Fallujah. It would come down to the privates, PFCs, lance corporals and corporals of the Corps.

U.S. air strikes began pounding targets in Fallujah, and hopes of any peace quickly vanished. Entire families began fleeing to nearby towns and villages. Sometimes residents who returned to check on their homes found foreign fighters camped out in their living rooms. One resident of Fallujah, Omar Daoud, a 35-year-old truck driver, made his way back into the city during a lull in the bombing. When he opened his front door he was surprised to find eight militants sequestered in the home that his family had recently fled. Of the eight fighters, only two were Iraqis—the rest were Syrian. Once admired as comrades in an anti-American struggle, foreign fighters had now become reviled and blamed for the

U.S. missiles that were flattening their homes and turning Iraq's City of Mosques into a battle zone.

Daoud demanded that the men leave his home immediately. The fighters slowly rose, reached for their weapons and told him he was being impolite. They told him they had come to "defend Iraqis and their honor and their families," Daoud said, "I yelled at them, 'Don't you know where my family is, the ones you came to defend? We're refugees. We are living in a school. If my house is destroyed, who will fix it?"

Daoud had two options. If he tried to kick them out, the militants would kill him as a traitor, and if he stayed, he would most likely die in the constant U.S. air strikes now hitting the city. Daoud took a final look at the insurgents, turned, closed his door and walked away from his home. He made his way out of the city, leaving it to the foreign militants and the U.S. military, now preparing to enter.

Fallujah residents, now mostly displaced, told of hundreds of non-Iraqi Arabs in town before the offensive began. They added that the ties of brotherhood had mostly unraveled, and the remaining foreign fighters had tried to intimidate residents into staying on as human shields against the looming American attack.

A rebel-allied cleric, Sheik Raafa, told of Iraqi rebels so infuriated by the disappearance of their foreign allies that one cell had executed twenty Arab fighters because they left an area they had promised to hold.

A Fallujah construction worker, Abu Ehab, 30, said, "We didn't want the occupation and we didn't want terrorists, and now we have both. I didn't think the Arabs would be so vicious, and I never thought the Americans would be so unmerciful."

During the bombings, someone witnessed a group of the insurgents moving through the streets, "I was with some of the Fallujah fighters earlier. They looked tired, but their spirits were high and they were singing. Recently, many Iraqis from other parts of the country have been joining the local men against the Americans."

U.S. aircraft began dropping leaflets in Fallujah that read:

> "Surrender, you are surrounded. If you are a terrorist, beware, because your last day was yesterday. In order to spare your life, end your actions and surrender to coalition forces now. We are coming to arrest you."

A Marine, Major Holdredge, said many years ago, *"It's entirely appropriate to kill a fly with a sledgehammer."* That's what the U.S. military intended to do in the city of mosques, use the sledgehammer approach on the insurgency. Outside of the city, the sledgehammer would be made up of some fifteen thousand U.S. Marines and Soldiers, with armored columns. They were backed by three thousand newly trained Iraqi troops. All were prepared to enter the city in a two-pronged assault from the north while other forces took up blocking positions around the cordoned off city. These forces would be the anvils.

The insurgents in Fallujah now had enjoyed nearly six months to gather their forces, train, and fortify the city for the coming storm that was to break upon it. They were well dug-in and prepared. The terrorists had set up zones of defense, ammunition supply points, mortar tubes, and had planted IEDs (Improvised Explosive Devices) all over the city. The insurgents were ready to fight and die throughout the city.

One of the battalions tasked to take the city was the First Battalion, Eighth Marines, from Camp Lejeune, North Carolina.

1st Battalion, 8th Marines

The 1st Battalion, 8th Marine Regiment left Camp Lejeune in late June 2004, destination Iraq. Before leaving the Marines said goodbye to their loved ones. The flight took two days. Battalion 1/8's advance party had arrived at Al Asad in early June. The main body of Battalion 1/8 joined their advance unit at Al Asad, Iraq on June 22. They were to replace the Marines of Battalion 3/4 who had put in a long stay and were looking forward to heading back to family and wives in the states. RCT-7 had a small part of the overall base. Tents had been erected and the Marines of 1/8 began settling in. They began running left seat, right seat rides with Marines from 3/4. From these forays out into their zone of operations, they began to learn the lay of the land and potential trouble spots. They also gathered information from the stories the 3/4 Marines told them about their fight in Fallujah in April.

Battalion 1/8 had twelve days to familiarize themselves with the area before the transfer of command. The Lejuene Marines of Battalion 1/8 unloaded equipment and learned their duties while trying to acclimate themselves to the scorching Iraqi heat. They learned which of the many snakes were poisonous and those that were harmless. The Marines walked around with lizards hanging onto their clothes for company and marveled at the giant Camel spiders that wandered around the land they would be calling home for the next seven months.

The transfer of authority took place on our Independence Day, July 4, 2004. Battalion 1/8 assumed the Area of Operation from Rawah, Haditha Dam, Al Asad to ASP (Ammunition Supply Point) Wolf, and the 3/4 Marines happily packed up, wished Battalion 1/8 good luck and urged them to watch their backs and then they went home.

1/8's battalion commander was an imposing Marine, Lieutenant Colonel Gareth Brandl. Just shy of six feet with a solidly built frame, Brandl, 43, a veteran of Iraqi Freedom I, found himself back in country with his battalion. A graduate of Penn State University, the Passaic, New Jersey, native loved the outdoors, especially fishing and hunting. Brandl's wife, Mona Rae, a teacher, and his five-year-old daughter Remington were home in North Carolina. Brandl was the type of Marine that commanded attention just by entering a room. Friends, family and cohorts called him Gary.

Brandl had taken over command of 1/8 from Lieutenant Colonel David Hough aboard Camp Lejeune right before deploying to Iraq. Battalion 1/8s only remaining link to the Beirut bombing, Hough, who had been a young lieutenant in Beirut, Lebanon, would miss going back to the Middle East with his old battalion.

In Battalion 1/8, Brandl had taken command of a veteran core of non-coms, a highly motivated young group of Marines, dedicated officers, many of which, like their commander, would be returning to Iraq for a second tour.

Battalion 1/8's main body stayed about ten days at Al Asad before Brandl, along with his Headquarters and Service Company (H&S Company), Charlie Company, and Bravo Company moved off to their very important objective, the Haditha Dam. Alpha Company stayed put at Al Asad. Upon arriving at the dam, Bravo Company moved off to ASP Wolf.

Haditha Dam, 75 miles from Syria, was a normal looking dam structure with two wings running out from the main spillway. Its military importance was that it supplied nearly one-fifth of all of Iraq's electrical power. The dam stretched out four and one-half miles including the earthen berms built to retain the lake water. A four-lane highway ran across the top of the dam. The highway was blocked by Marines and used only for military purposes. The main part of the dam was only about 800 meters wide. The Azerbaijanis controlled both wings of the dam and the Marines used it for their operating base. In the Marines' section of the structure the dam harbored old office spaces where the Marines set up their base.

The Haditha Dam stood some ten stories tall. On the top floor was located the battalion aid station (BAS), with a four-bed trauma center.

The combat operation center or COC was located on the ninth floor. A large conference room was situated on the eighth floor. A company office, chow hall, port-a-johns and showers were located on the seventh floor. A room the Marines dubbed "The Internet Café," was located on the sixth floor along with the Lieutenant Colonel's office. Company grade officers were billeted on the fifth floor with the junior staff NCOs. The battalion chaplain was located on the third floor. Troop berthing was on the second and third floors for Charlie Company, H & S Company, and Weapons Company Marines. On the first floor, the Marines had set up a small PX and some additional troop berthing.

While stationed at the dam, Battalion 1/8, nicknamed Task Force Hunter by Brandl, conducted operations in support of RCT-1 in the vicinity of Fallujah with half of the battalion, and continued operations at Haditha Dam and ASP Wolf. In this three-and-one-half week stay near Fallujah, Battalion 1/8 suffered their first casualties in Iraq.

On July 20, a sniper, Corporal Todd J. Godwin, 21, from Zanesville, Ohio, was killed in action near Fallujah. He was hit with shrapnel to the back of his neck, just below his kevlar, when an IED exploded on the right side of the Humvee he was riding in. Driving the vehicle was Corporal Nick Ziolkowski and sitting across from Godwin was Corporal Adam Golden. Godwin was seated in the back working the radio and was the only one hit from the deadly flying shrapnel. Also in the Humvee were Corporal Chris Lawler and Sergeant David Battles who were untouched by the explosion.

Riding in a Humvee directly behind Godwin's vehicle was fellow sniper Corporal James Mendenhall. Marine snipers work as a team, spotter and the shooter. "We had passed a lot of people on this mission. Then we saw some kids standing around and pointing at us. We waved at them and usually they would wave back, but not this day. When the IED went off it stunned us for a few seconds."

Riding in the same Humvee as Mendenhall was his team leader, sniper Brad Watson, 22, from Fresno, California. "It was mid morning and I remember seeing an Iraqi wearing a turban pulled down almost over his eyes when I heard what sounded like a gunshot. The man didn't even flinch. We halted and got out and formed a perimeter around Godwin's vehicle. There was a man standing in front of a child. We let them go. Corporal Adam Golden walked over and told me, 'Todd got hit and he doesn't look good at all.' That was the first I had heard he was hit."

Todd Godwin was proud to be part of the U.S. military and especially proud of being a Marine. The epitome of the boy next door, Godwin had wanted to be a Marine since his early high school years. He loved playing basketball and performing martial arts.

Neighbors of Godwin's parents, Bill and Kathy, in Zanesville had tied a yellow ribbon around a post in their front yard and flew the American flag when Todd had been deployed to Iraq. Todd had made sure that the American flag was displayed properly at this parent's home before he left. His family had also hung yellow ribbons on their porch and sent pictures to Todd to show him how proud they were of his service to the country.

Captain Mike Pretus, in command of the battalion's snipers, remembered the first casualty taken in the battalion, "I had just gotten off a shift when a runner came up to my tent and told me Godwin had been killed. I was shocked. I ran to surgical to see Godwin. Before I went in I saw the Humvee, weapons, and the other Marines who had been in the vehicle, and they were covered in blood. I walked back to the tent as Corporal Lawler cleaned the Humvee. Afterwards all of my Marines were very quiet and later Lieutenant Colonel Brandl came over to talk to the Sniper Platoon. Everyone was just in shock. There was no eye contact among the men and Ziolkowski was very shaken up over Godwin's death."

Sniper Platoon Staff Sergeant, Ben Alicea, remembered, "When I heard over the radio that a sniper had been killed I asked who it was? A Marine came over and told me the name of the person who had been hit but I couldn't understand him. He had a strong accent. Finally he said the name slowly. He told me it was Godwin. All I could say was, 'Oh wow.' I immediately went over to Bravo Surgical and saw the Humvee he had been riding in. It was covered in blood. The only person hit was Godwin and an outside mirror on the vehicle."

Captain Pretus took time to write to Todd's parents, "Todd is one of the most honest, hard working and loyal Marines I have ever known. No matter what was going on. Todd always remained happy go lucky."

Lieutenant Colonel Gary Brandl took Godwin's death hard, "He was my first loss in combat. I don't care what unit you're in, that first loss is the hardest."

"Todd's body had been taken to Camp TQ and they forgot his dog tags," Watson recalled. "I took a helicopter over to the camp to put his tags with his body. I also put a sniper round in with Godwin's body bag."

Medic Shawn Johns, who assisted Godwin, said, "Upon returning to Camp Fallujah with Todd's body I could see everyone stop what they were doing and salute as we drove by."

On August 18, two days before his 25th birthday, Sergeant Richard M. Lord, 24, a member of Weapons Company, was on a mounted patrol when his vehicle hit an improvised explosive device just east of Haditha. The popular Marine was in the right front seat when the flying shrapnel hit him. Lord died a short time later on the operating table. Lord was engaged to Rosanna Powers, 22, also a Marine corporal based out of Cherry Point, North Carolina, near Camp Lejeune.

Rosanna Powers' brother, twenty-one-year-old Lance Corporal Caleb Powers had been killed on August 17, the day before her fiancé, Lord. Powers was killed by sniper fire while standing guard duty in Al Anbar province.

Lord and Powers were planning to marry and settle down in Florida to raise their 10-month-old son after his stint with the Marines. Instead, Rosanna Powers attended her brother's funeral in the state of Washington and then flew on to Florida for her fiancé Richard Lord's funeral.

On September 13, two Marines from H&S Company, Lance Corporal Michael J. Halal, 22, from Glendale, Arizona and Lance Corporal Cesar F. Machado-Olmos, 20, from Spanish Fork, Utah, were traveling on a night convoy mission with their headlights turned off. They were on the road between Haditha Dam and Al Asad Air Base when the highback Humvee they were riding in flipped over. Both Marines lost their lives. Machado-Olmos died one week before his 21st birthday.

Battalion 1/8 had been in country for three months and had seen very little of the enemy. There had been a few firefights, but nothing serious. The Marines of Battalion 1/8 were fighting a "faceless enemy" according to their Lieutenant Colonel. Frustration was starting to set in with the Marines of 1/8 with the loss of four of their own.

On October 15, the cigar smoking Lieutenant Colonel Brandl tasked a group of his officers to go to Al Asad to plan the attack on Fallujah should the order come. The planning stage went on for about a week before the officers returned to their base at the dam.

A Michigan State University graduate, by way of the Culver Military Academy, Captain Stephen P. Kahn, 33, had been part of the planning stage at Al Asad. Married and the father of two children, Alexandra and Tanner, the ten year Marine was company commander of Weapons Company. His wife was home on Lejeune with the children. From a military family, his father, Captain Thomas Kahn, was retired from the Navy.

"There are two pieces to combat operations," Captain Kahn said, "One was, hey this is what we train for, let's do it, kind of the Gung Ho side of it. The other side of it, the Marines understand more now than they ever would what the price will be. Everyone knew that if we went to Fallujah we would take casualties, no matter how good we are and how well we train. That's the nature of warfare. I think our mindset at this time was, we'll do what we have to do to accomplish the mission."

The Marines also understood that a move to the insurgent-held stronghold of Fallujah would bring them face-to-face with their, up to this point in time, faceless enemy in Iraq.

Captain Kahn recalled, "Those of us that went to Al Asad submitted our plan and returned to the dam and conducted some other small ops. A couple days after arriving back at the dam, on October 22, we were tasked to go back to Al Asad for final planning to stage into Fallujah."

Lance Corporal Greg Nichols, 19, a native of Holden, Massachusetts, was a member of Weapons Company in Lieutenant Lee's 1st Platoon. Nichols, who planned to go to college when his enlistment was up, recalled hearing about going into Fallujah. "We heard there might be something going down in Fallujah. We talked about it and basically just blew it off. Most Marines thought that if we did go to Fallujah it would be just a ghost town, like Rawah where we had been. We felt everyone would leave."

Weapons Company Marines, mounted in the Humvees they called trucks, were like the cavalry of the Old West, except much better armed. These trucks were armed with .50 caliber machine guns in a turret, Mark-19 grenade launchers, as well as TOW missiles. When the other companies had trouble they called the cavalry of the battalion, Weapons Company, who seemed to arrive in the nick of time with their heavy firepower just like their cousins in the Old West. The trucks in Weapons Company also were tasked with escorting other vehicles around on the battlefield.

With most of the battalion still at the dam center, the battalion staff officers and company commanders met for an emergency conference on the seventh floor. Lieutenant Colonel Brandl passed on information that he had received from regimental commander, Colonel Craig Tucker, of RCT-7. Brandl told his Marines that they would likely be tasked to help take back Fallujah and that they had to be ready. He said that a date had not yet been set and told them to plan as though it would be tomorrow. He ordered them to start packing up, to get the vehicles up and running, and to be ready.

The Marines, hearing this from their commander, tensed up. They had been patrolling around the dam center for four months and had become familiar with the area. The move to Fallujah caught most of them off guard. If they went to Fallujah they knew it would be a tough urban fight. They would suffer casualties. Staff officers knew a lot of preparation and packing had to be done before moving from the dam.

The word filtered down to the grunts. Another of the many young men who joined the service after the horrendous events of 9/11, Lance Corporal David Houck, 25, wrote to his parents in Mount Ulla, North Carolina:

> *Well, I can't say that it's beginning to feel like Christmas, but a change of mood is definitely in the air. We got word two days ago to pack for a change of scenery. Once more, Bravo Co. is scheduled to go back into harm's way in a matter of days. Now obviously, I can't say precisely where I'm going, but it promises to be quite interesting. Apparently, the powers that be have decided they are getting bored and need stimulation in the form of urban combat. Personally, I am looking forward to it. Things have been getting somewhat slow around here, so a new area is actually a pleasant thought. Oh, so that's the bad news and now for the good-physically and mentally, I continue to enjoy excellent health.*

In October the battalion mounted offensive operations in the towns of Hit and Rawah. Firefights netted a few enemy insurgents KIA (killed in action) but it was Fallujah that was continually on everyone's mind.

Captain Kahn remembered his stay at the dam center, "We considered the dam to be a pretty big target, but in terms of living there, mission wise it wasn't too bad. Ironic, living at the dam there was no running water inside the center. None of the restrooms or showers worked. We couldn't swim in the lake. It just wasn't clean enough. Pretty much everything was running into it. Our Doc kept checking the water and it never got within what he would feel comfortable with, so we set up our own showers."

Lieutenant Colonel Gary Brandl finally got the order to move his battalion to near Fallujah. On October 26, 2004, he led an advance team of key leaders, including company commanders, to find quarters for the battalion who were scheduled to arrive in two days.

"We found a really good position in an old Iranian Training Camp (ITC) where defectors from Iran had been trained. This place had been completely bombed out, but the thick walls were still intact. My focus, whenever we did anything, was when we get down there we can tweak our plan for the actual fight but we had to take things sequentially. Let's make sure we get down there (Attack Position) with all of our combat power intact," said Lieutenant Colonel Brandl.

Battalion 1/8 had several Iraqi interpreters working with them at the dam. When the interpreters found out the battalion was going down to Fallujah, five of the Iraqis refused to go with the battalion. Six of the eleven interpreters decided to stay with the battalion and go south to the city.

The battalion would go in stages to Al Asad Air Base. Packing up the 7-ton trucks and Humvees, the last unit out, H & S Company, left the dam near midnight. Battalion 1/8 was replaced by a company from a Marine reserve unit. After a quick stop in Al Asad, they moved on to an Iranian Army training camp located near Camp Fallujah. They left late on the night of October 27 and arrived early the next morning at the Iranian Training Camp. The Marines of Battalion 1/8 were quartered in a large building at the training facility that had all its windows and doors broken out. The trip had been very quiet and routine for the battalion and they were now positioned only a few miles from Fallujah.

Riding in a Humvee in the strung out convoy, Virginia native Second Lieutenant Brandon Turner, 26, 2nd Platoon commander, Charlie Company, remembered the push to the Iranian Training Camp and the daylight arrival. "We left late at night. We were in twenty-five vehicles and were strung out for three miles, the entire convoy, 7-tons, Humvees, up armor, everything. It took us about three hours and we were tired and worn out from the ride when we arrived. The convoy was huge. We had been to the area of Fallujah in July and when we came in this time we could see that things had changed. We could make out the city off to our right and you could see that in the past few months how part of the city was starting to get leveled from our arty, air strikes and tanks."

PFC Paul Volpe, 19, a member of Weapons Company from Glen Rock, New Jersey, was riding in the convoy with four other Weapons Company Marines. "We knew we were going to be part of the big assault on Fallujah. We were joking on the way to Camp Fallujah. We were trying to stay upbeat. We were confident in our leader, Sergeant Smith, who is an awesome Marine."

First Lieutenant Paul W. Steketee, 23, a member of H & S Company, was one of the last Marines to pull out from the Haditha dam. The six-foot-two lanky Marine was a graduate of the Citadel Military Academy in South Carolina. His new bride, Gretchen, was home awaiting his return. "There were enough buildings at the training camp to stage the entire battalion. Being in the buildings was protecting us from mortar fire. Some of the leadership was a little stressed-out on the ride to Fallujah because we had gotten the warning order to go only 36 hours before we stepped off to the Iranian Training Camp," Steketee recalled.

"We had been preparing for it for about three weeks. We knew something was coming."

PFC Volpe, remembered arriving at the camp, "Once we got there we set up bunk beds in the ITC, a one-floor concrete barracks building. The date kept changing on when we would attack into Fallujah but we knew it was getting closer. The Marines are the best fighting force in the world and we were prepared to go into the city."

Captain Kahn, Weapons Company recalled, "The advance party had arrived before us and had everything set. We then moved into the place where we were going to live. Marines rolled in, got in our barracks and bedded down. From that day onward it was just straight up training. At this time we still had not received firm orders that we were to go into Fallujah."

Commander of Bravo Company, Captain Read Omohundro, remembered keeping busy the two days before the rest of the battalion arrived. "We did a lot of planning and looking at a lot of maps—got as much intelligence update information as we could, identified enemy positions, how we were going to go into the city, how we were going to execute the attack. This time we knew we had to go in there. Fallujah was the focal point where most of the attacks were coming from."

Alpha Company's 1st Platoon commander, Second Lieutenant Elliot Ackerman, 24, born in Los Angeles, was a graduate of Tufts University. His platoon was tasked by Captain Cunningham to be the lead element in the company attack on the Government Center once in Fallujah. He recalled the days of waiting at the Iranian Training Camp. "It was like something you would see in a World War II movie. We studied a mock-up of the Government Center, and what each of our tasks was when we attacked the complex. We sat there for days wondering how it was going to be. We had a foreboding and felt it would be heavily defended and we would suffer heavy casualties in the fighting," Ackerman said.

The date of launching Operation Phantom Fury was set for November 8, but on the night of November 6, the Marines of Battalion 1/8 mounted up and moved toward the city. At the last moment they backed off. Trying to keep the insurgents in the city off-balance, they had faked an attack on Fallujah. Captain Kahn recalled, "We loaded up and did basically a rehearsal of our movement to the Attack Position. It was basically a feint."

U.S. Naval Academy graduate and H & S Company commander, Captain Jacob Jenkins, 32, father of two from Marlton, New Jersey, recalled, "I did a leader's recon to find out where the area where we would stage would be. We couldn't find an area that had cover, and

24

settled for a position two klicks from the city. We needed bulldozers and D-9s to help dig the positions for the Marines and mortars."

First Lieutenant Steketee, H & S Company said, "From October 29, we did training, we did preparation, rehearsals. We set up the command center. A lot of things were established during that week, prior to going into the city. A lot of long hours of work went into trying to get everything ready before we stepped over the line of departure. On the night of November 6, Major Treble and everyone walked us through the plan. Up to the last minute they were still adding attachments of platoons, companies, and different units outside the battalion to us. Force Recon guys joined us at the last minute. Also, an Army medical unit was attached to us at the last minute."

Battalion Chaplain Denis Cox, 41, was also busy at the ITC. The Protestant minister, a member of the Assemblies of God, was performing communion services for the Marines and Navy personnel readying to go into Fallujah. His Protector Corporal Jonathan Zeno, armed with his M16, always closely followed Cox.

Chaplain Cox from Columbus, Ohio, graduated from Ohio State University with a degree in Criminology. His wife Karen, pregnant with their second child, held the home front down along with their seven-year-old daughter.

Cox recalled how he got the calling, "I gave my life to the Lord when I was twenty-six and went on to the seminary. In 1999 I received a phone call from our Bishop. He told me the church needed active duty chaplains, so I joined the Navy."

Cox had hurt his knee on board a previous deployment while giving martial arts training and had it recently operated on before coming to Iraq with 1/8. The knee was still bothering him, which caused a slight limp. Cox recalled, "It's funny. When we were at Haditha Dam the Marines called me the, 'Dam Chaplain.'" The 'Dam Chaplain' was going to be going into Fallujah with his Marines, under fire, with the rest of the battalion.

Commander of the battalion's Sniper Platoon, Captain Mike Pretus, 29, one was of the many officers in the Marine Corps born in the South, New Orleans, Louisiana. He had been a Marine for seven years, enlisting in 1997. His Sniper Platoon had only 18 members including himself and his Staff Sergeant Ben Alicea, making up four teams.

Ever the historian, Pretus compared the coming fight in urban combat to Fredericksburg, Virginia during the Civil War when Union forces forced their way across pontoon bridges and fought Barksdale's Mississippians for possession of that city.

Earlier, knowing they probably would be going into Fallujah, Pretus had approached Brandl to increase his platoon strength so he could field a total of six sniper teams. The call went out for volunteers from the battalion and five Marines stepped forward to join Pretus' Sniper Platoon. One of those volunteers was Lance Corporal Jeffery Walker, 19, from Lenoir, North Carolina. He had applied twice to enter Annapolis but had been turned down by that academy.

"I thought that the snipers were an elite unit and worked in smaller teams and did things their own way," Walker recalled. "We grew longer hair and beards before coming into Fallujah. I loved being a sniper. Before Fallujah we had to get rid of the beards and long hair."

Pretus' Staff Sergeant Ben Alicea, 30, was from Elizabeth, New Jersey. The married Alicea loved playing paintball and fishing when back at Camp Lejeune. When the new sniper recruits were added to the platoon Alicea began working with them. The snipers eventually went on a mission to guard an intersection near Haditha and acquired some more much needed training.

Most of the Marines prepared for the upcoming fight by writing a final letter home to their anxious loved ones.

A twenty-year-old fun-loving Marine from Bravo Company, Lance Corporal Jeffery Holmes from White River Junction, Vermont dashed off a quick two page letter home to his parents and younger brother, from the ITC:

> *Dear Mom, Dad & Cory,*
>
> *How is everything going...Well I wish I could have called but they turned the phones and Internet off for security reasons. It is the night before we go into the city. We are supposed to be in for a few days. By reading this I don't want you guys to get all worried but I figured I would tell you a few things.*
>
> *It is going to be crazy. The enemy has built up their position in the city. Some are saying it is going to be a huge fight. It won't be easy.*
>
> *I want to tell you that I feel we have all trained very hard and everyone is confident. We should be able to get it done and give the city back to the people.*
>
> *Just in case I always live by a saying. Sometimes "shit happens." I like to say it this way because it doesn't sound all sensitive. If anything is to happen I want to let you all know that I love you very much. I would not be here and who I am if it wasn't for you. You don't know how much I love you guys for that. I want*

you to know that I love my job. I love what I do and you
support me through this.
        Sometimes things happen but I do believe there is a
reason for this.... I got to go to get rest now.
        I love you all so much and hopefully in 2 months I'll
be back home.
                        With all my love, Your son Jeff

Lance Corporal Holmes knew all the words from almost every war movie and entertained friends by reciting them. Now he would be participating in a real war, far from the lush Green Mountains of Vermont.

The Army would be supplying two armored ambulances and their crews for use by the Marines in the city. SFC Cary, SFC4 Cook, Second Lieutenant Wilson, Staff Sergeant Brennan, SPC4 Strock, SPC 4 Ferrell and Sergeant Hurt began running classes on putting wounded Marines into the ambulances. The Marines weren't familiar with the Army vehicles and a few seconds delay in getting a wounded man in the ambulance could mean his life or death.

The Marines would later be impressed with the Army crews and their dedication in getting the Marine wounded from Fallujah, under fire, and in the process saving countless lives.

Sergeant Major of the First Marine Expeditionary Force, Carlton W. Kent, told troops on a Sunday visit to the Iranian Training Camp that the coming battle of Fallujah would be no different than the historic fights at Inchon, in Korea, the flag-raising victory at Iwo Jima, or the bloody assault to remove the North Vietnamese troops who had occupied the ancient citadel of Hue during the 1968 Tet Offensive. Kent went on to say, "You're all in the process of making history. This is another Hue City in the making. I have no doubt, if we do get the word, that each and every one of you is going to do what you have always done—kick some butt."

The Marines responded as they shouted, 'Oohra." Battalion 1/8 was good to go. All that was needed now was the final word to move into their Attack Position just to the north of Fallujah.

At the Iranian Training Camp, a large room had been set up for Battalion 1/8 as a conference room. A hanging tarp was strung up at one end to section off the area from the rest of the large building. First Lieutenant Steketee remembered the meeting held the night before they were to enter the city, "We had a projector set up and had drawn a large map on the floor. All the different units were there. We squeezed in as many people as we could have in the room. We basically walked stage by stage through the operation. What do we do when we're here? What do we do when we meet this objective? Once we take the Government Center, what's the next objective? Guys like me who wouldn't be going into the city were involved in part of that understanding of what was going on in Fallujah."

Officers pored over the map of Fallujah drawn on the floor with a marker while Brandl told them exactly how the operation to take Fallujah would go. In the coming attack, Brandl's battalion would be the tip of the spear. The hardest fighting in the city, it was felt at the time, would be in the Jolan District, and not in the path of Battalion 1/8. Intelligence had shown that the Jolan district hosted most of the hard-line enemy insurgents, the real hard-core foreigners. The Marines of Battalion 3/1 and Battalion 3/5 were tasked to take that part of the city.

Brandl had slept very little in the days leading up to Fallujah and was under the constant pressure of having a thousand or more Marine's lives in his hands. One of his main concerns on entering the city was the enemy ramming car bombs into the flanks of his attacking Marines. In the briefing with his officers Brandl said, "There's nothing out there that will defeat us. This is a right fight for us, this is a good fight for us. And we're going to win it. And we're going to do it with professionalism and honor." Brandl instilled confidence in his young officers who in turn passed it on down to the non-coms and enlisted men.

A series of objectives had been set up for the battalion. Bravo Company would attack first through a breach into the city and secure a foothold in the north. Charlie Company, who had the battalion's far left, would cross through the breach and take the Braxton area, then push to Phase Line Beth, and then on to Phase Line Cathy. Then Bravo Company would attack south from their foothold and take the Cultural Center.

The Marines dubbed the north-south highway that separated Charlie and Bravo Company, Route Ethan. Charlie Company Marines would prep the Al Hydra Muhammad Mosque, which was known to harbor the insurgents' command center in the city, for the Iraqi forces to take. Alpha Company was to enter the city and take the Government Center. Once the Government Center fell to Battalion 1/8, it would be used as the battalion's command center in Fallujah. The next objective of Bravo Company would be the Iraqi National Guard (ING) facility. Charlie Company was tasked to secure the Janobi Mosque. Phase Line Fran, Highway 10 that bisected the city from west to east, was the battalion's next objective. It was expected to take four days of stiff fighting to reach Phase Line Fran in the center of the city. The battalion would catch their breath and regroup before pushing south to the Queen's area and finally Phase Line Jenna, the most southern boundary of the city limits.

In the conference room, as a large picture of Saddam Hussein, dressed as Saladin, stared down at the Marines, Lieutenant Colonel Brandl met with the press and fielded several questions. He was asked if the rebels would stay and fight? Brandl answered, "I would be quite happy if my Marines could just walk into Fallujah, but they are ready for a fight. The Marines that I have had wounded over the past five months have been attacked by a faceless enemy. But the enemy has got a face. He's called Satan. He lives in Fallujah. And we're going to destroy him."

The media jumped all over Brandl's statement and his use of the word, Satan. The liberal-leaning press accused him of bringing religion into the fighting. They asked how a Marine officer could compare Muslim insurgents to Satan? Brandl stood by his statement, and what his Marines found in Fallujah would later prove him right.

Iraqi Security Forces were to join in with the U.S. Marines and Army Soldiers when the attack order came. U.S. commanders expected about 2,000 members of Iraqi troops, but General George W Casey, Jr., the top American commander in Iraq, acknowledged that an unknown number of the Iraqis did not show up.

Brandl integrated the Interim Iraqi forces (IIF) and Marine tanks from Alpha Company, 2nd Tanks, in with his battalion. The companies conducted training with the M1A1 Main Battle Tanks and Charlie Company of the 2nd Amphibious Assault Battalion while at the training camp. The 15 vehicles were under the command of Second Lieutenant Morris. A normal AAV (Amphibious Assault Vehicle) platoon consists of 12 vehicles, four per section, with three sections. A platoon of AAVs can carry a company of infantry.

Long Island, New York native Captain Christopher Meyers, 26, an eight-year veteran of the Corps was commanding the tank force that was attached to Brandl's battalion. A graduate of Villanova University, Meyers' force was based at Camp Fallujah and his tankers were very familiar with the Fallujah environs. They had arrived in country from Camp Lejeune in September 2004.

In September and October, his tanks had been part of the shaping operations on Fallujah. "The only units that were allowed close to the city at that time were tanks. My sister company, Charlie Company, 2nd Tanks, and my command conducted a lot of attack by fires around the city. Regiment would give us an op order to conduct a feint on this day and what we would do is, the entire company would go to that portion of the city whether it was the Jolan or Queens. We would look for obstacles, berms, ditches and barriers and destroy them," Meyers recalled. "As soon as we got close to the city we would automatically attract enemy fire. Within fifteen minutes of being there you would see an RPG coming your way. Different types of RPGs can penetrate an M1A1 Tank. During these missions we had a couple of IED mine strikes on the tanks which we repaired. We suffered no casualties in those feints."

Colonel Tucker, RCT-7 Commander, and all company commanders, conducted a rehearsal of concepts and live fire rehearsal of loading to the Attack Position. On Sunday November 7, the battalion issued the final operation order for Operation Phantom Fury.

The Marines of Battalion 1/8 spent the day loading assault packs for the fight and Alice packs for follow-on gear and studying the terrain model one last time. All platoon commanders and platoon sergeants reviewed the scheme of maneuver with the Marines on the terrain model. Every Marine would know what his job was and what was expected of him in the coming urban battle. The Marines of Battalion 1/8 would not enter the fight blindly.

Two Marines in Alpha Company's 3rd Platoon, Lance Corporal Joshua Bush, 19, and his good friend Lance Corporal Bradley Faircloth, 20, like so many other Marines in the battalion bracing for what was coming, wrote their *death letters*. Both friends agreed to send the other's letter home to his family if something bad happened to the other. Both young Marines hailed from Alabama.

In his letter home Faircloth asked his mom to use his insurance money to help complete a senior project he had started at Murphy High School. His class had wanted to erect a statue of a panther, the school's mascot. He also described the kind of funeral he wanted and included names and phone numbers of his friends he wanted to be present. Faircloth wrote:

> *I know it sounds dumb, but all I wanted to be when I was a little kid was to be famous. I wanted to be talked about when I was alive and missed and remembered when I was gone.*
>
> *Make sure it's a good ceremony. Make them laugh and cry too.*

Captain Read Omohundro talked to his Bravo Company Marines while at the camp. "I explained to them, you take care of each other, make sure you're doing the right thing. Go forth, fight, and let's all come back and drink beer afterwards."

Battalion taps sounded at 2000 the night of November 7. They would mount up and move to their Attack Position early the next morning.

The British Black Watch Regiment had already moved into positions east and south of the city to help block any escape routes of the insurgents still in Fallujah. The Army's Black Jack Brigade had joined them in encircling the entire city.

In the first stage of the assault, a Marine unit and other troops including Iraqi forces would seize two strategic bridges and a hospital situated on a peninsula formed by the Euphrates River. The hospital and the peninsula were considered a possible fallback zone for insurgents when driven from the central sectors of Fallujah. The hospital was also being used as a center for enemy propaganda to inflate civilian casualties. The hospital was to be secured by the newly formed Iraqi 36th Commando Battalion backed up by the Marines. The Iraqis were then tasked to keep the hospital open for expected civilian casualties.

The hospital/bridges missions were carried out promptly and efficiently in the shaping phase of the battle. On November 8, the air and artillery assault on the city began in earnest. The massive strikes were executed for twelve hours prior to the main attack on Fallujah. When the Marines from Battalion 3/5 took the bridge where the Blackwater men had been hung, they wrote: *This is for the American's of Blackwater that were murdered here in 2004. Semper Fidelis. Battalion 3/5 God Bless the US Marines. P. S. F*** you.*

Battalion 1/8's Attack Position

Under a curtain of artillery and air strikes, the Marines of First Battalion, Eighth Regiment staged at 0230 on the morning of November 8. Marines still trying to wake up trudged with their weapons and gear to waiting vehicles. Breakfast would come later. Right now they had plenty of butterflies to fill their stomachs. Bravo Company was transported in AAVs and the remaining companies packed into trucks. They departed the staging area at 0515 and arrived at the dispersion area along Route Miami. After staging, events would begin to click in rapid fashion for entry into the city.

"Two days after the feint to Fallujah we woke up at 0230 at the Iranian Training Camp, we walked to our vehicles and we moved right into our Attack Position to the north of Fallujah. We would remain in the Attack Position for twelve hours before entering the city," Captain Stephen Kahn, Weapons Company remembered.

Second Lieutenant Brandon Turner recalls the early morning at the Iraqi training center as two regiments loaded up, "That night, once it turned dark, artillery was pounding the city so we hadn't gotten much sleep. It was pouring rain with lightning, which was odd for Iraq. We marched to the loading position and that's when we saw this massive gathering of the two regiments. Trucks as far as you could see, along with tanks and AAVs. Before arriving near the city the rain tapered off, but the Harriers were still dropping bombs and artillery was still going off. The mood of the Marines was pretty quiet. Everyone was just waiting for it to happen. I had talked to them when I knew we were going to go into Fallujah. We talked about the Blackwater men and what had happened to them."

One of the hardest jobs some of the Marines had to perform was to stay back and not go into combat in the city with their fellow Marines. First Lieutenant Paul Steketee, H & S Company was tasked, along with forty other Marines, to remain at the Iranian Training Camp. He was not envied by any of his fellow Marines. His job was to compile the paperwork on the wounded in action (WIA) and killed in action (KIA). Steketee had to identify those Marines, those friends of his, which came back in body bags or those who had been wounded.

"A quarter-mile from where I was in the Iranian Training Center, and closer to Fallujah, we had set up the Logistics Support Area (LSA), but to get there, we had to drive all the way around the training center to get in the main gate. What we wanted to do was have all the supplies and the medical support forward enough to where they could come straight out of the city to that Logistical Supply area," Steketee said.

Other Marines, stuffed into their vehicles were lost in their own thoughts on what to expect, as they moved closer to Fallujah.

"We had to halt on the cloverleaf because the Army Black Jack Brigade was taking indirect fire. We had to wait for that to finish before we could leave and move up to the Attack Position," Captain Omohundro recalled.

Captain Kahn, Weapons Company, had one of the more stressful jobs in the coming battle. He was to coordinate all indirect fire and all air support for the battalion. Some of these missions would be called to within 200 meters from the forward Marines. "As soon as they arrived in the Attack Position, the Marine engineers dug in hasty firing positions for the battalion with D-9 bulldozers. We were waiting for a hand off of the battle from division. The 81 mortars were quickly set up and in place. My platoons were in their positions to support. They were isolating our flanks in our zone and we had one platoon that was ready in support of Alpha Company. We got the word the operation kicked off in our zone with a strike on the northern edge of the city. We had been told that basically every route into the city had been set with IEDs. We called in the strike to allow our tanks and troops to move up to the edge of the city without casualties or damaged vehicles. This all started at 1850. Our kickoff had been set for 1900. We would remain in the Attack Position for twelve hours before entering the city."

One of the many Floridians in Bravo Company, Lance Corporal David Ojeda, 20, a graduate of South Lake High School in Mont Verde, Florida, lugged his M249 Squad Automatic Weapon (SAW) and clambered with the rest of his 1st Squad into the back of an amtrac. A member of 2nd Platoon, the paintball loving Ojeda had plans to go on to college after his enlistment was up. As the Marines piled out of the amtracs, what greeted them seemed all so unreal. "I remembered the amtracs dropped us off a few miles outside of the city. We were there just watching everything while we dug our skirmish trenches. The soil was real hard to get through with the 'E' tools (Entrenching Tool) and they kept on breaking. You could look at the city and see the artillery just blowing stuff to hell. Air strikes were coming in from left to right and I thought to myself, *Holy crap this is for real. This is not a drill or training, this is for real.* It seemed like we were there for three days when it had only been a few hours. Sure you're a little nervous and a little scared, but your adrenaline is going and you want to get in there and get some," Ojeda said.

Located 2,000 meters north of the city at the Attack Position, Brandl called a meeting of his commanders. Charlie Company Commander, Captain Bethea was in attendance. "We had a Key Leader brief at 1030 at an AAV and the meeting went for about an hour. The press was briefed from imagery that we were getting from the overhead vehicles. Artillery was still being adjusted on targets in the city and air strikes were still strafing."

Lieutenant Colonel Brandl had the D-9 bulldozers make a berm up across a highway leading from the city through his position. "We didn't want any suicide vehicles driving down that road into our position and any indirect fire hitting us. We knew we would be there all day long," Brandl remembered.

Bravo Company had arrived at the Attack Position at 0800, and Charlie Company Marines arrived at 0850 under cloudy, misting skies. Staff Sergeant Olalde made liaison with platoon commanders and guided them to their defensive sectors. The Marines that would be going in the first wave dug trenches, hydrated, ate chow and rested.

To the west of the city, Marines from Battalion 3/1 and Iraqi troops in RCT-1's zone of operation had secured the hospital and the two vital bridges coming into the city from the west. Operation Phantom Fury had begun. The Marines of Battalion 1/8 could hear the firing and watch tracers emanating from that part of Fallujah. They also watched as thousands of tracers were flying into the city from the attacking force.

Sitting in an AAV, the command and control amtrac, Captain Kahn said, "I was in the C-7 located behind my mortar firing position. We were the FSCC (Fire Support and Control Center). I was the fire support coordinator. The artillery liaison officer, First Lieutenant Greenwell, our battalion air officer Captain Green, and then I had Corporal Van Allen, who was my mortar rep. He knew his stuff real well, so we pulled him up to that position. Intelligence officer Captain Starace and operations officer Major Trimble, who had Sergeant Gonzales with him, rounded out our group. We had every seat in the vehicle used."

Including the Marines, the C-7 vehicle carried an array of electronic equipment and gear stuffed in every available space. It looked like Star Wars with all the lights and gadgetry flashing and glowing.

In the coming weeks, the Marines in the FSCC amtrac would get to know each other very well, as well as they would their cramped vehicle. The amtrac became their motel on wheels in the battle for Fallujah.

Captain Kahn said, "We knew the enemy was going to do two things. We knew the enemy was going to try and hug us as tight as they could, to prevent us from using our indirect fire. We didn't want to let them succeed so we knew we would have to bring our fire in close. The other thing that the enemy had gotten very good at during our time in Iraq was, when indirect fire goes off, they moved away. So if we drop an adjust fire round, then they knew what was coming and they ran away. So we had to fire for effect."

Back in July over half of 1/8, including Lieutenant Colonel Gary Brandl, two companies, and part of Weapons Company had gone to Camp Fallujah. After only being in the country a few weeks, part of the battalion was reassigned from RCT-7 to RCT-1 for close to a month. In that time they got to know the area around Fallujah and that was one of the reasons they were tasked to join in the retaking of the city.

"When we went to Fallujah in July we did not go into the city. Our charter was basically the southern outskirts of Camp Fallujah. We were there when the Fallujah Brigade had control of the city. While we were there in July we saw the city every day, but we stayed out of it. There was a lot of firing going on in the city and we took mortar and small arms fire directed at Camp Fallujah from within the city. While we were there, it became obvious the Fallujah Brigade couldn't control the city. It was my feeling that when we left Fallujah in August that we would be back. By being there we had gotten a situation awareness of Fallujah and we felt if someone was going to get to do this, it ought to be us. We felt ready," Brandl explained.

In their Attack Position just north of the city, Battalion 1/8 was set to attack up the belly of the beast. Lieutenant Colonel Brandl was positioned in his command Humvee, in the Attack Position, awaiting zero hour. He had had an operation on his back the previous year and every so often it continued to stiffen up on him, but he was good to go. He would be pushing into the city with his battalion. He believed in "Command from the front," and Fallujah would be no exception.

"We had taken casualties from a faceless enemy. We wanted to stand up and fight. We were going to do the job the right way, the way we wanted to do it. There were specific objectives given to the regiment, and since we were the main effort for the regiment, we would be taking those objectives. We did have a zone that we would be fighting through. I set up battalion objectives that would facilitate taking those critical regimental objectives. We would be hunting down the enemy, destroying them and turning the city back over to the Iraqi Interim Government," Brandl recalled. "We had a common sense rules of engagement. We had to positively identify enemy that was attacking us." One of Brandl's main concerns in the coming attack on Fallujah was minimizing civilian casualties as much as possible.

Lieutenant Colonel Brandl and Major General Natonski walked among the troops and spoke to many of the Marines.

Captain Read Omohundro, Bravo Company, turned to his First Sergeant, Ronald Whittington, confiding in him a prediction that getting into the city wouldn't be the hard part of the attack, but that the first regimental objective, the Cultural Center, would be the hardest for the company.

At the Attack Position morale was high, even though rockets began flying over the battalion, exploding to the north of their dug in lines. A BBC reporter on the scene, Paul Wood, heard a wiry, tough-looking Staff Sergeant say to his 1/8 Marines, "We're not going into Fallujah to give out fuzzy bears and warm hugs." The Marines knew it wasn't going to be easy. They were bracing for what would come.

In the background and off to the east, the Marines could hear the sound of Marine artillery, 155mm Howitzers, pounding targets in the city. Planes were continually unleashing rockets on suspected enemy targets in Fallujah.

That night, Arab media reported they witnessed insurgents moving about in the city as they manned their fighting positions. As the fighters moved they were heard to chant, "There is no God but Allah, and Mohammed is the messenger of Allah." They felt they would be doing God's work by killing American Marines and Soldiers in the coming battle for the city, and felt they needed their God's help to win. They also knew that world attention was now focused on Fallujah. AK-47s were cleaned and loaded and the insurgents began spreading RPGs throughout the city for quick use by their roving fighters. The insurgents planned to win the battle or die trying.

1st Battalion, 8th Marine Regiment Order of Battle in Fallujah

Alpha Company-Captain Aaron Cunningham
1st Platoon-Second Lieutenant Ackerman
2nd Platoon-Second Lieutenant Hunt
3rd Platoon-Second Lieutenant Barnes
Weapons Platoon-Lieutenant Malcom

Bravo Company-Captain Read Omohundro
1st Platoon-Second Lieutenant Eckert
2nd Platoon-Second Lieutenant Berch
3rd Platoon-First Lieutenant Wilkens
Weapons Platoon-First Lieutenant Noble

Charlie Company-Captain Theodore Bethea
1st Platoon-Second Lieutenant Rhoades
2nd Platoon-Second Lieutenant Turner
3rd Platoon-Second Lieutenant Littell
Weapons Platoon-First Lieutenant Miller

Weapons Company-Captain Stephen Kahn

1st Platoon-Lieutenant Lee
2nd Platoon-Lieutenant Risler
3 rd Platoon-Lieutenant Kutilek
Mortar Platoon-Gunnery Sergeant Gilkerson

Headquarters and Service Company-Captain Jacob Jenkins

Supply-Lieutenant Hagh
H & S Truck-Lieutenant Lodestro
NBC-CWO1 Fair
Snipers-Captain Pretus
H & S Motor T-Lieutenant Dieckhaus
CEB-Lieutenant Devine
S-1- Lieutenant Steketee
S-2- Captain Starace
S-3-Major Trimble-CWO2 Athey (Battalion Gunner)
S-4-Captain Maryahin
S-6-Lieutenant Stepp
Air Officer-Captain Greene
BAS-Medical Officer-LCDR Jadick & Lieutenant Kennedy
JAG-Captain Nodine
Battalion Chaplain-Lieutenant Cox

Attached Tanks-Captain Chris Meyers

Second Lieutenant Lee
First Lieutenant Klingensmith

Attached AAVs- Second Lieutenant Morris' 2nd Platoon, Company C, 2nd Assault Amphibian Battalion

Artillery-Marine Battery C, 1/12 was the lead artillery battery supporting Battalion 1/8

Battalion 1/8 to the Breach D-Day for Operation Phantom Fury

To transport his Marines to the Attack Position, Lieutenant Colonel Brandl had the use of 15 Amtracs from Company C, 2nd Assault Amphibian Battalion under the command of Second Lieutenant Morris. This unit also hailed from Camp Lejeune and had been with 1/8 since arriving in Iraq. Morris' amtrackers were to patrol streets, provide medical assistance, handle re-supplies to their fellow Marines fighting in the city and carry 1/8 troops in and out of the battle.

Driving one of the AAVs was a young Marine who like many others enjoyed listening to hardcore rock music, Lance Corporal Jonathan Olexa, 21, from Burlington, Connecticut. As Olexa drove his vehicle loaded with Marines stuffed into the back he stared ahead at the city, which seemed to glow from thousands of incoming and outgoing rounds. Then he glanced at an American flag displayed inside the vehicle on the right side for all the Marines to see. His good friend Corporal Lucas Pickard had helped him mount the flag in their AAV. It was an old weathered American flag that had a story behind it. Like most Marines who had acquired or been given some token, cross or memorabilia for luck, Olexa had this flag.

In 1983 Olexa's father, John, had taken the flag with him to the Middle East and upon his return he had stored it for special occasions. Following 9/11, then a member of the Connecticut Air National Guard, he carefully packed the flag for his next mission to Kuwait in Operation Southern Watch. The flag again returned safely with its owner to the states. John then carefully packed it away for safekeeping.

In January 2003 the old flag was once again taken from its chest and prepared with its owner for their next mission, deploying with the 103rd Fighter Wing attached to 410 Fighter Wing as part of Iraq Freedom. During this deployment the flag flew high over Iraq on the wings of an F-16 Falcon Fighter. The flag again was taken home and stored away in the chest.

In September 2004, the old flag that had seen so much of the Middle East was once again readied for battle. This time not in the hands of the man that had cared for it all these years, but in the steady hands of a young Marine, his son, Jonathan. It had brought him safely through all those trips to the Middle East and he told his son it would do the same for him.

AAVs had brought in Bravo Company to the Attack Position on a road north of the city and railroad tracks to where the Breach Zone was located and then disembarked its load.

One of the Marines riding in Olexa's track was Sergeant Lonny D. Wells with his 1st Squad from Bravo Company. Wells had taught the grenade course at MCT at Camp Geiger, North Carolina in 2003 and Olexa had gotten a kick out of Wells' teaching manner.

As the Marines off loaded, officers began shouting out orders as a mortar round impacted where the AAVs tried to maneuver to return for Charlie Company. The vehicles where having a tough time turning around due to the lay of the land. Rounds from the direction of the city were continually flying over the infantry and vehicles.

AAV Marine, Lance Corporal Olexa said, "We got a lot of fire from Fallujah when we started dropping them off. We were bringing 1/8 in by company as RPGs and tracer rounds were coming from the city. After Bravo Company we then went back for Charlie Company."

High in the sky, an Air Force AC-130 Spectre Gunship, code name Basher, with fourteen crewmembers, continually circled over Fallujah. The AC-130 is a giant flying artillery platform. Its center fire-control systems can pinpoint an individual structure or level entire areas in a matter of seconds. The AC-130 has the added benefit of being refueled in the air, allowing it to remain over its targeted area for extended periods while supporting the infantry in the city below. The plane is armed with 20mm rotary cannons, 40mm cannons, and a 105mm Howitzer cannon.

The Marines felt a little more comfort knowing they could call on the AC-130 when needed. During the coming battle, the AC-130 would earn the respect of the Marines slugging it out on the city's streets. The AC-130 is basically a flying killing-machine.

To the west of the city at Camp Fallujah stood the 155mm Howitzers of C Battery of the 1st Battalion, 12th Marines, ready to assist the infantry of Battalion 1/8 when called on. Their artillery pieces stood on the field like mighty dragons breathing their hot breath on Fallujah. But until the infantry called on them, the battery was busy taking out Intel targets in the northern sectors of the city hoping to make the job of the advancing Marines a little easier.

Captain Read Omohundro, 34, a Desert Storm veteran, who was the unflappable commander of Bravo Company, rode in with his Marines. The native of Fort Worth, Texas had three sons—Tarrant, Alec, and Gavin—all home in Oklahoma City, Oklahoma, with his wife of ten years, Nicole. The six-foot Marine, a graduate of Texas A & M, loved motorcycle riding and puttering around with mechanical things when home in the states. Along with carrying an M16A4, M9 sidearm and a sharp Ka-Bar knife, he also carried an axe. From a military family, his father had served in Vietnam, and his grandfather in WWII. His Bravo Company would form the right fist of Lieutenant Colonel Brandl's two-company push into the battalion's attack zone in the northern sector of the city. Omohundro would lead Bravo Company from the front.

"When we found out we were going to Fallujah, of course we were a little nervous, but we were excited. We were ready to finally do what we were trained to do, and that was to be an infantry company and take care of business," Captain Omohundro recalled.

One of Omohundro's Marines was a twenty-nine-year-old Lance Corporal, Dimitrios Gavriel a native of Haverhill, Massachusetts. Known to his family and friends as Dimmy, he had enjoyed wrestling while enrolled at Timberlane High School. Gavriel was a graduate of an Ivy League College, Brown University in Rhode Island. From there he went to work on Wall Street as a broker. He quit his job when two of his friends were killed in the attacks on the World Trade Center September 11, 2001, because he wanted "to make a difference in the world."

Because of his age and several wrestling injuries, Gavriel had to convince the Corps to finally accept him. Shortly before he went into Fallujah he wrote a letter to GOYA a Greek Youth Organization, explaining his reasons for the drastic job change:

> *...I moved to a small apartment next to Central Park in New York City and began the long hours of the "grind" of Wall Street. I remember those years as some*

of the best of my life, surrounded by close friends and good times. So how, after all this, did a guy like me end up in Iraq? The answer is pretty simple when I look to the young Marines at my right and left. I wanted to make a difference. I wanted to do something, no, give something, to deserve all the good things we, as Americans, enjoy and sometimes take for granted as we move through the years of the good lives we lead under the safety and freedom of our flag. Everyone lost something on that terrible day of 9/11. I lost my close friends, brothers you might say. Guys I grew up with, team mates, pals, mentors, and confidants. I watched the towers fall, helpless, from a block away in the streets of New York and made a promise before God that I would do all I could to keep something like this from happening again. I left a job I loved, said goodbye to a circle of close friends and joined the Marines, the perfect place for a guy who wants a front row seat to the sweeping changes the world is currently experiencing. No man can know just exactly how much his effort has changed the world out here, but together we have chased much evil away from power and have shown those who, for one reason or another, hate our way of life, that we are a nation of people who refuse to live under the threat of terror. We are out here for the things we miss most, green grass, football games, flowers, and the fresh cool breeze of home. Most importantly, we are out here for you, the people who make our land so special. ...

A reporter from the New York Times asked him shortly before entering Fallujah if he and his fellow Marines were ready for what awaited them in the city. Gavriel confidently answered, "Locked, cocked and ready to rock. That's about how we feel."

The left fist of the battalion's push would be thirty-three-year-old Captain Theodore C. Bethea's Charlie Company. In the battalion book commemorating their service in Iraq, a Marine wrote, "Captain Bethea's real name is 'Joe Marine, good to go?' There has never existed an officer more completely Marine Corps than Captain Bethea." The 5-foot-10-inch Bethea hails from New Orleans, Louisiana and graduated from Sewanee University of the South in Tennessee. Like his battalion commander, he loved to fish and hunt when he found the time at Camp Lejeune. The captain was married, but to the Marine Corps. Bethea, like the other company commanders in the battalion, would lead his men from the front carrying his M4 carbine.

"My company had been in contact with the enemy on a weekly basis throughout the entire deployment. We had had Marines that had been seriously wounded. When we got word we were going to Fallujah, we were ready," Captain Bethea explained.

In charge of a machine gun squad and an assault squad, Sergeant Robert Frederick, 25, belonged to First Lieutenant Miller's Weapons Platoon in Charlie Company. A native of Newburgh, New York, a small town splashed along the Hudson River, Frederick recalled the mood of the Marines prior to entering the city. "We were excited, we knew this time we were actually going in and clean the city up. We didn't get too much sleep the night before we went in."

Another Marine from Charlie Company, Lance Corporal Thomas Tribou, 19, from Torrington, Connecticut, 1st Squad, 1st Platoon, recalled, "I remember the Iraqis holding up signs when they killed the Blackwater guys, saying that Fallujah was a graveyard for Americans. We wanted to change that perception."

Lance Corporal Dominick Giusti, 21, from Union, New Jersey, Charlie Company, a member of Second Lieutenant Littell's 3rd Platoon, 3rd Squad recalled the 20-minute ride in the buttoned up amtrac to the berm. "We were all either saying prayers or telling each other that we're going to get through this and bring everyone back. There was no joking."

PFC Michael Johnson, 19, a native of Olean, New York, and a member of 2nd Platoon, Weapons Company recalled the trip to the outskirts of Fallujah. "When we left Camp Fallujah it was raining, cold and miserable."

Navy Corpsman, HA (Hospitalman Assistant) Ernest Argueta, 19, a medic, was armed with a pistol and an M16. In the military for only one year, he remembered the wait to go into Fallujah. "At first we were planning not to dig any fighting holes but we were wrong. As soon as we put up the Battalion Aid Station (BAS) we received incoming rocket fire. Luckily for me and HM2 Johns and a good buddy of mine HM Stedman, the rocket landed thirty feet from us and didn't explode. It was a dud. It would have killed us all had it gone off. So then we really started to dig our holes."

Also at the BAS was Chaplain Denis Cox. "I was standing beside the BAS tent when the rocket came over my head and landed about 15 feet behind me. Everyone hit the ground. Thank God it was a dud," Cox said.

Another corpsman who was assigned to the BAS, HM2 Shawn Johns, 28, from the small Indiana town of Monon, remembered, "They read a message from the Iraqi Interim Prime Minister and I thought, *Holy shit we're going in.* When we drove in to the edge of the city to set up our forward aid station (FAS), one of the units that was to supply security on the roadways was already in contact with the insurgents. I remember watching the .50 cals going off and grenades being thrown in these buildings, and then I realized it was the real deal. There's no turning back now. This is what we get paid to do and what we wanted to do. When we arrived at checkpoint eighty-four, we quickly set up the forward aid station, which consisted of a tent with four litters inside. LCDR Jadick and approximately thirty-five corpsmen manned the station. When we were standing in front of the aid station you could just hear BOOM! BOOM! in the background. I said, 'Quiet!' and just then, a small rocket landed beside Stedman, Argueta and me. It was a dud. While at that position we also treated an Iraqi soldier and one of the Americans working with the Iraqis who had been hit in the shoulder."

LCDR Rich Jadick was a thirty-eight-year-old former Marine captain who had volunteered to go to Iraq with 1/8.

Navy Corpsman HM3 Milton Jones, Jr., 23, Heidelberg, Mississippi, was attached to Bravo Company as one of their combat medics. "I remember trying to get some sleep along the berm, waiting to go in. I got some food in my system, some MREs (Meals Ready to Eat) and we just waited."

H & S Captain Jenkins recalled, "The first element down was the engineers, the breach team supported by Weapons Company. I was with Lieutenant Devine centered up on the breach site supporting the engineers, who were actually doing the breach. I watched while they dug the ramps over the railroad tracks for the breach force to move in. We couldn't get my gun truck over the railroad tracks, so we dismounted the M-240G and put it up on the railroad tracks. As soon as the gun was in action, there were targets. There were three insurgents in a hut, which we could see through our thermal sights. RPG rounds were hitting in front of us. The railroad tracks offered us good cover position which stopped most of the shrapnel."

Battalion 1/8 was now poised at the tip of the spear in America's fight against terrorism in Iraq. Bravo Company was to lead the attack through the breach and gain an initial foothold in the city, which would enable Charlie Company, the battalion's main effort, to attack towards their first objective, the Braxton complex. The other line company, Alpha Company, was kept back in the staging area until called on to take the Government Center.

The Marines were under constant sniper and RPG fire since coming to the outskirts of the city. The trenches dug in along the berm gave them some protection from the erratic enemy fire. The Marines joked about the heat in Iraq, "There is heat, dry heat, humid heat, Lejeune heat, and 29 Palms heat, then there is Iraqi heat." Iraqi heat had them all beat.

At 1800 the tanks, mobile assault platoons, and engineers moved slowly down Route Dave to the breach point. Marine tanks, now ideally positioned near the railroad tracks, began firing on targets in the city, in particular the Braxton complex, shaping the area for the infantry attack. Indirect artillery fire from Camp Fallujah was also brought down on the Marines' first objectives. The fire would help to mask their move into the city.

"I made a decision to use the obstacle clearing team we had in place for the breaching. We had Force Recon in the breaching area to draw some sketches for us. My concern was the railroad tracks between us and town would slow us up. The banks were high and sandy, and I felt we would get bogged down on the railroad tracks," Lieutenant Colonel Brandl explained. "Our plan was to send four tanks down there after we pulled Force Recon back to our position, who had done some shaping for us by calling in indirect fire on some targets. Our engineers used 1,000 pounds of C-4 line charge (MICLC) to explode mines and IEDs in our breaching area. We brought in four tanks, two on either side of the breach. When the breaching team was ready to go in, we would send in a smokescreen to cover their movement. Another line charge was used in the traffic circle down one of the main roads. They disabled any IEDs, and it was also a shock effect to the enemy."

Driving Marines in his AAV, Lance Corporal Olexa was startled when the line charge exploded. "I got all spooked when it went off, thinking it was an RPG. It looked like it was coming right at us when they fired it."

His vehicle commander, Staff Sergeant Christopher Shaw mounted in the commander's turret yelled to his crew, "It's just the line charge and not an RPG. Just keep going! Go! Go!"

Shaw, 26, hailed from Liberty, Missouri and had been in the Marines for seven years. He wanted to make a career in the Corps. The third member of Shaw's AAV crew was Lance Corporal Budd. "We had talked among ourselves in AAVs before going in and knew we were going to be under fire in this operation," Shaw said.

This traffic circle located on the outskirts of Fallujah was important to the battalion. It was situated on the highway that came into the city from the north. The highway turned west at the edge of the city, and ran along the rim of Fallujah. A number of streets ran directly south from this highway into the main part of the city. The first major street that ran south from this highway was the main street the battalion would attack, Route Ethan. Brandl needed the traffic circle in order to secure his main re-supply line into Fallujah. The traffic circle had a clear view back along the highway to a bridge to the north. The bridge and highway were needed to get supplies in to his troops.

The combat engineers deployed their line charges and breached the railroad tracks while heavy enemy fire continued coming from within the city. Tracers flew skyward and fell slowly to earth. A short time later a second line charge was set off at the traffic circle, at Phase Line April and Route Ethan for use by Charlie Company. The Second line charge didn't explode and a corporal from the combat engineers made his way out in the open, under fire, to manually set it off. It went off with a thundering explosion, clearing any mines and IEDs in the area in preparation for the Marine infantry attack. Any nearby insurgents in that sector were stunned or killed by the blast.

Tank commander Captain Chris Meyers sent First Lieutenant David Klingensmith, 28, Norwich, Connecticut native, forward with a platoon of four tanks to assist Charlie Company's entry into the city. Meyers would keep a section of two tanks back with him at the logistics support area near the Attack Position, until needed. This was also the position where the tanks would come back out of the city for refueling and rearming. Meyers had three additional tanks, if needed, on call at Camp Fallujah to replace any damaged tanks in the coming urban fight.

Meyers' tankers had made a sweep outside the northern outskirts of the city earlier on the night of November 5 and had come under fire at the position he now manned. Looking into the city brought back memories of a few days earlier when his tanks dueled with the insurgents in Fallujah. "We ended up getting in a firefight just at the train tracks. We were receiving fire from the enemy in the Braxton complex," Meyers recalled. The fight went on for three or four hours until Meyers' tanks finally withdrew before daylight. Now he was back to stay.

Weapons Company vehicles were set up in a half moon position on the railroad tracks facing the city, about a mile from Fallujah. A section leader in Weapons Company, Staff Sergeant Richard Choquette III, 26, a native of Providence, Rhode Island, had four vehicles under his command. "As a lead element we knew we would get attached to tanks. We arrived at the attack zone and basically set up in a support by fire position, and my platoon was tasked with registering the 81 mortars. Our support by fire was to suppress the edge of the city enough to allow a line charge to be blown, to clear out the IEDs. We were firing about two hours before Bravo punched into the city. We were catching a lot of RPG and mortar fire. One of our Marines, Corporal Joshua Ray, was near an RPG when it exploded. His amtrac had been behind a train car when an RPG round hit the train car. It basically knocked him out. When he awoke, he was ok." Corporal Ray also suffered shrapnel burns to the back of his neck from the same exploding RPG round.

Klingensmith enjoyed what he was doing, leading tanks in combat. A graduate of Penn State University, he was a career Marine. He had met his calling and it was in an M1A1 tank. His tankers are trained to field strip every weapon on the M1A1. These young nineteen and twenty-year-olds are put in charge of driving these 4.5 million-dollar machines around on the battlefield. A Marine for five years, Klingensmith gave the order to push forward in preparation to link up with Charlie Company.

Lieutenant Colonel Brandl was located about two thousand meters from the breaching position. Close enough to keep an eye on things, but not too close to get in the way of his company commanders. He was the type of battalion commander that set the objectives and then let his company commanders do their thing but he wouldn't be too far away from the action.

"I put my Alpha Command group in an amtrac, and for the past four months I was driving around in my own mobile command element which consisted of four vehicles that were armored Humvees. For the initial breach I remained back at the Attack Position. What I didn't want to do was gum up the works with another moving part down there," Brandl recalled.

At 1830 Bravo Company moved south to the breach line located on the western side of the traffic circle and began to stage for their attack. They had four hours to prepare before launching their lead company attack south into the city. They stayed in the amtracs for protection from enemy fire.

It had rained earlier when the Marines first left the Iranian Training Center and a misty rain continued to fall over the city. It fogged up the Marines NVGs, which cut down on one of their advantages over the insurgents, night vision. With the night vision goggles the Marines owned the night, without them, it was more of an even fight.

After one hour, at 2200, Captain Omohundro gave the order to close up the distance to the breach site located to the north of the train tracks. Upon arrival, the Bravo Company Marines began dismounting their buttoned up amtracs at the breach line. Captain Read Omohundro, carrying his M16A4, got out of his vehicle and directed his officers to get their platoons organized in preparation for going through the breach. Walking upright while exploding bursts of mortars and RPGs littered the air with shrapnel, Omohundro checked his one hundred and fifty men hugging the berm.

"We had to wait to link up with a Force Recon unit. We're behind the railroad tracks and I'm on the phone with this Recon unit trying to figure out where they were located. I'm talking to them and they asked, 'Can you see my strobe?' We're looking through night vision devices to the north. I told them I can't identify you because every tank, vehicle, amtrac, and Humvee has a red strobe." Captain Omohundro, Bravo Company explained.

Lifer, Sergeant Shawn Gianforte, 28, from Caledonia, New York, had a wife, Lisa, his high school sweetheart, and a daughter, Zoie, at home in the states. A Weapon's Platoon member, he was a part of Bravo Company's FiST Team. This was his second tour of duty in Iraq, the first came March to October 2003. Holding his M16A4 he stared into the smoking city and focused on what he had to do upon entering. "We were a support team that was in charge of calling in mortars, air support and artillery."

Weapons Company Marines strung out along the railroad tracks and facing into the city were already in a serious firefight with insurgents located on the outer rim of Fallujah.

Staff Sergeant Choquette's Weapon's Company, sitting with his vehicles on the railroad tracks some 198 meters from the city, remembered, "We were to hold the flank off so nothing would come from other zones into the rear of our line companies as they pushed south. From this position we were calling in air and artillery support."

Lance Corporal Sven Mozdiez, 21, a five-foot-eleven Marine in Lieutenant Rizler's, 2nd Platoon, Weapons Company, a native of Holliston, Massachusetts, describes the action positioned up on the railroad tracks. The city lay before him like a panorama picture of history in the making. "Our platoon moved up on the railroad tracks with 1st Platoon to set up a base of fire for the line companies to come in on the amtracs and enter the city. As they were setting up the line charges, we were taking fire from the city. There were red streaks, which were RPGs coming from the city and going over our trucks. They weren't very accurate, but a couple came pretty close. A platoon sergeant in Lieutenant Lee's 1st Platoon had a pretty close call with an RPG, and my vehicle commander, Lance Corporal Harry Johnson, took some shrapnel in the throat from one of the mortars that knocked him unconscious. He turned out to be all right. An RPG team of three guys came out of the city. We saw this one guy get down on one knee. When an RPG team sets up, one guy comes up behind the handler of the weapon and digs a hole so the back blast from the RPG won't fry their legs. The guy who fired the RPG at us had failed to pull the pin, so the back blast shot backwards but the rocket didn't come out of the launcher."

Lance Corporal Mozdiez and the other Marines in Weapons Company watched as the RPG rocket, still in the weapon, exploded and lit up the three-member RPG team in a field of blazing light. The three insurgents were staring at one another trying to figure out why the rocket hadn't launched when Mozdiez told his Mk19 gunner on the Humvee to bear down on the lit up area. The fumbling RPG team was quickly dispatched. A Mk19 has a firing rate of over 350 grenades per minute, with a range of over 2200 meters. The insurgents tangling with Lieutenant Risler's Marines were easily outgunned on the outskirts of the city. Risler's men helped to clear the path for Charlie and Bravo Companies to punch in to the city.

"Right after that, we saw a guy up on the third level of a house near the outskirts of the city. He kept coming over the railing and jumping back down as he strafed us with AK-47 fire," Lance Corporal Mozdiez recalled. "We got a bead on him and Lance Corporal Weyrauch fired a TOW missile in that level of the building and we didn't receive anymore fire from that position. That problem was taken care of. We saw another guy on a balcony on one of the spires of a mosque. He was hanging out there spotting our movements. We launched a Javelin missile right through the spire and took care of that guy. We shot three or four more TOW missiles that night taking down people firing at us."

Lance Corporal Brian Koskey, 20, a native of Princetown, New York, Weapons Company, was with the mobile reserve located farther back from the railroad tracks, in a half moon position facing the city. "We could see the firing to our front, and after a while we moved up in our Humvees to the railroad tracks."

Weapons Company was providing security for the 81mm mortars located outside the city. Lance Corporal Danny Myers, 21, from Pinola, Mississippi, a member of 1st Section of Lieutenant Kutilek's 3rd Platoon, was watching the light show to the south near the rim of the city. "My good buddy Corporal Smith and I were sitting around talking about how in two and a half years we had never seen combat. We felt this was going to be one of those times that we would be so close to seeing combat and never get the opportunity. We felt we wouldn't get in to the city. Little did we know that when the next day came, we would be right in the middle of it."

"During the work up for the attack, everyone was getting hyped up and a little nervous." Lance Corporal Greg Nichols, Weapons Company's, 1st Platoon said, "For me, I really knew the shit hit the fan when we were rolling out and everyone is talking about the bombs and the bullets. We set up on the railroad tracks in an L formation. For a time it was quiet, a little artillery and phosphorous dropping on the city, but not that bad. When all of a sudden a red light flew over the hood of our truck and we all kind of looked at each other and agreed this wasn't going to be another Rawah. Then everything went to hell with mortars and rockets raining down around us. One of the infantry companies staged right in front of us, and we couldn't return fire anymore. I remember some Delta Force guys that were working with the Iraqi forces and they kept tripping over the train tracks. We were laughing at them."

Lance Corporal Adam Lew, 19, a native of Macedonia, Ohio recalled being one of the most advanced units near the city. Lew, a TOW gunner, belonged to Weapons Company, 1st Platoon, 2nd Section. Lew always felt he didn't belong in a Weapons Company. He had to learn a lot of new weapons systems, but felt that being a gunner had helped his self-esteem. He felt it showed they had trusted his abilities by moving him to Weapons Company. "When we were up on the railroad tracks we were one of the first units in the battalion to fire into the city. A good friend of mine, Lance Corporal Kevin Weyrauch from Rochester, New York started shooting first. He was one of the first ones up on the railroad tracks and got the first shot off," Lew recalled as he set up in the turret. "When we first pulled up we had to wait while the other trucks pulled into their positions. We set in a very vulnerable spot and I remember thinking, *this was going to be crazy.* At that moment, an RPG round flew over the hood of my truck and right in front of my face. I felt the heat from it as it flew behind us and impacted a hundred meters or so away. I looked down at my driver, O'Donnel, and said, 'I think we should move.' We eventually moved to another position. When Weyrauch got ready to fire his first TOW shot, my driver O'Donnel told me they were going to fire. Our truck was right behind Weyrauch's truck. When you fire a TOW you have to allow for a back blast and I said, 'no they're not we're right behind them.' Right then everything just exploded as the TOW blast came right back at us. I felt the intense heat, but no one was injured."

"Lieutenant Morris' vehicle along with my AAV were called on to run up and pick up the Lieutenant Colonel and get him up to the Forward Command vehicles," AAV member Staff Sergeant Chris Shaw recalled.

Brandl and his four-vehicle mobile command element, which had positioned themselves with the Force Recon Marines, now moved closer to the breach to get a better assessment of the situation. Brandl said, "I realized very quickly that I wasn't going to gain anything there so we pushed up to the breach site. I was positioned there when Bravo Company and Charlie Company were pushing through the breach site and into the city. It was amazing to me to see the amount of RPGs and indirect fire coming out of the town. The enemy tried to attack us from the rear with indirect fire, rockets, and automatic weapons fire. It didn't surprise me when they attacked our rear, but it did make it interesting. The Army's Black Jack Brigade took care of the enemy behind us."

Reaching the berm near the breach in their convoy, Brandl climbed out. He and some of his staff climbed the berm to get a better view of Fallujah. As Brandl and his command group stood outside the city, it began to rain again. Brandl and his staff had spent countless hours of preparation in the battalion's plan of attack into Fallujah. Hours of preparation went in to making sure his Marines had everything they needed for the coming battle before entering the city. As the rain began falling, regimental commander Colonel Tucker arrived at his position. Brandl, dripping wet and standing beside the colonel, felt a little sheepish. He had spent all that time on preparations for his men, but had forgotten his own rain gear. "I didn't even think about bringing my Gore-Tex, but Colonel Tucker had his on. He looked at me like, *'I guess that's why you're a battalion commander and I'm the regimental commander.'* I was basically getting soaking wet," Brandl laughed as he recalled.

Sergeant Major Anthony Hope was positioned with Brandl in the falling rain along the berm. Sergeant Major Hope, 45, the oldest Marine in the battalion, was a native of Shelby, Alabama, and the father of two, one was a twenty-two-year-old sergeant in the Marines. Hope carried an M16. Hope, like his commander Brandl, enjoyed hunting and fishing in the Carolina lakes and forests. "Everything was going well at this time," Hope recounted.

Brandl, who had been up since 0200 from the night before, kept glancing over his shoulder to where he heard noises in a nearby clump of bushes. He turned to Battalion Gunner Jonathan Athey, also standing beside him on the rock-strewn berm.

"It sounds like someone shooting a twenty-two rifle right next to us, over there in those bushes!" Brandl said. He then gestured to the underbrush.

Athey glanced over to the bushes before answering his battalion commander. "Sir, those are rounds snapping over our heads."

"Oh yeah. There are a lot of them." Brandl commented as he turned his attention back to the city and Bravo Company's coming attack to secure a foothold for the battalion.

Throughout the early morning hours Brandl kept close tabs on what was happening with the battalion by monitoring the incoming calls. "The way we had our command and control set up, since we had formed such a tight CP in the months leading up to Fallujah, I could monitor the calls the operation officer, Major Trimble, was getting. If I started to feel there was some friction, then I could interject by getting on the radio," Brandl said.

Located two kilometers north of the battalion's Attack Position was Brandl's executive officer, Major Mark Winn, 41, a native of Pleasanton, California. The good-natured Winn had been a company commander in the Gulf War. A graduate of Rutgers University, Winn was commander of the Main Command Post mounted in seven Humvees and code-named C-7.

Winn recalled, "We would set the vehicles up in a certain formation so that we could hook all the radios up together. When Brandl went forward to the berm, we took command of the fight while they were moving. We had close to forty Marines in our command unit at Fallujah."

Bravo Company gets a Foothold in Fallujah

At 2130 Bravo Company was positioned along the railroad berm and was preparing to advance in one hour into the city. Indirect fire was still being brought to bear on their first objective. Captain Omohundro had eventually linked up with the Recon Marines. "Once we linked up with Recon and a Navy SEAL unit, I gave the command to move out. We went through the breach and passed through a garbage dump," Omohundro recalled.

Second Lieutenant Andrew Eckert's 1st Platoon was tasked to be the first platoon of Bravo Company and of the battalion to enter and grab a foothold. The battalion had a five-block wide wedge attack zone to enter into Fallujah proper. Eckert, 23, from Baltimore, Maryland, was a Michael J. Fox look alike. Carrying an M4 carbine, Eckert looked out at the open terrain they would have to push across to reach the city.

"This was a rehearsed event. Everyone in the company knew the exact way we would be making entrance into the city. The engineers cleared a lane about fourteen meters wide for us to push across," Lieutenant Eckert recalled. "Engineers went out and marked the lane we would be going on by dropping chem lights on either side."

Corporal Nick Criddle, 23, Assaultman Squad Leader, attached to Eckert's platoon adjusted the two SMAW rockets and an additional 50-

pounds of demo explosives he had on his back. The Cleveland, Tennessee native turned to two members of his squad, Lance Corporal Robert Kelly and Lance Corporal Sean Evans who were also positoned along the railroad bank. "Keep your heads down and I'll see you in the city." All three Marines carried M16A4s.

The assaultman's job, like the combat engineers, was to help breach buildings with their SMAWs and the demo explosives they carried. "We joked that the assaultmen were the 'Bastard children' of the infantry," Criddle said.

As tracer rounds and RPGs streamed from Fallujah, Eckert turned to his 1st squad leader standing beside him. The Marine he turned to was a twenty-three-year-old Marine from Stoudsburg, Pennsylvania, Jacob Knospler. His wife had just presented the Marine with a baby daughter a few months before in September. Being in Iraq, Knospler had yet to see his newborn daughter. Like most Marines he enjoyed motorcycles and hunting. "We were watching RPGs coming from the city at the tanks positioned to our front. It was all unreal," Knospler recalled.

Eckert got set to issue the order to push across the marked lane when he turned to his 1st squad leader and said, "Corporal Knospler, let's go!"

Knospler took a deep breath and answered his lieutenant, "Alright sir!" Then he quickly asked, "Right there with the blue chem lights?"

"Yeah! You see them? Follow them to that alley and take the first building," said Eckert.

"Roger!" Knospler answered as he pushed out with his 1st Squad. Corporal Jacob Knospler's squad would be the first Marines from Battalion 1/8 to enter the city of Fallujah with Knospler leading them in.

Knospler remembered, "I led four Marines into the city and Sergeant Sam Williams followed with the rest of the twelve man squad." The five Marines steeled themselves for the advance into the unknown, the depths of Fallujah. Leading his riflemen from the front, Knospler clutched his M4.

The unmarried Sergeant Samuel Williams, 24, from Traverse City, Michigan, carrying his M16 along with the eight remaining men from 1st Squad, followed by the remaining Marines in Eckert's 1st Platoon, picked themselves up and joined Knospler's squad pushing over the railroad tracks. The forty-six Marines in Eckert's platoon, pumped with adrenaline, started running across the open field in a sprint. Earlier the men in the platoon had likened their expected advance across this open field to the D-Day invasion of Normandy. They didn't know how much fire they would be receiving as they crossed the open terrain. Forty-six pairs of boots were pounding the loose sandy gravel as the Marines ran between the chem lights toward the city. They ran over rocky ground that was also littered with rusty junk. All they could hear as they ran was the sound from their boots, heavy breathing along with the noise of equipment and ammo rubbing together. To them it sounded like a small herd of elephants on the move. Were they attracting the attention of the hidden enemy? There was firing going on in other parts of the city but the Marines blotted it out as they ran. They finally reached a road and quickly ran across it holding their collective breaths, fully expecting the enemy to open up on them with machine guns and RPGs.

Another Marine crossing the road in Knospler's squad was the 3rd Fire Team Leader Corporal Kyle Mastropasqua, 21, from Winston-Salem, North Carolina. "We were ready to go. As we moved forward we couldn't see very well with the NVGs and had to use our thermals to get a good idea what was to our immediate front. It was real chaotic at that time."

"There was firing going on at the time, but none was directed at us," recounted Eckert. "At least we didn't think so, we were focused on getting across and into the city. My radio operator PFC Sanabria rolled his ankle as we were running. He continued trudging on with us even though his ankle was killing him. He fell about thirty-feet back before he finally got across with a few of the rear guard Marines. We made it to that first house and we called back and told Captain Omohundro we had the building."

"There was willy-pete being fired by us and it was falling near us," recalled Assaultman Corporal Criddle. "First Sergeant Whittington kept telling guys not to step on it for it only caused it to flare up again."

Sergeant Sam Williams explained, "There was a lot of confusion when we first entered the city. It was hard to orient with all the smoke and fire. For an hour to two hours before they had been prepping the city with white phosphorous and it was still burning on the ground. I asked one of my Marines to stomp on it and his boot caught fire. We learned you had to throw soil on it to extinguish it."

The run to the building had taken the Marines all of forty-five long, and what seemed like, drawn out seconds. But those forty-five seconds seemed an eternity for the members of Bravo Company as stray rounds cracked around them. The out of breath Marines of 1st Platoon finally got across and piled into the empty building. They began setting up firing positions from the doors and windows. A few Marines went to the rooftop.

Tank commander Captain Meyers said, "Lieutenant Klingensmith's tanks were to be attached to Charlie Company and once they got a foothold in the city, would then assist Bravo Company in their push into Fallujah. I was back with two tanks at the Attack Position and we were monitoring everything that happened. Both Charlie and Bravo Companies began pushing simultaneously into the city. It was evident that both needed tanks. Klingensmith stayed with Charlie and I pushed forward to Bravo Company with a tank section consisting of two tanks."

Corpsman HM3 Milton Jones, Jr. carrying an M9, followed a tank through the breach and into the city. There were two corpsmen attached to each line platoon and the second corpsman in the platoon was HM3 Nadermann. Jones didn't know it at the time, but he was attached to the company that would take the brunt of the casualties in the coming days in Fallujah. "We secured the first building we came to. I was just thinking, *I hope I don't get hit and none of my guys get hit.* The Marines around me were doing real good suppressing the enemy," Jones recalled.

Staff Sergeant Ben Alicea attached to Lieutenant Wilkens' 3rd Platoon led his sniper team up the stairs to the roof of one of two buildings Bravo had taken at the edge of the city, the first foothold for Brandl's battalion in Fallujah.

"I saw a guy just walking up the street," Alicea said. "I asked 'Ski' if he could see him with his night optics. The man advanced to about 50 yards from us and then made a right turn. 'Ski' said he couldn't see him."

Positioned nearby, a team of Navy SEALs saw the walking man and opened fire.

Corporal Knospler was one of the Marines on the rooftop. "We looked down and could see that our tanks in the street were the main targets of the enemies RPG rounds," Corporal Knospler said. "We stayed about two hours on that first rooftop and didn't receive too much in the way of enemy fire directed at us. We kept wondering when they would discover us up there and fire at us."

Second Lieutenant Andy Eckert was positioned with his 1st Platoon to the western-most sector of Bravo's objective to establish a support-by-fire position for Charlie Company's attack on battalion objective F, the Braxton complex. Eckert's Marines, the first unit into the city, now would cover the movement of the rest of Bravo Company as they set up in a hasty 180-battle position on the west side of the traffic circle near the edge of Fallujah.

When the rest of the Marines of Bravo Company, loaded with upwards of ninety pounds of equipment each, climbed over the railroad embankment they were witnesses to an assortment of vivid red and blue flares. The flares were being fired by the insurgents to try and nullify the Americans' night-vision goggles. It was as if the Marines were at a 4th of July fireworks display or a rock and roll light show. Tracers were streaking into and out of the city. Some of the buildings were on fire and the whole city seemed to be wrapped up in smoke.

With hearts in their throats and butterflies in their stomachs, they pushed down from the embankment. They stepped down onto a rocky and junk littered railroad yard located on the edge of the city. The Marines of Bravo Company moved quickly through the debris in the open area to the safety of the two houses they would occupy.

One of those Marines was a lanky twenty-two-year old Marine from Elysian Fields, Texas, Corporal Thomas Hodges, who had four brothers, three of whom served in the military. In his second year at Panola College, when 9/11 occurred, Hodges felt that his freedom was precious enough to join the Marines and help defend it. Hodges talked with a slow Texas twang. "I wasn't scared going into the city. This is what I had enlisted for. I was excited and looking forward to going into Fallujah."

In the background, a "psy ops" truck began blaring old AC/DC songs like, *Hells Bells* to counter the propaganda coming from the cities many loudspeakers located on the mosques. It was like a scene out of a Francis Ford Coppola movie:

> *I'm a rolling thunder a pouring rain*
> *I'm coming on like a hurricane*
> *My lightning's flashing across the sky*
> *You're only young but your gonna die*
> *I won't take no prisoner won't spare no lives*
> *Nobody's putting up a fight*
> *I got my bell I'm gonna take you to hell*
> *Hell's bells*
> *Yeah Hell's bells.*

The small arms fire had slacked off a little. Marines now began pushing in to the web of streets and alleyways where one sniper could hold up an entire company for hours, even a day.

"We were receiving intense fire as we moved in, including RPG rounds. Once we got into the building we began returning fire," Captain Read Omohundro explained.

From his vantagepoint in the secured house, Eckert could see fire coming from the south up Route Ethan. "We were concerned about how far Charlie Company had advanced before we returned fire."

Captain Omohundro pushed across with Second Lieutenant Steven Berch's, 2nd Platoon in the second wave. First Lieutenant Christopher Wilkens, 24, from Brewster, New York, brought his 3rd Platoon across the railroad tracks and moved into the smoky city. After Bravo Company had secured the western side of the battalion at the traffic circle, it set in motion Charlie Company's move.

"I positioned the Recon, Navy SEALs and our snipers to cover the far western area. They had the better night vision scopes and better long distance shooting capability to keep that area clear. There was a lot of firing going off to the west and east of our position," Captain Omohundro said.

A member of 3rd Platoon, Team Leader Corporal Anthony Silva III, 22, from Oakdale, California, with a wife and two children at home (one born while he was deployed in Iraq), remembered the first hours in the city as being very chaotic. "It was real confusing. No one knew what was going on. At the small leadership, we didn't know exactly what was going on around us and what was supposed to happen. The first night we weren't at the right place at the right time."

Lance Corporal David Ojeda, 2nd Platoon, echoed the words of his friend Silva about the push into the city, "After we got in the city everything was chaotic, nobody really knew what was going on. Everybody was running around trying to get their bearing. Once everything got organized, we started to break off and everything started getting better."

A member of Silva's team, Lance Corporal Edwin Maldonado, 21, from San Juan, Puerto Rico, lugged his twenty-pound weapon, the SAW gun, into the dark city. "Everyone was anxious and excited, even though we didn't know what was going to happen. We were Marines and we wanted a taste of war, but we would get more of a taste than we wanted."

A young Eddie Murphy look alike, Lance Corporal Xavier Forester, 23, who hailed from Tampa, Florida, was armed with a MK-153 SMAW (rocket launcher) and moved forward with his squad. Some of his fellow Marines even called him 'Eddie' after the movie star. "I had gotten in a little trouble before coming to Fallujah, so I was kind of on the shit list. I hated life at that point, but once we got into the city it changed. I never had that feeling before. It was like happiness mixed with the biggest adrenaline rush that I ever had. It was a combat high all the time. It was like a big hunting trip."

In fact it was a hunting trip, the Marines had to hunt the insurgents and eliminate them from the city. The only difference was that here, the targets they hunted had AKs, RPGs, RPKs and would be firing back. The Marines would get to know the insurgents' weapons of choice—the AK-47, RPG, RPK, and the deadly Dragunov sniper rifle. And each one held their own terror for the Marines, and all were extremely deadly. The Russians, who were now supposedly our allies, had designed the weapons during the Cold War. Now, these same weapons were killing our Marines and Soldiers.

A member of Weapons Platoon, commanded by First Lieutenant Vince Noble, Sergeant Shawn Gianforte, was sitting up on the railroad tracks getting ready to go through the breach and into the flaming city. "I told myself, *Here goes nothing. I have to haul ass, keep my head down and if I get through there, I'll be good.* We ran as fast as we could. To my surprise, we made it through the breach with very little resistance at all. We went in one building and got set up and let everyone figure out where we were. Then the platoon started moving. Lieutenant Noble was running the show and Captain Stroud was our FAC (Forward Air Controller). As the line platoons moved forward we fell in with them, and once they cleared a house and got up on the rooftop, we would move in and set up shop on the roof. We would bust out the binos and get the radios up and wait for anyone to call for help."

Captain Read Omohundro set up his company headquarters in a corner house that had received some damaging artillery fire. The lower floor was completely destroyed. The command unit made their way through the rubble and up the shaky stairs to the rooftop. He relayed his company's position back to the lieutenant colonel, "All we could see up there were vehicles to the south of us. The enemy was using cars to drop off fighters. We could see our tanks firing on targets and the enemy was concentrating on them, not realizing that we were in the buildings yet. We also were watching for Charlie Company to push into the city to the east. Comm was good and we were getting reports from intel that enemy fighters were moving in and where they were coming from. The reports were coming in so fast that it was difficult to get an understanding of what they were seeing in relation to our position and whom they were attacking. It started raining again around 2400. I didn't want to stay in the same place too long, then they'll pinpoint our position and start firing." Omohundro remembers.

After entering the city, Noble's FiST Team set up on one of the rooftops. They sat there for a few hours waiting for a call for assistance, but none came. They observed the clearing operation unfolding below them in the streets and alleyways of the city. They, along with the infantry, were getting the flow and feel of the battle and how it was developing. After the first few hours, calls for indirect fire for support began coming in.

Sergeant Gianforte recounted a close call from friendly support fire. "3rd Platoon got stuck in an area and started to receive contact. We were trying to figure out where they were. It took awhile, but after using their strobe lights we located them. We moved and linked up with them and then called in some artillery. I remember Lieutenant Collins called it in and he said, 'Hey Gianforte get down it's going to be pretty close!' I asked, 'Sir how close do you mean?' He said, 'About 175 meters.' I figured that isn't too bad, but I watched as Lieutenant Collins got down, so I thought, *Yeah, I'd better get down too.* I looked up and could see the glow of the round going over us, and when it hit, it sounded like it was right next to us. Later, when we left the city, I met one of the Marines from the Fire Control Center who told me that specific call for fire was only 86 meters away from us. They said it was one of the closest ones they could find for a combat call."

A Weapons Company Marine attached to Bravo Company's 3rd Platoon, Lance Corporal Andres Llerena, 25, a graduate of Tappan Zee High School and a native of Sparkill, New York, pushed into the city and recalled receiving fire that first night. "We made our way through the streets trying to get to the houses we were going to. At one house we moved into the Iraqis began firing at us with small arms and then with RPGs. The other SMAW gunner and I went up to the rooftop to see where the fire was coming from. We figured it out and began firing along with our snipers. We took care of the problem. We stayed up on that roof for a couple hours."

Climbing up to the same rooftop that Lance Corporal Llerena was on, SAW gunner Lance Corporal Maldonado found out there were too many Marines on the roof and had to go back down. "I took another position on the second deck on a balcony. I started to open fire across the street. In the return fire I took a little shrapnel," Maldonado remembered. He felt a burning on his body and had the corpsman check it out, "He told me it was just a scratch. We laughed about it and kept going. There were guys getting hit worse than me."

Located on the rooftop was a sniper team that had been attached to Bravo Company. Californian, Corporal Bradley Watson, commanded the team. His spotter was Lance Corporal Jeffery Walker. Also part of his team were Corporal James Mendenhall and his sniper/spotter Corporal Kirk Bosselmann. Mendenhall, 27, hailed from Chicago, Illinois. The graduate from Southern Illinois enjoyed sky diving in his spare time. Here in Fallujah he carried a SAM-R, sort of a jazzed up M16, used by Marine snipers.

Mendenhall recounted his entering the city, "We set up on two adjacent buildings and our team got its first kill that first night."

Corporal Nick Criddle's Assault Squad went to the rooftop along with Sergeant McDade and his machine gunners. "While on the rooftop there was a violent explosion off to our right in 3/1's area of operation. They must have hit a weapon's cache because there was a big mushroom cloud and the shock wave from the explosion rocked our building."

Llerena and his fellow Marines checked out their first kill as they began pushing south with the rest of the company. "We got moving again and stopped in the house where we had taken fire from. We saw the dead individual and the weapons he had been using, including RPGs," Lance Corporal Llerena said.

"We had some trouble maneuvering troops into where 3rd Platoon was positioned," FiST member Gianforte said. "Basher the AC-130 came on site over us and we began working with them."

Corpsman HM3 Jones, pushing down the street with the infantry, was relieved the company hadn't needed his help. "We kept moving forward and got no sleep that first night. In fact, we pushed forward twenty-four straight hours, suppressing the enemy as we moved. Luckily we hadn't received any casualties."

Texas native, Corporal Tom Hodges recalled pushing farther into the city. "We went about six blocks and entered a building to take a rest. It was maybe three or four in the morning. We set up to hold our ground with Marines going to the rooftop. From that advantage point they saw movement in the street below. Three individuals were coming down the street toward us. We opened fire on them. Early the next morning we moved out and saw the bodies lying there with guns, grenades and RPGs lying beside them. There was a blood trail going over a short wall where one of them had gone."

Assaultman Criddle remembers, "We left the rooftop and went down into the street. We were cutting across an alleyway when I heard a Marine Cobra above us. I looked up and it was firing off 8 missiles at a building near us. Chunks of the building began raining down on us." No one was injured and Bravo Company pushed on.

Off to Captain Omohundro's west lay around 150 meters of open and unoccupied parts of the city. Beyond that was the right flank of the Army's Battalion 2/7. In the original drafting of the battle plan, the Iraqi Security Forces were to sweep and clear both flanks, as well as policing the rear of Battalion 1/8.

Charlie Company goes Through the Breach

Charlie Company commander, Captain Theodore Bethea, proud of his New Orleans roots and upbringing had used the call sign, *Cajun* for his Charlie Company. Bethea's orders for the coming battle were specific. "It was a very clear mission statement. Attack and destroy enemy in zone in order to seize designated objectives. If there were enemy that needed to be destroyed, we would destroy them. If not, we continued to push south to our objectives using fire within the rules of engagement," Bethea explained.

At 2200, the 185 Marines in Charlie Company conducted their mechanized movement in eighteen amtracs to the Attack Point. On the push up, Second Lieutenant Brandon Turner rode in the lead amtrac with some of his platoon, followed by Captain Bethea in the second vehicle.

After arriving they grabbed their weapons and dismounted just north of the railroad tracks, north of the city. They searched out their squads in the darkness and gathered them along the berm and settled-in, their weapons pointed toward the city while they waited for the order to attack.

Lance Corporal Craig Wintrow, 19, from the quaint, little tourist town of Mount Dora, Florida, and a member of Turner's 2nd Platoon recalls the push to the breach line, "Coming up to Fallujah we rode in the amtracs. We really didn't see where we were going, but I remember them telling us that as soon as we dismounted the amtracs, people were going to be shooting at us, just a whole bunch of chaos. They shouted out 30 seconds, 20 seconds, 10 seconds, then the doors dropped and we ran off. You just start shaking and you get scared. We all ran off screaming, 'Yeah. We're going to get you mother f***ers!' We were trying to motivate one another and keep each other in the fight. When we dismounted there was a 30-foot berm in front of us. There wasn't anyone going to shoot us behind that berm. At that point my knees got weak and I almost fell down because it was such a relief to arrive safely. We waited there until everyone got on line."

Lance Corporal Joshua Thompson, 20, a native of Swainsboro, Georgia, 2nd Platoon, 1st Squad, clambered out the back of the amtrac carrying his twenty-pound weapon, the SAW (Squad Automatic Weapon), as well as an additional seventy-five pounds of equipment and gear. Taking a position with his squad along the rocky berm, he peered out into the surreal looking city. "When we got out, we set up as we had hundreds of times before in training. We watched the city getting lit up from artillery and planes and everyone was pumped up, ready to get in there and get some, although everyone knows deep down inside they were scared to death."

Lance Corporal Dante Di Pasqua, 20, Boca Raton, Florida, another SAW gunner in Turner's Platoon, 2nd Squad, remembered the awesome firepower delivered on the city by U.S. forces on that first night, "It was just amazing watching the jets and the line charges going off. The explosion was enough to shake you a mile away. The engineers sent out a rocket with 1,000 pounds of C-4 that detonated the mines in our path."

The explosion created a 50-foot fireball and cleared out any mines or IEDs the Marine might encounter.

Sparta, North Carolina native, Lance Corporal Jason Carpenter, 20, a member of Second Lieutenant Rhoades' 1st Platoon, 2nd Squad, recalls running out the back of the amtrac, "It was all noise when the door dropped, mostly from the planes lighting up the city. Explosions and rounds were going off everywhere. My squad found each other and got together and set up a support by fire position near the berm. It was like the 4th of July with all the fireworks."

Another member of 1st Platoon, 2nd Squad, a native of Sunrise, Florida, nineteen-year-old, Lance Corporal Rafael Peguero clutching his M16A4, watched the planes, tanks and artillery soften the city in preparation for Charlie Company breaching the line. He had lost his father from a heart attack just four days before his birthday, four days after Peguero's wedding, and just six days before his deployment to Iraq.

"The city glowed. My biggest fear before we entered the city was IEDs. We had heard the IEDs were all over the place. Everyone was warning us to be alert, stay focused. The NVGs we used were only good for defensive operations and not that good for offensive fighting." Peguero's new bride Waleska was awaiting his return in Jacksonville, North Carolina. When bored he would scribble his thoughts down on paper. He wrote, "The true heroes in the world are those who feel it at heart and apply it in actions, leaving the cowards at only words." These Marines lived by their actions.

1st Platoon, 1st Squad member, Lance Corporal Stephen Ross O'Rourke, 19, from Lebanon, Ohio, stared in awe as the city was continually softened up by air and artillery, "We rolled in there on amtracs, AAVs. One broke down and we had to get out, distribute seventeen Marines between the other three amtracs. Bodies were lying on top of each other. We were just stuffed in with bodies, packs, weapons and equipment. Artillery and air support was just nailing the city. The planes would just light up the city with its machine guns. It was unbelievable. I had never seen anything like that in my life. You'd hear explosions left and right. When we dismounted the amtracs we could see RPGs flying over our heads. They were firing at us already."

Lance Corporal Giusti, 3rd Platoon, 3rd Squad, who wrestled in high school and enjoyed lifting weights, now found himself lugging and wrestling his SAW from the amtrac and up the berm. He set up with others from his company along the rim of the tall berm, "We were all pumped up and we hoped, whatever happened, we would get through there safely."

Captain Bethea received a full accountability of the company from First Sergeant Andrade, positioned just north of the railroad tracks.

Second Lieutenant Brandon Turner linked up with Captain Schauble's Marine Force Reconnaissance Platoon and the D-9 Bulldozers section that now were under the direct command of Captain Bethea. The D-9 bulldozers were to lead the attack through the breach. The battalion had two D-9s on the scene to assist in getting through the tall berm and for later use in the city, if needed.

Turner, 26, a graduate of the famed military school in Virginia's Shenandoah Valley, V.M.I., was from the neighboring state, North Carolina, and the small town of Newton. Married to wife Amy, with one child, Turner enjoyed the outdoors, especially skiing and rock climbing. Now moving through the sandy rubble along the train tracks with his M16, he was far from ski country. He would have to look far and wide in Iraq to find some rocks high enough to climb.

"My Marines wanted to get it over with. We were ready. When we arrived, we got in a defensive perimeter behind the railroad tracks and waited," Turner remembered.

Lance Corporal Wintrow remembers hugging the thirty-foot high berm, "To show you how aggressive the insurgents were, they shot an RPG from a street at us, while we set outside the city. I remember just watching the RPG fly by. It just moved slower than you expect. There were also countless tracers coming from the city toward us."

Carrying his 249 Squad Automatic Weapon, Lance Corporal O'Rourke tried to stay focused on the coming attack on the city. "I was looking to my Team Leader for what was coming next. With RPGs flying overhead, we wondered what the city would be like once we went in."

Captain Theodore Bethea and Force Recon Captain Schauble conducted a face-to-face liaison before he ordered his company forward to the breach line. Around 2230 Bethea ordered the D-9 bulldozers through the breach and got his company moving along behind. The first D-9, which also carried mortar ammunition for the company, went up and over the railroad tracks and plunged down the far embankment into a thick muddy morass from the recent light rain. Turner's 2nd Platoon was following close behind. No sooner had the order been given to attack, then Murphy's Law quickly intervened. The D-9 tried to maneuver out of its plight but was hopelessly stuck and apparently no further use to Charlie Company that night. The second D-9 couldn't maneuver around the stuck bulldozer. Turner stared at the immobile D-9s, shook his head and reported the bogged down bulldozer to Captain Bethea. There's a saying, "Always have a backup plan because the first one won't work."

Turner remembered, "Pushing across the breach we had the D-9 dozer in front of us and it got stuck in the mud. The whole plan started to go to shit in a heartbeat. I said, 'What the hell!'"

Turner got the go ahead to by-pass the bulldozers and to conduct the assault on the city. Staff Sergeant Nash, 1st Platoon, posted a squad for security on the stuck D-9. Corporal Paz, 1st Platoon, supervised the removal of mortar rounds from the stuck D-9 to the second bulldozer. First Lieutenant Miller had them add a collection casualty cart to put the mortar rounds into and attach it to the second bulldozer. They needed to get the ammunition, eventually, up to the Braxton complex.

"Lieutenant Matt Rhoades detailed some of his Marines for security on the dozer and we kept pushing," Turner recalled.

"The engineers had marked the breach and so we made sure the Marines stayed between the markers to prevent hitting landmines," Captain Bethea said.

It started drizzling harder, and the Marines, like their lieutenant colonel, hadn't brought their rain gear.

"We followed the D-9 through the berm and over the tracks as it cleared land mines and stuff, and then it got stuck in the mud," said Lance Corporal Joshua Thompson, 1st Squad, 2nd Platoon.

Thompson and his friend Corporal Di Pasqua squinted toward the smoky city trying to make out what was going on. Thompson said, "We finally got on line near the city, in fact we were right across the street from the city. Myself and Lance Corporal Di Pasqua in my squad, if we wanted to look around, the only NVGs we had was the scope on our SAWs."

Lieutenant Turner, who as a V.M.I. cadet had hiked forty-eight miles with the other cadets from his school to the famed New Market Civil War battlefield site, now hiked with his Marines into the rim of Fallujah and into history.

A Marine in Turner's platoon, Lance Corporal Dante Di Pasqua, who planned to become an engineer after his enlistment was over, lay hunkered down behind the thirty-foot berm with his platoon. He didn't know how far from the city they were. He recalled the platoon finally moving forward, "No one told me we were that close to the city at that point. We got up on the road and I hadn't looked through my NVGs, so I figured we had to hike quite a bit to get there. They told us to take a knee, so I said to myself, *The hell with it. I'm going to see how far we are.*" Di Pasqua didn't have to look far. His 1st Squad was right across the street from the city of Fallujah. "The city was just right there. If they had opened fire on us, I would not have been prepared for it. Then we got the word to push in."

Floridian Lance Corporal Wintrow also describes the initial push into the city, "We got the word 'go!' It was real chaotic going in, tracers, AK fire, but as we hit the main part of the city it got real quiet. The officers were hollering out general instructions, 'Make sure you keep your dispersion. Make sure you keep security. Move up and make sure you have cover. Use the rubble or buildings for cover.'"

The Marine tank platoon, commanded by First Lieutenant Klingensmith, was on line along Phase Line April supporting Charlie Company's initial push south into the rim of Fallujah.

The remainder of Charlie Company breached the line and went up and over the tracks and joined Turner's 2nd Platoon in the Jeghaiti neighborhood. They were met with a surreal picture as shells continued pouring in and out of Fallujah. The company seized their first real estate in the city, a foothold at the northern edge of their first objective, Objective Braxton, located on the eastside of Route Ethan.

Staff Sergeant Corey Lohr, 29, 3rd Platoon, Charlie Company, a native of Westbrookville, New York, had a wife and two children home in Jacksonville, North Carolina. When at home, Lohr, enjoyed riding and working on motorcycles. He recalled going through the breach in a letter home to his wife of ten years, Cindy:

"We crossed the train tracks through this mud and rubble. Once we got to (Phase Line) April the platoon spread out on line. Lieutenant Littell then instructed 1st squad to assault forward and clear out a house. 2nd and 3rd squads remained back with us. We then started receiving sniper fire from our east. 2nd squad covered our East flank and returned fire in the direction of the sniper. The .50 cal on the tank then started to shoot down our flank. 2nd and 3rd got pushed forward to avoid getting shot. 1st Plt rolled in with the D-9 and assumed positions to our East...RPG/mortar fire started coming in close to our positions."

Whether by plan or because of the bombardment from air strikes, artillery and tanks, most of the enemy positioned along the northern rim of the city seemed stunned. Some had been killed by the heavy bombardment, while others had been totally surprised by the sudden advance into the city and pulled farther south into the center of Fallujah. For whatever reason, it became ghostly quiet in Charlie Company's initial zone of attack.

Staff Sergeant Lohr describes what the Marines of Charlie Company saw moving through that eerily deserted part of the city, "When we got on line there was nothing but rubble. As we pushed on into the built up area it started drizzling again. The firing in the city created a light show that reflected off the wet buildings and streets. About twenty-five percent of the houses we came to were destroyed. The neighborhood was just house after house, maybe an inch between each house. They all had walls six feet tall with gates. Countless electric lines draped on houses and hung down onto the deserted streets. Some houses looked like they were set up as enemy battle positions but it looked as though they had pulled back. It was real hot and the city had a musty odor."

When Second Lieutenant Brandon Turner first entered the city he was amazed at what he saw. He stood on top of a pile of rubble looking around, trying to get his bearing. He was looking for the house they were to set up in. But, because of the heavy bombardment from the air and artillery, nothing looked as it should. He couldn't make out anything recognizable as he stared off into the darkness. He stood motionless on the house he was to secure which was now a pile of rubble. "We had seen imagery before of what the city should look like. When we got there that house was leveled except for rebar and concrete sticking out of the ground. We were thinking, *Why is it so quiet?* I mean it just got real quiet. No shooting! Nothing! Then we got 100 feet farther into the city, then it was game on."

Staff Sergeant Lohr's radioman, the single Lance Corporal Chris Willson, 22, from Renton, Washington recalled, "When we first went into the city I didn't use my NVGs and was having a hard time seeing. We scaled the rubble of a destroyed three-story house in the dark. The piled rubble was the height of a one story house and with the radio and all my gear I felt I was going to fall and twist an ankle or knee."

The insurgents shook the cobwebs from their heads caused by the heavy bombardment and struck back. "RPGs started popping over head." An RPG round went WHIZZING by Turner's head. "My corpsman grabbed me and it exploded behind us," Turner said.

In the misting darkness the quietude the Marines of Charlie Company had first experienced after entering the rim of the city came to an abrupt end. RPGs came flying at them from the south, as well as small arms fire snapping and cracking around them. The Marines' mouths became instantly dry from the tension. Their training began to kick in.

Sergeant Robert Frederick, Weapons Platoon, was amazed at seeing his first RPG streaming by his men. "We were taking heavy fire a couple of times as we pushed south to our first objective, the Al Hydra Mosque. An RPG round flew right in the middle of two of my gun teams and exploded a hundred meters behind us. The RPG round was actually pretty as it flew by us."

The Marines tried to stay near the walls and out of the open street as they surged forward in the darkness. Every window and door they passed could be hiding an insurgent armed with an AK-47. Every rooftop they passed beneath could conceal an enemy fighter with an RPG or grenades. The Marines moved in teams and entered houses in stacks watching one another's back. Constant communication between the stack members is critical in this environment. The training kicked in. When assaulting a house from the ground floor, the Marines would seize the front courtyard first, then the two seating rooms, followed by the central hallway. The Marine stack, supporting one another, would then move to each successive upper deck. Finally they would climb the ladder to the uppermost rooftop of the house. When tanks were assisting them, the Marine infantrymen would utilize them for cover and move along behind.

Carrying his heavy M-240G, Lance Corporal Jason Carpenter, who had wrestled and played baseball in high school, pushed off the berm and entered the city with Second Lieutenant Rhoades, 1st Platoon. "It was unreal. We moved over near a tank and watched it open up on a couple of buildings just outside the city. We got the word to push and came upon our first problem. 3rd Platoon, 3rd Squad, Corporal Sill's squad, was pinned down by sniper fire. Staff Sergeant Lohr told my squad leader, Sergeant Brooks, that he needed a machine gun team to help them out. We fired on a couple of buildings to provide cover for them to get out," Carpenter recalled.

Another member of 1st Platoon pushing forward, Lance Corporal Stephen O'Rourke remembered, "As soon as we got in the city, there was a little bit of confusion at this traffic circle. We had to link up, under fire, with the other platoons so we could get on line as a company. We cleared a two-story house and then realized there were enemy snipers on the roofs to the left and right of us. Force Recon attached to us yelled, 'We got the roof!' Lance Corporal Maldonado armed with an M16 and I got on the roof with the Force Recon guys. They said, 'On the count of three, we're going to fire on the house we are taking fire from.'" Firing on the house located to the east of their position, the Marines wiped out the enemy fighters. "That was the first time I had fired and it was pretty crazy."

Lance Corporal Giusti, 3rd Platoon, moving through the dark streets far from home became a target of the gathering enemy fighters. "We got through the first block and my fire team Leader and I and two attachments to us, Lance Corporal Crowe and Lance Corporal Leduc, who were our assault men since our fire team was shorthanded at the time, were pushing into the city. We crossed over the road and all of a sudden it was like a wall of lead coming down the street from a building that had insurgents inside. I lay down some suppression fire with my SAW on the enemy. Corporal Arroyo with his M203 sent about two HEDP rounds inside the building." A violent explosion followed each firing, quickly killing the insurgents in the building. "The firing stopped and we figured the enemy snipers were KIA. We got moving again and crossed the street to provide security for 2nd and 3rd squads of 3rd Platoon."

The Marines of Charlie Company pursued the enemy fighters down rain slick streets and alleyways. The glare of muzzle flashes, flares and air strikes reflected off the streets causing their NVGs to be almost useless in the darkness. Explosions reverberated off the houses and buildings causing the Marines' ears to start ringing. Whenever they received fire from dark shadows, open windows or rooftops, they would set up to root the enemy fighters out. The Marine fire teams are no different than a well-trained basketball or football team, except for one important difference, their lives depended on one another, and no one could make a wrong move. They knew when to enter a house and what to do once inside. They were trained to react on instinct to threats found inside. The Marines knew when to move and to always cover each other's back. But most importantly, they knew the unwritten rule—never leave a fellow Marine behind, wounded or dead. It goes to the core of every Marine infantryman to get the downed Marine out.

With the insurgents defense steadily stiffening, Second Lieutenant Turner got his 2nd Platoon pushing deeper into the dark city. He began issuing orders to his squad leaders. "My platoon sergeant pushed off to the left, 1st Squad with their sergeant pushed off to the right, and I pushed up the center. Second Lieutenant Mark Littell, 3rd Platoon was to my left. Mark and I were on line with each other. At one point 3rd Platoon got held up and I kept pushing. We went so far ahead of the rest of the battalion, we began to get hit harder and harder. We got a hundred meters in front, and in the desert or woods a hundred meters is nothing, but here in a city fight, it became a real problem."

Captain Bethea, who had waited until the Iraqi Coalition troops were accounted for, now pushed farther into the city and moved to a building situated behind his 2nd Platoon. "I encouraged Lieutenant Turner to get into a defensive position, while getting 3rd Platoon pushed up to maintain our formation. 2nd Platoon was along the route of attack, 3rd Platoon adjacent to them on the left, and 1st Platoon covered our flank, less one squad who was posted to the stuck dozer to our rear. This prevented the enemy from getting in and enveloping us. We were in a U-shape defensive formation," Bethea explained.

A member of LCDR Richard Jadick's medics, Texas native, HA Argueta, still outside Fallujah, recalled watching the city explode in colorful lights. "That's when we started receiving casualties coming in to our aid station. We also started receiving calls telling us of Marines getting hit with small arms, IEDs and RPG rockets. Our first casualty that came in had been hit in the leg by an enemy sniper. As the wounded came in we heard them talking to each other about the fighting in the city. We marveled at the camaraderie and the esprit they had. We could tell they cared very much for each other."

The D-9 dozer was finally helped out of the mud by a tank retriever vehicle, commanded by Staff Sergeant Rocky Hutton. "Hutton didn't know how to drive a D-9," Remembered Tank Commander Captain Chris Meyers, "So he walks into this minefield gets in the D-9 bulldozer and looks at the controls and calls me over the net."

"Yeah, I can figure it out," said Hutton

So Hutton drove the D-9 bulldozer out of the quagmire of mud into the city and back into the fight.

Sergeant Major Hope was positioned at the berm near the breach line as Charlie Company and Bravo Company punched into the city. Hope said, "Initially we hit a lot of resistance when we first entered the city. Our main objective was getting a foothold in the city and get down to the Government Center and take that. We knew once we took that, we would be able to pour through, build up, and make our command post there. I know that Charlie Company hit some pretty rough stuff that first night."

Alpha Company Sits Tight Outside the City

.

While Charlie and Bravo Companies fought for a foothold in the city, Captain Aaron Cunningham's Alpha Company waited outside the city. Cunningham, 31, his hometown in historical Marietta, Georgia, had a wife, Jennifer, and three-year-old son Mason at home in the states. He carried an M16M4 rifle and had a 9mm pistol strapped to his body. Standing among his men, he watched the initial stages of the battle developing before him as both of his sister line companies punched through the breach and into Fallujah. He witnessed the constant firing and explosions as he walked among his Marines.

He knew his men were anxious to join their comrades in combat in the city, but he also knew there would be plenty of action left for his company in the coming days. Cunningham's Alpha Company had been tasked to enter the city, at the discretion of Lieutenant Colonel Gary Brandl, to secure the Government Center that would then be used as battalion headquarters, and more importantly, the forward aid station. He expected a heavy fight for his company at the Government Center.

A young Marine, Private Ross Caputi, 20, from Leominster, Massachusetts, went almost everywhere his commander, Captain Cunningham went, but he did it carrying a 50-pound radio on his back.

Caputi and Corporal Mineholtz both carried radios for Cunningham's use. One radio was for battalion and the other was the company radio.

Caputi remembered looking at the city when the other two line companies attacked south, "We were in trenches. It was night and the sky looked like a fireworks show. It started to drizzle a little. The next morning we loaded up in the amtracs and moved to a highway where we were to go in. We dismounted early in the morning and used the time to get some chow and smoke. Early the next morning we mounted back in the amtracs, they shut the doors and drove us right into the city."

PFC Paul Volpe and Staff Sergeant Stephen Davis

"I didn't go into the city in the first mission that my platoon went on, November 9," PFC Volpe recalls. "I stayed back to drive a truck with supplies in it that morning. I was pissed that I didn't get to go in with them on that first mission. They came back out of the city at 0830 and said that they would be going back in about ten minutes and I would be going in with them."

A member of that first casualty Medevac mission from Weapons Company was PFC Michael Johnson, proficient in the SAW, TOW, Mark-19 and M-240G machine gun. "We went in with eight trucks, and as we drew closer to the city, the noise got louder and louder. I asked myself, *What the hell am I doing?* We were security while the Army's M-113 armored ambulance picked up the wounded Marine. One RPG just missed our truck by going over the top. I could feel the heat of the rocket as it went over and blew up on the other side of a wall. Everyone was yelling trying to keep comm with each other and it wasn't working. Tracers were coming from every direction. We came back out of the city and then we heard of more casualties. We prepared to go back."

The turret gunner for the lead truck in that first mission, Lance Corporal Danny Myers, Weapons Company, along with his buddy, Corporal Smith, felt they would never get the opportunity to see combat but were now on their way into Fallujah. Sometimes you have to be careful what you wish for. "The first mission into the city went pretty well. To get into the city, we had to go up an incline to get over this bridge. When we were up on the bridge we could see the city was all smoke and fire. Things click, and it clicked right there, *We were in the shit*," Corporal Myers related.

Talking to his fellow Marines in Weapons Company, PFC Volpe was told that things were crazy in the city with RPGs and a lot of gunfire. He could hear explosions and gunfire from inside Fallujah, and the returning Marines confirmed that they were receiving fire.

Carrying his M16, PFC Volpe, a member of 3rd Platoon, climbed into the last of the eight Humvees that made up the convoy that would be returning to the city. Staff Sergeant Stephen Davis was the Section Leader of the 3rd Mobile Assault Platoon, Weapons Company. Lieutenant Kutilek's 3rd Platoon was tasked to support the battalion attack in the city. While mounted in Humvee gun trucks, the platoon would respond to multiple casualty evacuations along the attack line in the city.

"I was ready to go in, that's what I had trained for. We were tasked to go in and get some wounded back out. We crossed over a bridge and entered the city. We dismounted our vehicles and began walking down the main highway. An M-113 armored ambulance was used to load up the wounded and then we got back in the Humvees. As the convoy turned around, my Humvee was now the first in the line," Volpe remembered. "Captain Ritchie walked up to me and told me there was a KIA down the street. I called Sergeant Smith over to me and told him the situation. So we headed down the road, looking for the KIA. We had no idea where he was, and that was the problem. There were Marines walking on both sides of the highway."

Only a few blocks in the city, Volpe and the Marines in the Humvee kept looking for the KIA they had been called in to pick up, until they came to an area that was considered a danger zone by the line companies. There were houses on both sides of the street with a large rolling field off to the right. They reached a corner on the street and Volpe leaned out and checked for insurgents. It looked clear. Sergeant Mathew Smith walked up behind Volpe and told him to go ahead. Volpe lugging his M16 started dog trotting across the street.

"I had to run about a hundred yards to get behind the cover of a wall," Volpe said. "As I was running I looked to the left down a side street and saw two guys, one in a blue shirt peeking out from a wall about one-hundred and fifty yards away. Then all I heard was gunfire. I felt two rounds hit my leg, one in the thigh and one in the calf."

As soon as he was hit Volpe dropped quickly to the ground. He found himself lying in an open courtyard, under fire, and started screaming to Sergeant Smith that he had been hit and was down. The insurgent continued to pump AK-47 rounds at the downed Marine. Volpe held his injured leg as he lay in the open, trying to stem the bleeding. He tried not to move. He didn't want to attract more enemy fire. It wasn't just two insurgents firing at Volpe, but also gunmen in three houses were working him over with an assortment of weapons.

"It seemed like I was out in the road by myself forever, but it was only a few minutes," Volpe recalled. The lifeblood was pouring from his wounds and time was of the essence to get Volpe urgent medical attention.

Section Leader, Staff Sergeant Davis ran over to the corner of a wall to find one of his Marines, PFC Volpe, critically wounded and lying in the open courtyard. Davis saw that Volpe was still pinned down by the intense small arms, machine gun and RPG fire originating from three fortified houses that surrounded the area.

Staff Sergeant Davis had only seconds to decide what he would do. With utter disregard for his own safety, he left the covered position he was in and ran fifty meters down a street, through an open field, exposing himself to a hail of enemy fire. Despite the heavy volume of incoming fire, Davis reached Volpe and said, "Volpe let's go." He began assisting Volpe back across the open field to a covered position. RPK and AK-47 rounds were cracking and snapping around Marines, Volpe and Davis, as they struggled back together.

"Staff Sergeant Davis came out and grabbed me and helped me up and I put my arm around him and he started dragging me, and then he got shot," Volpe said. They had moved only ten meters when Davis took a painful round to his left hand. Both Marines fell clumsily to the ground. "It hit him in the pinky finger and the round went on into my forearm. Davis' finger was dangling off of his hand. He picked up his rifle and fired at the two men I had seen earlier down the street. He was firing inches from my head and it was the loudest thing I had ever heard. He got the two Iraqis down the street. Davis had to leave. He couldn't help me anymore," Volpe recalled.

Volpe's ears began ringing from the close muzzle blast of Davis' rifle. Although wounded and in pain, PFC Volpe managed to pick up his M16 and squeeze off thirty rounds at the enemy while the blood continued to pour from his wounds. Volpe was getting steadily weaker second by second from the loss of blood. Gunnery Sergeant Hill and Sergeant Smith now ran into the open area and both began helping Volpe back out of the enemy kill zone. Rounds continued to snap around them kicking up dirt and rock on the hard ground.

Other Weapons Company Marines had been supporting Volpe with a heavy volume of fire, trying to suppress the insurgents. Lance Corporal Harry Johnson worked his Mk19 like a violin against the enemy fighters. The grenades he was shooting detonated against the houses, tearing mortar and bricks from the walls helping to keep enemy heads down. Some rounds crashed through windows and blasted nearby rooftops. He fired rounds into the large open field to try and keep the enemy at bay. Johnson ended up firing fifty grenades from his Mk19 at the enemy fighters in the short firefight. His fire continually kept the insurgents off-balance while Volpe was finally brought to safety.

"Lance Corporal Harry Johnson saved me by laying down fire with his Mk19," An appreciative Volpe later explained.

Lance Corporal Danny Myers, Weapons Company, remembered his 1st Section arriving on the scene of the firefight, "Lance Corporal Johnson was there just putting Mk19 rounds across an open area with two buildings on either side of it. That's where all the action was going on."

One of the rescuing Marines now became a main target of the enemy snipers. Sergeant Matthew Smith, while out in the open, took a piercing round to his right shoulder.

Located in the last Humvee of the column, and not privy to the firefight going on to his front, PFC Michael Johnson, was surprised to see Sergeant Smith pass by with his right sleeve covered in blood. "I yelled over to him, 'Sergeant Smith where is the casualty?' He was just staring blankly off into space. The Gunner answered, 'Sergeant Smith is the casualty son!' Our lieutenant told me to, 'Go get the other trucks and tell them to get back over here because we have to go back in!' I ran over to the other trucks and that's when I saw Volpe. He was white as a ghost. I thought he was already dead. When I was standing outside the vehicle checking on Volpe, Sergeant Davis came by and he had had his pinky finger shot off. We had three people shot in our platoon in one day."

"Staff Sergeant Davis came over to our truck and got into the front seat. We thought he wanted to use the radio, and it was a few seconds before we realized he had been shot in the hand," said Lance Corporal Danny Myers. "They brought Volpe back and stuck him in the backseat of the Humvee. When they put him in there I thought he was dead. He was lifeless. We realized he was still alive when he mumbled. We had to get Volpe to our corpsmen. When we reached them they both jumped in our truck. Sergeant Croll was cutting the glove off of Staff Sergeant Davis to try and save his finger. We headed out of the city with Staff Sergeant Davis in the front seat and Volpe in the back seat while the two corpsmen worked on him. I was sitting Indian style in the turret trying not to fall out. After we got back out of the city we were tasked to provide security for the 81mm mortars. Corporal Smith and I were talking about how the night before we had wanted to see combat, and now, a half hour into it, we both agreed we didn't want to see anymore."

Just outside the city, an upset Lance Corporal Koskey and another Marine had to stay back and watch two trucks being used for supply while their platoon was in Fallujah. "I was listening to the radio and hearing about our platoon going in and taking casualties. A million thoughts were rushing through my head. I wanted to be there with my Marines. With all the injuries we had suffered, we had to reorganize our platoon," Koskey recalled.

Volpe said, "I was bleeding profusely and my legs were hanging out of the Humvee. I looked at Sergeant Smith and he looked at me and said, 'Volpe if you don't get your legs in the damn Humvee you're going to die!' I put them in and Doc Joseph Maston and Doc Joel Dupuis saved my life. I was in there bleeding to death and they were working on me the whole time. They put an IV in and gave me some morphine while they tried to stop the bleeding. I kept wondering when the vehicle was going to take me back. My friend, Lance Corporal Losito, heard on the radio that I was pronounced dead. They took me to the forward aid station where Commander Jadick and Petty Officer Johns helped save my life. They cut my clothes off of me and began squeezing more IVs in me. From the time they pulled me from the Humvee I only lost consciousness for about five seconds."

The Humvee pulled up near Doc Jadick and a young Marine hopped out and ran quickly up to him. A friend of Volpe's, Lance Corporal Joel Dupuis, began telling Jadick of Volpe's serious plight. Jadick hurried over to the wounded Marine in the back of the vehicle and realizing the seriousness of the wound began immediately issuing orders to his corpsmen. Blood covered the back of the Humvee.

HM2 Johns said, "Volpe was as white as a sheet when they brought him into us. Maston and Dupuis had worked their butts off to keep him alive until he got to us. He was going what we call, tits up. It seemed he wasn't going to make it. Doctor Kennedy and Doctor Jadick realized he was bleeding from a femoral artery. We began putting Hespen in him through the IV. As we worked on him his color began coming back. If there had been a thirty-second delay in getting him to us, he would have died."

Volpe was told by a corpsman, "If you go to sleep you'll never wake up!"

PFC Paul Volpe managed to stay alive thanks to the corpsman and doctors who worked on him and the Marines who risked their lives to save him in the mean streets of Fallujah.

Charlie Company Pushes to the Braxton Complex and Then to Phase Line Beth

In the Braxton complex the enemy had a perfect view of the bridge and the highway that came into the city from the north. For Brandl's battalion to use the bridge and highway safely, the Braxton complex would have to be swept of the enemy. "We knew the enemy was there, we had received fire from them. It was a good position for them. It was a choke point for that part of the city," Brandl recalled.

Charlie Company commander, Captain Bethea, got his Fire Support Team moved into a building in the Braxton area to get an elevated view of the city to the south. Captain Bethea then gave the order to First Lieutenant Klingensmith, tank platoon commander, to begin his attack down Route Ethan in direct support of Turner's 2nd Platoon. Bethea had Second Lieutenant Mark Littell's, 3rd Platoon, attacking south adjacent to 2nd Platoon, while Second Lieutenant Rhoades' 1st Platoon was tied in physically with 3rd Platoon which protected the company's flank.

As Charlie Company began moving south in the pitch-blackness of night, Marines could see the rubble left from the earlier bombardment of this part of the city through their NVGs. Telephone and electric lines lay tangled in the streets. Broken doors, glass, shattered bricks lay scattered before them in the roadway. The debris, mixed with the stench of trash and dead animals was covered with glistening raindrops. The Marines had to work their way around damaged cars left abandoned in the surreal looking streets. To add to the craziness, the Marines could still hear the music playing, but not the AC/DC that played earlier.

Lance Corporal Wintrow heard music as they moved through the wet streets and alleyways, "Psy ops was playing weird noises to try to psyche out the enemy, but at the same time it's affecting us. I was asking myself, *Where is our music?* We were told they were going to play some hard rock music and they didn't."

"Our squad was the first one to push into the city and we were tasked to clear the first of four buildings. We looked around for our building and then we realized we were walking on top of our building. It was nothing but rubble after the air had put a five-hundred-pound bomb on it and leveled it before we got in there," recalled Lance Corporal Joshua Thompson, 2nd Platoon, 1st Squad. "Earlier they had been getting sniper fire from the building so they went and leveled it for us. Corporal Turner, 1st Team Leader, 1st Squad led us into another house to clear it. We had flashlights taped to our weapons as we were kicking doors in. It was crazy and scary even though no one was in that house."

Things had started off on a sour note with the D-9 bogging down, but the good news was, no casualties had been reported to Captain Bethea on Charlie Company's initial breaching of the city.

Charlie Company now formed in a defensive U-position in the city, which afforded maximum firepower to their front, with the west flank guarded by tanks and the east flank guarded by 1st Platoon. All platoons were tied together in the defensive perimeter and First Lieutenant Miller got the 60mm mortars to establish a firing position at the Braxton complex in support of the company. Then Miller linked up with the Iraqi Emergency Response Unit (ERU) that Charlie Company would be working with in the city in taking the mosques. Captain Sims, the mentor for the Iraqi unit, along with First Lieutenant Jones, the battalion's liaison officer with the Iraqis, were told where to assemble and insert the Iraqi force.

With the addition of the seventy-seven men of Force Recon, seventy-seven men of the Iraqi ERU, and ninety-four men of the Iraqi Security Forces, Captain Bethea now had a swollen company of 385 infantrymen along his drawn up U- position in the Braxton complex.

Second Lieutenant Littell's 3rd Platoon was immediately hit with heavy small arms fire from the east. 1st Platoon was moved over to support the company's eastern flank in trace of 3rd Platoon.

Charlie Company's first enemy contact in the city was a violent welcome from the insurgents. Lance Corporal Giusti saw something in the sky streaming at them, "It was a big white and red light. I thought, *It's some sort of signal*! When all of a sudden a rocket came right over our heads and hit about ten or fifteen feet away, near Corporal Sarka. That made me realize it was time to get serious and do what we're trained to do."

Corporal Robert Sarka, 22, from Imlay City, Michigan, 3rd Platoon, was in the prone position looking down the street when the rocket-propelled grenade came soaring straight out of the darkness and exploded in a blinding flash only ten feet from the surprised Marine's feet.

"I was looking in my NVGs but they were all fogged up. The insurgents were firing RPGs over buildings at us from about two blocks away. Some were hitting about 100 yards behind us. I saw a bush about 200 feet to my right and I got up and moved over to it for some cover," Sarka recalled. "Just then there was a flash were I had just been."

Sarka was knocked to the ground and momentarily dazed from the concussion of the exploding grenade and hit by flying pieces of shrapnel. Positioned to his left Lance Corporal Storey and to his right Lance Corporal Carter began calling Sarka's name and for a corpsman to come up. First Sergeant Andrade, Staff Sergeant Lohr and Doc Pine ran over to the dazed Sarka to check out his condition.

"I tried to get to my knees and then I felt pain in my elbow," Sarka said. "I look around for my weapon but couldn't find it. Andrade told me my eyes were as big as dinner plates. My best friend Lance Corporal Curt Ward came up to me and asked if I was leaving the city."

Corporal Sarka slowly sat up and shook the cobwebs out of his head. Regaining situational awareness, he demanded to stay in the fight even though he had cuts from the shrapnel. He wanted to push on with his fellow Marines.

Just a few feet away from the exploding RPG round, lying in the prone position, were Lance Corporal Carter and Lance Corporal Zachary McWilliams, 19, a native of Raleigh, North Carolina. McWilliams witnessed the explosion, "Carter and I were near Sarka when the RPG hit just to the right of us. The explosion caused our ears to ring and threw debris on us."

Thinking his friend Carter had been hit, he yelled out. "Carter! Carter!" When the dust finally cleared, and the ringing in his ears subsided the relieved McWilliams could see his friend Carter still lying on the ground and covered in dirt, but moving. "I realized he was alright," said McWilliams.

Lance Corporal Dante Di Pasqua, 20, remembered, "About thirty minutes after breaching the city, we were staged inside a courtyard of a house and I remember thinking, *The battle isn't anything they've made it out to be.* One of our machine gunners was lying out in the road and I went out and lay down next to him. I pulled my bi-pods out and then tried to see if I could spot anybody. I saw this big red thing coming towards me in the night. It was like a big red tracer. I asked myself, 'What the hell is that?' Sure enough, an RPG went over our heads and I think it's the one that hit near Corporal Sarka. I realized this shit was for real. Then we started getting hit with heavy machine gun fire."

"I told Andrade that I wasn't going to leave," Sarka remembers. "I was pissed off and I wanted to find the m***** f***ing guy who did this."

First Sergeant Andrade, realizing that Corporal Sarka was good to go, allowed him to remain with his platoon. Then the Marines that had gathered around the shaken Sarka scattered. As Andrade walked away in the darkness he tripped over Sarka's missing weapon and handed it back to him.

As Di Pasqua and the machine gunner lay in the middle of the street, the bullets began impacting all around them chipping up pavement as the rounds hit. Reacting fast, Di Pasqua and the machine gunner began returning fire.

Lance Corporal Thompson saw his friend Di Pasqua lying in the middle of the road working his SAW. "The M-240G and Lance Corporal Di Pasqua with his SAW laid up and lit up the road. After a few minutes no fire was coming back at us from that position," Thompson said.

"The machine gunner took the guy out that was shooting at us," Di Pasqua recalled.

At 2230, Westbrookville, New York native Staff Sergeant Lohr also had a close call from the RPG round:

> *"Corporal Sarka took shrapnel from an RPG round that landed within five feet of his position. Doc Pines, Lance Corporal Willson and myself headed to aid Corporal Sarka...Corporal Sarka was hit in the left arm and dazed. He also told everyone he was good and wanted to push forward and fight. Lieutenant Littell then commanded the platoon to push forward through the 1st row of houses. 1st squad led with 2nd / 3rd squads in trace. I then proceeded to push with 3rd squad. We made our way through the 1st row of houses, got to an alleyway and started to the next set of houses...Lance Corporal Willson and myself noticed movement on the*

roof. I challenged them with voice commands. After no response, I then attempted to throw a white chemical light toward the roof to illuminate what was up there. The chemical light fell short and illuminated our position. Doc Pines then ran into the open, grabbed the chemical light, and chucked it away from our position. I then looked through my NVGs and still noticed movement. PFC Carter and I both gave verbal commands then opened up with rounds. Lance Corporal Veazie came over and saw three individuals moving around our position carrying weapons. He threw a hand grenade up and the targets were neutralized. We then proceeded through the house and pushed toward company objectives. We held up at the next house with comm (communication) lost."

Lance Corporal Veazies' quick decision of using the fragmentation grenade, most likely saved Marine lives. When the Marines eventually advanced to where the grenade had exploded, they found six dead insurgents scattered haphazardly about the ground.

Sticking like glue to his Staff Sergeant Corey Lohr was radioman Lance Corporal Chris Willson. Along with the company radio, Willson carried an M16 rifle. Willson weighed 150 pounds soaking wet and carried an additional 80 pounds of equipment including the radio and three days worth of batteries. "It was hard keeping up with Lohr with all of the weight I was carrying. We had only gone a few streets when our tanks began shooting near us. At that time we had worked our way out to a large street with a tree-covered medium. When an RPG went off near us, the corpsman came up and checked Sarka out and First Sergeant Andrade said he was good to go. The men we saw on the roof must have taken off."

Second Lieutenant Mark Littell, in his mid 20s, worked well with his Platoon Leader Staff Sergeant Corey Lohr, who said of his lieutenant, "Lieutenant Littell believed in advancing behind fire in the city."

Lance Corporal Thompson, a Georgia native, remembered pushing through the rubble and trash strewed streets of the city. "Our 2nd Platoon had split up to go down different side-by-side alleys. It was weird, at first you're out there with a whole bunch of guys and a few minutes later you're moving with only a squad. We then pushed down the main road with two tanks right beside us. It was good and bad because the tanks attracted fire. As we pushed we started receiving RPG rounds, machine gun fire, and tracers from down the street."

Captain Bethea, positioned with his Fire Support Team and the headquarters unit, began moving in the darkness through the city with his company. He had to dive once to escape being hit by RPK fire as they maneuvered through the dark streets. Picking himself up off the cement, he brushed the dust from his M4 carbine and started moving forward again. Earlier, Bethea had been feverishly working the radios to his platoon commanders and battalion. Now, his main concern was which way the company should take to get to the mosque they had to secure. He lifted his eyes from the map and stared out into the darkness. Bethea saw a series of narrow alleyways that led south and the wider more open street Route Ethan. He didn't want to get his men into those alleys which he felt could be used as killing zones by the insurgents. He chose to push with his Marines down the wider Route Ethan, which allowed the tanks more maneuvering room.

In the pitch-black of night, Bethea, carrying his M4 carbine, was walking with his Marines when he had an unexpected visitor drop in near him. An exploding mortar round. Other Marines heard the sudden BOOM and saw the flash but Bethea never heard the explosion. "It felt like someone had hit me in the back with a baseball bat. The next thing I remembered was lying face down in the street. I didn't know what had hit me until I was told later that a mortar had landed near us," explained Bethea. Because of the darkness and the blinding flash of the explosion, no one had seen Bethea go down from the impact of the mortar round. Luckily no one had been wounded from the flying jagged shrapnel. It was only a few seconds before Bethea shook the cobwebs out, wiped the dust off, and with the help of a good dose of adrenaline, he managed to pick himself up and get back in the fight. *Good to go.*

Turner's 2nd Platoon began receiving enemy machinegun fire and multiple RPG fire from the south, which hindered any further movement for the moment. The Iraqi insurgents were starting to crank things up on Charlie Company. Marine riflemen and machine gunners began to suppress the reconstituted enemy force to their front. The suppressive fire would allow Turner's 2nd Platoon to begin to move again farther south.

First Lieutenant Miller, mortar section, reported receiving mortar, machine gun, and sniper fire while in the defensive perimeter back at the Braxton complex. The Iraqis had recovered from the initial shock of the indirect fire directed on them by Klingensmith's tanks, the artillery and air strikes. Their fighters were coming out of their hidden positions and fighting back. Other groups of insurgents were surging north to meet the attack from the Marines of Battalion 1/8.

In Second Lieutenant Rhoades' 1st Platoon, Lance Corporal O'Rourke recalled the only time he became scared in the city, "The whole time I was in Fallujah I wasn't scared for my life except one time. We exited this house we were in with a group of Force Recon Marines to sweep on. We needed to link up with 2nd Platoon so when we swept forward we wouldn't leave any gaps in the line. We had a hard time finding 2nd Platoon for they were heavily engaged. So we held up in this alley with no cover for at least a half-hour. In combat, a half-hour is a long time. It was 2:30 or 3:00 a.m."

Hugging the walls in the dark alleyway, O'Rouke and his 1st Squad, 1st Platoon tried to make themselves invisible to the enemy snipers, but to no avail. "There was just nothing to hide behind. Then we heard a machine gun light up behind us. You can see the green tracers right in the middle. I'm the front man where the intersection meets the other road. The rounds are coming down and I said, 'Oh shit!' as I hit the ground and lay as flat as I could. Platoon Commander Lieutenant Rhoades hollered, 'Get down!' By that time we were all down. I think it was the Marine tanks' M-240G machine gun firing at us. I felt helpless. I wasn't afraid of the insurgents, they were lousy shots, but our tanks will kill. Eventually they stopped shooting and we left to link up with 2nd Platoon." No one was hit by the errant friendly firing.

First Lieutenant Miller, positioned with the mortars at the Braxton complex, was surprised to see the Iraqi Emergency Response Unit out on the roads marking the company's lines with their chemical lights. Incredulous, Miller ran out and ordered them to stop. The chemical lights were actually drawing enemy RPG fire on the company's position at the Braxton complex.

After the chemical light problem was taken care of, Gunnery Sergeant Cauley reported that the company mortars were now fire capable at the Braxton complex and ready to support the company in its push farther south when called on.

Carrying his machinegun, Lance Corporal Carpenter, 1st Squad, 1st Platoon, pushed down the wet streets of the city. "We found a couple of Iraqis in an alleyway. One was dead and the other was wounded with a loose grenade lying on the ground, probably five or six feet from him. They looked as though artillery rounds had hit them. We helped the wounded one out as we hunkered down in the alleyway for two or three hours. We had lost our comm and had to stay put," Carpenter recalled.

As Turner's 2nd Platoon moved through the streets, Lance Corporal Wintrow looking through his NVGs set up security for the squad at a corner. "I was making sure no one came down the street. I had a couple of other Marines to help me. The AC-130 was coming over and firing into the city and all of a sudden there is a guy just walking down the side of the road. He's not a Marine. He's wearing Iraqi clothing and acting real suspicious. We lit him up, got our guys out, and stayed put in the building until we pushed up," Wintrow recalled.

Sergeant John Megahan, 26, from Pennsylvania coal country in Ligoner, moved through the dark along Route Ethan. He was 1st Squad Leader in 2nd Platoon. "We were moving on the right side of the flank providing support for the tanks. The tanks were attacking and rounds were ricocheting off the armor. We kept our distance. Then RPGs began whizzing down the street."

A member of 1st Squad, Lance Corporal Dante Di Pasqua, 2nd Platoon, remembered learning a bitter lesson fighting near the tanks on a corner in the city. "I was posted on the corner for security. We had the tanks on our right. They had told us before that when we work with tanks don't get in front of them. The tank turned his gun near me and fired and pretty well knocked me out. It was lights out as I hit the ground." The shock wave from the tank's main gun slammed him to the ground. With his ears ringing and his body shaking he sat there trying to shake out the cobwebs. "My buddy came over and shook me and asked me if I was all right. I thought I was dead from the concussion of the gun."

At 2315, 2nd Lieutenant Rhoades, 1st Platoon and the Force Recon Marines seized a house on the company's eastern flank and killed three enemy fighters hiding there. 2nd Platoon attacked south, down to Phase Line Beth and encountered enemy resistance from three directions. Enemy fire was not only coming from the south but also from the west and east.

In battle it is advantageous to take, hold and if at all possible, fight from the high ground. In Fallujah it would be no different. The insurgents had plenty of time to take and hold the high ground in the city. There weren't any tall hills or mountains to set up as defensive positions, but in Fallujah, it was the thousands of rooftops, second and third floor balconies, and the mosques' tall minarets. It would be a guessing game for the Marines moving through the streets, difficult to tell which roofs held the hidden enemy fighters waiting to kill them. Fighting from above was one of the few advantages the insurgents had over the Marines. As in every war, the Marines would have to take the high ground from the insurgents, and whenever possible, fight from the tops of the buildings to counter that advantage.

Masked insurgents roamed freely through the streets and alleyways of the city. One group of four fighters, carrying weapons and draped with belts of ammunition, moved north through the narrow passageways of the city. Every so often they would stop, set up, and fire on the Marines with small arms, machine guns and hand held mortars. From a nearby mosque, the enemy fighters could hear loudspeakers blaring out, "God is great" in Arabic. The four insurgents eventually moved to the high ground, to the second deck of the city, the rooftops, to better direct their fire on the advancing Marines. They pulled grenades from their pockets and placed them within easy reach on a ledge that surrounded the roof. Then they silently waited in the darkness as they heard the sound of movements coming up the street from the north.

Carrying his twenty-pound 249 SAW, Lance Corporal Wintrow moved through the dark alleyways of the city with his 2nd Squad, carefully checking rooftops as they pushed forward. It was still misting on the Marines in the street but soon it would be raining grenades on them.

"Right before we hit Phase Line Beth, 1st Team of 2nd Squad got hit by multiple grenades. It's pitch black, we can't see anything, it's raining and our NVGs (night vision goggles) are fogging up. Everyone is yelling, but as soon as our guys got hit no one was yelling anymore. We all knew what to do," Wintrow said.

Corporal Nathan Dolan, 2nd Platoon, was advancing in the dark alley when one of the enemy fighters hiding on the rooftop of a nearby house threw a grenade down at him. It exploded on the street wounding Dolan with flying shrapnel to the face, left arm and both legs. He fell to the wet pavement, bleeding profusely from his wounds.

Two fellow 2nd Platoon Marines, Lance Corporal Matthew Knapp and PFC Ronald Charleson rushed to Dolan's assistance. They too were quickly brought under attack from the enemy on the rooftop.

The four hidden insurgents began raining more grenades down on the Marines positioned in the alleyway. Another grenade quickly exploded sending shrapnel biting into Corporal Adam Pyrka's left cheek, just inches from his eye and shrapnel wounded PFC Juan Vasques, Jr. in the left arm. In the darkness of the alleyway other grenades began exploding sending shards of metal hurling toward other Marines. Lance Corporal Knapp suffered injuries to the lower extremities, right arm, right femur and also his right eye. PFC Charleson was hit with shrapnel in the left leg and right arm.

"Three or four grenades went off around us, one right after the other. Within an hour of entering the city, we had suffered five casualties," Turner remembered.

Other Marines from the 2nd Platoon ran to assist the wounded men lying in the open alleyway and managed to drag them out of further harms way. Weapons Platoon Marines joined the Marines of 2nd Platoon and Klingensmith's tanks to bring fire on the enemy held rooftop.

Sergeant Frederick recalled the fierce firefight, "When the Marines got hit with the grenades, I shifted my Marines, Lance Corporal Lance Carlson, Corporal Alberto Saenz, Lance Corporal Evans Bledsoe and Lance Corporal Guillermo Fargas. They took out the threat. There was so much going on that it didn't hit the Marines right away that five had gone down." Together, the infantry along with the tanks killed the four insurgents.

Tank platoon commander, First Lieutenant David Klingensmith said, "I pushed my wingman, Sergeant Taylor's tank to the other side of the casualties and then I pushed up another tank alongside the wounded Marines to basically watch the other tank's back. When they were positioned there, I told them to only fire machine guns. As my wingman Sergeant Taylor was facing to the south, insurgent after insurgent kept running down the street trying to cross an alleyway. He killed about twenty or twenty-five insurgents."

"We posted security and some guys came up and got the Marines who were knocked out of the fight. From all the training and all of our drills we knew what to do. Everyone took their own initiative. Two of the Marines that were hit were good friends of mine, Charleson and Knapp," Lance Corporal Wintrow said.

Lance Corporal Rafael Peguero, 1st Platoon, 2nd Squad, who enjoyed the Corps so much that he was already planning to reenlist and become a lifer, told of when it got real for him in Fallujah, when he heard over the radio that Corporal Dolan had been hit. "It just kicked in that, oh shit, we're in the real deal here in the city."

Florida native, Lance Corporal Dante Di Pasqua, 2nd Platoon, said, "I remember waiting a couple times because our 3rd Squad had gotten ambushed. I heard our guys on the radio calling for casualty evacs for Dolan, Charleson and Knapp, all wounded from the grenades. We (1st Squad) became the casualty evac team. I remember helping Corporal Dolan into the amtrac and his head was wrapped. He could walk but he had his arm around me. He kept telling me, 'Don't look at my face. Don't look at my face.' His face was all bloody and his trouser and sleeves were just red with blood. He kept telling me not to look at him and right before I let go of him in the amtrac he said, 'I'll see you back in Lejeune.' That's when it really hit me that it wasn't the movies now, it's the real shit."

"We had suffered some five wounded by this time and I remember some of them were screaming pretty hard from the pain. After the AC-130 pounded the enemy on our flank, our tanks were able to push in front of us and block off our front to the enemy. They started to launch rounds down range. The Army M-113 armored ambulance escorted by Mobile

Assault Platoon (MAP) came in and got the wounded out," Turner remembered.

Captain Bethea immediately called in a medical evacuation from battalion. PFC Vasques and Corporal Pyrka refused to be medevaced out and continued in the fight. Here were young men who have been wounded and have the right and the opportunity to be taken out of the fight, but refused. No one would have questioned them for leaving the city. To put it in prospective, the Battle of Fallujah happened over three years after 9/11. America doesn't always get to pick its wars; sometimes the war picks us. Most of these young Marines had enlisted after the United States had declared war against terrorism. They understood we were at war and what was at stake. Those that joined the military at this time understood they were putting their lives at risk. By now, most of the military men who didn't want to see combat had opted out, or been transferred to a non-combat unit. Those who enlisted and served only in peacetime, known as sunshine warriors, knew better than to join the military at this violent period in our nation's history. The Marines in the city wanted to be there. They chose to be there. They knew what was at stake: the defeat of terrorism. They would not let their buddies down in Fallujah unless absolutely forced to leave with a serious wound.

A two tank section from Klingensmith's Tank Platoon, known as White 2, deployed to the east of Turner's 2nd Platoon's left flank and also assisted in the casualty evacuation. White 3, the second tank section, was kept busy during that night on Phase Line Beth scratching White Two's back, Klingensmith recalled. The tankers were using their .50 caliber machine guns that could call on 900 rounds, throughout the night lighting up the enemy attempting to attack their tanks with grenades. During the fighting in the darkness toward Phase Line Beth, Klingensmith's tankers accounted for thirty enemies confirmed killed while supporting Turner's 2nd Platoon.

Second Lieutenant Turner's 2nd Platoon, after suffering five casualties, renewed their effort and punched down to company objective two, the corner of Phase Line Beth and Ethan. Turner was barking out orders in the southern drawl that is typical of the part of North Carolina he came from.

Basher, the AC-130 gunship, now supporting Charlie Company from high above Fallujah, confirmed that the enemy was reinforcing their position in the twisted alleyways on Charlie Company's flank.

In the push into the city Turner fired a half of a magazine in the fight, but mainly worked the radio calling in air support for his advancing platoon. "I was talking to the company FAC and the executive officer about our location. We had an AC-130 overhead and he saw about thirty insurgents off to our flank, which would have been in front of Mark's 3rd Platoon. The AC-130 began pounding the enemy and people stopped firing on us right then," Turner remembered.

Captain Bethea, 32, who had long ago lost his New Orleans-Cajun accent, was thankful for all the help the AC-130 provided in the push through the city. "We had thirty-one confirmed kills from Basher the AC-130. The problem was the enemy was so close, 60 meters from 2nd Platoon's lines, which I had to authorize the fire danger close. The AC-130 fired one grenade from the 40mm cannon. When Lieutenant Turner radioed back and said that the grenade had hit the enemy and his forces weren't in danger, he then activated his strobe lights and all his Marines took cover. Once all those three criteria were met, I called the AC-130, which then engaged the enemy at will."

Captain Richie, the company Forward Air Controller, reaffirmed that Basher could see the tank platoon on Route Ethan and all friendly strobe lights before authorizing the AC-130 to engage the enemy within 60 meters, with 40mm grenades only.

Carrying their AK-47s and RPGs, the insurgents were preparing to mount an attack on an unsuspecting 2nd Platoon. It was one of the few times insurgents used the night as a cover to neutralize the Marines' superior firepower. From their vantagepoint above the city, Basher saw between thirty or forty Iraqis and foreign fighters creeping beside the walls of the alleys, drawing closer to Turner's hunkered down Marines.

Waiting in an alley, Turner recounted the action, "We were lined up in an alley and I got on the radio with the AC-130, who told me he saw two different groups and he didn't know who's who. He said, 'I'm going to light you up with the infrared.' So he turned it on and all of a sudden my entire platoon becomes like bright green. I said, 'Holy shit' this guys going to kill us. I jumped on the radio and hollered 'Negative! Negative! We're friendlies.' He said, 'Roger!' and immediately shoots his strobe off to my left. It was no more than 30 meters from me, just across a wall. I told the pilot that's not us. When he lit up again to my left he just started pounding them. It just sounded like mortars going off beside me."

Basher, in his pattern high above the Charlie Company position confirmed that the entire enemy force within danger close was destroyed. Turner and his Marines hunkered down in the alley and breathed a sigh of relief.

Lieutenant Turner said, "I informed the captain that we had taken the position and we weren't receiving fire from it anymore. He told us to hold our ground. When the sun rose the next morning there were constant firefights back and forth. Our guys on the rooftops were firing on the enemy to the south."

In the darkness, Klingensmith was stunned to see a tank coming north up Route Ethan straight toward his tank's position. He knew his Marine tanks were leading the attack in Fallujah and that intel had informed them that the insurgents didn't have any armor. As the oncoming tank drew closer to his position, he identified it as a U.S. Army tank and was horrified to see that they were preparing to fire on him. The Army tank assumed the Marines were insurgents and fired their main gun at the startled tankers. The shell impacted only 25 meters in front of Klingensmith's tanks, blowing up rubble when the round impacted. Klingensmith had seconds to decide a course of action on the errant Army tank. Concerned, he gave the order to prepare to fire. A round was pushed into the Marine tank's main gun. "I didn't know what was going on inside that tank," Klingensmith confessed. For all that Klingensmith knew, the insurgents could now be manning the U.S. Army tank in a ruse. Klingensmith's gunner tensed as he waited for the order to fire on the onrushing tank, kicking up dust as it came down the street.

Marines could make out the outlines of enemy fighters advancing behind the tank as it grew closer to them. The insurgents were actually using the Army tank as cover to push north closer to the hunkered down, Charlie Company Marines along Phase Line Beth.

Finally, the Army tank realized their mistake and pulled up to the Marine tanks. Klingensmith's tankers got the Army tank's frequency and began yelling at them for losing their way and firing on them.

"I gave him quite the counseling statement, we'll call it," Klingensmith said.

One of Klingensmith's tank sections was going back to the logistics support area for re-supply and he told the Army tankers to follow the Marine tank back. The Army tank followed the Marine tanks only a short distance north before heading out on their own again. Klingensmith, still upset at being fired on by the U.S. Army, watched in amazement as, "They turned west back into the city." Shaking his head in disgust, Klingensmith got his tankers to focus back on the fight in Fallujah.

Charlie Company's 3rd Platoon finally got in line with 2nd Platoon along Phase Line Beth. Fighting and moving on foot in the rubble of the Braxton complex had slowed them down.

SAW gunner Lance Corporal Tribou, Charlie Company's 1st Platoon, recounted, "We made our way up to a rooftop. I was the first one up along with Corporal Shawn Hefner, the 2nd Team Leader. We saw insurgents trying to maneuver around our flank. I saw a guy running for an RPG. I raised my weapon and started firing near Corporal Hefner's head. As I squeezed the trigger he fell to the ground. I thought he had been shot, but it was just my muzzle noise that had caused him to take cover. I helped him up and we looked down an alleyway and saw another whole group of guys trying to run out of the city. Other Marines came up and we started to light up that alleyway. I shot at least two of them. One insurgent tried to hide next to a wall, by a ledge. We could see his arm sticking out. Someone fired and hit his arm and then he got up to run and everyone opened up on him."

Lance Corporal Peguero, 1st Platoon, 2nd Squad, recalls the end of the first night's action, "They wanted to drop a five-hundred-pound bomb on a target near us, so we went firm in this house for the remainder of the night."

Usually, going firm for the night didn't necessarily mean rest and sleep for the tired sweaty Marines. This precious time was spent cleaning, brushing and oiling their weapons with well-practiced hands. Then, re-supplying, grabbing a quick meal, loading magazines with rounds, taking care of bodily functions, and then maybe, just maybe, if the tanks weren't firing at targets close to their position that night, try and get some much needed sleep. Maybe two or three hours of sleep, if they were lucky.

Lieutenant Colonel Brandl said, "I used the Iraqi forces down there to not only maintain control of that traffic circle, but also to picket the road leading to the mosque. I didn't want to have to take our Marines and put them in positions along the route which we needed for re-supply."

As the Marines continued to push to the south, most of them had the twenty-must-haves for any infantryman in urban fighting in Iraq. Advanced optical gun sight or binoculars, Energy bars, kevlar cushions for their kevlar helmets. Elbow and kneepads, which allowed them to take a quick trip to the hard pavement and not scrape their knees or elbows in the process. Personal role radios and global positioning system. Extra socks, to help keep their feet dry. Some Marines would go four or five days without changing their socks and always regretted it later. Gloves to help going over walls and for protection from broken glass. Baby wipes, which they used for multiple purposes. They didn't have time for personal hygiene, so the baby wipes came in handy. Three-point slings to better carry their weapons. Alice, or day pack, which carried most of their gear. Night vision goggles, which gave the Marines the advantage over the insurgents at night. Most Marines had the personal hydration system. They didn't have to wrestle with a canteen, all they had to do was pull the cord up to their mouth, and it holds more water. Compass and AA batteries for their NVGs and handheld radios. A poncho and poncho liner for cold nights. The Marines would sweat during the day, and then at night, freeze in their wet clothes. Ballistic goggles to protect the eyes from shrapnel and flying debris. A multipurpose portable tool kit, carabineers which they used to attach anything to their flak jackets, and a high-powered flashlight to help see in the dark smoke-filled houses.

These twenty items made a Marine's life in Fallujah a little more comfortable and tolerable. In some cases they actually helped save Marine lives.

Bravo Company Pushes South to Phase Line Beth

At midnight Captain Read Omohundro, Bravo Company, got the word that Charlie Company had seized their first objective, the Braxton complex. His men now in position, he set his attack in motion, south towards Phase Line Beth at 0100. Bravo Company had encountered little or no resistance during their initial push into the rim of the city, just as Omohundro had predicted earlier to First Sergeant Whittington. Now his main concern was the Cultural Center. He told his platoon commanders that they would do a penetration on line with Bethea's Charlie Company. The two companies, now abreast, would attack south in tandem and roll up the enemy in that area.

Bravo Company began bounding by platoons deeper into the city by establishing over-watch positions on the rooftops of houses strung out along the alleyways and open streets.

"At 0200 I talked to Captain Bethea and we received orders to take our objectives. Charlie Company had the mosque, and we would take the Cultural Center by first light." Omohundro explained.

Second Lieutenant Andy Eckert's 1st Platoon and Second Lieutenant Steven Berch's 2nd Platoon moved past Phase Line Cathy at approximately 0230 to establish SBF (Support by Fire) positions for First Lieutenant Chris Wilkens' 3rd Platoon. The 3rd Platoon would launch the attack on the Cultural Center and Recon was attached to 3rd Platoon to help bolster their attack.

First Lieutenant Wilkens got his platoon moving again and pushed up to join Captain Omohundro at Phase Line Cathy. On the push up some of his Marines spotted a blood trail that led them to a weapons cache. After leaving the cache to the engineers, they got into a sharp firefight that slowed them down from joining up with the other platoons. After suppressing the enemy fire they pushed up.

Moving on foot with his Marines, Captain Omohundro, carrying his M16A4, was coordinating the coming attack with Captain Meyers of tanks on the street. While 3rd Platoon was getting set to launch the attack, three white phosphorous shells exploded about 20 meters above their position raining fire all over the area. White phosphorous rounds create a screen of fire that cannot be extinguished by water.

"While we were waiting on Captain Bethea to get up to where we were at, we received white phosphorous rounds on our position. I was standing outside a tank talking to Captain Meyers, company commander for the tanks, when all of a sudden I heard a POP. I looked up and saw the explosion. We looked at each other and both said, 'Oh shit!' He ran to the east and I ran to the west," Omohundro recalled. "I kept thinking to myself, *This is going to hurt!* I jumped over some shrubs and went in to a forward roll and forgot I had my night vision devices on my helmet. The rounds were initially supposed to be further down, to provide a smoke screen for Charlie Company to come up through. Luckily we didn't receive any casualties from the friendly fire. We moved back about 100 meters to get out of the smoke and make sure everyone was okay. Once we found that everyone was alright, we moved back south."

At Main Command outside the city, Major Winn recalls the steady voice of Captain Omohundro during the friendly fire incident. "Omohundro was on the radio, very calm and in control. He was so calm that it kept everyone calm in the COC and the CP," Winn said.

Captain Pretus, Sniper Platoon, also remembers the steady Omohundro, "I remember being on the radio with Captain Omohundro and all kind of firing and explosions were coming over the radio and he was so calm, it was like he was giving a daily briefing back at Lejeune."

Tank commander, Captain Meyers said, "Captain Omohundro and I were standing outside the tank talking about how we were going to take the Civic Center when the phosphorous shell detonated over our heads and covered our tanks. I tried to get back in the tank, which was pretty funny because my Marines had closed the hatches. I was banging on the tank yelling 'Let me in! Let me in!'"

Also in the line of fire of the white phosphorous shell was tank platoon commander, Lieutenant Klingensmith who suffered his second run-in with the 'Willy Pete' friendly fire. "It's just one of those things; you look up and just hope it doesn't hit you."

SMAW gunner Lance Corporal Andres Llerena looked up to see fire falling from the early morning sky. "We were walking down the street, making our way to the next objective, when overhead we heard that whirling noise and then a round of 'Willy Pete' went off above us. There was fire burning everywhere, giving off smoke. We all took cover and the people with phosphorus on them were trying to get it off before it burned through their clothing to their skin."

Staff Sergeant Ben Alicea, sniper, saw the phosphorous coming down around him. "I decided I was just going to stay out in the open and try to run around and dodge the raining fire illumination shell. I took cover before the second one came."

Bravo Company Marines were trying to make themselves as small a target as possible as the red-hot phosphorous fell on their exposed position in the street. Charlie Company had called for the indirect fire that went astray over Bravo Company that morning.

FiST Team member, Sergeant Shawn Gianforte said, "We were moving through while Charlie Company's preset phosphorous smoke screen was going up. We were coming around the corner when the round went off. You could hear it whistling in and I caught a red glow out of the corner of my eye. I thought at first it was an RPG round. I got close to the wall and crouched down a little. Lieutenant Collins was behind me and he yelled out, 'It's a white phosphorous!' I grabbed the old shit and took off. I looked back as I was running, the white phosphorous had an umbrella shape to it. A few of the FiST Marines got it on their packs."

Luckily, there were no casualties from the errant shake and bake rounds, but the run-in with the exploding phosphorous did slow Bravo's attack on the Cultural Center.

Captain Omohundro got his company moving again as they pushed on toward Phase Line Beth, where he would again consolidate the company before pushing forward. Enemy activity got heavier as they inched closer to the Cultural Center. By 0600, Wilkins' 3rd Platoon was staged to attack, with 1st and 2nd Platoons in support, when a black vehicle traveling south approached Eckert's 1st Platoon position. Fearing a suicide car bomber, fire was immediately called in on the vehicle.

"1st Platoon encountered an enemy vehicle full of insurgents. Lance Corporal Russell, an M-240G gunner, turned around and mowed them down as they were getting out of the black vehicle. Some of the insurgents started to explode because they had explosive belts around their chests," Omohundro recalled.

"Then we saw about 16 guys with weapons, four had RPGs the rest AK-47s heading south," Staff Sergeant Alicea remembered. "The insurgents began to fire over their shoulders as they ran south. We opened fire and killed one outright. The others ran to a courtyard wall. I shot one and he fell down, then got back up and ran. We followed a blood trail to a huge weapons cache. The engineers came up and took care of the cache."

Bravo Company, staging for their attack on the Cultural Center, had advanced farther south than Charlie Company had. Bethea's Charlie Company had run in to intense sniper fire on their front and eastern flank from snipers. Because of this, Bravo Company's left flank was now hanging in the wind. Omohundro's Marines were now exposed to enemy fire from that direction.

"It was just starting to become daylight and we began receiving heavy fire from the west and the Al Hydra Mosque to our east," Captain Omohundro confessed.

Charlie Company's Push to Phase Line Beth

Positioned to Bravo Company's east, Lance Corporal Rafael Peguero, 19, was up early in the house that his 2nd Squad, 1st Platoon, Charlie Company, had going firm that first dreary, wet night. With his M16A4 in hand, he walked over to his friend Lance Corporal Michael Rodriguez of 1st Squad. Rodriguez was posted at the front gate of the house. "We were just shooting the shit about what we had seen the previous night when I looked outside the gate and saw a head pop up about two blocks down. He was like peeking out at us. I pointed my weapon down the alley just as the guy ran across the street. I had him sighted in, but I didn't pull the trigger because I wasn't sure I would have hit him, and I wanted to see how many there were." Peguero watched as a second man quickly ran across the same road. Now sighted in, he was ready if a third insurgent dared to run across the open street.

Peguero patiently waited to see if there was going to be another insurgent boldly showing himself on the road. "When the third one came out, I was ready, and that's when I popped him. The round went through his rib cage and out the other side and he went down. I fired again and the bullet hit him in the ass. He just lay there so I assumed he was dead. I kept looking down the alleyway for about twenty minutes when I saw the insurgent doing self-aid. He was wrapping a T-shirt on his wound. I stepped out in the open and he saw me. He reached for his AK-47 that was lying to his left. He pointed it in my direction." Bad move on the insurgent's part, for Peguero squeezed the trigger and fired a quick burst of rounds from his M16A4, swiftly finishing the wounded insurgent off.

A short time later 1st Squad, of 1st Platoon, came along the same alleyway and got a glimpse of the earlier handiwork of 2nd Squad. Lance Corporal Stephen O'Rourke, who takes courses at Coastal Carolina Community College when back home at Lejeune, was carrying his SAW through the streets of Fallujah. He also carried another 75 pounds of equipment strapped to his body as he cautiously walked along the street. He was second in line and remembered seeing his first dead Iraqi in the city, "We pushed down this road. Maldonado, a little in front of me, was on the right side and I was first on the left side of the street. We saw these three dead bodies. One is lying in the middle of the road. There were puddles on the road and you could see the blood mixing with the mud. This guy had his ass cheek completely blown off. One insurgent is in the middle of the street and one insurgent is about twenty feet in front of him bleeding from his stomach. I didn't notice any weapons as I walked over to the third one next to the wall. I kicked the one in the street to make sure he was dead. His body was hard. I went to the next guy and kicked him."

The kick startled the wounded Iraqi and he began moaning. The loud moan from a supposed dead man surprised O'Rourke. He jumped back. He could see the man was badly injured. The insurgent's leg was bleeding and his arm seemed broken. "He kept pointing to this house. I guess he was trying to tell me he lived there in that building. I knew he was full of shit, I could see a bandoleer of ammunition with a grenade attached lying in the street, about three feet in front of him. I said to the lieutenant, 'We have a live one here sir!' We tried to treat him, but I don't think he made it."

After trying to help the wounded Iraqi, Second Lieutenant Rhoades got back to pushing his 1st Platoon deeper into the city. They were now the left flank of Charlie Company and the battalion's left flank. At the end of their line there were 500 meters of open space which ran to the right flank of the Marines of Battalion 1/3. Rhoades dropped 2nd and 3rd Squads off to secure a house near the Al Hydra Mosque and to provide security on one of the D-9 bulldozers that had gotten stuck in a second muddy sinkhole. The D-9s had come untangled back at the mud hole thanks to an assist from one of Meyers' tank retrievers and was back in the fight, at least until it got stuck again. Rhoades kept his 1st Squad pushing south toward the first mosque that they were tasked to help secure.

Nineteen-year-old Lance Corporal Stephen O'Rourke, also a member of 1st Squad, who had a girlfriend, Jay-Me Bailey at home, recalled the push south to the first mosque. "When we're walking, I noticed this road coming from the east to my left when all of a sudden I hear machine gun fire. As I turn with my weapon to face down the road, I see a tracer go behind me and then a tracer go in front of me. They were definitely firing at us. We had machine guns attached to us so we had fire support. We squeezed against a wall for cover. Lance Corporal Wilson and I got on either end of these eight-foot walls and we do this thing with talking guns down the alleyway. I would fire and then take a break while he would fire. The heavy M-240G machine gun was also lighting up the building and street. I expended about 400 rounds in that fight."

Lance Corporal Joshua Thompson, 20, 2nd Platoon, 1st Squad said, "That night we pushed up to where we were going to set up to take the mosque at Phase Line Beth. We took up a position at a grocery store that still had some food on the shelves, but it was a mess. A tank had put a round into the store. We took a breather and everyone was just chilling out. We had a watch going. Corporal Williams, a SAW gunner in my team, and I sat there just shooting at the insurgents. You couldn't see the enemy it was so dark but we saw their muzzle flashes. The tanks setting beside us were taking pings off their hulls. They were lighting stuff up and down the street. The tanks saved our asses many times in the city."

Lance Corporal Thompson had a fairly comfortable night at the grocery store until finding out how close the enemy had been positioned to them during the night. "That next morning a couple of our guys hopped over a wall on the top level to a building directly behind us. They found three live insurgents in that house but didn't pop them. Our squad leader Sergeant John Megahan went up and took them as detainees. We found some homemade RPGs and IEDs and took them to the weapons collection point," Thompson explained.

"The enemy was just shooting and running," recalled Sergeant Frederick, 1st Squad, 2nd Platoon. "They didn't seem to be aiming at us, just harassing us."

The insurgents appeared to be doing two-second drills. From within a house they would dart in front of an open window and fire a quick burst before running for cover. From a doorway of a house they would step into the open street, fire their AK and step back in the house. The Marines sometimes would just catch a fleeting glimpse of the enemy fighters in the shadows or darkness of alleyways, rooftops and windows before the shadows vanished.

Staff Sergeant Corey Lohr, 29, in a letter home to his wife, described the push under fire to the mosque, on the second day of combat deep in the bowels of Fallujah:

> *"We continued to push south. We then had 1st squad push through houses to the West, 3rd in trace and 2nd to the East down the alley Road. I proceeded with 2nd. We bounded down the alley and came to a...open field to our East. We bounded through. When half the squad got through, what sounded like an RPK opened up on us from the east. We pushed forward and gained a foothold in the house directly south. 2nd Squad cleared the house and found a cache (weapons). 3rd Squad pushed forward and we laid down suppression fire for them to get inside the stronghold. 1st was in trace of them. Once the platoon was together the platoon commander (Second Lieutenant Littell) looked at the situation and the mission and decided to push forward. 1st squad and snipers pushed through the back of the house to another. Sergeant Eggersdofer and Corporal Watkins noticed an RPK inside the house set up down the hallway. Corporal Watkins fragged the room. Sergeant Eggersdofer and his squad entered. At that time Lance Corporal Thomas was the lead person for that squad, entered the house and shot 1 individual. They continued to clear the house and called for the rest of the platoon. They also found another cache.*
>
> *A Sergeant Owens from Recon was four houses down to our east. Lance Corporal Willson, Doc Pines, Corporal Black, Lance Corporal Hughs headed to his position. He gathered a big cache and asked for us to blow it as they continue South. Corporal Black and Lance Corporal Hughs rig the cache. 2nd Squad cleaned a house just 4 houses east of the platoon and notices another cache. It is now midday and we see the company Gunnery Sergeant running us down some water. We then hold up and blow all the caches in our area and reconsolidate. 50-100 meters South is Phase Line Beth. The Lieutenant tells the squad leaders to push south."*

Lance Corporal Chris Willson, Lohr's radioman said, "It was daylight and we were clearing houses by moving through back courtyards and climbing over high stone walls. When it was my turn to get over this one six-foot wall, I handed my M16 up to Doc Pine and I tried to get over with the radio and all my gear strapped on. I just couldn't do it. Lohr and Pine had to grab me by my straps and hoist me over." With a little help from his friends, the 150-pound Willson managed to get over the wall and get back into the fight.

Corporal Rob Sarka recalled, "We were pushing across a large open space during the daylight hours. Lieutenant Littell carrying an M16 was leading from the front and we were all running as fast as we could to get across. Rounds were impacting all around us when I looked up and noticed that Littell had vanished. I got to a large hole and when I jumped over it, as I looked down, I saw Lieutenant Littell in the bottom of the shell hole. He had fallen in and when I looked back Corporal Vendetti was giving him a hand and helping him out. We made it to the building without suffering any casualties and I went to a window on the second floor and began firing south. Lance Corporal Brodie joined me and we began popping rounds into windows in the direction we would be pushing. Brodie went back downstairs and I realized that I had my weapon resting on the ledge and sticking out the window. By doing that I was attracting fire and just as I pulled it in I heard a whizzing sound. A sound I had heard before, an RPG. I dove to the floor just as it struck the side of the building a few feet from my window. Brodie came running back upstairs and yelled, 'What the f*** happened!' I told him and we went back downstairs and Staff Sergeant Lohr said, 'You're an RPG magnate Sarka.'"

Corporal Rob Sarka had escaped being killed twice in less than 24 hours by an enemy fired RPG.

The battalion's two-company attack into the city was going much faster than first expected, but a problem had arisen. Captain Bethea's Charlie Company had met the most enemy resistance in the east of the battalions sector in his push to their objective of the Al Hydra Mosque, and wasn't keeping abreast of Captain Omohundro's Bravo Company, who was now positioned outside their objective at the Cultural Center. Directly across the street from the Cultural Center stood Charlie Company's objective of the Al Hydra Mosque. Captain Omohundro's left flank hung in the air and they were receiving stiff fire from their east. Several other problems also cropped up that slowed Charlie Company's drive to the mosque.

Captain Bethea had his own open left flank to the east to contend with. A five hundred-meter gap now lay between Bethea's company and the Marines of Battalion 1/3. This intentional gap was set before the attack to try and cut down on friendly fire between the two Marine battalions. But now, the enemy was taking advantage of the open seam by using it as a safe haven from Marine fire. Charlie Company also had to watch out for Bravo Company Marines on their right flank. And most importantly, Bethea had to contend with 171 Iraqi Coalition troops that were to be used for photo ops when Charlie Company took the mosque.

Charlie Company had to prep the mosque first by taking out any insurgents and then bring the Iraqi troops up to be photographed entering the structure. Welcome to PC (Political Correctness) in the military. The Iraqis were sometimes a little reluctant to enter the fray and had to be cajoled into advancing with the Marines. In their defense, the Iraqis lacked U.S. quality training, had no NVGs, and didn't want to attack at night.

To Bethea's front to the south, persistent sniper fire was harassing the company's movement forward. All of these factors did their small part in slowing the advance of Charlie Company's final push to the Al Hydra Mosque, some five or six city blocks into the city.

In the military, as in civilian life, shit flows down hill and Bethea quickly got on the radio with his lieutenants. He knew the problems facing his platoon commanders but he urged them to hurry their push toward the Al Hydra Mosque and begin to prep it for the Iraqi Coalition forces.

Staff Sergeant Corey Lohr wrote:

> *"Lieutenant Littell told the squad leaders to push south. We cleared a couple more houses and reached Phase Line Beth. The snipers and Lieutenant Littell headed to the top of our building to get a good eyes view, while the squad leaders and I got consolidated. We began receiving rifle fire from the west. We returned fire and it went on for a good ten minutes. Lieutenant Littell then decided to use a SMAW round. Corporal Farmer, Lance Corporal Crows and Lance Corporal Bourns headed out there with Corporal Quintana to shoot two SMAW Rounds into the building we had received sniper fire from."*

After the two SMAWs leveled most of the building, the sniper fire abruptly ceased. The Marines of Charlie Company began to set up in houses and buildings along Phase Line Beth in preparation of pushing to Phase Line Cathy and securing the mosque.

One of the D-9 bulldozers took an RPG round off its reinforced armored hull. As the RPG harmlessly exploded the D-9 barely shuttered as it continued doing its work establishing blocking positions to prevent suicide bombers from attacking Charlie Company from their eastern flank.

Captain Bethea called battalion again and informed them of another friendly fire incident involving Marines from Light Armored Reconnaissance (LAR). No friendly casualties were taken from the errant fire but it again underlined how chaotic and mixed up things could become on the flanks of the advancing battalions.

One of the Marines manning Phase Line Beth, Lance Corporal Rafael Peguero, posted on a rooftop overlooking the ravaged city, saw some movement to his front. "Lieutenant Miller was next to me when about three or four insurgents crossed a field and started shooting at the Force Recon guys and then started running away trying to get around a corner. I popped a couple of shots that missed and then when the last one reached the corner I popped him in the back. He just dropped, sliding down as he fell. That was my second kill that day." These were some of the same insurgents that had been harassing Bravo Company's flank, to Charlie Company's west.

In the darkness, with a heavy wet mist still falling, Second Lieutenant Turner walked among his men strung out in their defensive position on the streets of Fallujah. It was a "How you doing Marine?" A pat on the back from Turner, a reminder to keep focused. "Once we pushed to Phase Line Beth, I was holding at a corner at the main avenue. I never went to a building during the night, not until the sun started to rise in the sky. I spent most of the night checking the lines to keep the Marines awake. The adrenaline rush was wearing off so I had to keep them focused," Turner recalled.

During the early morning hours the company was conducting a re-supply of ammo and water for the resting platoons. Busy cleaning weapons and swapping stories of the nights action, Marines filled their water bottles to help slake their thirst in the coming days fight. Charlie Company Marines were relieved that no one in the company had been killed in the fierce fighting leading up to Phase Line Beth.

"Our mission the next morning was to take the Iraqis and have them seize the mosque. They didn't have any NVGs and didn't want to attack at night. At this time we began receiving friendly fire from our flank coming from Battalion 1/3. We suffered no casualties, but I knew from the color of the tracers that it had been friendly fire. I got on the radio and told them to shut it off," Captain Bethea said.

At 0330, First Lieutenant Miller, with the Iraqi Coalition forces informed Bethea that the Iraqi Emergency Response Unit refused to move down Route Ethan at night. This again slowed the attack on the mosque planned for the next day.

When things go bad, they go bad in bunches. At 0500 Captain Bethea got word that the D-9 was stuck in the mud again, and he had to line up security for the big iron beast again. Bethea was most likely feeling that the D-9s had become a white elephant strapped to his back. But the D-9s would prove their worth later by saving Marine lives in the fighting to the south.

At 0515, First Lieutenant Miller finally got the Iraqis moving down Route Ethan toward Phase Line Beth and the Al Hydra Mosque.

Weapons Company Commander Captain Stephen Kahn, still positioned outside the city, remembered his sobering conclusion after the first days fighting in Fallujah, "It was my understanding that they expected this fight in Fallujah to take ninety-six hours from start to finish. The whole battle! It was after that first day that we realized we're going to be here a little while. The battle wasn't going as fast as we anticipated because the enemy was offering more resistance than we initially expected. We expected most of the enemy to be in the Jolan District. At this time we said, we've either hit the wasp nest or the enemy isn't where we expected them to be."

A physician at the Fallujah hospital which was located far to the west of Battalion 1/8s fighting position in the city, told reporters, that some of the corpses of the Mujahedeen that were brought in were burned. Other corpses were melted, most likely from white phosphorous shells used for screening the infantry.

Charlie Company Advances South to the Al Hydra Mosque

Major Mark Winn, positioned in the Main Command CP, located two kilometers outside the city, got the order to move up. Winn recalled, "Colonel Brandl told us to come forward so we displaced down to the breach and set up there. We took control of the fight, which allowed Colonel Brandl to go into the city. At this time everything was going as planned. Bravo Company had a tremendous amount of success on the eastern side of Route Ethan."

On Tuesday, November 9, Charlie Company got moving at 0600 on its push south from their position along Phase Line Beth to Phase Line Cathy and then set up to take the Al Hydra Mosque. Of Fallujah's one hundred and thirty mosques, sixty of them, almost half, would be found to harbor terrorists in defensive positions. Under international law, religious structures used for military purposes forfeit their protected status.

With the breaking of dawn the intersection of Phase Line Beth and Route Ethan became a hornet's nest of enemy sniper fire and activity and Charlie Company became the main target.

It would become a predictable pattern by the enemy in the next few days. With the waning of the sunlight the enemy would retreat south or go to ground. When the sun came up, the enemy would come to life and move back north and attack the Marines. With the beginning of the second day of action in the battle for Fallujah, the Marines had to be extra careful of becoming targets for the enemy snipers.

When the Marines of 1st Platoon, Charlie Company cleared up one trouble spot another would crop up. They began receiving heavy fire from the west. Lance Corporal O'Rourke watched rounds impacting along a nearby wall. "It just started happening. I saw impacts on the wall and the gate that I was leaning on. There were two bullet holes in the gate. We had reporters who were with us and they were scared at this point. We eventually killed the enemy fighter in the house."

Turner's 2nd Platoon also began receiving and suppressing heavy machine gun and sniper fire from their immediate front. Sergeant Dustin Stout and his snipers were brought in to help clear the enemy snipers to the southeast of Second Lieutenant Turner's platoon.

Sergeant Stout, 22, was leader of his sniper team consisting of Sergeant Adam Earls and Lance Corporal Dan Merkle and in addition he commanded both his and Corporal Quintana's team attached to Charlie Company. Stout from Bellefontaine, Ohio was one of the most experienced snipers in battalion 1/8, second only to Sergeant David Battles.

"We set up on a rooftop to the north of the mosque with a squad of Marines from Turner's platoon," Stout remembered. "The lip of the roof had a wall about three feet tall surrounding it and we set up a hasty position. Earls, Merkle and I blended in with the other Marines. Earls had a view about 250 yards and I had a clear shot down an alley for about 350 yards."

Captain Bethea requested a white phosphorous artillery mission at 0600 near an enemy strong point located along Phase Line Beth and Route Ethan. He needed smoke to cover the movement of his Marines now under heavy fire. A little shake and bake could also clear the rooftops of hidden enemy snipers. These were the three phosphorous rounds that fell among Captain Omohundro's Bravo Company in the streets just to the west of Charlie Company. No Marine casualties were reported from the friendly fire incident.

At 0600, First Lieutenant Conner and his Fire Support Team seized a building at the intersection of Phase Line Beth and Route Ethan. From the rooftop this building held a commanding view of the Al Hydra Mosque and the terrain surrounding it some 300 meters to the south. Klingensmith's tanks had pushed farther south than its accompanying infantry and were busy fending off RPG fire as they were locating and destroying the enemy along Route Ethan. The tankers under heavy fire were fighting by instinct, loading and firing without thinking, taking out targets.

Bravo Company's Fire Support Team called in an artillery mission near the tanks positioned along Route Ethan. First Lieutenant Conner contacted Tank Section White 1 to warn them of the upcoming artillery mission in their vicinity. The tanks began double timing it back north, up Route Ethan, to escape the expected friendly barrage. But all the tanks weren't fast enough. Artillery rounds came screaming in and exploded, scattering shrapnel and damaging one of the retreating tank's communication gear.

"It was at this point in the city we were hit by friendly artillery fire," Villanova graduate Captain Meyers said. "It was quite an experience. The rounds hit right on us. First Lieutenant Klingensmith's tank was damaged, his antennas were broken off. Half of our water bottles were shattered from the shell barrage." An irate Meyers quickly got on the radio and was screaming, "Cease-fire!" when the firing finally stopped.

"I went back and switched out tanks and got right back in the fight," Klingensmith explained. "I didn't sleep the first five days in Fallujah." Luckily, there were no casualties among the tankers from the artillery mission.

Charlie Company's Marines were kept busy clearing the streets around Phase Line Beth and Route Ethan. As the Marines dodged in and out of the narrow alleys and littered streets, snipers continually tried to pick them off. The enemy resistance in this sector of the city had stiffened and the Marines had to continually out think the enemy, to stay alive.

3rd Squad of Rhoades' 1st Platoon, located near a D-9 dozer, identified an enemy RPG squad maneuvering near them. The Marines opened fire with their M16s and SAWs and quickly took them out, killing all three insurgents. Snipers attached to Charlie Company were also busy working the enemy over near the intersection.

It was sniper against sniper on the streets and rooftops of the city. Sniper Corporal Quintana, after establishing a firing position on a rooftop, engaged and killed an armed insurgent off to his south. Nearby, another member of Quintana's sniper team, Corporal Joe Watkins, with 3rd Platoon, set up an advantageous position with a view of the enemy fighters. Watkins squeezed the trigger of his rifle bringing down an insurgent preparing to fire on the Marines. Corporal Josh Munns was the third member of this sniper team attached to Charlie Company.

The Marines marveled at the weapon caches they found throughout the city of Fallujah. Another three caches were found on just the push to the mosque. Corporal Black, Lance Corporal Hughes, and Lance

Corporal Holmes personally found and destroyed three weapon caches on this one day of fighting. Of Fallujah's approximately 1,000 city blocks, 203 were found to contain weapon caches and ammunition storehouses that were set up to feed the insurgents a steady stream of ammo and weapons during the rolling battle.

At 0800 Corporal Turner, leading his fire team from 2nd Platoon, captured three insurgents in a building along Route Ethan.

A persistent enemy sniper position was holding up the advance of Lieutenant Littell's 3rd Platoon at an intersection. At 0900 Captain Bethea met up with Littell at the hotly contested corner and ordered Littell to destroy the sniper position so he could commence the final push toward the Al Hydra Mosque.

Only moments before, Littell had his Marines take out another nearby sniper position with a shoulder launched multi-purpose assault weapon. Corporal Farmer, 3rd Platoon, had engaged the enemy snipers located in a green house, who had been holding up the company. Using two shoulder-launched multi-purpose assault rockets they neutralized the sniper nest, killing the two insurgents.

Once again, Second Lieutenant Littell turned to the winning duo of Corporal Farmer along with Corporal Quintana's sniper team to attack south of Phase Line Beth to engage the elusive and harassing enemy snipers.

Motorcycle enthusiast Staff Sergeant Corey Lohr wrote of the action around the contested intersection of Phase Line Beth and Route Ethan:

> *"We then received sniper fire from our west. We return fire and it goes on for a good 10 min. Lieutenant Littell then decided that we need to use a SMAW round. Corporal Farmer, Lance Corporal Crows and Lance Corporal Bourns head out there with Corporal Quintana and shoot 2 SMAW rounds into the building we received sniper fire from. The sniper fire ceased and we were preparing to push forward with the rest of the company."*

Marine tanks also were in action at the disputed intersection. "I had my wingman, Sergeant Taylor, orient off to the east at the intersection of Cathy and Ethan, and his tank killed five or six guys that had been flushed out and trying to cross the street," Tank platoon commander, Klingensmith explained.

The chaotic fighting continued around Phase Line Beth and Route Ethan hour after hour. Five insurgents were seen maneuvering south of 3rd Squad, 1st Platoon's position along Phase Line Beth. Marines firing their M16s and SAWs opened fire on the maneuvering enemy. The noise from the small arms and the tank's .50 cals was deafening as the enemy fighters were destroyed or pushed back, but ever so slowly.

1st Squad, 1st Platoon spotted two 60mm and two 82mm mortars set up in mortar pits in an open field to their south. Force Recon Marines swung into action by engaging and destroying one of the threatening mortar pits with direct fire.

The enemy snipers were succeeding in slowing Charlie Company's attack down to a crawl. Throw in some RPGs being fired at the Charlie Company Marines and it all made for a perfect scenario for the insurgents in slowing the Marines down and making them pay dearly, in blood, for the city.

Another more immediate problem cropped up for Captain Bethea. Force Reconnaissance Platoon was trapped about a hundred meters east of Charlie Company's Fire Support Team. Apparently, one team from Force Recon had attempted to cross an open field between their position and 1st Platoon under heavy enemy fire. One of those Marines was Sergeant David Caruso, 25, a native of Naperville, Illinois, an assistant team leader with Force Recon attached to Charlie Company. Caruso loved the outdoors and the Chicago Bears football team. He had wanted to become a Marine while he was still in junior high school. When he was young and watching a parade in the states he noticed that people grew tired of waving the flag and laid them on the ground. The patriotic Caruso confided in his mother, "Mom don't they know that the American flag should NEVER touch the ground!" He spent the day picking up any flag that he saw on the ground and handed it back to its owner. He was the type of young man that believed in giving back to his country. That was one of the main reasons he became a Marine. He once asked his mom, "What are you doing for our country?" Her answer to her son was quick in coming, "I gave them you."

Sergeant David Caruso lost his life for that flag and his country while running across that open area far from home in Fallujah. He was hit in the head by a round fired by a hidden enemy sniper. He crumpled to the ground and lay motionless out in the open as the fight swirled around him. The remainder of Caruso's team took cover in a house directly south of Charlie Company's 1st Squad, 1st Platoon's position. 1st Squad joined the Recon Marines firing in support of their downed comrade.

A 1st Squad Marine viewing the furious action was Ohio native, Lance Corporal Stephen O'Rourke. Watching the Recon Marines as they ran forward under fire, he saw one drop to the ground. "When he (Caruso) went down, me and four or five other people went out, picked him up and carried him back. He had blood and tissue matter on his weapon from a head wound. He was dead when we reached him. At this time the Force Recon Marines were taking fire, hard core. We covered for them." It was alien for the Marines to leave one of their own out in the open. Sergeant Brooks had led the group of Marines out into the enemy fire zone and brought Curuso's body back.

After a three-hour stay in a building waiting for communications to come back up, Lance Corporal Carpenter's 1st Squad, 2nd Platoon had been pushing down the alleyways deeper into ravaged Fallujah. When passing Phase Line Beth, they bumped into six insurgents in a building across from where the Recon Marines were pinned down. All hell broke loose in the firefight. The noise in the house was deafening as the Marines took the insurgents out, face to face, one by one, room by room. "We held up in a building and there were six Iraqis, one had an RPG, another an RPK and the rest were armed with AK-47s. We engaged them, shooting down four of six," recalled Carpenter. "Across the street, where the Force Recon Marines were operating, we saw they had a man down in the middle of the street. Sergeant Nash said, 'We have to get that guy out, he's dying.' Six guys ran across the street and picked him up and carried him back to the house. He was dead when we got him in the house. We set up in that house for a few hours and it was the first time I had gotten some sleep for two days. While there, we watched the Cobras come in and attack the city. It was cool."

Captain Bethea called for a medical evacuation for the downed Force Recon Marine. He was the first Marine in, or attached to, Charlie Company to die in the fighting in Fallujah.

Lance Corporal Danny Myers, Weapons Company, 1st Section, 3rd Platoon, recalled his second mission into the smoke filled city in support of wounded Charlie Company Marines. "We drove up to a large intersection by the Al Hydra Mosque. My platoon commander, Lieutenant Kutilek, wanted us to block the intersection to supply security for an APC picking up casualties. The only people in the two trucks were the gunners and drivers. Everyone else had dismounted and they were walking around beside the vehicles. We drove to the right and I saw there was no cover, so we parked next to the APC. Corporal Smith went to the left with his vehicle and parked. We set there waiting for the APC to load up the casualties. A building was on fire to the right of us and smoke was pouring out into the street. Some Marines from the line company informed us that there were enemy units to our front. Finally the APC loads up and peels out. I told my driver, Lance Corporal Adshire, to start backing up, and as I looked forward an RPG flew by, missing my head by inches. I looked down and saw my driver was all curled up in the truck yelling 'Shoot that mother f***er.' The RPG round hit a tank behind us and bounced off. I started to lay rounds down range from where the smoke trail had come from. As we were leaving the city we got a call of more casualties."

"We were attacking down Route Ethan with the headquarters unit, 2nd Platoon and then the Iraqis in that order," said Captain Bethea.

As the day began slipping away, Operations Officer, Major Trimble (Hunter 3) asked Captain Bethea when the assault on the Al Hydra Mosque would commence. Lieutenant Colonel Brandl was concerned with how slow the attack on the mosque was developing. The battalion was moving faster than they had expected and he wanted to continue the momentum.

Bethea's Charlie Company had been in continuos enemy contact since seizing their initial foothold in the Braxton complex and the attack south. The entire company was now fully engaged along Phase Line Beth with enemy snipers continually peppering their front line. They would neutralize one enemy position, only to move a few meters farther south and run into another sniper's nest.

Captain Bethea was not only fighting to eliminate the enemy to his front and get his casualties out, but now he also had to contend with the Iraqi Emergency Response Unit to his rear. The friendly Iraqi troops were experiencing multiple negligent discharges from their weapons in a building the company was using for their headquarters. That was a nice way to say that the fire was careless and that the Iraqi troops were incompetent. First Sergeant Andrade ordered Clint, a mentor to the Iraqis, to stop their negligent firing.

Meanwhile, Captain Richie's Fire Support Team had Lance Corporal Hunter set up a laser designator and began lazing a target where they were receiving fire. An RPG round went off near Captain Richie's group as he talked an aircraft onto the target. The exploding RPG round pelted the group of Marines with jagged shrapnel along with chunks of cement and rock that could seriously injure a Marine. The Fire Support Team brought serious fire down on the enemy position and eliminated that threat in the building, and then immediately pushed on.

Staff Sergeant Lohr described the exhausting and confusing fight south toward Phase Line Cathy, in a letter to his wife, Cindy and their two children, Tyler, 9, and Kaylin, 8:

> *"The Lieutenant then told Corporal Farmer to breach the wall in front so we could get through our zone and spread out. Corporal Farmer shot 3 SMAW rockets into the wall and did very little damage. So 1st Squad went over the wall. 2nd Squad pushed East around the wall. Recon had an over-watch to our east*

side and yelled saying they will provide cover fire. 2nd Squad pushed South on the east side of the wall once they were out of sight, I traveled with 3rd in the same route. As we got up to the east side of the wall, Recon said they will suppress. We received fire from down south and further east. On the South side of the wall we see 2nd Squad holding a strong position. We are receiving fire all the way into their position. 1st Squad pushed all the way through and realized they had to back track for there was no exit on the south wall. I sent Corporal Arroyo and Corporal Black around to the front to our east to break the lock on the gate to a courtyard. Once they broke the lock he said 'It was clear to move in.' At that time 3rd Squad was lead element in clearing that courtyard. Corporal Quintana threw a white smoke (grenade) to screen 1st Squads movement into the courtyard. 2nd and the remainder of 3rd laid down suppressive fire to cover for 1st Squad. 2nd Squad then pushed west and cleared another house. We push west to a stronger position with better visibility as we hold up and wait for word from the Lieutenant. Marines then start refilling magazines and providing security positions and resting. At this time the platoon is exhausted and pumped of adrenaline waiting for the word and watching for the enemy. A mortar hit the southwest side of the building throwing glass and rubble in the courtyard. Corporal Arroyo was hit in the right elbow and back with pieces of glass, rubble and shrapnel. He was burned by the blast. We get word to link up with the Company CP just shy of Phase Line Cathy. It is mid afternoon when we push down and link up, receiving sporadic fire."

This fight with the enemy snipers went on for nearly three hours as Charlie Company fought its way the final 300 meters to Phase Line Cathy. Finally positioned at Phase Line Cathy, Charlie Company was now located directly across the street from the Al Hydra Mosque. To their west was Captain Omohundro's Bravo Company preparing to take the Cultural Center.

In that final push to the mosque, Turner's 2nd Platoon secured three buildings along Phase Line Cathy right across from the Al Hydra Mosque allowing them to set up their Attack Position.

Bethea, First Sergeant Andrade, Clint and Snake, (aliases) the two handlers of the Iraqi forces went to one of the houses Turner's 2nd Platoon had just taken. They climbed to the second floor of the building and out onto the roof. The Marines of 2nd Platoon, 1st Squad, covered them. While on the roof they were continuously under attack from enemy small arms fire. The Marines of Turner's 1st Squad were kept busy returning fire on the enemy snipers in buildings adjacent to the Al Hydra Mosque. The Iraqi forces, which had been moved forward to take the mosque, were acting up again and Turner was ordered to go firm because of their erratic friendly fire. The Iraqis errant fire wounded one of their American mentors, Snake, and one of their own soldiers in the leg.

U.S. handlers were encouraged to adhere the words of T.E. Lawrence, (Lawrence of Arabia) the legendary British author and officer who wrote in 1917, *Do not try to do too much with your own hands. Better the Arabs do it tolerably than you do it perfectly. It is their war, and you are to help them, not to win it for them.*

Captain Theodore Bethea called in a medical evacuation for the Iraqi Response trooper that had been wounded in the leg. Clint told him that the mentor, Snake, would wait to receive medical treatment once the mosque had been taken. The Medevac mission was cancelled.

Nearby, Marine snipers, led by Sergeant Dustin Stout, 3rd Squad, 2nd Platoon were busy in a fierce firefight, a deadly duel, that accounted for four enemy killed at around 1000 hours. 3rd Squad, 1st Platoon engaged a group of insurgents and brought down five more of them in steady fighting in their sector.

Stout remembered, "We began seeing a band of insurgents moving from east to west across an alley. We tried to get a clear shot at them but they continued sprinting across the opening."

The enemy was found to be trying to reinforce the mosque. Spotted by 2nd Squad, 2nd Platoon, the reinforcing insurgents were brought under a steady fire that accounted for another three enemy fighters killed.

From a secure rooftop, 1st Squad, 2nd Platoon saw a group of enemy fighters running along Route Ethan toward the south. They opened up on them with small arms fire and brought down two more of the insurgents.

1st Squad, 1st Platoon, saw a parked vehicle in an alley, east of the green house on Phase Line Beth and engaged it with an M203 grenade launcher. The impact of the grenades on the vehicle caused it to burst into flames. Seconds later fifteen secondary explosions and 3,000 rounds began cooking off which tore the vehicle apart. Apparently the insurgents were using the vehicle to run ammo and weapons to their fighters. Also the 1st Squad killed one enemy sniper in a window located about 150 meters south of their rooftop position. Lance Corporal Giusti,

3rd Platoon, 3rd Squad recalled seeing one of the Marine snipers in action against a fighter who continually stepped from cover and fired his weapon, and just as fast, stepped back. "The insurgent came out again and the Marine sniper nailed him in the chest, knocking him back about three feet before he crumpled to the ground. The insurgent then managed to crawl into a house. Our sniper loaded up an M203 on his launcher and fired it into the house he had just crawled into, basically destroying the building. If he was still alive, he wasn't a happy man."

Littell's 3rd Platoon, 3rd Squad found itself held up by sniper fire coming from south of their position. Corporal Shrivan, tired of being shot at by an insurgent, loaded his grenade launcher and fired. Right after the grenade impacted, the sniper returned fire. Shrivan fired a second grenade. Again the sniper fired back at Shrivan. Thoroughly angered by now, Corporal Shrivan reloaded with a third grenade. He aimed, fired again and then he quietly waited. After firing the third grenade, there was no longer any return fire from the enemy sniper. Shrivan had fired three 40mm grenades to finally neutralize the threat to the 3rd Squad.

At 1100, the Iraqi Security Forces linked up with Second Lieutenant Matt Rhoades' 1st Platoon in preparation for the assault on the mosque.

The enemy fighters stayed active around the mosque as Charlie Company prepared to attack. At 1200, 1st Squad, 1st Platoon, spotted six armed enemy fighters moving from the west across their immediate front. The Marines engaged the enemy with small arms fire. 1st Squad Marines, firing their M16s and SAWs, created a cacophony of noise with bullet casings covering the rooftops and flying into the street below. The Marines went out and checked the dead enemy. They had dropped four of the insurgents. They recovered a PKM medium machine gun and an RPG launcher.

With daylight fading, Klingensmith's tanks punched south of Phase Line Cathy, and using their night scopes, fought it out with several entrenched insurgents. They got the best of the enemy fighters, killing ten of them. Captain Bethea got on the phone and requested the tanks destroy the enemy sniper positions still working them over adjacent to the mosque. Bethea then ordered the tanks to fire their main guns and create three breach holes on the north wall and two breaches along the west wall of the mosque for entry. Fearing a car bomb threat, the tanks used their main guns to destroy a parked vehicle along the north wall of the mosque.

Bravo Company Attacks the Cultural Center

On November 9, a six-lane highway lay between Bravo Company and their first big objective, the Cultural Center. The center was located on a corner near a large open area along a four-lane highway (Phase Line Cathy), which was divided by a cement median. On the western side of the Cultural Center, a row of garage stalls stretched out along the highway. The stalls had tin roofs weighted down with old car tires to help keep the roofs from blowing off. A small blue mobile shed sat alone on one corner across from the center. On the eastern side of the intersection set Charlie Company's first big objective, the green domed Al Hydra Mosque with its tall minaret dominating the area skyline. An abandoned blue truck with broken windows sat haphazardly on the trash littered street. The highway Bravo Company would have to cross was still wet from the overnight rains. Captain Read Omohundro attached his FiST team with Andy Eckert's 1st Platoon during the push on the center. Eckert's platoon along with Berch's 2nd Platoon would supply covering fire for the coming attack on the center from across the street.

"As the sun came up we approached Phase Line Cathy and Route Ethan," Second Lieutenant Eckert remembered. "My platoon was tasked to support by fire position in the taking of the mosque and the Cultural

Center. We moved to a house that was a little west of the intersection and I went to the roof to establish the support by fire position."

Six Marines from Eckert's platoon were still pushing south down the street to join their lieutenant in the house when a Jeep Cherokee suddenly pulled up behind them and came to a complete stop. Out looking for Marines to kill, the occupants of the SUV had stumbled on a hornet's nest. Six insurgents manned the vehicle. In the twilight hours the surprised Marines in the street quickly opened fire just as the insurgents jumped from the vehicle with AK-47s at the ready. Lance Corporal Andrew Russell dropped to a knee and opened fire with his SAW cutting a few of the enemy fighters down.

"Staff Sergeant Brown called us down from the rooftop with our SMAW rockets," Assaultman Nick Criddle explained. "As we set up we noticed there were two bodies lying beside the vehicle. Lance Corporal Kelly fired and his rocket went high over the vehicle. I then grabbed one and fired and mine went right through the front window and out the back window and exploded against a wall."

Staff Sergeant Eric Brown, Corporal Jason Huyghe, and Corporal Steven Archibald then added their firepower to the lopsided fight in the street. SAWs and M16s began playing a tattoo against the car and the remaining insurgents.

Corporal Jacob Knospler said, "Most of the platoon was on the rooftop looking south in a fire support position when I heard all kind of firing behind us. I went over to the other side of the roof and looked down to see what everyone was firing at. Some insurgents were just exiting a vehicle and everyone was firing at them. I began firing and two of the insurgents crawled into a courtyard. There were a lot of rounds being fired."

Sergeant Samuel Williams, on the same rooftop, heard someone behind him shout, 'We got company!' He ran over and looked down on the alley below. "Everyone was firing at this white vehicle. We fired two rockets and several grenades. The insurgents didn't have a chance to get a shot off," Williams said.

Four of the insurgents were killed immediately by the hail of gunfire as the two wounded insurgents made it into an adjacent courtyard off the main street.

"Huyghe and Miller followed them over to the courtyard and tossed a grenade in before pushing into the gate and finishing them off with small arms fire. I saw bodies lying around the charred and chewed up Jeep," Eckert recalled. The insurgents had been trying to get additional weapons from the trunk of the Jeep. Later when the Marines checked the vehicle they found machine guns along with RPGs in the back of the SUV.

Knospler said, "One of the insurgents blew himself up and the other one was killed by a Marine grenade."

The company's FiST team got busy and called in artillery around the Cultural Center for approximately thirty minutes to prep it before the attack. Omohundro tasked Wilkens' 3rd Platoon to push across Phase line Cathy at 0700 and launch their daylight attack on the Cultural Center. Force Recon Marines had earlier entered the mosque and secured it, but the surrounding buildings had not yet been searched for enemy snipers.

Tank platoon commander and Penn State graduate, First Lieutenant David Klingensmith said, "Bravo Company was attempting to cross Phase Line Cathy to get over to the Cultural Center. To do that, they had to cross a large wide-open area. I was still attached to Charlie Company, but I tried to get their attention, to at least put my tank in between them and the open area. I wasn't able to reach them before they attacked."

Wilkens' 3rd Platoon was tasked to go into the Cultural Center while Eckert's platoon supported by fire from their position, and Berch's 2nd Platoon to the west of Eckert's platoon also supported by fire.

Corporal Brad Watson and Lance Corporal Jeffery Walker, attached sniper team, had moved over with Bravo Company to the north of the Cultural Center. They had pushed across the street to the center and now would go back across the street they had just traversed, this time under enemy fire. Lance Corporal Jeffery Walker lugging his M16A4 and an M203 followed his team leader, Watson.

Walker recounted what happened. "Brad went first and I followed. We got half the way across the wide street when I heard all kind of firing to my left. When I looked over I saw muzzle flashes from a building on the Cultural Center side of the street. Then I felt something like a baseball bat hit my left upper arm. The round jerked my hand off my weapon. I looked down at my arm and it was gushing blood from an artery. As I continued running I got off a few rounds at the muzzle flashes with my right hand. When we made it to a wall across the street we were still in the line of fire. I saw a green gate that led into a courtyard. We ran into the courtyard and I found myself staring at a house that hadn't been cleared. I sat down and called out to Brad, 'I've been hit!' He was looking out the gate and didn't hear me with all the firing going on. I yelled again and he still didn't hear me."

"I kicked the door down and we ran into the courtyard with some mortar men following us. I told Walker to train his rifle on a window and I began counting guys as they came into the courtyard," Watson recalled. "Up till then as we pushed it didn't seem to be as bad as I thought it was going to be."

Finally Walker strolled up to his Team Leader, Corporal Bradley Watson crouching near the green courtyard gate. "Excuse me Corporal can I get permission to go over and see the corpsman?"

Watson stared at the Marine and asked him "Why?"

"I've been hit in the left arm," Walker said.

Surprised, Watson looked down at Walker's arm and saw the blood oozing out of the gunshot wound and said, "Walker if you've been shot you don't have to ask permission to go and see the corpsman, just do it! I got on the radio and put a call in to Doc Rex Goodman. Before Walker left I gave him a hogs tooth sniper round on a necklace."

Walker said, "Doc Goodman from 2nd Platoon came over and cut my sleeve off to get at the wound. He gave me a shot of morphine and put some quick clot on the wound. I made it over to a waiting Humvee to take me back. We drove off and then they received another call saying Bravo had more casualties so we turned around and went back to near the Cultural Center. When we arrived back I saw the faces of the Marines when they were loading guys on the track. They were all in disbelief. Just then I saw an RPG round coming right at the Humvee. I thought *'That's it, I'm dead and even if I survive I'll be messed up.'* Just then the RPG flew past us and exploded on a wall behind the Humvee. The driver of the Humvee said, 'let's get you out of here!'"

Sniper Corporal James Mendenhall recalled, "Walker was then medevaced out of the city."

Sniper, Corporal Brad Watson said, "We tried not to use rooftops in the city but tried to find windows but the way the houses were laid out we had to go to rooftops a lot. After Walker left, I along with another Marine went to a small balcony to provide supporting fire. I dropped four or five insurgents about three hundred yards across an open field by the Cultural Center. Two were behind a wall and three were advancing up an alley. "

"Fire erupted 360 degrees around our rooftop. Once the first insurgent fired at us, it started a chain reaction and we were all in a fire fight on the roof," said Eckert. "Before they pushed out we had been firing thousands of rounds at the Cultural Center, the mosque, and a line of apartments right across the street and behind a parking lot. We had fired some SMAWs at the mosque right before they punched across."

Sergeant Lonny D. Wells' 1st Squad was called on to punch across the open highway and get a foothold at the center. Sergeant Wells and Corporal Anthony Silva's team, consisting of Lance Corporal Derek Cheek, Corporal Maldonado along with Corporal Ngo, were the first Marines to cross the wide-open street. Once across the highway they were to link up with the Force Recon Marines already in the Cultural

Center. A Marine combat photographer, Staff Sergeant Knauth, also accompanied the first team as they started to dash across the street. There is a reason why they call them COMBAT Photographers and Knauth was about to find this out.

Corporal Silva, Team Leader of 1st Squad, 3rd Platoon, recalled the chaos after they reached the open street. "Captain Omohundro was saying, 'There is a hatch! We need to go in the hatch!' We didn't get much cover fire or smoke to help mask our identity as we crossed the road. Captain Omohundro said, 'Go!' and Sergeant Wells said, 'Let's go!' It's a big open road and the first thing I'm doing is looking for this hatch as we ran across, praying as fast as I could. I have a big black pack on with a SMAW rocket attached and I'm carrying a lot of ammo for my M203. As I'm running across all I heard was POPPING and shooting everywhere. I'm going! I'm going! I'm going! Sergeant Wells was running beside Corporal Ngo who carried the radio. Lance Corporal Cheek later told me that bullets were skipping at our feet. A bullet hit Maldonado's helmet. I don't know how Ngo didn't get hit. He was right beside Wells as they crossed. Halfway across the road I heard something hit my back. BAM! When I felt that I got really scared, but I kept running. A bullet had hit my sappy plate, went through my pack, and hit my camel back, which caused it to explode. I felt like I was bleeding. I finally made it across the road with Cheek and the combat photographer. We all took cover and then Lance Corporal Cheek began checking me out. The plate had stopped the bullet before it entered me. Everyone began firing. It was real chaos."

From his vantagepoint on the rooftop across the street from the Cultural Center, Second Lieutenant Andy Eckert could see the 3rd Platoon Marines running across the street. He stared in horror as Wells fell to the street. "I thought to myself, *Oh crap, here's where it gets violent!* I saw the blood coming from Sergeant Wells and I thought, *He's dead or in critical condition*! They had taken fire from the mosque not the Cultural Center. I started firing my weapon in support, in fact everyone was firing when they moved across. It was the first time I had fired my weapon in Fallujah," said Eckert.

Lance Corporal Edwin Maldonado, with his wife Sonia waiting for him at home, was one of the first Marines bounding across the open street. "When we started running, the street just started to light up with rounds. You could see the bullets just hitting the pavement. I tried not to think about it but just kept on running, that's what we're trained to do. I couldn't run fast with all my equipment weighing me down. When I reached the door I jumped inside and that's when Corporal Johnson, who was right behind me, said that a round had hit my helmet. I never felt it and didn't know it had even happened."

Immediately the Marines crossing the open street came under heavy fire and Sergeant Lonny D. Wells, 29, from Vandergrift, Pennsylvania, married and the father of five, two sons and three daughters, was hit with shrapnel to his chest, left leg, and abdomen. He immediately went down. The most serious of the three wounds was in the leg where the femoral artery had been nicked. He lay on the road, face down, as the other Marines scattered for cover. As they looked back at their fallen sergeant they could see the blood staining the pant leg of Wells' uniform.

Lance Corporal Llerena was right behind Sergeant Wells as they punched across the highway. "Fire was coming from everywhere. Rounds were bouncing off everything as I ran across the street to the Cultural Center. I was directly behind Sergeant Wells when he got hit. We had to keep moving. Everyone knew it wasn't the time to try and assist anyone. When we got across we got behind a small wall. We didn't know where the door was to get in. After a few minutes we made a dash to get into the Cultural Center. Another platoon supplied covering fire for us as we got inside. We began to set up an area of security within the building. Corporal Straub and I were in one room shooting out the window at a couple of insurgents that kept running from the cover of a wall and firing at us. Lieutenant Wilkens authorized a SMAW shot at the target. Corporal Straub fired from within the room. An AT-4 has a 60 meters back blast. We did it in an eight by ten-foot room. The blast was deafening and it stung a bit, but it took care of the insurgents."

Located in a house about fifty yards from where Wells' Marines were crossing was Lance Corporal Michael Rodriguez, 20, a member of 3rd Squad, 3rd Platoon. Rodriguez from New London, New Hampshire, who wanted to become a history teacher upon leaving the Marines, heard the firing. "We were getting ready to cross the street and get in the Cultural Center when we heard the shooting. Someone yelled 'Wells is hit!' We then started to haul ass across the street. Lance Corporal Holmes and Lance Corporal Gilg were right beside me as we finally entered the building. Sergeant Sheik, a member of recon began directing us to the windows to provide covering fire. About eight or nine rounds of artillery, RPGs or mortars fell nearby. My triceps were lacerated from the shrapnel," Rodriguez said.

Marines are trained to quickly adapt to chaotic battle situations. To do that, they have to come to grips with their fear of exposing themselves to enemy fire in order to support a fellow Marine. Gunnery Sergeant Ryan Shane, 32, of Danbridge, Tennessee, 2nd Platoon, quickly ran out on the open highway to try and pull Wells to safety. Navy Corpsman Joel

Lambotte joined Shane in the open as they both began pulling on Wells. An enemy sniper took careful aim and fired again. The round hit Shane in the buttocks and traveled up to his bladder. He immediately stumbled backwards before falling down in the road fifteen feet from where Lambotte was trying to help Wells. After seeing Marines being hit by enemy fire, still other Marines began going out into the open street to assist their wounded buddies. The unwritten code—*Never leave a Marine behind*—kicked in.

Navy Corpsman HN Joel Lambotte was then targeted by the enemy snipers and took a round to his ankle. He managed to crawl back out of the line of fire. That left only one corpsman to care for the 50 Marines of Wilkens' 3rd Platoon, Corpsman HC3 Luis Ruizpupo.

North Carolina native, Lance Corporal David Houck, a member of 3rd Squad, helped Lambotte by doctoring the wounded corpsman's foot. Luckily, Houck had completed a Battlefield Casualty Course just before their deployment to Iraq.

Standing near his lieutenant, Corporal Jacob Knospler remembered, "I turned from the north side of the roof where 1st and 2nd Platoons had just taken care of the Jeep Cherokee full of terrorists and looked to the south down the street to the Cultural Center. When I did, I saw two Marines down in the street. It looked as though no one was doing anything so I turned and took off down the stairs."

Knospler ran past some of his squad members positioned in a walled courtyard area at the street level of the building he had been on. Corporal Kyle Mastropasqua, 3rd Fire Team Leader, recalls, "I saw him pass to my left and run toward the street. At that time, because of our position, we couldn't see what was happening to our guys under fire in the street. We were supplying suppressive fire against enemy positions to our left."

Knospler didn't hesitate as he made his way down the stairs from the rooftop and into the chaotic street below. He yelled to Staff Sergeant Brown that there were Marines down in the street and he was going to help get them out. He dashed the hundred yards to where the fallen Marines were lying. Other Marines began to react and followed Knospler under fire and into the open to rescue the wounded Marines.

Corporal Nathan Anderson, Sergeant Kenneth Hudson, Sergeant Michael Ramirez, and PFC Samuel Crist all ran out under the enemy fire to help retrieve the two wounded Marines. Joining them were Corporal Jeremy LaForce and Santa Maria, Texas native, Corporal Thomas Hodges. Both LaForce and Hodges ran toward the seriously wounded Wells. The accurate fire of the enemy machine guns and snipers began to find Marine targets. A round hit SAW gunner PFC Crist, who took a gunshot wound to the left thigh and right shoulder and Sergeant Hudson was hit in the left arm.

Just down the street from where Wells' squad was under attack, Corporal Tom Hodges had heard Marines shouting 'Go! Go!' "I started running across the street as rounds were impacting against the pavement. I saw Marines lying in the street while others were running past them. I thought, *Why are these guys running past him? Marines don't do that.* I ran over to Wells and grabbed the straps of his daypack to pull him off the street but when I yanked on them, they broke. Anderson ran up and we both grabbed Wells' flak jacket and pulled him off the street and into a cubbyhole by the Cultural Center. I saw Sergeant Hudson get hit by a round in his left arm and drop his weapon."

The six-foot tall Knospler reached Gunny Shane. "Now there were five wounded Marines down in the street. I glanced over and saw Corporal Hodges and Corporal LaForce helping Wells. I ran over to Shane just as Corporal Anderson joined me. Anderson had already pulled one Marine from the street and was returning to help. I remember thinking we both had this *oh shit look on our faces* as we began to carry Shane from the f****** open street."

Ohio native Corporal Nathan Anderson who grew up in the Apple Valley area of the state had drug one Marine to safety then ran back out into the fire zone to assist Knospler with Shane. For a hobby Anderson enjoyed bull riding and had wanted to be a Marine when he reached ten years of age. He came from a family of five, three sisters and a brother.

Anderson and Knospler began pulling Shane from the street. Knospler recalled, "He seemed to weigh about 350 pounds with all of his gear on. Rounds were impacting around us as we got him back to this small alcove adjacent to the Cultural Center."

Still positioned up on the rooftop, Sergeant Sam Williams recalled, "I got a call on the PRR that said, 'Hey we need you guys down here now!' We ran down the stairs and linked up with Staff Sergeant Brown and then pushed across the highway toward the Cultural Center. All hell was breaking loose. We made it across the street and turned a corner to climb the stairs into the building. There were like thirty steps to climb. Gunny Brown yelled 'let's roll!' I felt like Rocky in the movie when he's training and running up the steps. It seemed to last forever till we burst into the entrance. I saw Sergeant Ken Hudson who had been wounded in the hand from friendly artillery rounds that were falling around the building. The fire had been called in earlier and was just being answered when we were in the Cultural Center."

Corporal Nick Criddle's Assault Squad was on the rooftop again, "Kelly and I went back up to the rooftop just as the suicide run across the street began. We were called on to create a breach for Charlie Company to enter the mosque. Both Kelly and Evans fired a SMAW rocket at the mosque 250 yards away and they just exploded harmlessly on the outside wall."

These were the first casualties that Bravo Company had suffered in Fallujah. After the initial confusion, the casualties were quickly evaced out of the city while 1st and 2nd Platoons suppressed the enemy in and around the Cultural Center and in an adjacent open area just to the west.

"We were in this room and found out it didn't lead into the main part of the Cultural Center. We were piling up. I saw Cheek checking Silva's back to see if he had been hit. A plate stopped the round. I looked out this small window and saw Sergeant Wells lying in the street. He had taught me everything I knew in the Marines. He was an awesome guy, a teacher, friend, everything. Finally we found our way into the main part of the building. Recon had already cleared the building for us. I saw Sergeant Mohammed Sheik of Recon who had been shot in the arm and was sitting down, relaxing. I asked myself, *What is going on?* We were still getting fire from all directions. This is when I got the wake up call in Fallujah," Maldonado remembered.

Marines, under enemy sniper and machine gun fire, continued to pour across the street. Corporal Silva stared out from the Cultural Center in disbelief as more Marines ran toward him. "A couple minutes later everyone started across the road and I'm trying to tell them not to come because we couldn't find the hatch to go inside. We didn't know where the enemy fire was coming from. Marines were still coming across the street and we were bunching up in this one room," said Corporal Silva.

The area where the Marines were bunching up did not have a direct door into the main part of the Cultural Center. The Marines had to leave the cover of the small room on the side of the building, and run back outside to get to the main entrance of the building.

Corpsman Luis Ruizpupo ran across the six-lane highway under the intense enemy fire and began administering aid to the casualties.

"I remember a track coming up to take care of the wounded," Knospler recalled.

Corporal Hodges explained, "When I was in the cubbyhole area I went over to calm the wounded Crist down. He kept telling me 'Don't let them take my arm! Don't let them take my arm! I told him that he was going to be all right, that his arm was okay. I saw blood in his crotch area and feared the worst but found out later the blood came from a thigh wound."

Doc Jadick arrived in an armored ambulance after hearing that two or more Marines of Bravo Company had been wounded in the fight around the Cultural Center. After dismounting the ambulance he found that not two but seven Marines had been wounded in the fierce fighting.

He began getting the Marines behind the safety of a low three-foot wall and out of the incessant enemy fire. RPGs began detonating around the makeshift MASH position.

Under fire, Jadick began stabilizing the wounded Marines before getting them into the back of the ambulance. Because of the severity of the wound to his buttocks and bladder, it was too painful for Gunny Shane to be carried and he had to crawl himself into the vehicle.

Sergeant Lonny D. Wells died from loss of blood while in route to the casualty collection point outside the city. Captain Omohundro was notified by radio of his sergeant's death. He was the first Marine killed from Bravo Company. "It was devastating. You never want to hear about one of your Marines dying. I had to focus on the fact that I had Marines alive and we still had a mission," Omohundro said.

Sergeant Wells' death was a heavy blow to First Lieutenant Chris Wilkens' 3rd Platoon, as well as for the entire company. At Camp Lejuene Wells had written letters to the parents of the younger Marines in his squad, assuring them he would look over them during their tour in Iraq. Corporal Anthony Silva remembered being in denial when informed of Sergeant Wells' death. "A Marine came up to me and told me Sergeant Wells was killed. I didn't believe him. Other Marines kept on telling me. I wouldn't listen. I was in confusion. My daughter was born while I was gone and I hadn't seen her yet. I was just shot at and I was totally out of it."

The tanks came to assist Bravo Company. "I moved a tank around to support Bravo Company and that's when my tank got hit by an RPG. It hit right off of my cupola," Klingensmith said. "It knocked me and my loader back down in the turret. The blast hit me in the face, hit my loader in the head with a sand bag, and destroyed five cans of ammo."

At this juncture in the attack, the Operations Officer Major Trimble talked to Captain Omohundro about calling in fire support. "He told me that, 'You are there, you got it. You can see what's going on, you call the shots with the tanks and the indirect fire.' It's not normally something that a company commander does," remembered Omohundro.

The fighting surged around the Cultural Center for about an hour before Wilkens' 3rd Platoon pushed all of his Marines across the street and forced their way into the building. Although Recon had secured the building earlier, the Bravo Company Marines went room to room in a clearing operation before Captain Omohundro established his COC in the building.

At 0900, the remainder of HQ Platoon and the FiST team moved from 1st Platoon's position, crossed the street and joined the company commander in the Cultural Center. 1st and 2nd Platoons remained in their positions across the street from the center in order to provide overwatch on Charlie Company's next objective, the Al Hydra Mosque, located to the east of the center. They also were positioned to secure the western flank of the company and the battalion.

Corporal Jacob Knospler said, "A few members of 1st Platoon were in the Cultural Center and we set up a fire support position firing to the west at some insurgents. Rounds were impacting against the walls of the building as other Marines from the company joined us."

At 1600, both 1st and 2nd Platoons moved under smoke to the Cultural Center to rest and prepare for follow on operations.

"I remember an enemy fighter came out from our east in an open area near the Cultural Center. He wore a yellow shirt with a white and black checkered scarf covering his face and he wore a dark hat. He was right out in the middle of the road shooting his AK-47. He became a big problem for us, we had to get Charlie Company to shoot at him, because our Marines firing from their position would have run the risk of shooting friendly forces," Omohundro said.

"This is when things got real crazy. I went up on top of the roof with a squad of Marines, two machine guns, and Lieutenant Wilkins, the 3rd Platoon commander. While up on top of the roof we began receiving fire from every direction but the north. We could see countless muzzle flashes on three sides of us," Captain Omohundro explained.

With a panoramic view of the city, Omohundro could see smoke coming from the west and east where the other battalions were attacking into the city. "We were up on the roof firing for about twenty minutes, shooting at enemy forces until we were able to get it clear enough to move down. I was orienting my fire to the east. I don't know how many magazines I went through," Omohundro said. "We found out that the enemy primarily occupied the upper stories of the buildings and houses. In buildings, they wouldn't fire from near the windows or doors, but from deeper in the room so their muzzle flash would be obscured. They could see you, but most of the time you couldn't see them."

Captain Meyers' tank was oriented directly south and his Executive Officer, Lieutenant Markley, had his tank oriented to the west. Both tanks were engaging insurgents on the streets to the west and south up to 600 meters away. Klingensmiths' Tank Platoon was positioned nearby, only a few meters away to the east. Klingensmith's tanks covered east and assisted with fire at the enemy to the south.

The two line companies that the tanks supported, Charlie and Bravo, were now less than a block apart. "Our tanks maneuvered on the main roads in the city, and in that position, we were fighting in a 360." Captain Meyers recalled, "I was shooting at insurgents down the alleys and Markley was shooting insurgents on Phase Line Ethan. The enemy was leaving the area around the Cultural Center and we were killing them as they left the buildings. Most of the work was done with our machine guns because of the proximity to our infantry. Our awareness in the tank is much less than an infantryman. We're basically looking through a straw when we're buttoned up in the tank. So for the most part I had my hatch open."

"Combat was what I expected in Fallujah. But I thought I would be spending more time directing more platoon size fights than working with supporting arm fires. I spent a lot of time coordinating tank fire and other indirect fires. A major from another unit said of Fallujah, 'It was a platoon commander's fight and a company commander's war,' Omohundro remembers.

"The one thing that stuck in my mind was as the radio traffic was progressing, Captain Omohundro was completely in control. He was completely calm," Major Winn remembered. "I was a platoon commander during the Gulf War and when bullets start flying around you, you tend to get a little excited. Captain Omohundro was completely calm on the radio. He obviously had complete awareness of what was going on around him. He was that way the whole attack in Fallujah."

"We rested at the Cultural Center with seventy-five per cent alert—two platoons on watch and one resting. I got two hours sleep during the day, and another hour and a half of sleep that night. The fighting seemed to have slacked off some and this was the first night in the city that we could rest. Lieutenant Colonel Brandl showed up and talked to me. He informed me that Sergeant Wells didn't make it and I told Lieutenant Wilkens what had happened," Omohundro said.

Corporal Watson's sniper team went to the rooftop of the Cultural Center to set up. Corporal Marcin Ochman replaced the wounded Walker as Watson's spotter.

Lieutenant Colonel Brandl and Sergeant Major Hope paid a visit to the Marines of Bravo Company at the Cultural Center. In the first Humvee rode Gunner Athey, then the Lieutenant Colonel. In the third were the Marines for security, and in the fourth Humvee rode Sergeant Major Anthony Hope. As they pulled up, blood was still visible in the street. "At the Cultural Center we lost Sergeant Wells. The mood of the Marines was tense because there were insurgents still down the street running around. An enemy fighter stuck his head up near us and all the

Marines with the COC opened up on him," said Sergeant Major Hope. "As we traveled the city's streets we never knew if they were secure or not. We would see unarmed people crossing the street and pick up weapons at one of their many caches and begin shooting at us. Nothing was ever clear until we pushed all the way south. It was hard to clear every single house."

"When I walked into the Cultural Center, one Marine came up to me and told me about another Marine that had been shot in the back and the plate had stopped the round. He brought it over and showed it to me. If we hadn't had the plates he would not have been with us today," Hope recalled. "We stayed there and talked to the Marines awhile. The Marines were excited and pumped up with adrenaline. I'm not right up there with them. It hurts to see them up there and me not there with them, especially when there's a loss. When I go in, I see the Marines are pumped up and I try to keep them pumped up, to motivate them and tell them what a good job they're doing. I let them know that the Colonel and everyone are impressed with the job they're doing. They're eighteen and twenty-one-year-olds and here I am forty-five, and I tell them in a heartbeat that they're as good a Marine as ever been in the Corps."

At 1400 Captain Meyers' tank section left the city and moved back to refuel and rearm. "Captain Omohundro said he didn't need us any longer. After refueling we were to be attached back to Avenger, Alpha Company and Captain Cunningham. We basically had to refuel every 12 hours, and when we came back into the city we would bring in MREs and supplies to the line companies. It took us two or three hours to refuel and the crewmen would take that time to get some sleep. When we were in the tanks in the city, to relieve ourselves, we would use piss bottles. For number two, we waited and took the opportunity when we were being refueled out of the city. Later that night I heard the AC-130 was overhead and radioed that one of our tanks in the city was being encircled. The AC-130 began engaging enemy around the tank. It worked out really well. Those gunships were phenomenal. We had one tank hit by an RPG that day. It hit the .50 cal ammo box. I was right next to the tank and no one was injured," Captain Meyers said.

At 0100 on November 10, Marines of Bravo's 1st and 2nd Platoons moved from the Cultural Center, south of Phase Line Cathy, to establish over-watch positions for Alpha Company's coming attack on the important Government Center. At approximately 0500, under the cover of darkness, Alpha Company conducted passage of lines with Bravo Company and commenced their attack.

Charlie Company Secures the Al Hydra Mosque

Insurgents, cloaked in red and black checkered headscarves, were seen carrying their fellow wounded fighters down the desolate streets that were littered with shattered concrete and several dead bodies. The enemy fighters carried them into the Al Hydra Mosque.

November 9, Captain Bethea, Charlie Company commander, tasked to get the photo op for the media of Iraqi troops taking the Al Hydra Mosque, now had his company in position. "We prepped the mosque, as well as destroying any enemy in the area, as well as laying down a smoke screen for them to cross the street and get into the mosque," Bethea said.

Eighty-six members of the Iraqi Emergency Response Unit formed up in a holding position in a building located directly behind Charlie Company's 2nd Platoon. "At 0600 we called for artillery fire," Captain Bethea explained. "Myself, First Sergeant Andrade, and the Iraqi liaison went up to the top of a building. Lieutenant Turner was right next to me on the rooftop. We had the tanks fire to create three breaches in the north side of the mosque and two on the western side. The liaison requested additional rounds be fired at the mosque. Across the street, Lieutenant

Turner's men are killing enemy as they were maneuvering back and forth."

"When we were at the Al Hydra Mosque, we set up support by fire positions, suppressed the mosque, then the Iraqis would move in and clear it out," said Lance Corporal Thompson, 1st Squad, 2nd Platoon.

Lance Corporal Di Pasqua of 1st Squad was on watch when he stared down the road and saw someone dart across. "I saw the first bad guy but the belt had turned over in my drum. I pulled the trigger and it just clicked. I called for Lance Corporal Thompson to get up here and take these guys out. Before Thompson got there, a second guy ran out. That was right before I was going to charge the weapon," Di Pasqua said.

Hearing his name called out, Thompson got up and quickly grabbed his SAW and turned to where Di Pasqua was struggling with his weapon.

"When I turned around, there were these guys starting to run across this very wide road," Thompson said.

"When Thompson reached me I told him what I had seen. From the bushes near a wall I saw a reflection of the sun off a barrel," Lance Corporal Di Pasqua remembered. Di Pasqua fumbling with his SAW finally managed to get it un-jammed.

"I dropped to one knee and fired at about the same time Di Pasqua got his weapon up and running. It was just talking guns. They made it across the street and ran into some bushes. We unloaded on the bushes until we ran out of ammo. We called the tanks over and got a re-supply of rounds," said Lance Corporal Joshua Thompson

Di Pasqua agreed with Thompson, "It was talking guns."

Both SAW gunners, Di Pasqua and Thompson, began raking the bushes kicking up dust as the heavy rounds tore into the greenery and the surface of the street. If the insurgents were still there, they were now dead insurgents.

"They told us to stand by for support by fire. They wanted the Iraqi forces to go in and take the mosque," said Lance Corporal Di Pasqua, 1st Squad.

Turner had snipers attached to his platoon executing targets down the side streets and alleyways around the mosque. "You could see quite a distance down the alleys so I called in some 81mm mortar rounds from the Attack Position," Turner recalled.

Hearing the mortar rounds being fired north of the city and seeing their impacts around the mosque, Charlie Company Marines knew they weren't forgotten along the front lines. If they needed help, it could be there in a matter of minutes.

Tanks were called on to run armored patrols up and down Route Ethan, as well as east and west along Phase Line Cathy. Some enemy insurgents were caught trying to flee the mosque to the south and were taken out by the tank's .50 caliber machine guns.

Klingensmith's tanks moved to take up supporting positions around the mosque while Charlie Company Marines gathered up their smoke grenades for the coming Iraqi assault on the building. "I ordered Lieutenant Turner to deploy smoke into the street. Once the smoke was deployed, the liaison led the Iraqis across the street and into the mosque. When entering the building he killed several insurgents," said Bethea.

Sergeant John Megahan was positioned on the right side of the street and provided support for the Iraqi forces as they entered the mosque. He belonged to 2nd Platoon and was their 1st Squad leader. "We popped smoke and then the Iraqis came out of the building in single file and marched across the street. It all looked staged. There was some firing from the building after they went in."

"The Iraqi troops went in through a breach in the wall where the tanks had blown large holes. We provided covering fire," Lance Corporal Craig Wintrow said.

With the smoke from the grenades curling around in the street, Clint and Snake led the Iraqis into the mosque. Inside they found three confirmed enemy fighters killed.

Captain Bethea, First Sergeant Andrade, along with a small security detail from Turner's 2nd Platoon entered the Mosque.

One of those 2nd Platoon Marines that entered the mosque was Lance Corporal Wintrow. "When I entered, I saw a dead Iraqi insurgent in the mosque with his face blown off."

"The Al Hydra Mosque was secured by 1300 of the second day of fighting for the city. Later I called 3rd Platoon up too and sent them into the mosque," Captain Bethea recalled. "We found an infirmary and also a weapon's cache in the Al Hydra Mosque."

After entering the secured mosque, Captain Bethea told a reporter attached to the battalion, "This is the nerve center of the resistance and we're here." He then ordered Littell's 3rd Platoon to cross Phase Line Cathy and establish security at the mosque.

To attest to the heavy fighting during the previous night and early that morning, SAW gunner Lance Corporal Joshua Thompson, 2nd Platoon, alone fired 900 rounds. "We set up in a building across from the mosque for the coming night. When they were collecting up all the dead bodies around the area, they pulled a couple of guys out of the bushes. I'm pretty sure that was us that got them. Eventually we got into the mosque and got some down time," Thompson remembered.

"We stayed at the mosque for awhile. I was up on the roof with one of the contractors, a former SEAL, who was working with the Iraqi forces.

He had already taken a round in his shoulder. It was bandaged. He was a tough guy," Lance Corporal Dante Di Pasqua, 2nd Platoon, 1st Squad, recalls. "Sniper fire began snapping by our heads. We couldn't figure out where it was coming from. The former SEAL had a scope on his weapon and he said, 'Alright, I think I know where it's coming from.' There was a water jug about 500 meters across and down the street near one of the houses. The sniper was firing from behind the jug. He shot and I saw the enemy sniper just fall out. The former SEAL guy shot him right through the jug."

"In the first six hours we were finding insurgents that were fighting but would fall their lines back. They weren't the die-hards. These guys wanted to survive. Later in the fight we met the real die-hards. What I was expecting and what I went through were two different things. What I saw, I never expected. It was a true three-way environment. You didn't know which way the rounds would be coming from. Up, down, left or right, from everywhere," Second Lieutenant Turner recalled.

Corporal Rob Sarka a member of 3rd Platoon inside the mosque remembered a few more close calls from enemy fire. "Inside the mosque was supposed to be safe so we didn't need all of our gear on unless we were on security. I was sitting in a lawn chair on the second floor and I took my helmet off and drank a bottle of water. I then rinsed off my forehead with the rest. My elbows were on my knees and I lowered my head. Next thing I remember I heard a loud crack next to my ear. I fell out of the chair to the right and put my helmet back and began firing my M203 grenades out a window in the direction the shot had come from. When I looked at the wall behind me, the bullet had hit no more than two feet from my head. Later I was waiting to go out on a patrol. The platoon had all our gear on, including assault packs on our backs. We were on the first floor in the courtyard of the mosque waiting for the large gate to open so we could leave. I was leaning against a short metal fence with my back to the gate. The gates were open and just as we stepped off we heard the rhythmic thump of a machine gun. The platoon scattered out of the gate."

Sarka tried to dive into the rubble filled room but couldn't move. He tried desperately to pull himself into the room but he still couldn't move. Like a puppet he stood out in the open with his pack hooked on the iron fence. The rounds were pounding and chipping up the cement all around him.

"I heard a burst of machine gun fire hit extremely close and I felt cement debris hitting me in the face and arms," Sarka said. "I watched as bullet holes appeared in the cement above my head. I knew they were close, so I dropped my rifle, pulled my arms out of the pack strap and dove for the cover of the nearby room."

Lance Corporal Rafael Peguero remembered his short stay at the Al Hydra Mosque, "They were really hyping the mosque up, that there were a crazy amount of insurgents in there, but it wasn't that bad. They told us after entering the mosque that we had six or seven hours to rest up. We started cleaning weapons and eating some chow and as soon as we finished, we were called back out to move. We were to take the second mosque, so we didn't even have a chance to get some sleep."

Sergeant Dustin Stout's snipers were kept busy with enemy snipers around the mosque, as two more insurgents were brought down by accurate fire along Phase Line Cathy.

At 1500, First Lieutenant Miller was ordered to bring up the company mortars to the mosque for fire support. They arrived just in time to support a fire mission called by Turner in support of his 2nd Platoon. Turner had spotted about eight enemy fighters moving back and forth in front of his position. It looked as though the enemy fighters were preparing to counter-attack the newly secured mosque. Miller's company mortars responded and killed five of the maneuvering insurgents.

Later, First Lieutenant Miller spotted a gray flak jacket hanging in a courtyard and instructed 2nd Squad of the 1st Platoon to clear the suspicious house. They found another large weapon cache including sixty or more RPGs, rockets, night vision optics, ammunition, and a U.S. military map of the city. While an intelligence detachment was documenting the site, five insurgents were discovered on a rooftop of a house to the southeast and engaged. The enemy managed to escape by moving farther south, out of the line of fire. In some instances the insurgents jumped from rooftop to rooftop like a frog uses lily pads.

Nearby, 1st Squad was brought under fire until a Force Recon FO (Forward Observer) employed air support to assist them. The aircraft appeared overhead and fired a Maverick missile to destroy the enemy position.

Lieutenant Colonel Brandl pulled up at the Al Hydra Mosque at around 1500 to pay a quick visit with the tired Marines of Charlie Company.

Brandl's battlefield entourage included four Humvees and nineteen Marines. One of the vehicles was a Highback Humvee loaded with six Marines. Sergeant Major Hope's Humvee held four more Marines, and Brandl's Humvee carried the lieutenant colonel and three other Marines. The fourth Humvee was Battalion Gunner Athey's vehicle, which held five Marines. All four vehicles had up guns in the turret for extra-added firepower.

One of the Marines in Gunner Athey's vehicle was Sergeant Kelley Starling, a native of the small Florida town of Live Oak. He had just turned twenty-six on November 6 while preparing to enter the city. He had come from another unit, Battalion 3/8, and upon his arrival to Battalion 1/8 he was put into Headquarters and Service Company. Starling was familiar with Fallujah. He had accompanied Battalion Gunner Athey when part of the battalion was tasked to support RCT-1 in the vicinity of the city back in July. Starling was carrying his second issued M16A4. His first rifle was blown apart when the vehicle he was riding in hit a roadside bomb during that July operation near the city.

Captain Bethea and his staff greeted Brandl, Athey and Hope, then showed them through the mosque. Of particular interest to Brandl was the Iraqi infirmary in the back of the large structure. In the Lieutenant Colonel's thirty-minute visit, Bethea informed Brandl that his Marines were ready to take the Al Janobi Mosque the following day. Brandl gave him the Marine "good to go" before walking out to his Humvee.

"We spent some time with Charlie Company, got an assessment of his situation," Brandl said. "My main concern that coming night was that there was going to be a counter-attack on the mosque. We're now getting far inside the belly of the beast. They know we're here. We had the NVGs, security out, and snipers posted. We were prepared."

Sergeant Starling remembered, "Right before we left the mosque, an old Iraqi man came out of a nearby building, and through an interpreter said he wanted to leave the city. We told him to go back inside the building, that he would be safe there. Then we drove back to the railroad tracks outside the city and stayed there for about four hours. Then the lieutenant colonel had us mount up and push back to the Al Hydra Mosque and Charlie Company. We arrived just as it was getting dark."

Brandl, fearing that a counter-attack might develop that night, wanted to position himself to oversee the situation. "I wanted to be there if they attacked," Brandl explained.

"We parked our trucks across the street under the outside pillars of the Cultural Center. Everyone went inside the mosque to get some sleep but I decided to sleep on the back of my truck. I took my flak vest off and lay it over me," Sergeant Kelley Starling remembered. "The tanks with their engines running constantly were also firing their main guns, off and on, all night. Then the AC-130 (Basher) came over during the night and fired a 105mm round at some insurgents in the alley about forty feet away from me. When it exploded, it scared the living shit out of me. I couldn't sleep so I told the guy on the gun in the turret that I would take his watch. I just sat there the rest of the night."

At the mosque, Brandl set up with his command element and his radio operator. He moved around looking at his Marines to check the resolution in their eyes that night. He wanted to make sure they were okay. Brandl could see that they were tired and trying to get some rest but they still had the fight in them. That night he found a spot on the bare concrete floor and tried to make himself as comfortable as possible. "The tanks started firing in very close proximity to the mosque. The building was so open that when the tanks fired a round it would reverberate through the building. I managed to get a few hours sleep. Later on that night Colonel Tucker came down to the mosque and we linked up. It was at this time we determined we could go ahead and attack the Government Center with Alpha Company early the next morning. One of my concerns was that the enemy had the whole city to run around in and not stay fixed," said Brandl.

Lance Corporal Thomas Tribou, 19, spent the night in the mosque, but doesn't remember getting much sleep. He recalled hearing the bone jarring tank rounds throughout the night. "The tanks located on the sides of the mosque were blasting away at targets all night long. A piece of glass jarred loose and fell down on Lance Corporal Charles, right next to me, cutting his shoulder. The medics worked on him and he stayed in the fight."

Although the tanks were loud and prevented the Marines from getting some much-needed sleep, they found comfort in knowing those steel beasts were posted right outside the door of the mosque.

Sergeant Frederick, 2nd Platoon, said, "I spent the majority of that night on top of a building that overlooked the mosque. Two snipers, my M-240G gunner Lance Corporal Carlson and I spotted some insurgents moving through an alleyway and we engaged the targets as they moved to the west to our front. We took out three of them. At the intersection there was a downed insurgent that had an RPG on one side and an AK-47 on the other side. He also had a chest rig filled with magazines and grenades. Through that day we engaged targets of opportunity. When night fell, to our east there was a small warehouse type building where we discovered a weapons cache. We left the cache and went back to our rooftop where we spotted three insurgents creeping down the street. We watched them through our NVGs and thermal sights as they entered the cache building. We could see them inside the building and we engaged them. We know we got one. When we checked that building out later, we noticed that they would have had a perfect RPG shot at us on the rooftop. We got him before he got us."

The main action in the fight for Fallujah was shifting away from Charlie Company. After securing the mosque Captain Bethea received an order to detach the two D-9 bulldozers from his company and to help support Alpha Company's upcoming attack on the Government Center. Around the same time, First Lieutenant David Klingensmith, Tank Platoon commander, requested permission from Bethea to leave Charlie Company to support Bravo Company in its expected attack on the Iraqi National Guard Headquarters.

There is an old saying in the Marine Corps that, 'The sergeants run the Marines, but don't tell the commandant.' The sergeants in 1/8 were kept busy in the fight south overseeing their tired men.

Staff Sergeant Corey Lohr recounted the taking of the mosque and a much needed morale booster, in a letter home to his wife:

> *"We got into the mosque and secured, I then set up a defensive position. 2nd Squad went to the roof. 3rd covered West and 1st covered South. We set up a rest cycle for the night. We got re-supplied with chow, water and ammo. We stayed there for the night receiving harassment fire, RPG rockets. Squad leaders and myself walked the lines numerous times...As the sun started to rise I woke all Marines with a Happy Birthday for it was 10 Nov. Psy ops played the Marines Hymn, which seemed to motivate everyone."*

The Marine Hymn echoed through the trash filled streets of Fallujah. Those Marines that heard the song stood a little prouder on that day.

"The enemy didn't attack that night and what we later found out was that they just didn't have the capabilities to attack us at night," said Lieutenant Colonel Gary Brandl. The insurgents knew the Marines owned the night in Fallujah.

At a news conference, the commander of military operations in Iraq, Lieutenant General Thomas Metz said, the assault on Fallujah had so far, "achieved our objectives on, or ahead, of schedule. I think we're looking at several more days of tough urban fighting. We felt like the enemy would form an outer crust in defense of Fallujah. We broke through that pretty quickly and easily."

Alpha Company Storms the 'Belly of the Beast,' the Government Center

Lieutenant Colonel Brandl conferred with the Regimental Commander, Colonel Craig Tucker. They agreed that with the minimal amount of resistance that Battalion 1/8 was seeing in the northern reaches of the city, Brandl could go ahead and push to the Government Center. The early morning hours of November 10, the 229th birthday of the U.S. Marine Corps, would be the day.

A course taught at the U.S. Military Academy, The History of Military Art, taught that the principle of the offensive was: *Seize, retain and exploit the initiative. Through offensive action, a commander preserves his freedom of action and imposes his will on the enemy.*

Brandl was retaining and exploiting the initiative in Fallujah. "We decided to go ahead and pick that (Government Center) off. When we put the plan together, common sense told me that once we got into the belly of the beast, they were going to come at us from every angle, which is what they did. This was fine with us because we would be in a defensible position and we could destroy them," Brandl explained.

Captain Cunningham, Alpha Company commander was informed that it was time for his company to take the Government Center.

Brandl would now have all three of his line companies in the city. Alpha Company had rehearsed the taking of the center days before at the Iranian Training Center. The Government Center, a walled complex, was the approximate size of one entire city block. Cunningham's line company would be reinforced with two Marine tanks commanded by Tank Commander, Captain Meyers and also AAVs to bring his fresh Marines into the city in their push toward their objective.

"We were tasked to enter the city at 0430 in the morning and attack the Government Center. It consisted of about eight buildings in that one city block area. At 0400 we had a half-hour to initiate the breach and enter the city. We would push past friendly lines at about 500 to 800 meters," Cunningham recalled.

AAV member Staff Sergeant Chris Shaw said, "We heard over the radio that the infantry had done so well in the fight that they caught up to where they needed to be...and there would be an early morning assault on the Government Center. My section number 3 AAVs would be carrying Lieutenant Ackerman's 1st Platoon into the city."

Number 9 AAV driver, Jonathan Olexa said, "We were really tired as we loaded up the Alpha Company Marines. We had been up several nights without much sleep. We tried to catch catnaps inside our vehicles when we could. Our air was just bombarding the city."

Early on November 10, under the cover of darkness, Alpha Company Marines buttoned up in AAVs that were closely following Meyers' tanks, roared past their fellow Marines from Bravo and Charlie Companies, who were either trudging through the wet city streets or hunkered down in dark houses along Route Ethan. The Marines in the streets knew where the Alpha Company Marines were heading and gave them the thumbs up as they pushed to their objective. Cunningham planned to have his Alpha Company, with a secure foothold, inside the center before daylight.

Captain Bethea, Charlie Company remembers, "At 2200, Charlie Company's 2nd Platoon maintained battle positions north of Phase Line Cathy. 3rd Platoon guarded the Al Hydra Mosque and 1st Platoon established battle positions along Route Ethan. Our mission was to picket Route Ethan and to guard the route so Alpha Company could have a secure movement in AAVs to take the Government Center,"

To Lance Corporal Olexa it was like a movie watching the bombardment from outside the city. He yelled up to Staff Sergeant Chris Shaw manning the .50 cal in the AAV turret, "Maybe they killed everyone and we won't have to go in." Little did Olexa or Shaw know that once they entered Fallujah, they would end up driving over 400 miles in support of Battalion 1/8 and their vehicles would use up 100 hours of engine operation before they would eventually leave the city.

Two of the AAVs had mechanical problems so only thirteen of Second Lieutenant Oscar Morris' vehicles would be bringing Alpha Company Marines into the city.

"An AC-130 led us from above as my two tanks led the way on the ground," Tank commander Captain Meyers recalled. "At 0400 we made a right on Phase Line Cathy, passed a water tower and entered an alley. Right behind us were the amtracs with Alpha Company and following the amtracs came the LAVs. We breached some holes in the ten-foot walls around the center with our main guns. We destroyed the walls and then I drove through and went straight to the center of the Government Center. The amtracs brought the Marines in and they began to clear the buildings."

Alpha Company Marines would be securing the Government Center under the watchful eyes of Lieutenant Colonel Brandl and Regimental Commander, Colonel Tucker. They were positioned nearby in their vehicles and witnessed the entry into the center by Cunningham's Marines. Brandl then went back north to meet up with his Operations Officer, Major Trimble.

Radio operator PFC Caputi said, "Captain Cunningham was sitting up front in his amtrac as we went into the city. I was in the back and couldn't see anything as we drove in. We dismounted from the amtracs when we arrived at the Government Center. It had been hyped up and I expected to come out of the amtrac into immediate enemy fire. But as we unloaded it was quiet. The only noise that night were the tanks and us. A tank fired a round to breach a ten-foot wall so we could enter. When the tank fired I expected it would attract enemy fire, but it remained quiet. Captain Cunningham didn't go through the breach for about a half-hour. He was busy on the radio outside of the wall, directing his platoons inside the complex in the clearing operation."

"We essentially created a couple of breaches by bringing up the tanks and blowing holes in the wall. We had good intel before we went in and we basically knew what the center looked like. Prior to going in, around November 4, we had built this replica of our objective to let the Marines know the distances from building to building they would have to travel once inside," Cunningham recalled.

Second Lieutenant Ryan Hunt, 24, 2nd Platoon commander who hailed from a small hamlet in eastern Washington, Grand Coulee, sat on the front left side of an AAV in the TC hatch. "It was pretty quiet compared to the first night of fighting. I remember my Marines had been worried about not seeing any combat, and I told them, 'Be careful what you wish for.' It was dark and overcast and the vehicles were blacked out. The drivers used their NVGs."

Another west coast Marine from the small town of Walnut Creek, California, Corporal Michael Ergo, 21, 1st Team Leader, 2nd Squad, Second Lieutenant Douglas Barnes' 3rd Platoon, Alpha Company, tells of the attack on the center. "We're riding in the AAVs into the city in the dark, around three or four in the morning. We could hear bullets ricochet off the side of the vehicles as Marines were on watch on top of the amtracs. Things were loud and reports of engagements are coming over the radio as we rode toward the Government Center."

Buttoned up inside one of the AAVs, Ergo and the other Marines were wondering when they would stop and begin to dismount and if they would be exiting under enemy fire. Finally the AAVs rolled up to the ten-foot walls, entered and then came to a stop. The back ramps dropped and the Marines with weapons at the ready and not knowing what to expect, quickly piled out into the alleyway. They stepped from the AAVs into the pitch black of night.

"I was the first one out on my side. I took one step, tripped over something and fell right on my face." Corporal Ergo confessed. "I was wondering what I had tripped over." Feeling a little foolish Ergo didn't have time right then to find out what had tripped him up. He quickly picked himself up and pushed off with his platoon in the clearing operation. The only sounds were the engines of the tanks, boots shuffling along, and the occasional blast as another door was blown open by the engineers. The Marine teams, positioned in stacks, pushed into the buildings fully expecting a firefight.

Later, when Ergo patrolled back with his squad to the area, he got the chance to find what had caused him to fall flat on his face. "I thought I would find some brush or a sack of potatoes or something, but it was a dead insurgent. His arm had been shot off with a .50 caliber machine gun and he was lying there just looking straight up at me. I was so pissed I kicked the corpse before pushing on," said Ergo.

Meanwhile in Hunt's 2nd platoon the AAVs were closing on the Government Center. "We turned left and drove toward the complex," Second Lieutenant Hunt recalled. "Cunningham asked me on the radio if we were in position yet. I said, 'Let me check!' I looked out from the open hatch and scanned really quickly to see if were getting closer."

"Hey sir we're in position, looking good!" Hunt replied as the AAVs sped through a narrow alleyway tearing packs from the outer surface of the vehicle. Unbeknownst to the AAV drivers, the enemy had dug a small tank ditch that was hidden in the darkness near the complex. The AAV hit the ditch hard, causing Hunt to fall partially into the vehicle.

With his left hand he clutched at the hatch to right himself just as the sixty-pound metal door swung closed. Hunt let out a loud moan as the hatch crushed all four fingers and broke several bones in his hand.

"Oh My God!" Hunt screamed aloud in pain as he began squirming around in the opening of the hatch.

Sitting on a bench inside the AAV near Hunt was a tall blond lanky Marine from Cicero, Indiana, Corporal Jonathon Brown, 21. Brown was in the 2nd Squad, Weapons Platoon, attached to Hunt's platoon. The ex-high school football player's wife, Kathleen was home in Jacksonville, North Carolina.

"I heard this loud BANG! 'Holy shit! Hunts been hit!'" Corporal Jonathan Brown yelled to the other Marines in the crowded AAV thinking that a sniper had shot his lieutenant.

Brown remembered, "Hunt didn't respond. I saw blood near his neck and felt he had been shot there. The blood had splattered everywhere in and out of the vehicle." This worried Brown.

Doc Turner quickly made his way over to the injured Hunt. Turner gingerly removed the left-hand glove from Hunt's hand to examine the injury. As he did, blood spilled out of the glove. Even in the dim light inside the AAV Turner could see bones protruding. Hunt was in excruciating pain as he fought to keep himself focused on the mission and not pass out.

Just then the vehicles came to an abrupt stop and the ramps were quickly lowered. The officer ran along with his Marines into the street near the walls of the complex. Hunt quickly got on the radio and requested tanks to come over and breach the wall for entry. Meyers' tanks quickly arrived and created a breach by backing into the wall, which allowed Hunt's Marines to push into the center.

After getting his Marines in place, Second Lieutenant Hunt and Doc Moody hurriedly ran back to the safety of the AAV to take care of his painfully bleeding hand.

Doc Moody made a quick assessment. "All four of your fingers are crushed and bones are also broken in your hand." Moody explained. He offered the lieutenant a morphine shot to help ease the pain. Hunt refused the morphine knowing the drug would basically take him out of the fight. Instead, he asked Moody for some Excedrin pills to help ease the pain. He took several Excedrin and picked up his M16 and climbed out of the vehicle to link up with his platoon.

The AAVs were putting fire on several of the buildings in support of Alpha Company Marines. Driver Lance Corporal Olexa painted a battlefield picture via the radio for Staff Sergeant Chris Shaw in the commander's hatch. Shaw began working over a building with his .50

caliber machine gun. Spent shells from the heavy gun flew from the chamber and rattled around inside the track.

"We had practiced earlier with Alpha Company on embarking and disembarking them because they hadn't worked with AAVs before. After we arrived, our AAVs set up in a 360 in the government complex, facing out. Command covered north as Third Section covered the western side, southern section covered by First Section and Second Section covered the eastern side in support of the infantry and the next day began running re-supplies for the entire 1/8," said AAV Staff Sergeant Shaw. "Staff Sergeant Plotzke and Staff Sergeant Collins' vehicles were detailed to handle any medevacs, if needed."

"We expected more resistance as we rolled into the Government Center with our vehicles," AAV member Olexa remembers.

Nearby, Second Lieutenant Elliot Ackerman's 1st Platoon dismounted along the upper west wall of the Government Center and quickly entered. Ackerman's 1st Platoon systematically began seizing the police station along with the government house.

Ackerman remembered, "I heard someone shout, 'corpsman up!' I thought, *Oh shit it's already starting!* But it wasn't anything serious, and we continued to secure the center. We cleared the high-rise building and went to our next objective, the power plant located in the southwest corner of the complex.

Lieutenant Hunt with his hand bandaged, now back with his 2nd Platoon, secured the parking lot and helped Ackerman's platoon with the clearing of the power plant. Second Lieutenant Matt Barnes' 3rd Platoon held the side street on either side of the center, and also provided security. The platoon leaders knew the distances between the buildings thanks to the replica they had studied earlier while at the Iranian Training Camp.

"We were pumped up like a football team getting ready to play as we exited the AAVs. We had practiced taking the Government Center many times and everything was going just right. We were using frags and they were going off inside this two story building," Corporal Jonathan Brown said.

Sergeant Daniel Stoy, 27, a native of Hudson Falls, New York, Weapons Platoon, attached to Ackerman's 1st Platoon, was section leader for the machine guns. He carried an M16 and had a 9mm-pistol strapped to his body for added protection. He had two brothers in the military. One brother was in the Navy, and the other in the Air Force. Both were serving in the same theatre of war. His brother Chris had been in the Pentagon on 9/11 when it was hit. "We breached the wall from the west. We went to the police station and I set up the machine guns on the outside, one at the east corner, one on the west corner of the building. When the building had been cleared out, we went up to the main government building. Two of the SMAW gunners took a shot at the north wall as we set up our machine guns on the eastside of the courtyard. They were trained on the front door as well as the top of the building. They moved in and cleared it out," Stoy said.

Ackerman left one squad at the power plant after receiving an order from Captain Cunningham to secure two buildings on the western side of the complex. The Marines dubbed the two buildings, Mary Kate and Ashley, after the movie actresses, the Olsen twins. Ackerman's Marines cleared the two buildings in just a matter of a few minutes.

Ackerman then positioned Corporal Adrian Bessant's 3rd Squad at the power plant, Corporal Jordan Latva's 2nd Squad at the west twin tower (Mary Kate) and he moved Sergeant Adam Banotai's 1st Squad to the east twin tower (Ashley).

So far Captain Aaron Cunningham had to be extremely satisfied with the results of the attack on the Government Center. Cunningham remembered, "We attacked in and received no fire between 0430 and 0615 directed at us. We did initiate with coax (machinegun mounted on the tanks) on suspicious vehicles, and we used the tank's main gun rounds to breach every door to disrupt any booby traps that might be waiting for us. We went in with overwhelming shock and firepower. Once we got the first series of buildings secured, I owned the whole north end of the center and the sun was just coming up. At daybreak we began to take fire from damn near everywhere, but mostly from the south, west and east. They had an overlook of the entire center. If I was the enemy, that's what I would have done."

Apparently, the insurgents had expected that the Government Center would be one of Battalion 1/8's main targets after entering the city and had moved outside the center into the surrounding buildings and minarets. Once outside the center the enemy waited for the Marines.

Captain Cunningham had all the tanks move to the middle of the complex parking lot for fire support. Meyers' tanks were to provide over-watch on a group of buildings across the street that looked down on the center. One was a four-story building that had a great view of the Marines inside the complex and an excellent field of fire.

The sun was just coming up as the Marines of Alpha Company finished securing the buildings at the center. The sunrise seemed to have brought every insurgent out to open windows and rooftops outside the center. Alpha Company Marines began receiving intense heavy small arms, machine gun and RPG fire. The insurgents also added sporadic indirect mortar fire to the mix.

"Captain Cunningham and I went to the roof of the police station to get the radio higher up in order to get a better signal. They began firing RPGs at us in the center when the sun came up. We were on that rooftop for about an hour," PFC Caputi recalled.

"You could tell that a few of the terrorists out there had sniper rifles with scopes and above average skill in using them. There was a mosque across the street that we began receiving fire from and we could see insurgents just moving all around it. It was located just south of the center in what we called the pizza slice. I pushed the tanks forward and they began engaging those buildings. We also called in artillery and mortars for support," Cunningham said.

It was dubbed the pizza slice by the Marines because of the way the roads intersected in the city forming a triangle that ran from east to west. The triangle contained a mixture of restaurants, shops, offices and a few homes. Cunningham's Marines would get to know the pizza slice much better in the coming days of fighting. Ackerman's 1st Platoon would get to know another infamous landmark of the city, the candy store. But now they had to contend with the enemy snipers around the complex. If they couldn't suppress the snipers outside the Government Center, the position would be untenable for the battalion to use as a forward aid station.

Captain Cunningham had Second Lieutenant Ackerman's 1st Platoon and Lieutenant Hunt's 2nd Platoon set up firing positions on the upper decks, the rooftops and windows of the buildings facing south from the center. Second Lieutenant Doug Barnes' 3rd Platoon was held in support.

Corporal Ergo, 3rd Platoon said, "I remember insurgents setting off smoke grenades in the minarets of the mosques. I don't know if that was to draw more insurgents or some sort of signal, but they began to rally their forces. All of a sudden RPGs began flying over our heads. It was like waking up a hornet's nest."

With the sun just popping up at the twin towers and power plant, Ackerman's 1st Platoon Marines also began receiving fire from the south. At 1000 the MAP Marines relieved Ackerman's 1st Platoon at the twin towers and all of his Marines consolidated in the power plant.

Brandl had driven back north immediately after Alpha Company pushed into the Government Center so he could confer with his Operations Officer, Major Trimble. When he returned to the center, the first thing he saw when he drove through the breached wall was a Marine lying on the ground, hit by an RPG. "I was gone maybe two hours and when I got back all hell was breaking loose." With the casualties starting to mount, Brandl told himself, *To focus on the mission. Get it done.* "After arriving I began assessing the situation. To alleviate the pressure on Alpha Company, I decided to push Bravo Company down to secure the Iraqi National Guard Center and Charlie Company to take the Al Jonobi Mosque," Brandl said

By assessing the situation, Brandl meant he was going to where the fighting was happening. He went directly to the building his Marines had aptly named Fort Apache. It faced south across Highway 10. Carrying his M16M4, with a cigar clenched between his teeth and wearing sunglasses, Brandl came striding across the rooftop to the wall that ran around the lip of the building. Brandl stood on the roof assessing the situation to the south. All the Marines, as well as a BBC news camera crew, were bent over trying to stay out of the path of the enemy sniper's bullets.

Winston Churchill once said, *"Nothing is so exhilarating as to be shot at with no result."* The Marines around the center were experiencing this feeling first hand.

The Marines had been taking heavy sniper rounds from all directions. When an embedded reporter asked about the situation, Brandl gave an honest and direct answer, "Our situation is good. The enemy is coming to us and we're killing him." Brandl's bold leadership on the battlefield of Fallujah helped steady the nerves of many of his young Marines taking fire.

Brandl quickly called in an air strike and moved the tanks up closer in support of his Marines under fire on the rooftops. Brandl left the roof and went down to the first floor of the building. In just two days of heavy fighting, Brandl's battalion had suffered two killed, including the Recon Marine and over forty Marines wounded and injured.

The fighting around the Government Center continued into the late afternoon, which kept the Marines of Alpha Company busy. The Marines took another casualty when an RPG round hit an LAV in the complex, slightly wounding the driver.

The enemy didn't have to be very accurate when firing an RPG that had a range of up to 2,000 meters. Their favorite way of firing the weapon was to run out in the street, take a quick aim, pull the trigger and then run back to the safety of a wall or house. Sometimes it worked, but most of the time it didn't, which pleased the Marines fighting in Fallujah.

Lieutenant Dan Malcom, Jr., 25, Weapons Platoon commander and FiST leader, from Brinson, Georgia, led his Fire Support Team up the stairs and on to the rooftop of one of the center's highest buildings, dubbed the high-rise. Earlier his FiST Team had been on top of the Iraqi Police Station. From these rooftops the FiST Team could call in fire to the south, across the main east-west artery that ran through the city, Highway 10, Phase Line Fran. The thin Marine officer, a graduate of the

Citadel in South Carolina, loved to play chess and would spend many hours working out difficult moves with other chess playing Marines. War was similar to chess in that you had to continually counter your enemy's moves and thrusts.

Malcom had developed an innovative fire support plan that took into consideration the multitude of friendly adjacent units, the ever-present possibility of civilians in the city, and the extreme danger close nature of the high intensity urban battlefield.

Upon reaching the roof the company came under intense enemy small arms, machinegun, RPG, indirect and sniper fire. Malcom calmly began coordinating calls for fire from the attacking platoons. He began calling in mortar, air and artillery missions on the enemy positions, some within 100 meters of the company's forward trace.

Across the street from the rooftop, where Malcom's men were positioned, stood two minarets that were much taller than the high-rise they were on. Several enemy snipers manned both of those minarets and began to turn their attention on Malcom's FiST Team. On the building where Malcom stood ran a foot and a half high wall which wrapped around the lip of roof. This wall provided little cover for the rooftop Marines. The two Georgia born officers, Cunningham and Malcom, were on the roof together when the sniper's rounds began striking the wall near them. Both officers made a mad dash for the safety of the low slung wall. With his Marines under heavy sniper fire from above, Lieutenant Malcom began trying to get his men off the roof and into the safety of the building's stairwell. A sniper's bullet ricocheted off Malcom's kevlar helmet. Malcom kept moving and continued to order his men off the roof. The sniper took aim and fired again. Malcom was just stepping back into the safety of the stairwell when the bullet hit him on the right side below the armpit, on the side his flak jacket. The bullet exited his chest and fell on the stairwell. Malcom died instantly. First Lieutenant Dan Malcom became the first KIA from Alpha Company and the third Marine to die from 1/8 in the fight for Fallujah.

"I was up on the roof with Lieutenant Malcom when we became heavily engaged with the enemy to the south. We hit the deck and spent about ten minutes being suppressed," Captain Cunningham said. "We finally were able to get some Marines up to put some fire where the enemy's fire was coming from, which allowed us to get back in the cover of the building. I told Lieutenant Malcom to relocate his Fire Support Team. I said, 'Let's go!' and a round hit off his helmet and impacted the wall next to me. He shrugged it off as no big deal. Then Malcom was hit in the doorway as we went into the building. He was turned facing me and we were talking when a round caught him in the back and killed him instantly. He dropped at my feet. We did what we could, but it was instantaneous. We were getting calls for fire. A young Second Lieutenant, my artillery Forward Observer, Lieutenant Williams, was there and I told him to grab Dan's maps and that he was now Fire Support Team leader."

Cunningham's radioman, Private Caputi remembered, "Most of these roofs have a retaining wall around the outer edge. We were pinned down around that wall for around fifteen minutes. The sniper fire was pretty accurate and was coming in every ten seconds or so. We couldn't tell where it was coming from. Captain Ramsey tried to call in an air strike but the bomb went in the wrong direction and injured two Marines from 2nd Platoon. I was next to the Captain as he was talking on the radio. He decided we'd better get off the roof. Some SAW gunners on the roof began to try to suppress the enemy's fire while everyone else peeled off the roof. About an hour later Malcom and I went up on the roof again. I was carrying the radio and we went to the north side of the stairwell hut for cover. When we were done we ran back into the stairwell, me first, followed by Lieutenant Malcom as the round hit his kevlar and impacted the wall. We were both joking about the round hitting his helmet. I went downstairs and ten minutes later Malcom, on the roof, was hit again above his vest in the back and the round came out his chest. At that time I was downstairs and I remember them carrying his body down."

Located in his Humvee in the parking lot of the Government Center below the high-rise building sat Sergeant Major Hope. "We were taking sniper fire at the center. I was monitoring the radio and Lieutenant Malcom was on the rooftop about 150 meters from me. I was taking down information on WIAs and KIAs to feed the information on to the colonel. I got out of the vehicle and walked up to the colonel and said, 'Sir we just had this and this,' and then I went back to my vehicle and that's when someone came back on the radio and said that Lieutenant Malcom had been hit. I went back up to the colonel's vehicle and said, 'Sir, we just lost Lieutenant Malcom.' You could just see the look on his face, obviously it bothered him when we lost Malcom," said Hope.

Positioned in the power plant with his 1st Platoon, Second Lieutenant Ackerman wasn't informed right away of Malcom's death but noticed that Malcom wasn't 'rogering up' on the company radio. "I knew something had happened. I was called on the radio to send a corpsman over to the high-rise building. I sent Doc Holtshulte over," Ackerman remembered.

First Lieutenant Paul Steketee, located back at the Iranian Training Camp near Camp Fallujah, recalled walking over to the hospital and talking to the wounded Marines, "I don't think a day went by that I didn't walk over and see all the wounded Marines. They told me how crazy it was out there. We had a satellite phone and I would ask them if they wanted to call their wife or family to let them know they were all right. The hardest thing for me was when I had to identify the Marines who had been killed in action. I remember when Alpha Company radioed back and said that Lieutenant Malcom had been killed. He was a good friend of mine from back when we both had gone to the Citadel together. It was tough when I had to identify him. I was frustrated that I couldn't be in Fallujah helping out."

Lance Corporal Christopher Lett, 20, 3rd Platoon, a native of Hurst, Texas, was positioned alone in a room of a building overlooking the southern part of the city. "I was on the top floor, just below the roof of a six story building. I had my 249 SAW resting on a piece of rebar and a bunch of cinder blocks in front of me. I saw a group of insurgents carrying white flags heading toward a mosque. There were from fifty to sixty of them." The Iraqis continued to walk out of Lett's sight into a nearby mosque. Five minutes after they had entered the mosque Lett heard firing from the other side of the building he was in. The Marines, out of Lett's vision, began firing small arms and then the tanks joined in with their .50 cals. Things remained quiet on Lett's side of the building, at least for a short time.

Alone in the room, Lett continued keeping watch out the window. "I heard a CRACK and all of a sudden the cinder block that my SAW was resting on suddenly blew up in my face. Then I heard another CRACK! Then I realized I was getting shot at. It scared the crap out of me," Lance Corporal Lett confessed. "I stepped back from the window and yelled for Sergeant Martinez, my squad leader, to tell him there was a sniper somewhere on a rooftop. I would look out every few seconds to see if I could spot the sniper. I kept moving around in the room when I heard another CRACK! I moved back to a corner and when I looked up at the wall I saw a huge bullet hole in it. Martinez came into the room and I told him to get down. I heard two more CRACKS! Martinez got on the radio and told everyone on the rooftop to get down that there were snipers. It was less than a minute when I heard, 'Corpsman up! Lieutenant Malcom has been hit!' I watched them carry him down the stairs to put him in the amtrac. I think the same sniper that had fired at me earlier had shot him. The airforce later dropped a five-hundred-pound bomb and took the mosque out."

The insurgents that Lance Corporal Lett had seen moving to the mosque came into the view of the Marine tankers still positioned in the Government Center.

Tank commander Captain Chris Meyers, with wife Heather home in the states, volunteered to move his tanks close to 2nd Platoon, who were receiving most of the fire. "I moved my two tanks up and we shot holes in the walls which allowed us to fire using a crossfire at the mosque across the street where all the fire was coming from. Now we began to receive most of the fire that had been directed at 2nd Platoon. My tank got penetrated on the right side with an RPG round. I thought, *I have ten fingers and ten toes, I'm good.* The insurgents were coming out of an alley to the main road and firing at our flanks. We saw one guy hiding behind a wall so we fired through the wall, killing him. We saw groups of guys leaving the mosque every couple minutes," recalled Meyers. "Later in the afternoon Lieutenant Klingensmith came and relieved me at the Government Center. Klingensmith had suffered one casualty when an RPG penetrated the side of Lance Corporal Richard Slew's tank. A heater detonated and Slew had taken shrapnel all up and down his leg. Slew was the gunner on Corporal Gantt's tank. I saw them coming back with Slew on top of the turret and I knew something was wrong."

Second Lieutenant Ryan Hunt's 2nd Platoon took a series of buildings after first entering the Government Center on the eastside of the complex they nicknamed the quad. Hunt went to the rooftop of the building that had a clear view to the south and Phase Line Fran. Some of his Marines were covering behind a small ledge that surrounded the roof. Hunt and his radio operator Corporal Anderson positioned themselves behind the wall of a downstairs room that jutted up to the roof. Hunt's Marines began receiving heavy fire from their right side, the south.

Lance Corporal Brett Dayton, 20, from Quinton, New Jersey, a member of 2nd Platoon who enjoyed collecting Spiderman items, lugged his heavy M249 SAW machine gun through the complex. A SAW fires up to 750 rounds per minute and can basically cut a man in half. "Our platoon took a four-sided building called the quad. A squad was sent in first to clear the building out and then the rest of us went in. We set up posts on top of roofs on either side. At daybreak we started to receive fire from across the street, from two hotels and a mosque situated between them."

Corporal Jonathan Brown said, "An RPG flew over the rooftop we were on and then all hell began to brake loose. I began placing my machine guns to answer the enemy fire. I put Corporal Jonathan Parker with his M-240G in position and then I pulled a ladder out and climbed up on a third floor roof. It was like a shed situated on the roof."

Corporal Cole, with his M16, joined Brown on the third floor rooftop. Both Brown with his M16A4 and Cole began returning fire. A SMAW gunner, Corporal Aragon, climbed up the ladder and joined in the firing.

The three Marines were peeking over the ledge when an RPG struck the corner of the rooftop and exploded, scattering small chunks of concrete.

"Hey what's going on?" Hunt hollered over to his hunkered down men on the other side of the rooftop.

A Marine yelled back, "Sir, someone is shooting at us and we're returning fire!"

"Good to go!" Hunt answered his Marine just as an RPG round struck the side of the building causing it to shake under the feet of the Marines on the roof. Hunt's platoon was receiving fire from 410 meters away, to the south, across Phase Line Fran, Highway 10. The Marines watched in amazement as some of the RPG rounds soared over the building before exploding harmlessly on the grounds of the complex.

"Corporals Eric Madden and Bradford Donaghy began firing M203 rounds at the enemy," Hunt recalled. "Staff Sergeant Pillsbury came up to the rooftop carrying AT-4s on his shoulder."

To find his injured lieutenant, Pillsbury had only to follow a bloody trail into the building and up the stairs.

Lieutenant Hunt asked, "Do the AT-4s fire RPGs?"

"Yes sir!" Pillsbury answered.

"Go for it!" Hunt yelled back to his staff sergeant. 2nd Platoon was answering enemy fire with appropriate fire, round for round. But the enemy fire continued coming in on the beleaguered Marines sprawled on the rooftop.

Hunt got on the radio and asked for the assistance of tanks, Panzer 5 and 6, situated below the building inside the center. "They pulled up and put two main gun rounds into a wall then pushed through and brought the enemy in the building to the south under fire," Hunt recalled. He had good comm with the tanks below in the street as he led them to targets, some visibly, others by firing tracer rounds. At times Hunt would walk them from one window of the enemy held building to another by voice or tracer rounds.

"It was great working with the tanks," Hunt later recounted.

Corporal Timothy Conners had led his 3rd Squad, 2nd Platoon, made up of young Marines, up to the same rooftop on the quad. The Marines ended up lying on the roof on their backs behind a small wall, as the sniper's bullets snapped and cracked above and around them. One of the Marines spotted a window where one of the snipers was firing, some 410 meters away. He quickly sat up and fired his M203-grenade launcher at the insurgent sniper. The round scored a direct hit right through the window and exploded violently. Another enemy sniper zeroed in on their position on the rooftop. The enemy fighters would only show themselves for a few seconds while popping up to fire before quickly jumping behind cover again. The insurgents across the street were also unleashing RPG rounds at the beleaguered Marines. The RPGs would streak toward them as they hugged the deck with some rounds impacting on the sides of the building, while others exploded in the street below. When impacting on the sides, the building would shake roughly under their feet.

"The firing had calmed down somewhat when I had Conner's Marines climb up on the roof of a room that jutted up from the rooftop. It only had a small ledge around the top," Hunt said. "I was trying to get better position for my snipers. Once there, they were pinned down by enemy sniper fire that had dialed in on them. At the count of three, we began working over all the windows in the building that we thought held the sniper."

Conners, Martin, and the other pinned down Marines on the roof shouted back and forth to one another while the insurgent's incoming rounds snapped and popped around and over head. Corporal Conners told the others he would pop up and fire his AT-4 shouldered fired rocket at the sniper. He told the others to support him by firing their weapons when he jumped up. The Marines would then throw three smoke grenades to conceal their move off the small roof. At the count of three, the Marines all popped up and opened fire on the sniper. Conner sat up, aimed, and fired the rocket. The rocket flashed across the street and scored a direct hit through an open window as the Marines on the roof gave out a lusty cheer. The three smoke grenades were quickly flung out and Conners' squad made their way off the roof, still under intense enemy fire.

Lance Corporal Drew Martin, 19, from Fairfax, Virginia, was a member of Conners' 3rd Squad, 2nd Platoon. He recalls the fighting on the rooftop. "When we were up on that roof it was chaotic. We were firing everything we had to suppress the enemy fire. We were firing at anything, windows, doors, and alleyways. We very rarely had a good target to shoot at. The insurgents would pop up and fire. Just shooting and moving to protect themselves. We had a dozen Marines on two roofs and everyone was constantly returning fire and it was hard to hear one another above the noise. We must have fired at least five or six AT-4s at the insurgents across the street. All I heard was the noise of the rounds going off and the ringing in my ears," said Martin.

"We were getting most of the fire from a nearby mosque. I glanced down and saw one of our tanks get hit by a mortar round. The shell caused the turret to spin but they stayed in the fight," Corporal Brown remembered.

Hunt had gotten on the radio with his CO, Captain Cunningham. Cunningham asked, "Do you want air on that and can you get your Marines down?"

"Hell yes! I can get them down, but give me a ten second splash call!" Hunt answered.

Another member of 2nd Platoon, Lance Corporal Steven St Claire, Jr., 20, who hailed from a small hamlet in Georgia, recalled being in the way of the errant bomb. "The fire opened our eyes when it happened. I was up on the roof, in a corner all day taking fire. They called in an air strike. I saw an insurgent go into an alleyway and I kept looking for him to come back out. I raised my rifle and kept a bead on him in case he came back. If he returned, I would take the shot. Corporal Brown, a machine gun squad leader, told me I had to move so he could position his machine guns there. I was pissed off and I told him, 'I don't want to move!' He insisted. Lieutenant Hunt then called me over," said St Claire. Carrying his M16A4, St Claire finally moved over near his lieutenant to see what was up.

"I had to get Cole and Lance Corporal Davenport and their machine guns in a better position. We saw three or four enemy pop out again and we fired, dropping one of them," Brown remembered. "I then moved myself five feet behind my machine gunners and got into a tucked position.

"Everybody down!" Hunt yelled to his Marines on the rooftop.

"When I reached the lieutenant, he told me that they were going to drop a bomb on the building across the street where we were receiving fire from. He told me to take cover, and said it was coming soon. We sat there for awhile and nothing happened," St Claire said.

"I was watching the attack come as the plane passed over us. I was looking for the ten degrees away from friendly forces that they give," Hunt said. "The sun was in my eyes and I couldn't see them (plane) at the time."

A Marine on the radio with Hunt announced the ten-second-splash time warning for his 2nd Platoon. Hunt yelled out again to warn his Marines of the splash time. Positioned near a wall, Hunt had the radio up to his ear when he glanced over his right shoulder. He couldn't believe what he saw, the falling bomb streaking straight toward their building.

Some of the Marines had seen the plane release the five-hundred-pound bomb. They expected a successful strike on the enemy sniper nests in the buildings to the south. In seconds their hope turned to horror as they watched the bomb plunge toward them.

"Everything went in to slow motion mode," Hunt said. "I thought, *Oh my God we're all dead from the bomb blast, falling debris or the building is going to fall.*" He had just enough time to scream, "Get down!" once more as he dove over his radio operator, Anderson, and tucked his wounded hand under his own body.

Corporal Jonathan Brown recalled, "I looked up and saw the fighter coming over us from the northwest and then it fired the LGB guided missile that came in just six feet over our heads. I could have reached up and touched it. It passed so close I felt the heat from the missile. Then the sky turned black and began raining small rocks and then bigger and bigger ones. I stayed curled up and tried to cover my head."

The five-hundred-pound bomb crashed into a courtyard near the street adjacent to the buildings the Marines were fighting from. A second later the bomb exploded with a thundering roar. KABOOM! Jagged pieces of shrapnel, along with concrete, dirt and debris were blown skyward, high above the prone Marines on the rooftop before raining back down.

Lance Corporal Steven St Claire said, "Then it hit. I looked up and there were big hunks of asphalt falling down on everyone. Brown had his right leg broken from the falling concrete. Then I realized, that's where I was sitting when he asked me to move. It could have been me."

Lance Corporal Martin recalls, "Everything flew up in the air and the raining debris fell back down on the rooftop. Everyone got in the fetal position to protect themselves."

Brown said, "I saw this huge chuck of concrete the size of a man falling and it landed on my arm and leg. I went into shock as I called out for a corpsman. No one responded. I screamed, 'I'm hit! I'm hit!' No one heard me so I got up and started running through the dust and debris."

After the debris had crashed back to earth, Second Lieutenant Hunt stood up on the roof and looked around at his Marines through the thick swirling dust. Limping through the swirling dust toward him was Corporal Jonathan Brown. Hunt grabbed his Marine and helped steady him.

Hunt quickly called off a second mission from the fighter jet by yelling, "Abort! Abort!" into the radio.

"Corporal Jonathan Brown was badly injured from the falling debris. His arm was crushed in several places and his leg was broken as he was trying to get one of his machine gun teams to take cover," Second Lieutenant Ryan Hunt recalled. "He was a great squad leader and very good at technical and tactical proficiency. He was excellent with the machine gun. He was an excellent Marine."

Lance Corporal Martin said, "The falling debris hurt a few of our Marines, especially Corporal Brown who was hit with a large piece of cement. The Marines close to Brown grabbed him and followed us over to the protection of a higher wall on the roof. Brown's arm had been broken and was turning a purple color. Docs Moody and Turner were working on him, putting a splint on his arm."

"They cut my boot off and put three tourniquets to stop the heavy bleeding," Brown said. "I ask the Docs if I was going to lose my arm. They told me I was going to be all right and not to worry. I asked if any of my team had been hit and they told me everyone was okay. They pulled my glove off and my thumb was just hanging there by a small piece of skin. We began receiving sniper fire again as they tried to get me off the roof."

Brown had to be taken from the rooftop to be evaced out of the city. Lance Corporal Dustin Swenson's team volunteered to carry the injured Brown downstairs to the waiting AAV. Enemy snipers were still sending rounds at the Marines on the rooftop. Sergeant Battles suggested that they fire on every window on all three levels of the building the enemy snipers were working from. With a count of three, the Marines opened fire with M16s, SAWs and M-240Gs. Hunt fired several magazines to help suppress the enemy sniper. Hunt yelled, "Go" and Swenson's team jumped up raised the poncho holding Brown and they all rushed downstairs.

Brown recalled, "I remember Davenport was like Rambo with his gun when everyone fired. PFC Sweeney was squeezing my hand and keeping me alert as we went down the stairs. He kept saying 'Your going to be okay.' He kept me awake."

"We carried him downstairs to the waiting amtrac," Lance Corporal Martin remembered.

The errant five-hundred-pound bomb also shook Marines positioned inside on the lower floors of the quad buildings. Standing near an open window at the time of the explosion, Lance Corporal Travis Desiato, 19, from Bedford, Massachusetts, was knocked out by the concussion of the exploding bomb. A few minutes later, surrounded by his fellow Marines, Desiato shook the cobwebs from his head and stumbled to his feet. The corpsman suspected that Desiato had sustained an upper leg fracture but because he was able to walk they ruled that out. Desiato, who had married his high school sweetheart just two weeks before shipping out to Iraq, refused to be evacuated from the city, and stayed with his platoon in the fight at the center.

Lance Corporal Brett Dayton, 2nd Platoon, recalled the air strike from the advantage of the first floor of one of the quad buildings, "The firefight got heavier around noon and air support was called in. I was down on the bottom floor on the left side of the building because all of the firing positions had already been taken up on the roof. I pulled a desk over to a window and put a chair and table on top of it. I then put my

249-assault machine gun on the furniture, aiming out the window. I started firing at the two tall hotels across the street. Lance Corporal Martinez was directly behind me. The next thing I remember was a big FLASH and then a loud BOOM and then the whole building shook. I was knocked to the floor. I thought an RPG had hit the building. I got up, grabbed my weapon and got out of the room and went up on the roof to see what was going on. There were huge pieces of concrete, the size of tires, scattered all about on the roof. Later, I found out that we had called in air support, a five-hundred-pound laser guided bomb. The bomb had malfunctioned and gone off target and landed next to us some 200 meters away. A Marine from Weapons Company, Corporal Jonathan Brown, had been hurt from the falling concrete. It also broke his M16 in half."

Another 2nd Platoon Marine, Lance Corporal Keith Dyment, 19, from Loudon, New Hampshire, who planned to go on to college when his enlistment was up, lugged his seventy pounds of equipment along with his M16A4 up the stairs of one of the quad buildings. "We're going up the stairs and I see the door to the roof. It was right after the five-hundred-pound bomb had been dropped. We were replacing the Marines on that building. As we stuck our heads out the door that led out to the roof, rounds began impacting on the wall right beside us. We were deciding how to get out under this fire when the men on the roof gave us some covering fire and we ran onto the roof. We were there a half-hour and my squad leader said, 'We need to get someone out on the edge of the roof to keep watch!' We looked at each other and I asked, 'Are you crazy?' He shouted, 'Trust me you'll be fine.' They lay covering fire as we ran to this three-foot wall on the edge of the roof. It seemed like we were running in slow motion. It was only twenty-five feet, but it seemed like a hundred yards. Along the wall we fired at muzzle flashes, and if we saw anyone in the windows we fired on them as well. Our .50 cal gunners on the tanks were shooting like crazy at the mosque and the two hotels across the street," Dyment recounted.

When things calmed down on the rooftop, First Sergeant Derek Fry saw blood all over the roof. It was mostly coming from Hunt's injured hand. He walked up to his lieutenant.

"You've lost a lot of blood on the floor," Fry told Hunt.

"Yeah I guess I have," Hunt answered as he tried to be nonchalant about his injury but the throbbing pain was excruciating.

A nearby sniper, Corporal Rob Lewis, saw the blood seeping through the bandages and asked his lieutenant if he needed his wraps for the wound. Hunt told him, "No thanks corporal, you hold on to them you might need them."

Just then Doc Mask came over to Hunt and began re-wrapping his lieutenant's bloody hand.

The executive officer of the company, First Lieutenant Krugman, came to the building and inquired about Hunt's injured hand.

"How bad is the hand?" Krugman asked.

"It hurts, but I'll be okay." Hunt answered.

Krugman added, "You're going to have to go back."

As was the case with most of the wounded Marines, Hunt didn't want to leave his fellow Marines in the city. He stayed with his platoon of fifty-two Marines until Gunny Sergeant Ramos stopped at the building with a re-supply of water, chow and ammo and took him back to the aid station. From there, he was taken to Camp Fallujah, then to Germany, then Bethesda Naval hospital, and finally back to where it all started, Camp Lejeune, North Carolina.

Second Lieutenant Ryan Hunt later said, "In Fallujah, as a platoon, I owed everything to those young Marines and the team cohesion we had. I had a great first sergeant and excellent non coms."

Lance Corporal Roopnarine, 24, a Weapons Platoon Marine attached to Lieutenant Ackerman's 1st Platoon in Alpha Company, remembered moving into a large school building in the center, "Across the street from us were some taller buildings that we were taking a lot of fire from. My Team Leader Sergeant Barton, told me to open fire on the insurgents on a rooftop of one of them. I fired killing four insurgents and then a tank came up and opened fire right after my last burst of the M-240G and completely blew the top of the building off."

Alpha Company Marines kept trying to suppress the enemy fire directed at the Government Center while the friendly Iraqi troops were brought south to the complex to raise their Iraqi flag.

"When we took the center, I brought the Iraqi forces down to the center to raise their flag," Brandl said. "For psychological reasons it was a good thing for the Iraqi people to see that we've taken the center of the government power in Fallujah. We played the Marine Hymn a few times to motivate our Marines and piss off the insurgents. We made a video of the flag raising and got it out for the nights briefing on Fallujah. I decided to combine my Alpha and Bravo Command elements so we could do 24-7 at the Government Center." A new flag now was flying over Fallujah, the Iraqi flag, raised by their own troops.

Now Weapons Company Marines were called in to help support Alpha Company in subduing the snipers with their heavy firepower. Lance Corporal Brian Koskey, Weapons Company, mobile reserve, recalled coming up to help support Alpha Company. "1st Section manned one building and 2nd Section manned a building right next door.

My team of five Marines was up on the roof and we were taking sniper fire and RPGs from everywhere, especially across the street from an apartment building. We were returning fire with a Mk19, SAW, and M16s. When artillery and air strikes were called in we would get some debris coming down on us. We tried to duck up close to the walls so as not to get hit with anything. It went on like that for several days and nights. We received very little sleep. When we came up the stairs, after getting some rest in the building below, those on watch would give us a quick report on what was going on and what to watch out for," said Koskey.

"Alpha Company needed some help with snipers and we were tasked to go in and help them. Our First Sergeant Daniels went in with us," said Lance Corporal Myers, 21, Weapons Company. He had just gotten married a few months before coming to Iraq and his wife, Marlena, was home in the states. "There were broken water mains and the road was covered in water. As we moved through the water in our trucks, we continually dodged unexploded RPG rounds. We came through the breach in the wall and then ramped up into the Government Center. The last truck, driven by Lance Corporal Palmer from Tennessee, took a round to the windshield, right where he was sitting. The bullet proof glass stopped the round."

"We had been in a couple of small firefights and a few IEDs had gone off around us, but this was the first time my Marines had been in a fight of this intensity. It was quite the eye opener for us," recalled Captain Cunningham.

Marine tanks, along with Alpha Company, had been in the thick of the fight against the insurgents all day. "We ended up having a great relationship with Alpha Company. Cunningham, his lieutenants were great. Staff Sergeant Pillsbury, who took command of 2nd Platoon after Hunt was hurt, was an incredible Marine," said Tank Commander Captain Meyers.

With Second Lieutenant Ryan Hunt now out of the fight, Staff Sergeant Pillsbury, commanding 2nd Platoon, got the word to move the platoon. "That night my squad was told we had to go to another building about a block away," said Lance Corporal Dyment, 2nd Platoon. "We crossed the open quad and went to the east-side of the Cultural Center. My squad leader told me to take point. We cleared the building and spent the night there. The next morning an amtrac came down the road and I saw two RPGs impact the vehicle. It started to catch on fire as it was still rolling down the road. The fire reached the interior and rounds started to cook off inside the amtrac. I told my squad leader about the burning amtrac and he told Sergeant Hastletine and me to run back to the CO and tell someone. Our radio wasn't working. On the way a couple of amtracs pulled up and we told them about the vehicle on fire. They told us that they already knew about it and that all the guys had gotten out and no one was hurt."

During the night of November 10, AC-130 gunships were brought in to work over the sniper nests in the outside perimeter of the center. The rounds from Basher were impacting danger close to the Marines in the Government Center but the AC-130 helped in keeping enemy heads down that night.

Bravo Company Takes the Iraqi National Guard Compound and the Michelin Building

At daybreak on November 10, Captain Omohundro got Bravo Company moving south again from their over-watch position that they had manned while Alpha Company was taking the Government Center.

While at the center Alpha Company came under heavy sniper fire and Brandl wanted Bravo Company to launch their attack on the Iraqi National Guard compound as soon as possible to help in taking the pressure off Cunningham's Alpha Company Marines.

"We called in artillery fire on the area to our west where we were receiving fire from," Omohundro explained. "We had a map that had printed on it, 'don't use for fire missions,' and when the rounds came in they were falling short." Fifteen artillery rounds screamed in, exploded to Bravo's east, which was very close to their position, before they could get the fire mission cancelled. "From then on we went to polar missions, walking the rounds in from behind the enemy fighters' positions."

Captain Omohundro and his Marines pushed toward Battalion Objective H, the Iraqi National Guard (ING) compound located just north of the main east-west artery, Highway 10, Phase Line Fran.

Bravo's 1st and 2nd Platoons moved out into the rubble-strewn street and moved south, followed in trace by 3rd Platoon. The Marines cautiously walked along the courtyard walls and the sides of buildings trying to stay out of the open street. When they reached an intersection the Marines covered one another while others dog trotted across with weapons at the ready. The farther south they pushed down the street the more sniper fire they began to attract. Some of the sniper fire was coming from a minaret at a mosque to their east. It was 0900 on the second day of the fight for Fallujah.

"As we moved toward the ING compound, my platoon and Lieutenant Steven Berch's 2nd Platoon came under some pretty heavy sniper fire that pinned us down in an open field," Eckert recalled. "We threw some smoke out and we all made a mad dash to a courtyard. We began suppressing across the street with mortar fire. The sniper fire was intense and we never did find out where the firing was originating from."

While moving toward the ING compound with his squad, a native of Belington, West Virginia, Corporal Romulo Jimenez, 21, 2nd Platoon, was hit in the left side of the neck with a round fired from a hidden enemy sniper. Jimenez, who had wanted to be a Marine since he was three-years-old, died before his fellow Marines could get him off the open street. He was the second Marine from Bravo Company to die in the battle for Fallujah. After the Marines managed to bring Jimenez out of the street, the sniper continued to take pot shots at them.

A good friend of Jimenez, Assaultman Corporal Nick Criddle, remembered seeing his friend near the Cultural Center the day before, "I saw my good buddy Jimenez and I told him to be careful and keep your head down."

Jimenez smiled and said to his friend Criddle, "I'm always careful."

After the death of Jimenez, Corporal James Mendenhall, sniper, remembered being hit by friendly fire. "The tank fired a round from its main gun and the errant exploding shrapnel hit my kevler vest in the chest and I went down. 'Doc Ski' (Lucas Jushinski) ran up to me and yelled, 'Open up your kevler!' My chest was beet red from the impact but it didn't penetrate my skin. I was shaken up from the impact and 'Doc Ski' just laughed and said, 'Get up you pansy!' I got up and we kept on pushing south."

Second Lieutenant Steven Berch, 25, a native of Killeen, Texas, got his 2nd Platoon into a mosque near their next objective, the ING compound.

A high wall surrounded the ING compound and would have to be breached before Bravo Company Marines could enter the building. A Marine tank came up and began pushing a parked bus into the wall to force an opening. This failed and the tank finally rammed the wall and created an opening for the infantrymen to enter.

Second Lieutenant Andy Eckert's 1st Platoon pushed into the ING compound at 1100 and quickly began securing the buildings and the grounds. Eckert's and First Lieutenant Chris Wilkens' 3rd Platoon set up to support by fire positions for Second Lieutenant Berch's 2nd Platoon's attack on a five-story building directly across the street from designated Phase Line Fran. A FiST team was brought in to support the attack of 2nd Platoon and began calling in artillery on the southern side of a threatening nearby five-story structure. Artillery rounds cascaded down on the target for twenty minutes in an attempt to prep it for the coming attack by Berch's platoon.

"We were taking a lot of fire from the south and from a tall minaret. At this point we hadn't seen any civilians on the streets. It was supposed to take us four days to get to Phase Line Fran, and it had only taken us thirty-six hours," Omohundro recalled.

Lance Corporal Maldonado remembered, "We were getting fire all day. One of our squads was receiving fire from within a house but we had to stay where we were. We couldn't go in because it would have made it worse. It was hard not helping them."

At 1600, Second Lieutenant Steven Berch led his 2nd Platoon across Phase Line Fran and into a large five-story building. Once that building was secure, Captain Omohundro moved his headquarters and FiST into the ING compound already occupied by 1st Platoon.

That five-story building south of Phase Line Fran was the Michelin building, so named by the Marines because of the large Michelin Tire billboard on top of the modern looking cement structure. On the eastside of the Michelin building stood an unfinished one-floor building. To the western side of the building stood a strung together row of one-story shops.

Amtracker, Staff Sergeant Chris Shaw, retells Bravo Company's push across the street to the Michelin Building. "We moved the vehicles out in front and flanked the infantry who was in between us. We were told to button up after a Maverick missile was launched near our position. After it hit we began to receive RPK fire some 200 meters down the road, from the west, aimed in our direction. We got the Bravo Company Marines in that quadrant and dropped off some supplies, turned around, picked up a casualty and started to return when mortars began falling around us. We didn't know if they were friendly or enemy rounds, but they were close."

Marines located in the ING compound also supported the Marines pushing across the street to the Michelin Building. Assaultman Corporal Nick Criddle, "Because of what had happen at the Cultural Center, everyone would support the Marines crossing the street with heavy fire from our side of the street. If anyone was around we would attempt to keep their heads down."

A Holyoke, Massachusetts, Marine who loved skiing and hunting, Lance Corporal Andrew Braunschweig, 19, Weapons Platoon, moved across Phase Line Fran carrying his M16A4 along with seventy-five pounds of equipment. He recounted the fighting around the Michelin building. "As soon as we got up on top of the building we could see the enemy running around below. We spent an hour just shooting at targets until they figured out we were up there and then we started receiving sniper fire. They were shooting through four-inch diameter holes in walls and buildings. Another hour and a half went by with the insurgents exchanging fire with us," said Braunschweig.

Eddie Murphy look alike Lance Corporal Xavier Forester, told of the fighting around the Michelin building. "When we crossed Highway 10 and moved up to the Michelin building, Lance Corporal Landis and I had to run out in the middle of the street and blow the doors open with rockets so the other guys could go in. While we were in the street all you could see were puffs of dust on the road kicked up by bullets. We hurried up and launched the rockets and we all went into the building. We cleared the building and I ended up on top of it. There were two insurgents inside. Up on top a firestorm started. You could see the enemy running around on the ground and I began launching some SMAW rockets, but most of the time I was using a rifle. Enemy snipers began getting into the tall minarets and firing down on us," recalls Forester. "At night they began walking the mortar rounds in on us. We were up on the wall that ran around the rim of the rooftop shooting down at the enemy, when one of them fired an RPG that hit where Lance Corporal Braunschweig and some Recon guys had been standing. I saw it sizzling toward us in slow motion and I yelled, 'RPG!' Everyone hit the deck and all you could see was a big explosion with a big puff of smoke. I thought they had all been killed but after the smoke cleared, they all got back up. The FiST Team came up and began sweeping everything out there for about 300 meters. They brought in everything, artillery, air, and when they were done there were no more snipers." Lance Corporal Xavier Forester, with a great view from atop the Michelin building, watched as the devastating power of U.S. air and artillery unfolded in a panoramic picture before him.

FiST Team member, New Yorker Sergeant Gianforte, 28, said, "We went to the Michelin building and set up and began helping them out in dealing with all those snipers. We ended up working the area most of the day. We kept shifting artillery having them repeat on the targets. The fire was just awesome to watch as it came in on the enemy targets. It was unbelievable how accurate the Marine artillery was from firing so far away. You could hear the report of the guns in Camp Fallujah and then the rounds would impact in the city in two or three seconds."

Now, a large building to the west of the just secured five-story Michelin building had to be taken. First Lieutenant Chris Wilkens led his 3rd Platoon in to search and secure the structure. With the structure secured, Bravo Company was ordered to hold the target buildings just taken until the next morning and to go firm for the night. No live enemy fighters were found in the buildings taken by Bravo Company, only a few dead insurgents scattered about inside.

Assaultman Corporal Nick Criddle said, "During the day we spotted a man in a field about 300 meters from our rooftop position at the ING compound. Billiot and Lance Corporal Irvin with their hand held 60mm mortars dropped six rounds in on him."

Around 0100, Omohundro, positioned on the lower level in the back of the ING compound, heard mortar rounds impacting. "That evening there were a lot of snipers and firing from five and six story buildings around us. We got heavily mortared with about twenty rounds that night. At the time we didn't know where they were coming from. I checked with Captain Kahn to see if there were any friendly fire missions. He shouted 'no!'" Omohundro recalled.

The mortar rounds kept pounding closer as the insurgents bracketed the ING building. One mortar would explode to the right of the building and the next one would hit to the left, each time coming in a little closer to the hunkered down Marines inside. Crowded into the hallways of the building, some of the Marines, silently and out loud, said their prayers as the exploding rounds shook the structure causing dust, broken glass and cement to fall on the men inside.

"Lieutenant Colonel Brandl, now at the Government Center, called me and asked 'You alright?' I answered, 'We're still alive, but this is getting hairy!' He said he knew something was wrong because I was getting excited on the radio," explained the usually calm Omohundro.

"Everyone was on edge when the mortar rounds began working us over. We had some intense moments that night," Second Lieutenant Eckert said.

A Marine from Brockport, New York, a small town located east of Buffalo along the old Erie Canal, Lance Corporal David Graham, 21, 1st Squad, 2nd Platoon remembered a harrowing night spent under heavy mortar and sniper fire at the Michelin building. "We were on Phase Line Fran and we had just taken the Michelin building when we began exchanging sniper fire with other buildings in the area. That night Lance

Corporal Forester and I were on the rooftop and all of a sudden mortars began falling. They kept shooting mortars and getting closer and closer to the building we were on. Someone had to be down in the houses near the building directing the mortars. They were walking them in on our position. I felt helpless sitting there waiting for them to hit us. We kept looking down on the streets and alleyways to catch someone moving around and using a cell phone that might be giving our position away. Forester lobbed a few grenades down the alley and hit somebody. The mortars were pretty close to us before they just stopped."

First Lieutenant Chris Wilkens called on Staff Sergeant Alicea and his sniper team as well as Staff Sergeant Parry to try and locate where the rounds were being fired. From their rooftop perch they looked south but couldn't see where the enemy's mortars firing position was located.

"The mortar rounds that were impacting around us were enemy 120mm," Alicea said.

"Then the mortars abruptly stopped. A few days later to the south we found a mortar tube with a round still stuck in it along with aiming stakes, in a courtyard," Omohundro remembers.

"After November 10, I gained one of my tank platoons back," Captain Meyers, tank commander recalled. "3rd Platoon led by Lieutenant Lee, had been supporting Battalion 1/3, which wasn't going to be pushing south. Now they were attached with Battalion 1/8. So now I had all ten of my tanks attached to Battalion 1/8. I attached 3rd Platoon to Alpha Company, and 2nd Platoon to Bravo Company. One of the tank sections in 3rd Platoon, led by Gunnery Sergeant Dixon, had been hit by an RPG that penetrated the fuel cell so that tank section had to be pulled out. I took over his role. So my section and Lieutenant Lee's section were both attached to Alpha Company in the push south."

A Bravo Company Marine, Lance Corporal Braunschweig, said, "The next morning the mortars started up again and my gunner, Lance Corporal Charles Becker, was firing his M-240G machine gun when it seemed like a puff of smoke hit him. He fell back and then stepped forward and started shooting his M-240G again. I noticed that blood was coming from his neck and dripping down his back. We took his kevlar off and noticed that a round had grazed his head. The bullet had gone through his goggles, through his kevlar, grazed his head, and went right out the back. He didn't want to go, but they medevaced him out of Fallujah. It almost felt like a game until you see the first person go down."

That morning 2nd Platoon was loaded into amtracs and driven 150 meters to a building on the eastside of the Michelin building across Phase

Line Fran. They quickly secured the building and the remaining units of the company were brought across in two more waves in the amtracs.

In the air war in and around Fallujah, two Marine Super Cobra attack helicopters were hit by accurate enemy ground fire and forced to land in separate incidents right outside the city. Both crews were not injured and were eventually rescued.

Battery C, 1st Battalion, 12th Marines, in Support of Battalion 1/8

Battery C, 1/12, was initially attached as part of Battalion Landing Team, Battalion 1/3 out of Hawaii, but once they arrived in their Area of Operation they were soon attached to RCT-7 and RCT-1.

On October 30, Battery C was the only battery firing in support of the feint on Fallujah in support of the tanks.

A member of Battery C, Staff Sergeant Baeza wrote:

We were the lead artillery battery for the assault and supported 1st Battalion, 8th Marines. We fired the initial smoke rounds to start the actual attack on Fallujah. The effort of my young Marines was unmatched. I would like it to be known to all what they did in the fight to free the people of Fallujah.

Battery C, 1/12 fired the most rounds for the operation, over 1,500 rounds during the attack in support of Captain Omohundro's Bravo Company, Battalion 1/8. Staff Sergeant Baeza later wrote:

The entire time out there my Marines would see the newspapers come in and when they received a break, whether it be five or ten minutes, they would never see anything written about them, including our own newspaper. So sir I would like to clarify our part in the attack and just let it be known of the outstanding job my Marines did during our deployment with the 31st Marine Expeditionary Unit.

Bravo Company Commander Captain Read Omohundro, the recipient of much of the supporting fires from the Hawaiian battery, said, "The battery did an outstanding job firing any mission that I requested. Once a mission was approved, rounds were down range without hesitation. The missions were extremely accurate and the adjustment of rounds made destroying enemy positions very easy. I was very thankful for what they did, and I am proud of their Marines for doing a great job."

If Battery C, 1/12, didn't receive the respect and appreciation they deserved from the media during the Fallujah fighting, they certainly got it from the Marines of Battalion 1/8.

Captain Stephen Kahn, who coordinated all indirect fire support for Battalion 1/8, commented on 1/12's support by fire. "They were outstanding. It was made difficult because all fire had to be cross-referenced with imagery and maps. Their timing was excellent," Kahn said.

First Lieutenant Paul Steketee, H & S Company, Battalion 1/8, located back at the Iranian Training Camp next to Camp Fallujah, felt he had to do something for his Marines fighting in Fallujah. He picked up his M16 and walked the two hundred yards over to Battery C's firing position. He talked to the artillerymen, thanking them for the great job they were doing for Battalion 1/8. He passed along some comments he had heard on the radio from the Marines in the city.

"I knew the guys firing were supporting our guys in the city. I went to the gun line and said to the commander, 'I want you to know that you're shooting for us out there. I want you to know your doing a great job' and I shook his hand," Steketee recalled. "Later, I got a couple of my Marines to go over there and pull a lanyard (firing) a couple of times. They all wanted to be involved."

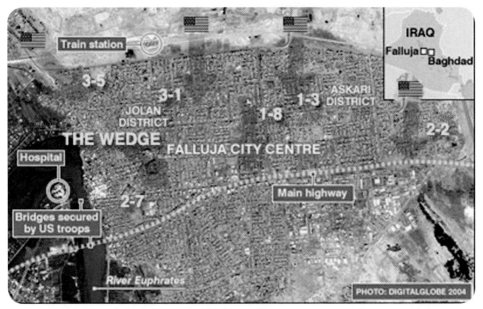

Fallujah City Center

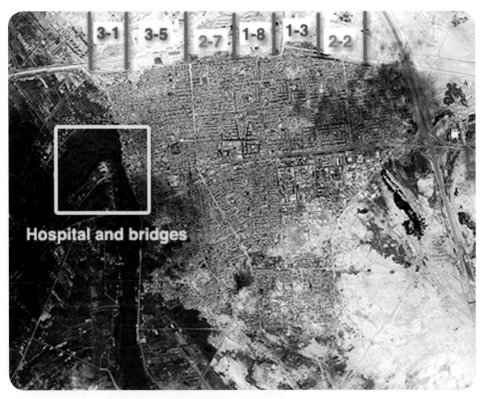

City of Fallujah and attack positions.

1st Platoon, Alpha Company Machine Gunners in the candy store.

November 10, Alpha Company Marines at the Government Center.

Five hundred pound bomb falling danger close to Alpha Company.

C Battery of 1/12 Artillery firing in support of 1/8.

AAVs in the fight.

Marines of Charlie Company securing a narrow street on
November 8, 2004.

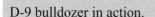
D-9 bulldozer in action.

Bravo Company Marines, Lance
Corporal Benjamin Voorhees
(holding mirror) and Lance
Corporal Patrick Lavey, look
over rooftop for enemy snipers
in Fallujah.

(Pictured left to right) 1st row: HA Avila, LCDR Jadick, HA Argueta, HM1 Zimmerman, HM3 Mcardle, HM3 Stahura, HM Stedman 2nd row: SFC Cary, SFC4 Cook, 2nd LT Wilson, SSgt Brennan, SPC4 Strock, Sgt Hurt 3rd row: HM Johns, SPC4 Ferrell

Marine tankers Lance Corporal Howe and Lance Corporal Walls.

Second Lieutenant Elliot Ackerman at the candy store calling in indirect fire.

Lance Corporal North, Charlie Company, trying to draw enemy fire.

Alpha Company Marines on a rooftop looking south with tanks in support.

Alpha Company Squad Leader Sergeant Adam Banotai and Corporal Jordan Latva.

Sergeant Daniel Stoy at the assembly area.

Staff Sergeant Dennis Nash reenlisting at the Mosque south of the Governent Center. First Sergeant Arturo Andrade and Captain Bethea perform the ceremony.

Captain Theodore Bethea II, Charlie Company Commander and Captain Meyers, Tank Commander.

Al Jonobi Mosque

One of the many Mosques in Fallujah.

Charlie Company Marines at the attack position outside Fallujah.

Cajun HQ with Major General Natonski.

Alpha Company Commander Captain Aaron Cunningham working the radio on a rooftop in Fallujah.

Iraqi forces raising their flag at the Government Center.

1/8 Marines securing a house.

60mm mortar manned by Corporal Jarvis and Lance Corporal
Parsons of Bravo Company.

Bravo Company Marines under fire at the Cultural Center.

Gunny Sergeant Ryan Shane assists the mortally wounded Sergeant Lonny D. Wells.

Corpsman Joel Lambotte joins Shane in trying to get Wells out of harms way.

Gunny Sergeant Ryan Shane is hit by enemy fire while assisting Sergeant Lonny D. Wells.

Captain Read Omohundro kneeling, working the radio outside the Cultural Center.

Bravo Company Marines outside the Cultural Center.

An armored ambulance picking up the wounded from the Cultural Center as Doc Jadick on the right works on the wounded.

Re-supply from Weapons Company Marines.

Bravo Company Marines with Iraqi detainees.

Iraqi forces after securing the
Al Hydra Mosque.

Michelin building that 2nd Platoon, Bravo Company, secured.

SMAW gunners from Bravo Company.

Marine Sniper trying to draw enemy fire from a rooftop.

Captain Omohundro along with his platoon commanders and his tank platoon commander Lieutenant David Klingensmith in the famous KA-Bar meeting.

Captain Omohundro pointing with his KA-bar to a map of Fallujah.

Bravo Company Marines patrolling the streets of Fallujah.

Charlie Company Commander Captain Bethea standing on the D-9 bulldozer.

Charlie Company's 3rd Squad, 1st Platoon with the D-9 bulldozer.

Marine Corps birthday at Cajun Forward Base 3.

Lieutenant Colonel Brandl cutting the
Marine Corps birthday cake.

Combat Engineer,
Joshua E. Lucero

(L-R) Protector Jonathan Zeno and Chaplin Denis Cox are pictured with a rocket on the ground between them.

Lance Corporal Dimitrous Gavriel in Iraq.

AAV driver Corporal Jonathan Olexa with his father's flag.

Lance Corporal David
Houck in action on
Thanksgiving Day.

Lance Corporal
David Houck's kevlar.

Sniper Corporal Todd Godwin

Lance Corporal David Houck's sandbag
flag with the names of the fallen
inscribed on it.

1st Lt. Elliot L. Ackerman, 26, receives the Silver Star from Brig. General Charles M. Gurganus, 2nd Marine Division assistant commander. Ackerman, a native of Washington, D.C., received the medal for his heroism in November 2004.

Sergeant David M. Caruso

Lance Corporal Jeffrey Holmes

Sniper Platoon *Back Row* (left to right): Cpl Quintana, Sgt Stout, Sgt Lawler, Cpl Mendenhall, Cpl Lewis, Cpl Hixson, Cpl Golden, LCpl Hague, Cpl Mudge, Sgt Earls*Third Row:* Capt Pretus, Cpl Bosselmann, LCpl McAnally, Cpl Munns, LCpl Irizarry, Cpl Esquibel Second Row: SSgt Alicea, Sgt Battles, Cpl Watson, LCpl Walker, LCpl Merkel, *Front:* Cpl Ziolkowski, Cpl Watkins

1/8 Commanding Officer
Lieutenant Colonel Gareth Brandl

(L-R) Lance Corporal Davis (CO's PSD), Captain Matt
Nodine (SJA), Lance Corporal Morris (CO's PSD) and
Sergeant Major Hope.

CPL TODD J. GODWIN
Scout Sniper Platoon
March 4, 1983 - July 20, 2004

SGT RICHARD M. LORD
Weapons Company
August 20, 1979 - August 18, 2004

LCPL CESAR F. MACHADO
H&S Company
September 20, 1983-September 13, 2004

SGT LONNY D. WELLS
Bravo Company
January 10, 1975 - November 9, 2004

CPL ROMULO J. JIMENEZ
Bravo Company
June 28, 1983 - November 10, 2004

1STLT DANIEL T. MALCOM
Alpha Company
April 5, 1979 - November 10, 2004

LCPL NATHAN R. ANDERSON
Bravo Company
May 22, 1982 - November 12, 2004

LCPL TRAVIS R. DESIATO
Alpha Company
November 25, 1984 - November 14, 2004

CPL NICK L. ZIOLKOSKI
Scout Sniper Platoon
April 21, 1982 - November 14, 2004

LCPL MICHAEL J. HALAL
H&S Company
May 19, 1982 - September 13, 2004

LCPL WILLIAM L. MILLER
Bravo Company
November 24, 1981 - November 15, 2004

LCPL BRADLEY L. PARKER
Bravo Company
July 22, 1985 - November 15, 2004

LCPL DIMITROUS GAVRIEL
Bravo Company
July 31, 1975 - November 19, 200

LCPL DEMARKUS D. BROWN
Bravo Company
April 8, 1982 - November 19, 2004

LCPL JEFFREY S. HOLMES
Bravo Company
July 28, 1984 - November 25, 2004

CPL GENTIAN MARKU
Bravo Company
September 19, 1982 - November 25,

LCPL DAVID B. HOUCK
Bravo Company
October 10, 1979 - November 26, 2004

LCPL BRADLEY FAIRCLOTH
Alpha Company
February 19, 1984 - November 26, 2004

CPL KIRK J. BOSSELMANN
Scout Sniper Platoon
March 24, 1983 - November 27, 2004

LCPL JOSHUA E. LUCERO
Combat Engineers
May 30, 1985 - November 27, 2004

Charlie Company Secures the Al Janobi Mosque

Around 0830, November 11, after Klingensmith's tanks had returned from assisting Bravo Company in their fight for the Iraqi National Guard Headquarters, Captain Bethea tasked them to create three breach holes in the Al Janobi Mosque. The breach holes would be used as entry points for the Iraqi forces in the securing of the mosque.

That morning while Captain Bethea concentrated on laying out plans for the taking of the Al Janobi Mosque, things were still hot for Charlie Company around the Al Hydra Mosque. Sergeant Stout's snipers and Turner's 2nd Platoon Marines were taking a heavy toll on enemy snipers positioned near the mosque where the Marines confirmed multiple enemies killed in the brisk morning action.

Charlie Company received orders at 1200 to attack and seize the Al Janobi Mosque situated along Phase Line Fran, some 1,000 meters to their south. Bethea gave the company a warning order to be prepared to move. The order of movement consisted of the tank section, 3rd Platoon, the Fire Support Team, Force Recon Platoon, and 2nd Platoon followed by the Casualty Collection Point Marines. He ordered the mortars to remain in a defensive position at the Al Hydra Mosque and to be ready to support the main advance on the Al Janobi Mosque.

Two and one-half hours later, at 1430 under sunny blue skies streaked with the smoke of battle, Charlie Company launched their attack south across the line of departure and directly down Route Ethan. The company was immediately pinned down by accurate machine gun and sniper fire coming from their west. It came from the area that Bravo Company had attacked through earlier in the morning. Apparently some of the insurgents had pulled east to Charlie Company's front as Bravo Company had punched through. With their knowledge of the city the insurgents were playing a cat and mouse game with the Marines.

Charlie Company had also run into another hornet's nest of sniper and machine gun fire to their immediate front. Second Lieutenant Littell's 3rd Platoon was tasked to locate and eliminate this harassing fire, but 3rd Platoon itself began receiving heavy sniper fire, and was now pinned down. Captain Bethea got on the radio and called Klingensmith's tanks forward to help tip the scale in the fight with the enemy snipers.

Making it all the more difficult, the insurgents were maneuvering back and forth between the buildings to Charlie Company's immediate front. Lance Corporal Ward led his team into the suspected building the snipers were working from. The stack of Marines worked their way through the house, but found it was now empty. Ward's Marines climbed up to the rooftop of the building for better observation and to help direct the tank section fighting in the street below. Klingensmith's tanks fired on numerous buildings and were unable to quell the intense enemy sniper fire directed at the Marines of Charlie Company.

Force Recon began setting up their own sniper positions on the Cultural Center roof to help eliminate or neutralize the enemy fire to the south, but to no avail. Then the Fire Support Team moved up and added its weight to the fight, but the enemy snipers were well hidden with excellent fields of fire. Charlie Company began receiving fire from a tall minaret. Lieutenant Conner and Corporal Brown repeatedly called in mortar and artillery missions on the suspected enemy locations, but were denied because of the close proximity of friendly troops.

Lance Corporal Zachary McWilliams, 3rd Platoon, 3rd Squad, who had just gotten married before being deployed to Iraq, was point man for his squad on the advance south. Under a blazing sun he cradled his M16A4 in his arms as he cautiously moved down the street, stopping, checking to his right and left, before advancing. Marines were strung out behind him, cautiously following his moves. It looked like a choreographed dance as they moved in unison over the rubble on the city streets. "Our tanks had gotten about 50 meters out in front of the platoon and we were trying to catch up to them. When we reached them, the tanks fell back to the center of the platoon. About then we began receiving fire from our right. I was behind a bush near a wall in the prone position. The firing increased and with the adrenaline high we were on, I didn't know I had been hit. I knew something was wrong and I kept looking at my right foot and I noticed the bottom of my boot was gone. My foot was both hot and cold and I could see blood. Corporal Sarka ran up to me and said he would get a corpsman," McWilliams recalls.

"I was positioned across and to McWilliams left and I could see rounds hitting all around him. He started waving his arms and yelling for a corpsman," recalled Sarka. "I didn't see anyone moving to him so I told Lance Corporal Veazie to start spraying and praying. I got up and ran cross the street. I didn't know where he had been hit so I started to take his jacket off and then he told me he had been hit in his foot. I could see where the round went in the top and out the bottom of his boot. A sniper team helped me drag him into a courtyard."

"They dragged me back into an open storage area near a house and checked me out. I was pretty calm and I remember asking Doc Lopez, 'Is my foot okay?'" Lance Corporal McWilliams said.

Under fire, First Sergeant Arturo Andrade, Gunnery Sergeant Berry and Corporal Brandt carried McWilliams from the courtyard and out of harms way.

A member of Littell's 3rd Platoon, Staff Sergeant Corey Lohr described the lurching movement forward to the Al Janobi Mosque and the wounding of McWilliams in a letter home:

> *"(We) began to push south. Not over 10 mins/100 meters down the road we received sniper fire. 3rd Squad led with the Lieutenant. 1st Squad went second and I traveled with 2nd Squad. Lance Corporal McWilliams went down and everyone took secure positions. Corporal Watkins and Corporal Munns grabbed Lance Corporal McWilliams and drug him to a secure position for Doc Lopez to work on him. At that time the Company CCP went to the front and got McWilliams out of the area. We were all pinned down for approx. two and a half to three hours. I made my way to the roof of the closest building with the FAC to get a better eyes on. The tank opened up on numerous positions. Our snipers were receiving fire, Marines behind us were receiving fire and all 3rd Platoon was pinned down. AAV and this tank popped smoke for us to fall back. The Lieutenant started to bound back as the last guy fell past my position, I took up rear security, along with Lance Corporal Kashner we covered the alley to the west. As the Lieutenant passed*

*me he told me 10 Marines are still up there. I got a head
count for the Lieutenant and provided security till the
last 10 made it into friendly lines."*

Lohr was about 100 yards behind point man McWilliams. Lance
Corporal Willson heard over the company headsets that McWilliams had
been hit. "We thought it had been one sniper but later discovered there
had been several at that time," Willson said.

As the casualty collection point team moved up to extract Lance
Corporal McWilliams, Staff Sergeant Olalde looked down an alleyway.
He was stunned by what he saw. An enemy fighter in the alley was
holding a weapon on a man, a woman, and two children. The insurgent
was using the family as a human shield as he cowered behind them.
Olalde didn't hesitant. He raised his weapon and with one well-aimed
shot killed the terrorist without injuring any member of the Iraqi family.
Staff Sergeant Olalde then turned and saw another nearby insurgent
using the same ploy. He yelled to Sergeant Eggersdorfer to engage the
second gunman hiding behind the civilians. Eggersdorfer fired his
weapon bringing down the cowardly insurgent.

In three hours of continuos fighting, Klingensmith's tanks had
expended their ammunition and now they were also running low on fuel.
They had to break off the attack and go back north to re-supply. Bethea
decided to consolidate his company back at the Al Hydra Mosque and
regroup until the tanks returned from their refueling and ammunition run.
Charlie Company pulled back into a defensive mode at the Al Hydra
Mosque while new plans of attack were formulated to take the Al Janobi
Mosque.

Battalion had voiced concerns by radio to Captain Bethea on when
Charlie Company would be taking the Al Janobi Mosque. Lieutenant
Colonel Brandl got on the radio and urged Bethea to secure the mosque
as soon as possible. Brandl wanted the battalion's momentum to continue
on in the battle for Fallujah.

"I would not press the attack without tanks. That would be playing
right into the enemy's hands," Bethea said.

Staff Sergeant Lohr wrote in a letter home:

*"The Lieutenant (Littell) went back to planning to get
to the next mosque. They decided to move at night, so we
prepared."*

Captain Bethea, meeting with his officers, decided on a night assault
on the Al Janobi Mosque but problems began cropping up almost
immediately. Snake, the Iraqi Emergency Response unit leader, told

Bethea that his Iraqis weren't trained to conduct a night movement in urban terrain. He went on to inform Bethea that the Iraqis would only conduct a night attack if they were mechanized. A call from Bethea to Major Trimble quickly produced three AAVs for use by the Iraqi troops. Force Recon was ordered to be inserted via AAVs, behind Bravo Company, using Route Frank not Route Ethan, and then conduct a foot movement to a Charlie Company over-watch position near the Al Janobi Mosque. Earlier, Lieutenant Colonel Brandl had said no to Bethea on the use of Route Ethan with the AAVs, due to the threat of RPG fire on the non-armored vehicles.

Bethea reorganized the company for the night movement with tanks leading the way, followed by 2nd Platoon, 3rd Platoon, 1st Platoon, and then the Casualty Collection Point Marines. The attack was set to start under the cover of darkness at 2200. Littell's 3rd Platoon had carried the brunt of the load in the earlier daylight attack, so Bethea moved Turner's 2nd Platoon to the front. Turner's Marines would follow the tanks leading the attack. "Tank and infantry integration was the key to our success in Fallujah," Bethea said. "I left my Weapons Platoon with the mortar section back to defend the Al Hydra Mosque."

At 2200, with the return of Klingensmith's tanks, the Marines of Charlie Company probed forward across the line of departure, and moved deeper into the city toward the Al Janobi Mosque. Klingensmith's tanks quickly drew sniper fire as they slowly lumbered ahead. In the darkness Turner's 2nd Platoon cleared the first row of homes to the west of the mosque. Clearing one of the houses Lance Corporal Timothy Steele went down after suffering a shrapnel wound to his right calf, as the Marines tried to blow a breach in one of the houses.

"When the door exploded it completely blew back on him. The metal from the door cut into his leg," Second Lieutenant Turner said.

Another 2nd Platoon Marine interested in going into law enforcement after his enlistment, Lance Corporal Joshua Thompson recalls Charlie Company's second push to the mosque and the wounding of Steele. "It was pitch black when we went down to the second mosque. We moved as a platoon and cleared every house on that street. It was quieter than hell as we moved down the street clearing house, by house, by house. Shrapnel from explosives used in breaching one of the doors hit Lance Corporal Steele. We set up a fire support position on the mosque until it was taken."

Second Lieutenant Littell's 3rd Platoon, working in the dark, cleared the first row of homes to the north of the mosque while Matt Rhoades' 1st Platoon cleared homes to the north of Littell's Marines.

A member of Littell's 3rd Platoon, Staff Sergeant Lohr wrote home to his wife Cindy about the second attack toward the Al Janobi Mosque:

> *"We go out the same route where McWilliams went down. We all hug the buildings to the East. Hearing rockets to the West and small arms to the South and West. We receive sporadic fire towards us every so often. We move then stop every 25 meters. I travel with 2nd Squad again in the middle of the platoon...1st Squad starts clearing houses. There is a real bad smell of gas as the Lieutenant pushes down the road clearing house after house...We are preparing to suppress the mosque for the Iraqi forces to go in and clear it."*

The homes in this area of the city were mostly large cement structures enclosed with tall walls, front doors made of wood and metal. The Marines had to blow breaches in the walls to enter almost every house in this neighborhood. Looking more like coal miners, the Marines with their flashlights attached or taped to their weapons, worked as a team going from room to room searching for the elusive enemy that had tormented them in the previous day's fighting. The Marines not only had to be careful of the enemy, but also had to watch out for several propane gas tanks that had been ruptured from earlier artillery bombardments. The gas was leaking into some of the houses and they didn't want to set off the gas with their explosive breaches, so the platoons had to avoid establishing battle positions in the homes where leaking gas was present.

"When we pushed up to the second mosque we received sporadic fire. Once we arrived we ended up clearing every building, about ten to twelve houses around the mosque," 2nd Platoon Marine, Lance Corporal Tribou said. "We weren't receiving any fire as we cleared the buildings before reaching the mosque."

2nd Platoon Commander Brandon Turner recalled the attack toward the mosque. "It was pitch black. I had my NVGs on. I had one tank in front of me and I told him to push up to the road the mosque was on. He moved up there and oriented his main gun down a road to give me some sort of guidance to where I was going. I immediately banked that way and started pushing. It was late at night and there wasn't much fighting going on in the darkness so we cleared out all the buildings around the mosque with no problems," Turner remembers.

The elusive enemy realized they couldn't fight the Marines on even terms at night. The insurgents found it much more to their liking to withdraw to the south and wait for daylight before moving north and making contact again. In the darkness, lugging their RPGs and RPKs, the

198

insurgents moved south closer to the center of the city to live and fight another day.

Thursday, November 11 (D+4). Once the entire area around the Al Janobi Mosque was secured, Captain Bethea directed his Fire Support Team to join up with Force Recon on the rooftop of a building adjacent to the mosque on the west. In the darkness Charlie Company had methodically cleansed the area that earlier had given them so much trouble. "We basically cleared and destroyed everything immediately outside of the mosque. When that was done, then and only then did I call for the Iraqis," Bethea remembered.

At 0300 Bethea got on the radio and ordered the Iraqi Emergency Response Unit to conduct their mechanized movement south to the Marine prepped mosque. When the Iraqis pulled up in the AAVs, Captain Bethea and First Sergeant Andrade met them. They informed the Iraqi's American handler, Clint, on where Charlie Company's positions around the mosque were located. Fearful of friendly fire coming from the Iraqis again, they pointed out all of their positions to Clint. Once the handler was familiar with where the Charlie Company's forces were located, he led the Iraqi forces into the mosque.

Recalling the movement Staff Sergeant Corey Lohr wrote:

> *"3rd Platoon gets a mission of going back north and maintaining a firm base in there. The Iraqi forces cleared the mosque and we load in an AAV and get driven back. All night we get harassing fire from the West."*

After the mosque was secure, Bethea received a call from the Operations Officer, Major Trimble, tasking Charlie Company to establish battle positions along Route Ethan. Bethea told Second Lieutenant Turner to establish a defense at the Al Janobi Mosque with his 2nd Platoon, while Rhoades' 1st Platoon set up along Route Ethan between Phase Line Cathy and Phase Line Beth in a large white house. Littell's 3rd Platoon was ordered back to help defend the Al Hydra Mosque.

A 2nd Platoon Marine, Lance Corporal Thomas Tribou, recalled entering the Al Janobi Mosque, "Our 2nd Squad were the only members in our platoon to get to go inside the mosque. It was pretty well destroyed inside. Later we saw some of the Iraqi troops attached to the battalion. They looked scared and I felt sorry for them."

Sergeant Frederick also remembered feeling sorry for the Iraqi troops, "The Iraqis didn't even have any water so I gave them some of mine."

The photo op now over at the mosque, the Iraqi forces were loaded back in the AAVs and driven back to the Al Hydra Mosque. By 0400 all Charlie Company forces were in battle positions around the Al Janobi Mosque.

Sergeant Stout's Sniper Team moved into position near the mosque. "We were on a rooftop and we began receiving fire from a government building 400 yards to our west. They had us pinned down until a Marine tank moved up to support us. I began talking him to where the enemy was located. He fired off two main rounds into the building and we leapt up and made it off the building."

"That night at 0400 we were all inside the mosque. I had fallen asleep on my pack at about 0430. At about 0600 I woke up to shots and bombs. I was drained at this time, but not to the point that I couldn't do my job," Second Lieutenant Brandon Turner explained. "When I woke up, shots were ZINGING through the mosque. We started ripping doors off their hinges, anything we could find to cover up the windows. We left holes so we could shoot out, but covered the windows enough so they couldn't see in. I immediately put fire teams on the rooftop with Recon."

Second Lieutenant O'Connor and Corporal Brown joined Force Recon Platoon on the roof of the mosque in an effort to identify the enemy locations south of Phase Line Fran. Sniper fire was impacting on the roof and the outer walls of the building. The impacting rounds tore chunks of mortar from the house. The Marines on the rooftop now found themselves pinned down and unable to leave the roof.

Turner's 2nd Platoon supplied suppressive fire while O'Conner called in an artillery strike on the suspected enemy positions. 60mm mortar fire was also called on a sniper's lair by Corporal Brown. The mortar rounds fell on enemy forces moving around along Phase Line Fran. In Fallujah, relief for the Marines was only a quick radio call away.

Battalion tasked Charlie Company to conduct a relief in place with Alpha Company who had taken the Government Center earlier that morning. Captain Bethea requested the use of AAVs to support the displacement because his 1st and 3rd Platoons and mortars were located in positions along the contested Route Ethan and the Al Hydra Mosque.

At 0830, Bethea met with Lieutenant Colonel Ramos, Commander of Battalion 1/3, at the Al Janobi Mosque to hand off the Iraqi Emergency Response Unit. Bethea informed Ramos of the do's and don'ts when conducting movements and missions with the friendly Iraqi troops. Bethea shared what he had learned from his experiences with the Iraqis.

At 1015, while attempting to load in the AAVs at the Al Hydra Mosque courtyard, the Marines came under sporadic sniper fire again. First Lieutenant Miller, in command of the loading operation, maneuvered across the courtyard to his radio and ordered the AAVs to move to the intersection of Route Ethan and Phase Line Cathy and orient to the west to better cover the Charlie Company Marines loading from the mosque.

Charlie Company Runs the "Fallujah 500" at the Government Center

"At 1030 on November 11, we got picked up by the amtracs to be taken to the Government Center," Sergeant Robert Frederick, a Weapons Platoon Marine in Charlie Company remembered.

"We were going in to relieve Alpha Company and assume the entire defense at the Government Center. Alpha and Bravo Companies were both preparing to attack south," Captain Theodore Bethea explained.

AAV Staff Sergeant Chris Shaw recalled, "We picked them up in three runs and dropped them off at a strong wall in the Government Center. The vehicles included the rest of my section, Corporal Grant Elliot and Sergeant Jose Jimenez. The last stick we picked up was Captain Bethea's group. While we were picking them up we began receiving sniper fire. I returned fire with my .50 cal in support while they were loading. After arriving back at the Government Center I moved my vehicles in place to support while Charlie Company made their movement. They began receiving fire from a water tower to the west. We began supplying counter sniper protection from our vehicles."

As the Marines in Charlie Company began unloading, they found themselves in the southern part of the complex. After piling out of their amtracs they were directed to go to a main building. Once there, they were then directed to go on to the theater/gym building. The only problem was, to get there they would have to cross a 400 to 500 meter open field, the quad, now under constant sniper fire. A Charlie Company Marine, Corporal Sean Heffner, dubbed this event the "Fallujah 500." Enemy snipers were still positioned in the higher buildings outside and surrounding the center. With the arrival of the Charlie Company Marines, the insurgent snipers now had fresh targets to work over.

Lance Corporal Thomas Tribou, 1st Platoon, standing by a large metal door in the mayors building told of what happened next. "We were standing in the mayors building when a Marine asked, 'You guys ready?' Before we could answer him, it was like the gates of hell had opened. I don't think anyone in this world would be ready for what we experienced when that big steel door was flung open. As soon as the door opened I could hear the CRACKING noise of bullets impacting. We started running as hard as we could with all of our gear. It seemed like everything went in slow motion as we ran. Lance Corporal Mercer and Corporal Pinto were in front of me leading the squad the 500 meters to the center's theater/gym building. Bullets riddled the ground as we ran. About half way across our legs began turning to Jell-O but we couldn't slow down. I was never so scared in all my life. Bullets were hitting the wall where our shadows were. Everyone was spaced about fifteen meters apart until we got to the theater building. Then we had to squeeze through a small door, one at a time to get into the building." The Marines began stacking up at the door while rounds were impacting around them. "Eventually we all pushed our way into the theater/gym building."

Also recalling the mad dash in the open, Lance Corporal Peguero confessed, "When we arrived at the Government Center we dismounted from the amtracs and had to run about 500 meters across an open field, under fire to get to our position. It was a scary hell of a run. I don't know how we survived that run. RPGs and sniper fire were coming in on us. I remember one of our senior guys at the center, Corporal Pinto, who had two RPGs fired at him. He rolled and dodged both of them."

"I was carrying 1,200 5.56 rounds linked for my SAW weapon, about five sticks of C-4, and two to four hand grenades." Lance Corporal Dominick Giusti was a running IED. He remembered making his way across the open field, "At the Fallujah 500 we had to basically sprint with our full compliment of gear across this open area. It took us five minutes to get across while friendly forces on our left and right supplied covering fire for us. Rounds were impacting behind us as we ran."

Pennsylvanian, Sergeant John Megahan, 1st Squad leader, Turner's 2nd Platoon, recalls the mad dash across the wide-open terrain, "We had to run to get to the building and get out of the snipers range. We didn't know where the firing was coming from."

First Lieutenant Miller conducted liaison with Alpha Company and began to conduct the relief in place. Charlie Company assumed defense of the Government Center at noon.

Second Lieutenant Turner remembers, "When we were coming to relieve Alpha Company I saw my roommate from college, Second Lieutenant Doug Barnes, who I had gone to four years of college with. We went through all of our instructions at IOC together and then came to Battalion 1/8 together. When I came to the complex, I got to relieve his platoon. When his platoon pushed across the street, my platoon gave him supporting fire. We were putting rounds down the street while they got across. It was just an odd coincidence we were beside each other again."

Lance Corporal Tribou, and the other tired Marines of Charlie Company, were met by an even more exhausted looking group of Alpha Company Marines. They had just lost a Marine officer, First Lieutenant Malcom, in the stiff fighting around the center.

Lance Corporal Tribou stared at the Alpha Company Marines and admitted. "The look in their eyes made us all worry. When we thought it couldn't get any worse, it did."

Corporal Rob Sarka said, "We ran up to the second floor of a building with hardly any roof and only about a six inch lip to give us protection from incoming sniper rounds. Four of us went to the roof and began piling up cinder blocks, tires any type of rubble for protection. Corporal Korey Vendetti and the rest of our squad stayed downstairs. We began firing into windows and anything suspicious across the street."

Lieutenant Colonel Brandl tasked Captain Bethea and his Charlie Company to clean out the snipers around the outside of the Government Center. Captain Jenkins and his H & S Company Marines would supply security for the Government Center while Charlie Company swept the surrounding buildings.

Lance Corporal Thomas Tribou was one of the first Marines on the rooftop after Alpha Company had withdrawn. The Marines found out that friendly fire isn't really friendly. Tribou said, "The whole roof was just covered in shell casings, and as I looked around I asked myself, *What the hell happened here*? Then I found out what they had been firing at because we began receiving sniper fire from the same places. My Team Leader told me to get down and I started firing at every dark spot that I saw. Finally 2nd Platoon pushed across the road, followed by my 1st Platoon. We took those three buildings outside the center. From there we patrolled west, and that's where our squad found the biggest weapons cache in Fallujah. This garage of weapons filled two 7-ton Marine trucks up and there were still weapons left over, so they just leveled it."

Tribou recalled a friendly fire casualty in the clearing operation. "Lance Corporal Richard Muston was injured with shrapnel to the leg when a Marine threw a grenade that bounced back and exploded. We were in the heart of Fallujah and about every ten minutes a fire team was sent back to bring up more ammo. I burned off about seven-hundred rounds in less than thirty minutes and I wasn't wasting rounds either."

A mosque's minaret, located 280 meters west of the center, was where the most accurate sniper fire was originating. The tall minaret had an excellent overall view of the Government Center. Lance Corporal Hunter hurriedly set up a laser designator in a window in the center while under fire from the insurgents. Captain Richie, FO, sat in the opening and designated the target for attacking aircraft above the city. Bullets continued to snap around the window chipping off pieces of mortar. The Marines watched as two guided bombs launched from the plane streaked toward the target. With a thunderous BANG! BANG! The bombs impacted against the minaret about halfway up the tall lanky structure. The Marines let out a loud cheer as the minaret toppled to the ground, taking the deadly sniper's nest along with it.

Captain Bethea said, "We did simultaneous clear. 2nd Platoon deployed a squad and cleared the western section, 3rd Platoon cleared the northern sector, and 1st Platoon cleared the eastern sector. Once they did that, we established squad battle positions outside of friendly lines in each sector. That effectively mitigated the enemy sniper fire on the center. During this sweep we were killing the enemy as well as capturing weapon caches. After that, at noon, we were tasked to seize the mosque directly south of Phase Line Fran because we were receiving accurate sniper fire from it, directly into the Government Center. So once again I tasked 2nd Platoon as the main effort to attack and seize the mosque beginning at 1400."

"That was the first time I really started to see the insurgents pulling back and start to disappear from the fight completely," Second Lieutenant Brandon Turner said.

The fight for the third mosque, located near the Government Center, seemed the charm for Charlie Company. The enemy didn't put up as stiff a fight as they had for the two previous mosques. Turner's 2nd Platoon, Captain Bethea, First Sergeant Andrade and First Lieutenant Miller, along with his headquarters Marines, entered the mosque.

A group of insurgents were seen moving toward the northwest wall of the mosque. Earlier the enemy had been using the mosque's loud speaker system to call for all the insurgents remaining in the city to assemble there and prepare for a jihad against the Americans. They were calling for a holy war against the infidels.

Joining in the fight was an attached Navy SEAL team. The SEALs along with Staff Sergeant Olalde and some casualty collection Marines from Charlie Company manned the rooftop of a tall building near the enemy held mosque. Marines and SEALs armed with M16s and SAWs pounded away at the gathering enemy in the streets below. During the sharp fight, some twenty-two of the enemy lay among the rubble in the streets, the remainder had scattered.

Bethea's Charlie Company went firm after taking the mosque and the four adjacent buildings. Bethea recounted the SEALs fight, "During this attack the Navy SEALs located in the high-rise building got twenty-two confirmed kills in the action to our western flank. The company had attacked and successfully seized four objectives within two hours of being tasked to attack."

Sergeant Dustin Stout talks of the fight at the mosque, "We began receiving fire from a building to the east. We went to the roof, which was wide open. There was just no cover so we went down and entered a minaret and climbed up to an opening. We had a view of the whole city. We tried to get an angle of fire and Earl was laying on my shoulder when we saw a group of about 20 fully armed enemy fighters about 700 yards to the south. That distance basically maxed the effectiveness of our weapons. Then we watched as another heavily armed group ran across the street and entered the same building. I got on the radio and tried to call in artillery fire or an air strike on the building. We were turned down. They said they didn't know if there were friendlys there or not. Then we saw a car come toward us and then make a sharp turn to the west near a schoolhouse. We were shooting at them but from that distance we couldn't tell if we were hitting them. Finally a stationary target stopped near the building and we fired. The guy fell down and then crawled around a corner. We were then ordered out of the minaret."

While at the mosque south of the Government Center, Captain Theodore Bethea and First Sergeant Arturo Andrade re-enlisted Staff Sergeant Dennis Nash into the Corps, while Charlie Company Marines stood post at the windows with their weapons at the ready. Nash, in the chaos of war, reaffirmed his dedication to the Corps.

Also the Marines of Charlie Company were paid a visit by the Battalion Chaplain Lieutenant Denis Cox. To reach the men at the mosque near the Government Center, Cox and his Protector David Zeno had to run across the open highway. They were familiar with the enemy snipers that had been working over the center.

Cox recalled, "As we were running across the highway, Zeno was zig-zagging. He looked at me and yelled, 'Sir, zig-zag, zig-zag!'"

Cox told him, "With this bum knee I'm not going to zig-zag! If they're going to hit me they're going to hit me."

Cox and Zeno made it safely across and spent time with the Marines of Charlie Company.

At 1345, Major General Natonski, Regimental Commander, Colonel Tucker and Lieutenant Colonel Brandl all arrived at the high-rise building in the Government Center to visit with the battle weary Charlie Company Marines.

Charlie Company, after several days in the center, eventually moved over to the industrial sector of the city and set up a firm base for the company at a soda factory.

Charlie Company continued patrolling and clearing houses under the blazing sun in Fallujah. On November 16, two Marines from 2nd Platoon were injured when a fragmentation grenade, used to make entry in a house, exploded wounding Lance Corporal Fair and Lance Corporal Muston with shrapnel.

"A few days after relieving Alpha Company in the Government Center we patrolled out during the night." Sarka recalled. "We came up to a white truck sitting beside the road. Lieutenant Littell asked me if I could see it in the dark. I said I could see the outline. An Iraqi with a flashlight was walking toward the truck just when I fired. The grenade hit the truck and there was a blinding flash. We moved on and began to clear a house. They had a couch wedged behind the front door. We managed to get it opened enough to throw in some grenades. We managed to get in and I saw a rifle leaning against the wall and fresh food still on the table. We knew someone was in that house. I kicked the bedroom door open and saw two guys hiding under a red blanket on a mattress on the floor. They were acting like they were sleeping so I kicked one in the back and told him to get up. He said, 'I no ali bada!' No bad guy. We zipped them both up to take them back."

Littell's 3rd Platoon Marines then moved on to a nearby second one-story house to initiate another search. Again they found food on the table and AKs in the first room.

Sarka describes the mindset of the Marines and what they had to face on patrol that night, "There were three doors coming into that first room and all were closed. We had lights on our rifles as we began trying to enter the rooms. We knew that behind the first door that we had a one in three chance someone was going to be there. Lance Corporal Storey kicked the first door open and it proved to be empty. With the second door it was a fifty-fifty chance someone was waiting for us. The second door was locked so Lance Corporal Ward shot the lock off. It also was empty, so now we knew there was a hundred per cent chance someone was in that third room. Lance Corporal Carter kicked at that third door but it wouldn't budge. He then stepped back and rushed the door hitting it with his shoulder and jarred it open. We rushed in and nine people stood behind a bed, all were military age. We zipped them up and got them out and later found out one or two of them were on a wanted list of insurgents."

Sergeant Dustin Stout, sniper, attached to Charlie Company, recalled he and his snipers joining Rhodes' platoon in a large apartment complex. "We set up a field of fire with an excellent view of that part of the city including the water tower and the school building."

Marine snipers are taught to never set up the same way. They learned how to be creative in setting up their positions in Fallujah. They had to keep the enemy guessing for their lives depended on it.

Stout describes how they positioned themselves in the building. "We set up in a corner of a back room that had a view out the door and into the next room and then out a lightly white mesh curtained window. We stayed there two nights but on the second day we switched our laser optics to day optics. Nearby the friendly Iraqi troops began receiving enemy fire and pulled out. It quieted down and I decided to get some rest. We slept in two-hour shifts in the city. I found some blankets in the apartment complex and curled up on the floor. Merkle was manning the radio and Earl the scope. I was sleeping maybe an hour when I heard a round being fired. I went over to where Earl was and he showed me what he had fired at. An armed insurgent had been moving along about two hundred yards away when he had fired and brought him down. I couldn't believe it because the guy just jumped back up and started moving along a wall. He stopped at a corner and Earl fired again and the guy went down before staggering back to his feet. Earl fired off four shots before the man remained on the ground."

On November 17, two more Marines, Lance Corporal Rendiero and Lance Corporal Orgereon, received fragmentation when a grenade was thrown short of its target, a vehicle-borne IED.

On Thursday, November 25, Thanksgiving Day, Major General Natonski arrived at the soda factory to pay Charlie Company another visit. Natonski promoted Navy Corpsman Pines during a platoon minus formation. That same day, Lieutenant Colonel Brandl and Regimental Commander Colonel Craig Tucker held a commander's meeting at the factory. Charlie Company was kept active with clearing patrols and operations throughout the city until the battalion left Fallujah.

The fighting in Fallujah had been a bitter one for Bethea's Marines. They had suffered twenty wounded by hostile action, and one Force Recon Marine attached to Charlie Company had been killed in the battle. They also suffered an assortment of minor non-battle injuries in their push through the almost destroyed city. Charlie Company's 1st Platoon, commanded by Second Lieutenant Rhoades accounted for twenty-three confirmed enemy killed in action. Turner's 2nd Platoon had fifteen enemy KIA, and Littell's 3rd Platoon had fourteen confirmed enemy KIA. Klingensmith's tanks accounted for another thirty or more. FiST accounted for thirty-four KIAs. Viper 2 had nine enemies killed. Viper 5 had five, and the Navy SEALs accounted for twenty-two enemy KIA. Charlie Company and its attached units accounted for a total of 152 KIAs in Fallujah.

"Urban fighting is extremely intense. We had a clear purpose. I had 191 lives under my responsibility and that kept me going every day in Fallujah. The key to urban fighting was made clear by the regimental commander. Assess the situation. Lead with fire. Fire with violent maneuver, and insure that you never leave a man behind. That you never get cut off, and you need to use over all force to destroy the enemy in an urban environment," Bethea explained.

To celebrate the Marine Corps 150th birthday, Lieutenant Colonel Brandl saddled up his small convoy and took a birthday cake around for each company of the battalion to enjoy. Brandl sliced the cake and served it to the gathered troops at the different Forward Bases of the units. There is a tradition in the Marine Corps that the oldest Marine present serves the youngest the first slice. Sergeant Major Hope, being the oldest Marine in the battalion, served up the cake to the youngest from the different companies. Each Marine savored a very thin slice of the birthday cake. Over a thousand Marines of 1/8 got a taste of cake.

Corporal Rob Sarka remembered the birthday cake, "It was a few days late but the Marine Corps birthday was held in the southern side of the city, south of highway 10. Charlie Company was based in a two story complex where we ran security patrols around the perimeter. The battalion commander came by and talked to all of us telling us what a good job we were doing and there was no better place to celebrate a Marine Corps birthday than in the heart of a combat zone. Then we had prime rib and corn on the cob and we all did cake afterwards. Then it was back to business, running patrols and keeping three-hundred and sixty degree security twenty-four hours a day."

"We could hear heavy fire coming from the south where Alpha and Bravo Companies were," said Sergeant Frederick, Weapons Platoon of Charlie Company. The focus of Battalion 1/8's fight in the city now shifted to Cunningham's Alpha Company and Omohundro's Bravo Company in their push south.

Other Units Move up to the Government Center

Major Mark Winn and his Main Command and Control vehicles were to join the lieutenant colonel at the Government Center. Winn said, "When I came in, I brought in fifteen vehicles with us, including two M-113 armored ambulances. Mobile Assault Platoon Two, under Lieutenant Risler with eight vehicles, also went in with us. It was night when we came in at 0100. We came down Route David that had a pretty severe island in the middle of the highway. Risler hadn't been down this far in the city. We were on the left side of the highway and couldn't turn right and find our way over the island. We kept driving south and found ourselves the most southern unit in the battalion. We eventually stopped the convoy and had all the vehicles turn around and drive back north. We started to receive sniper fire. Staff Sergeant Choquette found a turn for us. Corporal Dewalt, who was my machine gunner, wanted to fire back but I told him we didn't know where our Marines were. We got across the island and made it in to the Government Center. It was real quiet when we arrived. I managed two hours sleep that night."

Tucked away in the back of one of the vehicles coming in with Winn were Chaplain Denis Cox and his Protector Corporal David Zeno. In his hand Cox held a Red Cross message for a corporal in Alpha Company.

The Marine's father was near death in the states and the corporal had one last chance to see him before he died.

"Upon arriving at the Government Center I went over to Captain Cunningham and showed him the Red Cross message," Cox said. "He told First Sergeant Fry to find the Marine and bring him back." The problem was the corporal was in Ackerman's platoon at the candy store.

Another Marine in the vehicle was Captain Mike Pretus, Sniper Platoon Commander, who had been attached to Bravo Command. "It was extremely dark when we came in. When we arrived we had to wait until daybreak to set up our command post."

H & S Captain Jacob Jenkins recalled his entry into the city of Fallujah. "At 2300 we stepped off in an eight vehicle convoy to head south to the Government Center. It took us about forty-five minutes and nothing happened on the way in. The COC was set up in a building that was a police station," said Jenkins. Jenkins grabbed a few hours of sleep before being awakened by the next wave of Marines arriving with the communication trucks.

Chaplain Cox said, "I found a busted up room in the police headquarters and managed a few hours of sleep. At 0500 First Sergeant Fry returned with the corporal whose father was dying. Sergeant Major Hope had told the Marine, 'You only get one father.'"

The Marine torn between leaving his fellow Marines in the city and his dying father finally jumped aboard the vehicle and departed the city.

"I remember the next morning walking over to the line of buildings where the Marines had taken fire the day before. It was no big deal on the walk over, but when I started back I saw Marines running. I asked them 'why are you running?' One said, 'Sir they're shooting at us!' I hadn't realized we were that exposed in the center, until then," Winn recalls.

A few days after the initial attack on Fallujah, LCDR Richard Jadick's medics moved in a three-vehicle convoy into the city and on to the Government Center to be closer to the fighting. The Division Hospital Corpsman motto was, "Through the gates of Hell for a wounded Marine," and the medical corpsmen and doctors in Fallujah lived up to the high standard of their unit's motto.

"It was dark and we stopped on the way into the center when the enemy started to walk mortar rounds in on us. We thought we were going to die but we made it safely into the center with no casualties," HA Ernesto Argueta, 19, said.

HM2 Shawn Johns remembered the trip into the Government Center, "Commander Jadick basically told us to, 'Grab your shit, we're going into the center in the city and set up the forward aid station.' The Army supplied the two M-113 armored ambulances for us to go in escorted by Weapons Company. There were nine of us including me tasked to go in. We arrived at the Government Center in the early morning hours of the third day. We knew where we were but it was dark, and we didn't know where to go once we arrived at the center. Alpha Company was taking sniper fire when we unloaded the ACPs. A few of our corpsman used their weapons to help provide counter sniper operations. Usually a forward aid station is set in a secure area, but here we were in a hot zone."

After arriving, they set up shop in a small one-story one-room building, in a 15x15 room originally used as a Muslim prayer room. Four cots were squeezed into the small space for the expected influx of wounded. All of the casualties suffered in the city would come through this aid station before being medevaced out.

"We were sleeping outside with the cats and dogs at night. Those cats would make noise all night long, fighting over food and what not. It was hard to get some sleep. I remember this one corporal who had part of his face blown off. He knew what was going on when we were working on him. You could see it in his eyes, and as I worked on him I was wondering if he would live or not. He did live," said HA Argueta. "I knew some of the KIAs that came in. One that came in at the center was sniper Corporal Nick Ziolkowski. I had gone out on the range with him before we came to Fallujah and he let me shoot his sniper rifle. He taught me how to use the weapon, but when I shot it, the recoil gave me a cut. He was still alive when he came in and we tried everything to save him. We would talk to the wounded Marines trying to keep their minds off their injuries. Seven KIAs came through our aid station at the center and HM3 Stedman, HA Avila, HM1 Zimmerman and I were tasked to put them in body bags. We had to take their personal items off of them and it really hurt when we came across pictures of their family, wife or girlfriend."

The young HA Ernesto Argueta was the most junior ranking medic at the Government Center aid station. One of his duties was emptying the plastic bags that were put inside empty MRE boxes that were used for latrines. Marines *improvise, adapt and overcome*.

"During the daylight hours of day three we didn't have any wounded brought in to the aid station, but the shit hit the fan that night," Corpsman HM2 Johns recalled. "We didn't have a radio with us at the forward aid station. The COC had one and sometimes they would receive a call that wounded were coming and would walk over to inform us. Sometimes they didn't. Sometimes we would get a report that three casualties would be coming in and six would show up."

"Day four we received heavy sniper fire during the day directed at our forward aid station. They weren't too accurate, though," HM2 Johns said. "But we were outside on the porch of the aid station treating casualties because we were getting so many coming in to us. I remember there was a point when for a few days we hadn't received any KIAs, so like baseball players, we didn't shave, hoping that would not jinx it. We eventually were told to shave. Although we corpsmen had stress, I knew the Marines coming in from the line companies had much more and I tended to give them space. We treated about four or five insurgents, giving them the same medical treatment as we would one of our Marines. Also some civilian Iraqis were treated. Apparently they had tried to stand-up to the insurgents by defending their homes and had been shot by them. I loved the camaraderie we had in Fallujah."

"When any casualties came in the aid station I would always go over there," Major Mark Winn said. "Rich Jadick, a good friend of mine, was working on some Marines and he looked up and saw a sniper on a water tower. He said, 'There's a sniper. Look up at the water tower!' I looked over and I could see the muzzle flashes. Here he's working on this kid and doesn't skip a beat when he sees a sniper. A section of Marines opened fire and got rid of the sniper."

Weapons Company commander, Captain Stephen Kahn, remembered a heart-wrenching scene at the forward aid station at the Government Center, "There was a day when Bravo Company had taken a lot of casualties. I saw our battalion surgeon, Jadick, looking defeated after he had stood outside for more than two hours working on these kids. He looked defeated because he couldn't save every one of them. He was covered from head to toe with blood. The corpsmen were cleaning out the floor of the aid station with buckets of bottled water because that's all we had. They were trying to keep it clean from the smell and the flies. It made for long days in Fallujah."

"Seeing your guys in the aid station on a stretcher is something I will never forget. I felt bad for the unit, but I felt the worse for the families. I had thought about how I would handle casualties before I left for Iraq," Lieutenant Colonel Brandl said. "At that time I had to compartmentalize that. I had a lot of live Marines, and I had to continue on with the mission. When we lost Marines we asked ourselves, is there something we're doing wrong? If so, we need to change our tactics right now. We did do some evolution of tactics when we punched farther south. We used the engineers and bulldozers to isolate the houses that held the enemy. In place of sending Marines in, we would bulldoze the house down with the D-9s. In Fallujah I saw enough acts of valor, bravery, and guts to last a couple of lifetimes. Uncommon valor is still a common virtue in our Corps."

Staff Sergeant Richard Choquette, Weapons Company, remembered his move from the railroad tracks and into the city. "Once the Government Center was secured we were moved to that position. At that point we were tasked with medevac procedures. The AAVs would pick up the casualties from the line companies, and occasionally we would roll up and run the wounded back to the center." Rolling up required leaving the Government Center and pushing out into the city under enemy fire and bringing wounded Marines safely back to the aid station. "They didn't want to push us in the street that much because of the RPG fire at that point. At the center we were still receiving a lot of sniper fire," he said.

"We got used to being fired on," Lance Corporal Greg Nichols, 1st Platoon, Weapons Company, remembered. Nichols' platoon was set up on a rooftop when he was tasked with bringing some ammo for the .50 cal up. Upon reaching the roof, he left the stairwell and walked around the corner when someone yelled at him.

"Hey! Hey!" The Marine shouted.

Nichols hollered back, "What's up?"

The Marine, looking incredulous answered, "They're shooting!"

"So what!" Answered Nichols.

The Marine smiled at Nichols, and then added the kicker, "At you!"

"I thought, *Oh shit!* When I reached the rooftop with the ammo, I expected a good-size wall around the edge. I popped my head over and there is just a one-inch lip. Everyone on the roof was just hugging the ground and I couldn't help myself as I started laughing. I threw the ammo over to them on the roof and went back down," Nichols recalled.

A few days later Nichols and his platoon were tasked to take care of a weapon's cache at the Government Center. "I was just sitting there looking around waiting for something to happen, when I felt a warm liquid running down my leg. I ignored it for a minute and then I looked at my pant leg and saw a purplish color. I thought, *Did I just get shot?* I started flipping out, I yelled out, 'I think I got shot!' I then climbed into the truck," said Lance Corporal Greg Nichols.

After climbing in the vehicle, Nichols hurriedly checked his pocket and discovered a container of grape juice had been the culprit and not an enemy round. The container had sprung a leak. The relieved Nichols leaned back in the seat and gave a sigh of relief.

Lance Corporal Adam Lew said, "We had been receiving inaccurate sniper fire at the Government Center when a round hit Lieutenant Risler's truck. We could hear Corporal Davila call over the radio that they had been hit. Then my truck takes a round right in the winch at the center of the truck in line with my head. We called and said that the truck had been hit and they tell us to get out and check it. When my VC Corporal Kendall gets out and checks, he told me the impacted round was right in line with my head."

There was a store located across the street from the Government Center where a Pepsi bottle sat in the window tantalizing the hot and thirsty Marines. A thirsty Major Winn finally decided enough was enough. He asked his good friend, Surgeon Rich Jadick, to cover him while he ran over to the store. Jadick looked at Winn like he was crazy. "I ran out and quickly covered the ten yards or so to the store. Firing started up when I grabbed the Pepsi." With Pepsi in hand, a thirsty Winn rapidly carried it safely back into the protection of the complex. "I opened the bottle up and it just turned to algae," Winn remembered. The crestfallen Winn tossed the bottle to the ground and he and Jadick had a good laugh at Winn's expense from the safety of the Government Center.

Alpha Company's, 1st Platoon Pays a Visit to the Candy Store on Haji Alley

Lieutenant Colonel Gary Brandl, who had met with Regimental Commander Craig Tucker the night before at the Al Hydra Mosque, recalled that they both saw eye to eye on the taking of the Government Center, but now Brandl wanted to take it slower on the final push south.

Brandl said, "With what I'm seeing, my gut feeling tells me we need to shape this a little bit more. I don't think it's a good idea to push everybody hi-diddle-diddle right now. We need to fix the enemy and gain an appreciation of how he is set up to the south. We need to try and shape as much as possible before we push through. They agreed to that and gave us twelve hours or so to do that. We pushed elements across to gain some high ground to see what the enemy was doing and we used the AC-130 on the night of November 10 and on November 11. Then later on in the day, kick off in force with Alpha Company and Bravo Company. The enemy we met in the north of the city were the local fighters, and the enemy to the south were the dedicated foreign fighters. I brought Charlie Company up to relieve in place with Alpha Company at the Government Center."

At midnight on November 11, Captain Aaron Cunningham received word that at 1400 he and his Alpha Company would attack south across

Phase Line Fran, the main highway that bisects the city, and into the pizza slice. At the same time Captain Omohundro and his Bravo Company would be stepping off from their position and attacking south. Both companies would be assaulting into the heart of the enemy resistance and if successful they would be breaking the back of the insurgency in the city.

On November 10, Brandl told Cunningham that he felt the insurgents would make their stand in the area of the pizza slice and to the immediate south. He told Cunningham, "Get a foothold behind those apartment buildings after dark and then proceed down to Phase Line Henry and roll them up," Brandl explained. Alpha Company had received the bulk of their sniper fire from those apartments the previous day.

"Our company and Bravo Company would attack south, while Charlie Company relieved us in the Government Center," Captain Cunningham recalled. "I was given two more tanks and I now had four to assist in the attack south. The night of November 10, I pushed Lieutenant Ackerman's 1st Platoon to a house across the street under the cover of darkness to get a foothold. In my mind, when the sun came up the enemy would not expect them there."

Second Lieutenant Elliot Ackerman was told at 1800 that he and his 1st platoon would leave the compound at 0400 and secure a foothold in the city to the south. He met with his squad leaders and told them of the upcoming mission. Ackerman tasked 3rd Squad as over-watch, 2nd Squad would supply suppressive fire and his 1st Squad would lead in the assault.

"My Marines were proud that we would be the main effort of the company in the attack south," Ackerman recalled.

The building that Ackerman would lead his Marines to was located only a short distance across the street and to the west of where they were positioned, in the power plant. The house was located in the pizza slice strip that also held a group of shops, offices and restaurants.

"I briefed our FO, Captain Ramsey, to prep the house in advance with artillery fire, and hopefully scare off any insurgents in the area," Ackerman said.

Ramsey answered, 'No problem.'

"Basher came on line and soon fifteen 105mm rounds began falling on the house," Ackerman recalled.

In the predawn hours, Tufts College graduate Ackerman, led most of his forty-six-man platoon across Phase Line Fran toward the building that he had picked out some 150 meters to the south. His 3rd Squad would stay in support at the power plant in the Government Center. Once Ackerman's platoon had cleared the building, 3rd Squad would join them. The platoon would go firm and await further orders from Cunningham.

Ackerman's 1st and 2nd Squads, weighted down with equipment, jogged across the highway in the dark and made their way through the eerily deserted intersection and streets to their objective. Because they had received such intense sniper fire the previous day, the stillness and lack of insurgents pleasantly surprised the jogging Marines.

As they moved on deeper into the city not a shot was fired; everything remained quiet. The insurgents had gone to ground or most likely pulled back farther south. Fearing the deadly combination of Marines, night vision goggles, and the darkness of night, they had slipped away to their safe house to rest, regroup, and wait for daylight before pushing back north.

When Ackerman and his Marines finally reached the building some 150 meters from the Government Center, the surprised Marines discovered that the prep fire had actually been too good, most of the backside of the building was rubble.

Ackerman said, "The front part of the house looked normal. Sergeant Adam Bonitay and I went up to the front and kicked in the door. When we walked in we noticed that the interior stairwell had completely collapsed as well as the back wall of the building from the artillery rounds. We climbed up to the top of three floors of rubble and looked around and decided we couldn't use the house."

With no back wall, the building looked as though it was on a Hollywood set. Staring at the pile of rubble, Ackerman had to make a snap decision, to either push a little farther west to find another building or go back to the Government Center. He felt that going back wasn't an option, so he pushed his platoon west about 100 meters and discovered a strong position in a solidly built two-story building, which could house his whole platoon. The colorful building had open areas surrounding the entire structure that would allow his Marines to set up fields of fire. The Marines dubbed the two-story retail confectionery store in the commercial district the "candy store."

Finding the door locked, Ackerman had his Marines blew it open. After entering the building the Marines moved through searching the rooms. With their weapons raised to their shoulders, they moved upstairs, calling to each other as they cleared rooms. Ackerman then radioed 3rd Squad to join them. "I told them to go to the house we had intended to secure and I would talk them in to us at the candy store. I had a Marine hold a strobe out the window to guide 3rd Squad to our building. We had to force open a few interior doors and my assault fire team actually had to blow one of the doors open," Ackerman said.

The noise the Marines were making didn't seem to be attracting any attention from the insurgents in the area; it continued to stay peaceful. The forty-six Marines began to make themselves at home among the stocked shelves full of tasty candy. They set up their firing positions looking out of windows in the solidly built structure. They piled boxes and pieces of furniture in front of the openings to provide cover and put curtains on the windows to keep the enemy from looking in. The Marines also dug and punched mouse holes in the walls to provide more firing positions.

Ackerman and his engineer Corporal Luke Davy went to the rooftop of the building to see if he could position his Marines there. The roof had only a foot and a half wall running around the edge and would provide only minimal cover for his men. Ackerman noticed that the taller buildings around the candy store had angles of fire directly down on to their roof and decided not to position any of his Marines on the low slung rooftop. The only firing position for his Marines was on the second floor of the candy store.

"I contacted Lieutenant Krugman, our XO, at the complex to let him know where we were now located. The way we were sent forward, in front of the battalion, would become an emerging tactic in the city," explained Ackerman.

One of those forty-six Marines with 1st Platoon was Brooklyn, New York, born and raised, Lance Corporal Carmine Castelli, 19, a SAW gunner. Castelli had been in high school only several blocks from where the Twin Towers had been brought down. "We began lugging bags of salt to the second floor, and built a bunker outside the room on a outside walkway."

Sergeant Stoy, Weapons Platoon, attached to Ackerman's 1st Platoon, remembered arriving at the candy store, "We crossed Phase Line Fran and the lieutenant moved to the candy store. I was put in a building, just north of the candy store to cover the platoon's movement. The first thing I heard on the radio was not, 'Hey Stoy bring up your machine guns!' but, 'Hey Stoy, we found a gold mine! It's all candy! We've got food!' There were candy bars, potato chips; they had everything you could think of in the candy store."

The Marines in the candy store turned the boiler room, located in the bottom floor of the building, into a latrine and a rest area. Most Marines managed to get a few hours sleep before daybreak.

Right before sunup, First Sergeant Derek Fry made his way to the candy store and brought the Marine, whose father was dying, back to the Government Center. Now Ackerman had one less Marine with him at the candy store.

When the sun came up on day four of the battle for Fallujah it found Lieutenant Ackerman and his 1st Platoon out on a limb, 250 meters away from the rest of Alpha Company who were still back in the safety of the Government Center. Two hundred-fifty meters in an urban setting like Fallujah may as well be one hundred miles when the enemy is all around, and they were. The members of 1st Platoon just didn't realize it yet.

SAW gunner, Lance Corporal Benny Matthew, 21, like Castelli, a native of Brooklyn, New York, remembers the early morning. "I was posted upstairs on the second floor. It was quiet except for a few pot shots every once in awhile. We didn't know where the shots were coming from. We were enjoying the candy while we could."

As the sun slowly rose, Ackerman's Marines stared out at three to five fully armed insurgent teams walking boldly about the street, fully unaware of the Marine's presence in the candy store. The daring move of pushing 1st Platoon to the south had completely caught the enemy fighters unaware. The insurgents believed that the Marines were still located north of Highway 10.

Second Lieutenant Ackerman, along with his Marines, gazed warily at the insurgents walking nonchalantly about the streets. His Marines opened fire. A blaze of M16s and SAWs opened up on the unsuspecting enemy fighters. Rounds poured from the second floor windows and the firing holes punched earlier through the walls of the building. The enemy fighters were caught completely off guard by the sudden onslaught.

"The insurgents looked to be moving to the west to reinforce. Since we only had the second floor to fire from, I began rotating my squads. Two squads would rest and eat downstairs, while a third squad worked the firing positions on the second floor," Ackerman remembered. He didn't want too many Marines bunched together upstairs making a good target for a lucky RPG, mortar, or rocket round.

The Marines cut down most of the surprised insurgents before they had a chance to return fire. The others, baffled, quickly scattered. The confusion among the insurgents didn't last too long as the enemy fighters quickly rallied. They surrounded the candy store and began to bring it under intense fire with RPGs, machineguns, and small arms.

Glowing RPGs lazily flew from across the street at the Marines holed up in the candy store before impacting in the street or against the walls of the building. RPKs rattled from rooftops and open windows. The sharp CRACK of Marine's M16s and SAWs quickly answered. It was dueling weapons between adversaries as both tried to suppress the other and get the upper hand. The noise inside the candy store became deafening as the firing of the weapons reverberated off the stucco and brick walls almost shattering the Marines' eardrums.

Ackerman found himself in a 360-degree fight in the inner bowels of the city. He recalled, "I was watching Corporal Bejrano pop rounds at insurgent after insurgent, bringing them down with his M16."

Lance Corporal Roopnarine manned a second floor window as he rested his M-240G machine gun on the windowsill and kept a wary eye on the street below. "We keep receiving sniper fire from the house across the street. We kept seeing this window blind on the third deck sway back and forth, but we thought the explosions were causing it to move," said Roopnarine. Three shots impacted on the wall directly behind him. One of the shots shattered some glass that went into the eye of Corporal Bejrano. "The corpsman came up and checked his eye and told him to go downstairs and take an hour break. We were continually moving teams up and down to conserve ammo. I looked across the street and saw the blind move and stay open. SAW gunner Corporal Opon came up and we both started working over the window." Roopnarine didn't recall receiving any more fire from the sniper in that particular window.

Meanwhile at the center, Cunningham received word by radio of the fight going on with Ackerman's Marines at the candy store. "His platoon was waylaid with an ambush. He was covered up with bad guys at close range at the candy store," Cunningham remembered.

Staff Sergeant Michael Cauthon saw that a sniper was beginning to zero in on one of his Marines, Sergeant Minard, on the second floor. A bullet bounced off Minard's kevlar as he was positioned near an open window. Cauthon quickly pulled him away from the window when Cauthon himself was hit with a round that skimmed through his kevlar helmet grazing his head. Cauthon tried to stand but stumbled to the floor.

"We were getting a lot of fire. As I was checking my machine gunners, Lance Corporal Roopnarine and Corporal Bianco, I remember Sergeant Cauthon doing a somersault and then standing up and saying he needed a cigarette and moving to the back of the room. Then he just fell," Sergeant Stoy remembered. "Due to the impact of the round hitting his helmet, his brain began to swell and he began losing feeling to his arms and legs." Cauthon was taken out of the fight.

Sergeant Michael Cauthon would later receive two Purple Hearts from wounds suffered in combat in Iraq. Earlier, he had received shrapnel wounds when the battalion was at Haditha.

Lance Corporal Mark Cabang, 20, from Fairfax, Virginia was posted with his SAW at a window looking to the west. He couldn't see anything moving when his Squad Leader Corporal Jordan Latva walked into the room. "He told me to go to the side of the building and put some rounds through a window where they had received sniper fire from. Corporal Lewis had an ACOG scope on his M16, and he identified a sniper and began firing. Brown had rushed over to the window and that's when he took a round and HM Steven Martinez came up and began working on him," said Cabang.

Lance Corporal Matthew Brown, machine gunner in Ackerman's platoon, got hit with a round but refused medical treatment until he had taken a bead on the sniper that shot him. Brown fired twenty to thirty rounds at the sniper until the enemy fighter was silenced. When Stoy reached his wounded machine gunner, Brown, all he saw was a pool of blood on the floor surrounding his bloodstained leg. A corpsman, Martinez, was working on the badly wounded Brown when he looked up and saw Stoy. The corpsman asked him to come in and help him out.

Stoy said, "He had been hit in the femoral artery of the left leg. The corpsman asked me to plug the bullet hole with my thumb to see if I could feel anything. He then asked me to lift Brown's leg, to see if I could find an exit wound. I watched as Brown went from tan to white with the loss of blood. We had pulled a picture out of his flak jacket and we had to tap him on the face to keep him with us. We showed him a picture of his girlfriend, and all he said was, 'Get her done!' We stemmed the bleeding and they eventually medevaced him out."

"The position where Brown was hit, I had manned earlier. We eventually joked about how it could have been me instead of him," said Lance Corporal Castelli.

"I was upstairs when we started receiving incoming rounds. We saw two or three insurgents across the street, and we were given permission to fire a SMAW rocket at the house," said Lance Corporal Matthews. "Lance Corporal Khoeler, Lance Corporal Rokos, and Lance Corporal Carl went to this carport rooftop, while Sergeant Corey Menard and I helped in suppressing the enemy in the building from our window."

Rokos told Ackerman he could make the shot on the harassing sniper but from outside and on top of the roof of the carport. That was the only angle for a shot.

Ackerman said, "My assault men were doing incredible things. I saw bravery. Corporal Hall, Lance Corporal Karl, Lance Corporal Khoeler, and Corporal Rokos went out on a garage carport roof to set up to fire a SMAW rocket. This was the only position they could get the shot off at the sniper who had been working us over for an hour. Another Marine had gotten in the way of where the back blast would come, and Corporal Rokos tackled him just as the SMAW was fired. No one was hurt." As the rocket fired, the carport shook violently as the Marines hustled back into the safety of the house.

Other SMAW teams began running out into the open fire zone of the street setting up and firing, before turning and running back to the safety of the candy store while under constant enemy sniper fire.

The Marines were continually screaming to one another when spotting an enemy fighter, "I've got one in the first building! Check the second story window! Did you see that curtain move?" Ackerman recalled.

It became a fight of microseconds as the insurgents only showed themselves for just a few seconds on the rooftops, or in front of open doors and windows, giving them just enough time to squeeze off a round or two at the Marines before quickly ducking back down. Marine eyes searched for a puff of smoke or a muzzle flash from a firing weapon. Smoke and dust from the battle began hindering the combatants' ability to focus in on targets of opportunity.

Marine tanks pushed up and joined in the fray outside the candy store. "We got in a heavy fire fight all around the candy store," Tank commander Captain Meyers recalled. "Lieutenant Ackerman is directing my fire to buildings across the street from the candy store by firing red tracers from their machine guns. I ended up destroying a diner and an electronics building." The insurgents reached into their bag of goodies and began returning fire with RPGs against the Marine tanks. "We were getting hit with RPGs from our sides."

AAV number 12 was commanded by Gunnery Sergeant Lindeman. Rear crewman Lance Corporal Chad Patterson, 22, from the small town of Owasson, Oklahoma was riding in the very back of the vehicle. They were called on to head to the candy store in the thick of the fighting.

Patterson said, "I was standing up on a bench seat with both of the cargo hatches open and the top part of my bottom exposed when we got a call to go pick up some additional casualties at the candy store. Our vehicle and Staff Sergeant Green's AAV went to answer the call. We came out of the Government Center and we made a right turn down Ethan. Once we turned west it was chaos. All we heard was POP-POP!"

The amtrac Patterson was in was moving on the street near the candy store, sent to pick up the wounded Marines and to conduct a re-supply when it came under heavy fire from the enemy fighters. An RPG sizzled through the smoke of battle and hit the moving amtrac through its closed back hatch. The vehicle shook from the impact of the exploding round but remained in operating condition.

"There was just a loud explosion, BOOM, and then a ball of fire just burst in the back of the track. It knocked all of us on our backs, inside," Patterson said. "I was blown back toward the turret. I got up and checked to make sure I still had my arms and legs. I got on the intercom and yelled 'Fire!' We all got out and climbed up on the top of the track and the driver didn't know we were hanging on for our life. We were still moving at a good speed."

Located back at the Government Center, Staff Sergeant Shaw and his crew heard over the radio that one of their AAVs had been hit.

Lance Corporal Jonathan Olexa recalled hearing about the attack over the radio. "We heard Pappy's track had been hit. I thought, *Oh God*!"

Hanging on the top of the burning track were Patterson and Corporal Andrew Paine. The driver, Sergeant McGill, began evasive maneuvers to prevent another RPG hit. The Marines on the back were frantically screaming to get the driver to stop the vehicle. The back was on fire and sixty grenades along with ammunition were in danger of exploding.

"As Payne, the AAV driver, was fish tailing the track, the flames were getting higher. Payne was already burned from the initial explosion," Patterson remembered. "The hairs on my face and arms were starting to burn when Gunny Sergeant Lindeman climbed out from the turret and began crawling to the driver's station while we were still going fast. Lindeman hit McGill on the head to get his attention and to stop and let us get off. McGill finally pulled over on the side of the median. When the vehicle came to a stop we all jumped off."

Ultimately the amtrac stopped and First Sergeant Fry began getting his Marines out from the smoldering vehicle. Several of the AAV members suffered painful burns from the RPG round. Corporal Andrew Paine received burns to his hands and face, and Lance Corporal Chad Patterson suffered internal injuries to his knee.

"By the time we stopped the whole back of the track was engulfed in flames," Patterson said. "We ran for cover next to a building. Staff Sergeant Green's AAV came up behind us and did a hard left in the street and gave us covering fire."

The Marines who had come in to remove casualties from 1st Platoon had now become casualties themselves. Fry and the amtrac Marines made their way back to the Government Center while grenades cooked off and the vehicle burned to the ground.

Patterson's stay in Fallujah lasted only a day and a half. His fellow amtrackers medevaced him out of the city.

Fry gathered up his Marines and got another amtrac and delivered his re-supply to Alpha Company.

Ackerman said, "First Lieutenant Sunny Risler heard about the track getting hit, and took four of his Humvees and pushed to the candy store to get our wounded out. Out in the street, his vehicles were shooting everything up while we loaded our casualties into the Humvees."

The fight around the candy store raged on and off for two hours as the Marines continued rotating shifts up to the second floor firing positions. The Medevac arrived to pick up the wounded Marines escorted by Captain Meyers and two of his tanks. So far, the pinned down 1st Platoon had only suffered two wounded Marines in the fight.

Staff Sergeant Choquette, Weapons Platoon, recalls getting a call to retrieve wounded Marines from the candy store, "I had four vehicles and we had a call for a Medevac in Alpha Company at the pizza slice. The location they told us they were, they weren't, and we kept looking for them." Choquette's small convoy, escorted by two tanks, kept turning down side streets and passing by alleyways as they searched for 1st Platoon. They eventually heard firing and aimed towards it. "We finally pulled into a road and I saw a tank firing at a building. We began receiving fire from the insurgents, and then we realized that Alpha Company was across this highway so we drove over the berm. Now we found ourselves between the enemy and the Marines. I had heard that a good friend of mine, Staff Sergeant Cauthon had been hit in the head and another Marine had been hit in the femoral artery. When we arrived at the building and dismounted, we fired to help suppress the enemy while they brought the wounded out. I checked to make sure all of the casualties were accounted for and then we left."

"They took the opportunity to move up behind my tank and get the wounded Marines out of the candy store," Meyers said.

Fighting began to slacken somewhat when Meyers and Ackerman talked to one another on the radio. "Lieutenant Ackerman said he didn't see any enemy moving around at that time, so I pulled back and returned to the Government Center to link up with Captain Cunningham and push south with him," Captain Meyers recalls.

Earlier, tank platoon commander, Second Lieutenant Jeffery Lee, fresh from supporting the Marines of Battalion 1/3, had joined up with Alpha Company at noon at the Government Center only to find out he would be immediately joining in the push south. "I met with Captain Cunningham to basically get an Op Order as he was screaming over the radio to Lieutenant Ackerman to push his platoon out from the candy store. Ackerman was telling Cunningham that he couldn't push right now. I was told to go to my tanks and get hold of Lieutenant Ackerman on the radio that we needed to talk. That's how I met Captain Cunningham and that was my introduction to him as he said, 'Hey we're getting ready to push across Phase Line Fran. Lieutenant Ackerman needs you on the radio. You need to go back to your tanks and link up with him,'" Lee explained.

Tank platoon commander Lieutenant Lee remembered the push out of the Government Center and his drive south to relieve Ackerman's 1st Platoon under heavy fire at the candy store, "I busted through a stadium area at the center and out on to Phase Line Fran. I came straight down the street until Lieutenant Ackerman on the radio yelled, 'I'm right here! I'm off to your left at a candy store!' I looked over and saw a very colorful building and told him, 'I've got you!'" Lee's two tanks were now on line to support Ackerman. "He said, 'I'm taking sniper fire from the beach house.' The Marines called the building the beach house, because of a big sign with a picture of the ocean painted on it that was attached to the top of the building. Ackerman told me, 'Take that beach house out!' My section of two tanks came up and we just leveled the two-story beach house. I think it was really a hotel."

At 1500 Ackerman received a radio call from Lieutenant Krugman informing him that Captain Cunningham wanted him to pull out from the candy store, push south and link up with the rest of the platoon at Phase Line Blue.

Ackerman felt they didn't fully appreciate his platoon's predicament. "Sir, you don't know what's going on down here. We need to stay here until nightfall!" Ackerman told Krugman on the radio.

Lieutenant Krugman told him, "Be prepared to push south to Phase Line Blue!"

Ackerman persisted, "Sir, I don't think you understand what's happening here. We're heavily engaged!"

Ackerman was told that the company did understand the situation of his platoon, but he was to move south with his Marines ASAP. Cunningham needed his flank covered in his move south to Phase Line Blue.

Ackerman signed off the radio then ran up the stairs to the second floor and yelled to his Marines, "Grab your shit, we're moving! My Marines were a little apprehensive about the move during the daylight hours."

There was another problem. The only door from the candy store was located on the west side of the building, and the enemy had an RPK machine gun covering it. The insurgents knew the building had only one exit and they waited.

Ackerman ran back down the stairs to the first floor and stood looking out the front door. He glanced over at three pigeons sitting on an outside wall. He flinched as he witnessed three rounds impact the wall causing the pigeons to flutter up in the air before gently landing back on the wall. Ackerman realized right then that it would be suicide for his platoon to exit the only door.

Sergeant Stoy said, "We were told to push south at 1530, down an open street during the daytime and under fire with insurgents shooting RPGs and RPKs all over the place. Lieutenant Ackerman jumped out the door and into the street to see if we could go that way. He jumped right back in under a barrage of fire."

Ackerman strode over to his engineer, Corporal Luke Davy, and asked if he could blow one of the walls. Davy nodded his head in the affirmative and said it could be done.

Ackerman quickly told his engineer, "Go make it happen!"

Davy was going to use two sticks of C-4 plastic explosives to blow the hole in the wall. The new opening would be on the east side of the building, so Ackerman had all the Marines try and shield themselves as much as possible on the west wall.

The charge went off blowing a good size hole in the wall, three feet wide and about five feet tall, big enough for the Marines to exit the candy store in a crouching position. The controlled explosion threw up dust and dirt, adding to the acrid smell of gunpowder that permeated the inside of the building where shell casings littered the floor.

Coughing from the dust, Ackerman waited for the room to clear before ordering his 1st Platoon to push through the breached wall and out into the fresh air and sunlight of the street.

"The lieutenant was yelling to us, 'Go! Go! Go!' as we pushed out the hole one at a time. When we got out into the street we were fast walking in a low crouch," Castelli remembered. The Marines of 1st Platoon were trying to make as small a target as possible for the enemy snipers as they got in behind the tanks by squad in the open alleyway.

"We basically were attacking south, in stride, to link up under fire with the rest of the company. We left the building and turned south down an alley," Ackerman said.

The forty-three Marines that remained with Ackerman got behind the cover of two tanks in squads and began to link up with the rest of the company at Phase Line Blue. They had only gone a short distance from the candy store when they ran into another fierce firefight.

"As we moved along Haji Alley we began taking fire from the rooftops, alleyways and buildings all around us. We tried to clear it as fast as we could. It was shoot and run all the time. We had only gone about 200 meters, but it seemed like miles," Sergeant Stoy said.

Meanwhile, Captain Cunningham back at the Government Center prepared the rest of his company to push across Highway 10, then move down a parallel alley and to link up with Lieutenant Ackerman's Marines along Phase Line Blue. He recalled his Marines of 1st Platoon being under fire while in the candy store, "During the fight, Lieutenant Ackerman's platoon sergeant, Staff Sergeant Michael Cauthon, was shot in the head with his helmet on. The round skimmed through and back out of his helmet. It knocked him upside down and into Disneyland. Ackerman took a few other casualties in there, and we pushed out the amtrac to bring the wounded out when it got hit broadside with an RPG round. The amtrac ignited as First Sergeant Fry was able to get all of the Marines off the amtrac. I'm sure Lieutenant Ackerman felt a little isolated at that time in the city. His Marines were fighting in three different directions. He was calling in mortar fire to support his platoon. His 1st Platoon did an excellent job. 2nd and 3rd Platoons, and the rest of the company, attacked at 1400 on November 11 from the Government Center."

A Marine in Weapons Company, PFC Michael Johnson, recalled his platoon getting a call for support, "Alpha Company was pinned down and needed support to get across the main highway and needed some machine gun platforms. We rolled up with eight of them as bullets were bouncing off of our vehicles. We worked our way up to this house and dismounted our .50 cals, Mk19s and M-240Gs and set them up inside the building. We set up there for two or three days. I remember walking into one room with a .50 cal manned by Corporal Myers, and the floor was just covered with brass from the spent cartridges."

Alpha Company Marines of Barnes' 3rd Platoon began moving south. Nearby stood Chaplain Cox watching them grab their gear and weapons and begin their push down Haji Alley. Cox said, "Staff Sergeant Tim Oberst ran up to me and said, 'I need a blessing!' Before I knew it Staff Sergeant Sebastian and other Marines lined up for a quick blessing."

Watching from a rooftop at the Government Center, executive officer for the battalion, Major Mark Winn had a panoramic view of Alpha and Bravo Companies pushing south simultaneously. "It was amazing, as soon as they got out of sight down the streets it was like the Fourth of July. You could see RPGs and tracer rounds just going everywhere. I think that was the heaviest fighting, according to what I saw and heard over the radio. Both Bravo and Alpha Companies were heavily engaged south of Route Ethan. At that time we began receiving a lot of casualties. One of the smartest things we did was use the Government Center for both a logistics staging area and the battalion forward aid station. From anywhere on the battlefield, our wounded were only ten minutes from the aid station," recalled Winn.

"We attacked south to link up with Ackerman's platoon. I was walking with 3rd Platoon and it seemed like every building had guys with RPKs, RPGs and machine guns. We got maybe 30 meters in when we walked into a hornet's nest. I don't think they expected us to push, for we were up close and personal with the bad guys," remembered Captain Aaron Cunningham. "The shock quickly wore off as the word got out among the insurgents that we were coming and they just poured up from the south. We started taking considerable casualties. It took us almost four hours to travel 250 meters. After the first five minutes we were fighting the whole way. The tanks were just blasting houses, creating breach holes for the Marines to enter the buildings. We were killing guys in the houses and making our way up to rooftops so we could support the tanks. We moved slowly south in this constant slugfest. We fired almost every tank's main gun rounds, all of the coax, .50 cal and almost every rocket we had in this fight. The firing was so loud you actually had to scream on the radio just to be heard."

"We pushed across Phase Line Fran and went down Haji Alley. As soon as we crossed the highway we came under enemy fire. RPGs were bouncing off of the tanks and exploding in the streets. Some rounds that didn't have the safety removed would hit and just spin around before rolling harmlessly to the ground," recalled Lance Corporal Drew Martin, 2nd Platoon. "We pushed a thousand meters that day, and six hundred of them were under fire."

AAV Lance Corporal Jonathan Olexa said, "Alpha Company pushed out on foot from the Government Center and began clearing houses on both sides of the road. We had two tanks in front of us and we were moving slow. We had a SAW gunner or two in our track with us." Each column moving south had two AAVs in support.

Lance Corporal Christopher Lett, with a wife, Mattene, waiting for him at home in the states, pushed across with 3rd Platoon into the Hell fire of Haji Alley. He carried his M249 SAW weapon. "Once we came out of the building a squad at a time, we began bounding forward. When we pushed across the highway we began getting cover fire from Charlie and Weapons Companies," Lance Corporal Lett said. "We made it to the buildings across the highway and waited for the tanks and amtracs to come up and give us support. 1st Squad of 3rd Platoon started to clear the houses on the left-hand side of the alley, our 2nd Squad started clearing houses on the right side. There were two tanks with us in this narrow alley and they barely had room to maneuver their turrets to support us. We had most of the company going back and forth across the street clearing the houses. Every so often I would hear an RPG round explode. I heard a rocket whistling overhead and ducked behind one of the tanks just before it hit. Positioned behind the tank, I felt like I was being fried from its hot exhaust." Looking out from behind the tank, Lett saw an insurgent shooting at someone. He raised his SAW and fired a burst at the enemy fighter right before he ducked behind the tank again to shield himself from another rocket explosion. "I saw Staff Sergeant Sebastian behind me telling me to, 'Go, let's go!' I got up and looked for the guy that I had shot, but I didn't see him. I followed Staff Sergeant Sebastian to another building. I was right outside the gate when I heard another RPG round coming in. I dove inside the courtyard, landing on some glass and sliding into Sergeant Leo."

When Lett finally picked himself up he was surprised to see a Marine combat cameraman putting himself in harms way. "He was just standing among the carnage taking pictures of the fighting."

Although still separated from his squad, Lett kept moving. "I was separated from my squad and I had a bunch of HEDP rounds. Sergeant Leo said he needed some HEDP rounds so I gave him all I had. He then told me to link up with my fire team. Corporal Martinez and I entered a house where I heard something moving. We go into the bedroom and I saw a guy hiding under the bed. When the enemy started to crawl out we noticed he had a pistol in his hand. Martinez started shooting. He missed him and I unloaded about twenty rounds into the bed with my SAW. We kicked the bed out of the way and the guy was all shredded."

Sergeant Ricardo Sebastian, 32, a married Cuban-American from Miami, Florida, pushed down Haji Alley with Barnes' 3rd Platoon. "The houses were all two and three story shops and stores crammed together on this narrow alley. We reached an entrance to an 'L' shaped street that contained townhouses. We began receiving RPK fire and I saw Sergeant Leo on a knee at the entrance returning fire."

Sebastian ran up and joined in the firing. The Marines were firing at muzzle flashes emanating from behind a blue gate at one of the town houses. Sebastian called out and got one of the machine gun teams over to put some fire on the front gate. Corporal Bolen and Lance Corporal Barnes lay down in the prone position and began firing. The RPK continued to fire from near the blue gate at the Marines strung out along a wall.

Now Sebastian called up a SMAW team, Corporal Lemire and Corporal Baker, and told them he would lead them to where they were to fire the rockets with rounds from his M16A4 rifle. Sebastian stepped out into the open street and began firing. The SMAW gunners spotted where the rounds were hitting, and put three rounds on the gate and finally quelled the enemy fire.

"I told Lieutenant Barnes that we were going to have to clear all the houses on the 'L' shaped street. He agreed, and Sergeant Leo and his squad along with the two machine gunners, and I moved to the next house. I ran low on ammo and went back to where Cunningham and

Barnes were and the FO gave me his spare ammo," Sebastian said. Sebastian grabbed the magazines, said a quick thanks, and rejoined his Marines now going house to house down the 'L' shaped street.

It would take Sebastian and his fellow Marines of 3rd Platoon close to four hours to fully subdue the enemy in the townhouses along the L-shaped street.

The alley or street the AAV units, tanks and Alpha Company found themselves on, was barely wide enough to fit one vehicle. AAV driver Lance Corporal Jonathan Olexa said, "There were RPGs shooting out of this building 100 meters off down this narrow alley. The RPG bounced off the first tank and spiraled off up into the air and then bounced off the second tank and rolled next to our track."

Behind the steering wheel of the AAV, Olexa braced for the explosion that never came. Luckily for he and his crew it was a dud.

"I could have almost reached out and swatted it away, it was that close. During the push south was one of the scariest days I remembered in Fallujah," Olexa said.

Alpha Company Marines would run up to Olexa's AAV and request fire support on certain buildings. Olexa would relay the request to Staff Sergeant Shaw manning the .50 cal up-gun in the turret. Rounds would snake forward from the vehicle to balconies and open windows where the Marines had received enemy fire.

Fighting to link up with Captain Cunningham and the rest of Alpha Company at Phase Line Blue, Lieutenant Ackerman's 1st Platoon was on the move again through the narrow twisting alleyways. The tanks were leading the way, with Ackerman's platoon following, and bringing up the rear were two amtracs that had joined them from the Government Center. Farther back, Iraqi Security Forces followed along.

"Muj rounds were coming in from the rooftops and hitting all around us and off the tanks," Ackerman remembered. "We were so close to the tanks that when the rounds from the main gun were fired it physically hurt. It felt like your guts were being pulled out through your asshole."

The noise was so earsplitting that Ackerman had a hard time communicating with his Marines and the tanks. Marines would run up to him to yell something and all he saw was the movement of their mouth. No sound matched their lips. The fighting was becoming chaotic. At times, Ackerman would run up to the back of the tank to use their radio to bring their heavy fire on enemy targets, and there was an abundance of enemy targets. He would ask the tankers if they saw the house with the red roof, second floor? They would answer, 'Roger that!' Ackerman would scream one word, 'Engage!' The main tank gun would take out the target and then move on. This is how it went hour after harrowing hour as they fought down Haji Alley.

Sergeant Banotai was knocked almost unconscious from the shock wave from the firing of a nearby tank's 120mm gun. Marines helped Banotai up on his wobbly legs as they continued pushing south.

It became hard to hear anything on the company radio with the entire company and the tanks all using it. And when Ackerman did get to use the radio, he couldn't hear half the words being spoken because of the cacophony of the fighting. Ackerman continually worked to keep the tanks from moving too fast down the alley and out running his Marines. Because of the many enemy fighters his Marines fought south at what seemed like a snails pace. A few days later Ackerman would lose his voice from shouting commands at the top of his lungs to his Marines and into the radio along Haji Alley.

At one point Lieutenant Ackerman went down on one knee trying to use the radio, while his radioman, Lance Corporal Nick Ames, protected him by firing his M16 at enemy targets along the rooftops. With the CRACK CRACK of Ames' M16 in the background, Ackerman worked the radio. He received a garbled radio call trying to tell him to keep pushing to Phase Line Blue. "Say again!" he shouted into the radio over the din of battle. The order was repeated and acknowledged. It had become a slugfest along Haji Alley. Ackerman and Ames ran across an intersection and both of them turned and fired their M16s, one firing down the street on the right, and the other working over the left street.

"We saw some insurgents on a rooftop firing down at us," recalled Lance Corporal Matthews. "We had two tanks with us which had escorted the casualty amtrac in to pick up the wounded at the candy store. One insurgent fired an RPG that wounded a corporal, and I took a round right through the buttstock of my SAW."

The Marines were taking so much fire from the rooftops and the open windows along the alley that eventually, according to the law of averages, some of the rounds began hitting the moving Marines. Lance Corporal Cabang said, "We entered this alley and Corporal Chris Hoffman took a round to the palm of his hand and started yelling, 'I'm shot! I'm shot!' He ran back looking for a corpsman. Corporal Latva yelled, 'Follow Me!'"

Rounds were impacting the walls of the alleyway, chipping pieces of cinder block and scattering them on the Marines. Cabang and Corporal Latva stared down the alley at four insurgent fighters only 50 meters away. One insurgent was on a knee on the ground and was preparing to fire an RPG at them. Cabang could see the face of the enemy fighter as he discharged the RPG that screamed down the alley toward them giving

Cabang and Latva no time to take cover or even drop to the ground. Cabang froze. "It came on so fast and hit the right side of the wall. BANG! It threw chunks of cinder and shrapnel at us. Latva went down with a wound to his right arm and leg. The concussion knocked me down and I took a small piece of shrapnel to my leg. I didn't know it had even drawn blood until later," Cabang said.

Ackerman said, "I saw the RPG round coming in. It looked like a football and exploded on the wall. Rokos and I ran over to Latva and grabbed him and pulled him out of the alley, while Opon with his SAW ran over, dropped down, and suppressed the enemy by firing down the alleyway."

"Sir, I got him! You don't have to worry about him!" Rokos told his lieutenant as he helped Latva back to the corpsman. Rokos knew his lieutenant had his hands full directing his platoon in the fight along the alley.

Fighting in the hot sun with all of their heavy gear, sweat ran down their faces and backs. It soaked their fatigues. Dust, dirt, and grime mixed with sweat coated their faces. The Iraqi heat was also thinning the ranks of the Marines as several passed out from heat stroke. They were either helped to the amtracs or carried along by their buddies.

"When we were in Haji Alley we were taking fire from every direction," Lance Corporal Roopnarine recalled. "We couldn't see where the fire was coming from because the insurgents were shooting through these mouse holes in the walls. Four rounds impacted into my machine gun sling. I was lucky not to lose an arm from those rounds"

An enemy fighter shot Lance Corporal Brian Passolt in the back as he fought his way through Haji Alley, and his fellow Marines helped Passolt into a waiting amtrac. In addition there was an assortment of non-hostile casualties taking its toll on the ranks, such as twisted knees and sprained ankles. One of Ackerman's medics, Doc Martinez, became a casualty when he blew his knee out while pushing through the littered alleyway.

Tanks had joined Captain Cunningham's Marines fighting south down a parallel street only a block over from Ackerman's 1st Platoon. The Marines who fought there called both streets Haji Alley. Marine tank commander Captain Chris Meyers said, "The heaviest most intense firefight I have ever been in was Haji Alley."

Cunningham watched as an insurgent fired an RPG round only 30 meters away from him. It whizzed toward him before landing a few meters in front of where he was standing. Bracing for an explosion he watched as the round skipped past him and went on down the street, failing to detonate. Other Marines saw the flash of RPG rounds being fired at them and detonating, some within 15 meters from them, adding more shrapnel to the already rubble filled streets.

The Marines of Alpha Company punching south continued to clear almost every house as they bounded forward. Most houses were empty of enemy fighters but when they found insurgents, they were routed out of their firing positions and killed. Alpha Company was moving like a well-oiled machine as they cleared one house after the other, from the first floor to the rooftops, in the process taking out any enemy fighters they found.

"We kept clearing the houses in a crisscross movement through Haji Alley. As we ran across the street, we could feel the hot blast of the exhaust from the back of the tanks. I ended up with another fire team in my squad who had two engineers attached to it," Lance Corporal Lett said. "We stacked up near the front gate of a house. We waited for the command 'Go!' The first man kicked the door open and we could see into the open courtyard."

Lance Corporal Lett recounted, "We approached the house and we couldn't find the door as it was all covered with vines. I looked through a window to see if I could see anyone. I asked Lance Corporal Gomez if he had a frag. He moved up to the window and threw it in. He screamed 'Frag out!' We ducked behind some cover as the grenade went off. We still couldn't get through the door, so one of the engineers put a plastic charge on it. The door didn't budge. While they were setting the second charge, I saw Lance Corporal Coffman on a wall looking down at the courtyard. He found another opening that led to the wall of the house. I yelled to the other Marines, 'There's another door over here!' Coffman was first, then me, followed by Lance Corporal Walleri all running to the opening in the wall. Before we reached the door we heard a rocket coming in from the west. It came in so fast and exploded against the house we hardly had time to react. It spread shards of metal and pieces of concrete all over us. We ran back where we came from. The engineer then blew the door. The door flew across to the other side of the building. We waited for the smoke to clear before we went in. Walleri and I rushed into the house. It was dark inside and smoky and hazy from the charge. We found no enemy fighters downstairs in the house, but a couple of the guys went upstairs and killed one insurgent."

Captain Cunningham said, "Urban fighting was intense. I had been in a couple of minor gunfights before, but nothing like that. The overwhelming intensity and ferocity was unbelievable. As a company commander my weapons are my radios that link me to my lieutenants. I didn't fire a shot in the city." Busy working the radios with his platoon commanders, calling in air, mortars or artillery, he sometimes lost awareness of what was happening only a few feet away. Cunningham admitted, "I had a great headquarters section that kept me alive. Sometimes I was oblivious to what was in front of me. I would see bad guys and see Marines drop them. The map of Fallujah was burned in my brain although I also had a paper copy on me. I envisioned myself in a hot air balloon above the city. I couldn't see the platoon next to me, even though they may have been only twenty feet away. By envisioning the city from above, I could control the tanks, indirect fire and platoons. When I didn't have great awareness five feet in front of me, that's when First Sergeant Fry or Gunny Sergeant Cully would tell me, 'Hey sir, get your ass out of the street!' They were my protection."

When Cunningham envisioned the part of Fallujah he was fighting in, he did it with the map of Fallujah in his mind. What he saw of the map right now didn't encourage him. The slice of pizza, down to Phase Line Henry, was a crisscross grid of streets and alleyways jammed clumsily together. All of the houses and buildings had rooftops that could harbor enemy snipers. The advantage was with the insurgents as they fired down at the Marines scrambling along the open streets below.

Meanwhile a block over, one of Ackerman's Marines, Lance Corporal Steven St.Claire, Jr., Weapons Platoon, recalls, "We were following the amtracs when they called a security halt and we maneuvered around some buildings. I looked over to my left 75 meters away at a building surrounded by a pretty high wall with a man lying beside it. No one knew if he was dead or not. I was keeping a watch on him when someone hollered that we're moving. So I got up and I looked down the road again and saw an RPG flying towards me."

Lance Corporal St.Claire was mesmerized. He couldn't take his eyes off the glowing red spiraling RPG round flying as if in slow motion from down the street and straight toward him. The round hit and bounced near his feet. As soon as it touched the ground it spun past him, careened on down the street and exploded. St.Claire turned to look at Lance Corporal Castle who had been standing by the wall directly behind him. "Castle had this weird look on his face, like he had just somehow escaped death. There was a hole in the wall where the RPG had finally hit." In fact, both Marines had narrowly escaped death from the RPG.

While fighting down the alley, Corporal Chris Hoffman took shrapnel to his right leg and forearm from an exploding enemy grenade or RPG round.

"The enemy was firing from every direction. An RPK opened up on us and the fire hit PFC Gary Koehler," Roopnarine recalled.

"The one I remember the most was PFC Koehler," Sergeant Stoy said. "He took an AK-47 round to the thick of the thigh on his left leg. He looked at me and asked me if he was going to be all right. I said, 'Yeah. You're fine.' PFC Gary Koehler, bleeding from the round to his left thigh, was helped to the safety of an amtrac.

"As we kept pushing down Haji Alley, 1st Platoon took several more casualties," Stoy remembered. "I remember piling a bunch of them in the amtracs. They had various wounds, from RPG shrapnel to AK-47 fire and were medevaced out of the city later that night."

At that time, Ackerman's 1st Platoon had quickly suffered seven casualties and he now moved his 2nd Squad to lead from the front. There were so many wounded that Doc Jordan Holtschulte had his hands full during the fight along Haji Alley. When they had to move, it took almost all of the unwounded Marines to help assist the wounded. At this time in the fight, there were just a handful of effectives to carry on.

Ackerman picked the first house in a row of houses south of Phase Line Blue to get his beleaguered platoon safely into. His sweaty and grimy Marines were strung out along a wall, seeking protection from the incoming enemy rounds. He screamed to his men to follow him into the house. No one heard him with all of the noise of the firing going on. The Marines in Haji Alley were now totally caught up in the chaos of the battle.

"Get in the f***ing the house!" Ackerman shouted again.

Once more no one heard him over the noise of the fighting. He started waving his arm to catch his Marines' attention and still no one noticed. Ackerman thought, *What the f***!* He now began waving both hands above his head and pointing to the house to get his men's attention. Finally he barreled his way through the gate and pushed into the two-story house. His 1st and 2nd Squads at last followed their lieutenant into the safety of the building. Ackerman's 3rd Squad ran to a three-story house across the street.

"We set up a casualty collection point in the house and the NCOs began to reorganize the men," Ackerman said.

1st Platoon was now south of Phase Line Blue. Ackerman got on the radio and was told by Captain Cunningham to 'Go firm! Go firm!' but they had to go firm north of Phase Line Blue, not where they were presently positioned south of that line. The tanks were going to be working over that area. Ackerman along with his 1st Squad left the house and bounded north of Phase Line Blue to the house already occupied by his 3rd Squad. Corporal Long and his 2nd Squad were expected to follow along immediately.

Corporal William Long was fighting in Fallujah for the second time that year. In April, Long had belonged to Battalion 3/4 during the first major fighting in the city. Now finding himself back again, Long's 2nd Squad started to leave the house south of Phase Line Blue and follow in trace of Ackerman when they were fired on from the upstairs inside the house. Rounds and grenades began shattering walls and windows as the Marines hurriedly took cover.

When Ackerman and 1st Squad joined his 3rd Squad in the three-story house, he found Sergeant Garret Barton upstairs with the Iraqi Security Forces talking to them in Arabic. Sergeant Barton had taken it upon himself to learn Arabic and now he had the Iraqis on the rooftop lighting up the insurgents below. Again, *improvise, adapt and overcome*.

Ackerman was surprised that his 2nd Squad was still back at the house that he had just left. He asked Sergeant Menard if he had seen 2nd Squad.

"No sir. I haven't seen them," Menard answered.

Looking back, Ackerman realized Long's Marines were taking fire from inside the house. He quickly grabbed the radio and contacted Corporal Long to assess his situation.

"We're stuck in the house sir and we've got to get out!" Long told his lieutenant.

Lieutenant Ackerman quickly ran outside the house picked up an Iraqi flag attached it to an eight foot pole and began waving it to attract the attention of four Marine amtracs idling down the street. Taking a page from the insurgent handbook, Ackerman continued waving the flag back and forth until the amtracs got the message and pulled up to where the 1st Platoon commander was standing. Marines had seen the insurgents signaling with flags in different parts of the city. This was yet another example of *improvise, adapt and overcome* by 1/8 Marines.

In the house with Corporal Long, Sergeant Stoy said, "As we pushed down Haji Alley, we ended up in front of a building on the eastern border of our zone. Lance Corporal Darlan Bastidas and several other Marines and I took some shrapnel and pretty much got cut off from the rest of the platoon. We found out they had pushed back and set up for the night in another house." Sergeant Daniel Stoy, Weapons Platoon, divorced father of twin boys, had taken shrapnel to his lower left leg from a grenade thrown in the house but continued to fight on.

"The insurgents were shooting RPGs and RPKs at us like it was candy going out of style. Finally, Lieutenant Ackerman found out we were separated from the rest of the platoon and stuck in this house. Ackerman jumped out in the middle of the road and did jumping jacks, while under fire, to get the attention of the Marines in the amtracs. He finally got the amtracs attention," Sergeant Stoy recalled.

"I had a face-to-face with Lieutenant Morris of amtracs," Ackerman said. "I told him that my 2nd Squad was pinned down in the building, and I wanted him to provide cover for them while they moved to my position. The amtracs pulled across the street and idled while Long's Marines loaded up and Morris brought them to where we were."

Second Lieutenant Elliot Ackerman's 1st Platoon was now re-united in the three-story house just north of Phase Line Blue. It had taken them almost five hours of fierce fighting to go barely 400 meters south down Haji Alley and then a short way back to where they were now located. Ackerman had six Marines positioned on the second floor, and the rest of his platoon on the rooftop shooting south.

Ackerman turned to Sergeant Menard and said, "I need to know how many effectives we have."

A few minutes later Menard returned to his lieutenant. "Hey sir, We have twenty-one effectives."

Ackerman only had twenty-one of the original forty-six Marines of 1st Platoon who had pushed south with him from the Government Center earlier that morning.

Surprised at just how few of his Marines remained in the fight, all he could say to his sergeant was, "Jesus!" Ackerman quickly got on the radio and passed along the amount of effectives he had in his platoon to his captain. "Captain Cunningham later told me, 'I was real worried about you guys right then,'" Ackerman said.

Ackerman and his Marines on the roof were working over targets to the south as well as marking targets for the tanks when a salvo of RPGs slammed into a ten-foot high wall on the back part of the roof. BOOM! BOOM! BOOM! And then, a second salvo hit BOOM! BOOM! BOOM! As the RPG rounds slammed into the cinder block wall they scattered shrapnel and deadly chunks of debris on the prone Marines. Shrapnel cut into the right shoulders of both Corporal Ronald Carrozino and machine gun Team Leader, Sergeant Garret Barton.

Picking himself up and shaking the dust off, Ackerman yelled to the injured Sergeant Barton, "Take everyone and get the f*** off the roof! I stayed along with Bejrano, who had the M-240G, and we took turns working over the row of houses to our south. The enemy was firing from the windows and we marked those targets for the tanks with tracer rounds." While on the rooftop, Ackerman began calling for indirect fire on targets to within only 90 meters of their position.

Downstairs, Executive Officer Lieutenant Krugman walked in and looked around at all of the platoon's casualties. He didn't see any officers and asked the Marines, "Who the f*** is in charge?" A low voice from one of the wounded Marines lying on the floor was heard to answer, "Doc." The medic was in charge downstairs with all the wounded.

"Krugman came upstairs and said to me, 'I know you guys had a hard day with all the casualties,'" Ackerman recalled.

"Our squad was down to three or four effectives at the end of the day's fighting," Lance Corporal Roopnarine of 1st Platoon remembered.

Captain Cunningham recounted, "That day was the most intense and longest we had in Fallujah. It was a four-hour long fight. After the first fifteen minutes there was so much fighting going on, I was too busy to call back to battalion. I didn't need any support, I was too busy fighting my company. Battalion heard the volume of fire and the operations officer, Major Trimble, called on the radio and asked my radio operator 'Do you have contact?' My radio operator didn't want to bother me because I was on the company phone talking to my platoon commanders, so he held the phone up next to a SMAW rocket as it was fired. Trimble hearing the firing said, 'I understand. I'll leave you alone.'"

Amtracker, Staff Sergeant Chris Shaw recalls the fight down Ambush Alley, "The distance we traveled was only about two hundred meters. We had started the attack about 1500 and it was dusk when we set in for the night."

To attest to the amount of RPGs and grenades being thrown and fired by the insurgents, the shrapnel wounds suffered by the Marines began to steadily mount. PFC Aaron Begley took shrapnel wounds to the right foot and was medevaced out, and Corporal Daniel Lemiere took shrapnel to his right forearm during the attack south. The ranks were thinning fast for Alpha Company.

Enemy fighters in Haji Alley took a heavy toll on the Marines of Alpha Company. Ackerman's 1st Platoon alone took twenty-five casualties during that one day of savage fighting, only two of which had happened earlier while they were holed up in the confines of the candy store.

Lieutenant Ackerman's 1st Platoon and Captain Cunningham, leading the rest of the company, finally linked up along Phase Line Blue. Alpha Company was now consolidated again. With darkness the fighting subsided, and the sweaty Marines worked over their MREs and tried to grab some much-needed sleep.

Many Marines began to actually admire the fighting abilities of the insurgents they met in Fallujah. They hated the terrorists and what they stood for, but as warriors themselves, the Marines could recognize courage in others. Outnumbered now by three or four to one, the insurgents fought the only way they could, from inside windows and hidden on rooftops and in some cases, fighting from tunnels beneath houses. Sometimes fighting alone or in small groups, the enemy tried to keep the pressure on the advancing Marines. Very seldom in the city did they attack the Marines with a large force. The insurgents fought against the massive array of firepower of the American forces and kept coming at them, and that alone created admiration from their Marine foes. The insurgents fought in Fallujah as the Marines had fought for centuries: they took casualties but kept coming. But in Fallujah, the terrorists had met their match. The Marines wrote the book on this kind of warfare, and they knew how to blunt the attacks. In Fallujah, the students were being taken to the woodshed by the masters of this fighting style. Though bloodied and battered, the Marines were relentless and to put it bluntly, they were kicking ass.

"We took over twenty casualties in that fight on November 11 and we were lucky that we didn't lose any Marines that day," said Captain Cunningham. "At 2100 we finally went firm for the night. At this point, I had only slept for an hour or two in over two days."

During that day, Lieutenant Colonel Gary Brandl, with only three of his four vehicles, pushed south from the Government Center to link up with Captain Cunningham and his Alpha Company fighting toward Phase Line Henry down Haji Alley. To mark their position for Brandl's three-vehicle convoy, Alpha Company popped a smoke round high above their fighting position along Haji Alley. The winds had caused the smoke to drift steadily eastward. The Humvees carrying Brandl and Gunner Athey sped toward the drifting smoke, and away from Alpha Company. After traveling a few minutes, Brandl and his Headquarters Company Marines now found themselves the lead element of the battalion deep inside the city among the dangerous winding alleyways.

"We had pushed some 600 meters south from the Government Center and still hadn't found Alpha Company." Floridian, Sergeant Kelley Starling remembered, "The lieutenant colonel received a radio call from Alpha Company saying, 'Stop, you are too far ahead of us!' Gunner Athey and two of the Marines dismounted the vehicles and with weapons at the ready, walked alongside providing security, while we began turning around to go back north. A head popped up near us and then an RPG round came whizzing over, hitting a wall right behind us and detonating with a loud BOOM! The Marines in the street hit the deck as I bumped the driver and yelled, 'Let's go! Go! Go!' Lance Corporal Federichi, Brandl's gunner, began working his weapon and took out three of the insurgents. Then we started taking fire from our rear. I fired eight rounds from my M16A4 at about five or six guys who were firing at us from inside a house. As we drove by one of the insurgents that Federichi had hit, I saw an RPG lying beside the body."

Lance Corporal Federichi, Weapons Company, attached to Brandl's group, screamed, "Muj everywhere!" As Brandl's three Humvee drivers tried to get their vehicles spun around and push back north, the cavalry arrived in the nick of time. In fact, it was truly the U.S. Cavalry from the Army's 2/2. An American Bradley fighting vehicle rolled down a street from the east, quickly assessed the situation, and fired into the house that held the insurgents. Gunner Athey and the other Marines hastily climbed back into the Humvees carrying the lieutenant colonel and began speeding back north to finally link up with Alpha Company in Haji Alley.

Bravo Company's Fight Pushing to Phase Line Grace

At 1400 Eckert's 1st Platoon, Bravo Company, stepped out from the Iraqi National Guard compound and secured a house located south of the Phase Line Fran and Route Ethan intersection. Now with all of his infantry platoons on line, Omohundro gave the order to move farther south to Phase Line Blue, at the same time Alpha Company was attacking down Haji Alley and stirring up a hornet's nest.

First Lieutenant Noble's FiST Team got into a fight right before sunset as they attacked south. FiST, which had earlier moved from the Michelin building and linked up with Wilkens' 3rd Platoon, held up in a house for a short time before receiving an order to keep moving with the company.

FiST member Sergeant Shawn Gianforte remembered the twilight action, "We were moving up trying to find another house for the night. As we moved we had our eyes on some armed insurgents in a house. Where we were located we couldn't get an angle on them. We called in some AAVs and when they pulled up they began laying suppressive fire on the house so we could move up the street. As we're running by the AAVs, I could see rounds ricocheting off of the vehicles. I said to myself, 'Oh shit here we go again!' I made myself get as low as I could in a crouch and still run. We were running to an area only 20 meters from where the amtracs were firing. It wasn't that far of a run, but as we were running there was a hole that was maybe six feet in diameter to get across before we went into the building. So, a whole platoon was trying to get over the hole at once and we started to get bunched up. Lieutenant Noble and I set up security while the guys ran across. Out of the corner of my eye I saw someone rolling around on the ground. I couldn't hear anything with all the firing going on with the amtracs supplying suppressive fire for us. I finally heard the man yell, 'I've been hit!' Then I realized it was Lieutenant Noble's voice. I turned around and the ground was just kicking up from incoming enemy rounds. I said, 'Oh shit!' I moved over to where Lieutenant Noble had gone down and I tried to give him some protection until Staff Sergeant Parry, Gunnery Sergeant Tom Scudder, and Lieutenant Collins came up and got Lieutenant Noble into the safety of a house. I was firing at muzzle flashes."

First Lieutenant Vince Noble, 26, from Philadelphia, Pennsylvania, Fire Support Team Leader, had taken a round in his left leg with the large caliber bullet lodging in the bone. 3rd Platoon's Corpsman Ruizpupo checked out the wound and administered to it. Lieutenant Collins picked up his fellow officer and all of his gear like a fireman and carried him out to the amtrac as Parry and Scudder went out to supply security while Noble was medevaced out immediately. Sergeant Gianforte posted up at the corner of the building to make sure the amtrac got out. "Whenever the enemy fired, the amtracs would quickly dump a lot of rounds at the enemies muzzle flashes," Gianforte said.

Captain Omohundro recalled, "I was standing behind a sand pile working the radio and didn't notice rounds impacting behind me along a wall. First Sergeant Whittington grabbed me by the collar and pulled me back to safety. He said, 'Damn it sir, get the f*** out of the way!' He was not only my first sergeant, but also a good friend. He saved me from myself quite a few times in the city."

After meeting very little resistance, at 1500 Bravo reached Phase Line Blue. "We began to secure a house and set up a base for the night but we ended up moving again. Lieutenant Collins took over command of our FiST Team as we pushed toward a mosque and went firm for the remainder of the night," said Sergeant Gianforte

Bravo Company was then ordered to keep pushing south to Phase Line Grace and to assist the friendly Iraqi forces in the taking of another mosque the next morning.

In the darkness of November 11, at 2200, Bravo Company was still pushing south to Phase Line Grace to establish a temporary firm base. As the Marines advanced they would leave small brown stains on the ground, sides of buildings and the floors of homes from chewing their Copenhagen smokeless tobacco as they fought and pushed through the littered streets of Fallujah. The Marines were Copenhagening the city as they moved. When not in action, the Marines would sometimes break into the Garth Brooks' country song about the smokeless tobacco:

Copenhagen, what a wad of flavor
Copenhagen, you can see it in my smile
Copenhagen, hey do yourself a favor, dip
Copenhagen, it drives the cowgirls wild

Captain Omohundro explained, "Just south of Phase Line Blue, 1st Platoon turned right at a corner and one of its squads entered a narrow alley. They made out some Iraqis 50 meters away dressed in the same desert utilities that the Iraqi Security Forces were wearing. Our Marines weren't sure if they were friendly or not, so they waved at the Iraqis. The Iraqis waved back and then opened fire with machine guns. The uniforms were so perfect, they even had the red and white tape to signify friendly Iraqis."

In the darkness of the alley in Fallujah, nine camo-wearing insurgents quickly dropped their charade and fired on the unsuspecting Marines of Bravo Company's 1st Platoon. Huntington, New York native, Corporal Scott Nolin's squad immediately came under heavy enemy fire. The uninjured scrambling Marines hid behind small cement steps or any other concealment they could find along the littered alley to help shield them from the accurate machine gun fire and sniper fire.

Assaultman, Corporal Nick Criddle said, "I had just cut the corner and moved 20 meters into the alley when the enemy machine gun began firing at our point man Lance Corporal Domenech, about 25 meters in front of me. Domenech, Russell and Anderson were all hit from the intense fire. One of my squad members, Lance Corporal Kelly, was walking opposite me and dove behind some concrete stairs for cover. I dove behind a bush. From up front I heard Corporal O'Brien who was unhurt yell, 'Contact! Guys down!' I could hear Russell screaming after being hit. Any time we tried to move, the insurgent machine gun would fire. We were pinned down."

The insurgent snipers were working from both sides of the alley, while their machine gun team fired from the middle, hitting three Marines. Corporal Nathan Anderson, 22, from Howard, Ohio was hit instantly from the initial burst of enemy fire. He was hit on his left side. Anderson who had wanted to be a Marine since he was ten-years-old had been one of those who had earlier risked his life at the intersection near the Cultural Center to help rescue the wounded Marines. Lance Corporal

Andrew Russell, 22, automatic rifleman from Fort Edwards, New York took fire to his right leg and fell to the pavement. His leg was almost severed by the impact of the large caliber bullets tearing at bone and flesh. A third Marine, Lance Corporal Carlos Domenech, took shrapnel to his left elbow and right shoulder. The wounded Marines were now totally pinned down as they lay in the alley.

Coming from the darkness Second Lieutenant Andy Eckert saw green tracer rounds coming out of the alleyway to his front. The enemy used green tracer rounds and the Marines red tracers. He tried to reach his squad leader, Corporal Nolin, on the inter-squad radio to tell him to pull back out of the alley. He got no response from his squad leader who was under heavy machine gun fire. A few seconds later, Nolin managed to reach his lieutenant saying that they were pinned down and had already taken three casualties. Now Eckert had to make a snap decision, to push into the alleyway and put more of his Marines in danger or try to find a more advantageous position to bring fire down on the enemy fighters.

"With the amount of fire coming from that alley, I felt that any Marine turning that corner would be cut down," Eckert said.

Moving behind 1st Squad, 1st Platoon Sergeant Sam Williams' job was to help stabilize any wounded Marine. He looked toward the opening to the alley and watched as green tracer rounds poured out of the darkness. "I ran up to the corner and yelled for SAW gunner Corporal Mora to follow me to the other side where we could lay some fire down on the enemy located in the alleyway. I ran across and slid into an IED with about eight 155mm rounds daisy chained together. I ran back across the alley and away from the apparently failed IED," Williams said.

At that moment someone yelled that there was an IED in the alleyway. Hearing that, Eckert decided to take Corporal Jacob Knospler's squad north to the next street and then push west. Once there, he would take the high ground in the upper deck of a building over looking the ambush in the alleyway. The Marines entered a house and ran up to the rooftop to find a fire support position to assist the pinned down Marines, but the house didn't have a view of the alley. Frustrated, the Marines quickly ran back down the stairs and entered the house next door and ran up the stairs to the roof. Once on the rooftop, they could only see a small portion of the alley. They couldn't see the enemy fighters or the pinned down Marines.

Meanwhile in the alley, rounds were impacting the street around the prone Marines chipping the pavement as they hit. Tracer rounds from the enemy machine gun continued to pour from the entrance of the alley.

The insurgents had set up a kill zone in the alleyway for the advancing Marines to walk into and had executed it to deadly perfection.

As Eckert, carrying his M4 carbine, was running with Knospler's squad to seek a better fire position, Staff Sergeant Eric Brown and Sergeant Aubrey McDade were running toward the alleyway that held the pinned down Marines. McDade rushed from the rear of the column toward the kill zone. Brown had heard on the radio about the casualties, and reaching the entrance to the alley, he kept leaning out to assess the situation. He would pull back when the enemy fire got close to him. Brown asked McDade if he could get a machine gun in the alley and lay down a base of fire. McDade from Weapons Platoon answered, "Heck yeah! I can get it done!"

Brown shouted, "All right, do it!"

McDade, along with Lance Corporal Kulbis, took the gun into the alleyway. Kulbis set up the machine gun in the street and began returning suppressive fire on the insurgents. Brown and a corpsman also ran into the alley and entered the first courtyard they came to.

Every time the Marines tried to reach their fallen comrades the enemy laid down a blanket of fire.

McDade with his gun in action ran out and to pull the wounded Marines out from the alley. Using his body to cover one of the wounded Leathernecks, he advised him to loosen his gear and then hoisted him over his shoulder. He carried the Marine to safety before returning to the kill zone in the alley for a second Marine. A combat photographer with the Marines jumped in and helped grab one of the wounded Marines.

Brown coordinated with Sergeant Williams, Lance Corporal Miller, Corporal Mora and Corporal Jason Huyghe, 22, a native of Dover, Ohio, 2nd Squad Leader, to climb up on the roof of the building from the courtyard with a few of his Marines. Corporal Huyghe, Sergeant Williams and the other Marines made it to the rooftop, and from there, the four Marines began pouring heavy fire down at the enemy fighters in the alley.

"We poured so much fire into the alley that our M16s were red hot." Sergeant Williams remembered, "I must have fired 200 rounds and I had to pry my magazine from the chamber of my rifle because it had expanded so much from the heat."

The Marines firing from the rooftop, along with those still pinned down in the street, and Corporal Kulbis working the machine gun, began to have an effect on the insurgents. The enemy fire began to slacken just when the tanks arrived and added their firepower to the mix. Four of the enemy fighters had been killed in the fighting which allowed a few others to escape.

Corporal Criddle remembered, "When the tank rolled up, McDade used the phone on the back of the tank to direct him where to shoot. Once the tank began working over the insurgents we pulled out."

Eckert, standing on the rooftop, could hear the firing below but still couldn't see the fighting, the enemy fighters or his pinned down Marines. "I passed Brown earlier and we didn't exchange any information. I should have taken a few seconds to communicate with him at that time. I basically had taken Knospler's squad and myself out of the fight. No one was manning the radio at that time which we should have been doing," Eckert said. "We heard the tanks and we went back to link up with the rest of the platoon. Although I had moved from the alley, I was proud of my Marines. They got the job done. Staff Sergeant Brown did a great job in that situation."

Earlier, after seeing Eckert run into a building followed by several Marines, Captain Omohundro had gotten on the radio and called in the tanks to support 1st Platoon in the recovery effort of the casualties.

Hearing the firing, Corpsman HM3 Jones rushed to assist the Bravo Company casualties being pulled from the alley. "They got the wounded back to a house on the corner and we began patching them up. They were in pain and asking for morphine and I was tearing up. One of them was one of the guys I was really close to. The Team Leader, Anderson, was already dead by the time we got to him. I tried to resuscitate him, but it was too late. I started throwing things I was so mad at losing a Marine. He was a close friend of mine. We put the poncho over him and called for amtracs. The other corpsman and I talked to each other about staying focused, keeping our heads up and staying in the game because we were losing a lot of guys," Jones said.

The uniformed insurgents were most likely former members of the Fallujah Brigade, another one of our ideas gone horribly wrong for the Marines who stumbled upon them in the dark streets of Fallujah.

Sergeant Williams said, "Basher told us that there were nine bad guys fighting us in the alleyway."

Captain Omohundro recalled the act of bravery during the fighting by one of his Marines, Sergeant Aubrey McDade from Houston, Texas. "Sergeant McDade, my machine gun section leader from our Weapons Platoon, who was attached to this platoon, ends up moving into harms way. He literally lay down suppressive fire and ran into the kill zone three times, to pull those wounded Marines back to safety. We dropped four insurgents in the fight," Omohundro said. "We set up a casualty collection point, and I called in tanks that oriented down the road and the amtracs came in and evacuated the Marines back to the Government Center. My Marines were shaken by the incident. I talked to one of my officers to re-orient him back on the mission. We had reached a quagmire, no one was moving. I finally said, 'We're moving!'" The tired Marines from Bravo Company picked themselves up and pushed south.

One of the hardest things a Marine officer has to be able to do is to continue to focus on the mission when suffering casualties under his command. The tragedies of having Marines go down is devastating to an officer. Usually a bond has formed over the months of serving together, especially when some of that time is spent in the heat of combat. A Marine officer is expected to have all the right answers to all the problems that might arise. It is unreasonable to believe that every decision will be a right decision. Is the decision right for the squad, platoon, company or the battalion? Only God can make all the right decisions. The Marines under an officer's command are like his younger brothers. You try and protect your younger brother, and when casualties happen it is hard on the commanding officer, whether he is a lieutenant, captain, major or colonel, it hurts. It hurts to the core of one's soul, a hurt that will remain for his entire life. But in the heat of battle, although hard, the officer tries to shut out those feelings. Those memories will be there later for him to think through and sort out. The officer must pick himself up and focus on the immediate fight.

Omohundro, trying to hold his company together, stepped in and ordered them to move south again. He shouted at them, "Damn it, get moving!" Whatever it took, cajoling, calmness, or a strong manner of leading from the front, he kept his Marines pushing forward to accomplish their mission. Omohundro, with a degree in Elementary Education, admitted that the battle had also put a strain on him too. "It's not like I didn't feel it, but if I were to show it, the whole thing would have come apart," Omohundro recalled.

2nd and 3rd Platoons met with sporadic resistance as they continued moving south into the inner bowels of the city. Both platoons then established over-watch positions just north of Phase Line Grace.

Second Lieutenant Andy Eckert's 1st Platoon pressed forward to Phase Line Grace. The plan was to occupy a building with an advantageous over-watch position on the mosque they were to set up for the friendly Iraqis to secure. It was a dark moonless night as the Marines trudged on.

"I had talked to the company commander and he told me the route I was going to take to reach the mosque, which was due south," Eckert said. "It was about 0030 the morning of November 12 as we moved straight down Route Ethan and took a right on Phase Line Grace and cut straight across to our morning's objective, the mosque. It was absolutely quiet when we arrived. We had tanks in support and their engines were the only noise. The mosque was on the corner of Phase Line Grace and Phase Line Frank."

Eckert's platoon finally approached a building that he had identified earlier as the support by fire position that they were going to secure. It had a good angle of fire on the morning's target, the mosque located almost directly across the street.

Corporal Kyle Mastropasqua, 3rd Fire Team Leader, recalls, "We knew we needed the house because of the proximity to the mosque across the street. I was right behind Knospler as we moved through the courtyard of the house. The door was locked so we tried shooting the lock off with our weapons. It wouldn't budge."

Corporal Criddle's Assault Squad moved forward to assist with a breach of the house. "I met with Corporal Knospler and he told me what he needed and we set the charge off," Criddle said.

"We moved up to the front yard and began making entry to the house. My 1st and 2nd squad leaders ended up in the building together and began searching the house, like a buddy team, as point men," remembered Eckert. "We had nine Marines in the house clearing the bottom deck and I was by the door waiting to hear that the first deck was all clear or not. Several Marines started to climb the stairs to reach the second deck. Corporal Knospler was point man with three Marines right behind. He had moved up several stairs when I heard a loud explosion."

Usually a PFC or lance corporal would be the first squad man up the stairs but Corporal Jacob Knospler was a leader and he chose to lead from the front. He was the first Marine up the stairs.

Mastropasqua remembered, "It was pitch black inside when we entered the house. We used our white lights on our weapons as we gained a foothold. There was a long hallway with a large room to the left and a large opening of a room at the end of the hall. Knospler went down the hall to the far room and I went to clear the room to the left. Knospler, Corporal Jason Huyghe and I all met at the foot of the stairwell. Knospler started up the stairs followed by Huyghe then me."

A hidden insurgent on the second floor either threw a grenade over the banister and down on the advancing Marines on the stairwell or set off a direction mine on the landing. The grenade or hidden enemy mine exploded right in the face of squad leader Corporal Jacob Knospler and shrapnel tore into his face, head and left leg.

Knospler recalls, "I had just moved up a few of the stair steps when a blinding flash exploded in my face. I staggered and went down on one knee. I didn't know what had happened to me." Part of his lower face was blown off from the enemy grenade.

Mastropasqua recalled, "Knospler had only climbed four or five steps and was leaning forward when there was a pop like a shotgun firing and then an orange flash. He absorbed all of the blast, neither Huyghe nor I were hit by the shrapnel. I saw Knospler straightened up before falling down on the stairs. His head had been badly hit. I grabbed his flak and pulled him down the stairs when I heard Huyghe yell 'grenade!'"

The insurgent took this time to unleash another grenade into the chaos swirling below him on the first floor of the house.

Mastropasqua said, "I left Knospler thinking he was already dead. I took two steps when I heard the grenade land and bounce then there was a bright flash that spun me around facing the stairwell again. I was hit and fell to the ground. As they were dragging me out, I passed out."

PFC Brandon Burleigh took shrapnel to his left arm. Shards of metal tore into Lance Corporal Michael Daly's right leg. Casualties in 1st Platoon were mounting fast as Corporal Jason Huyghe went down with shrapnel wounds to his left leg. Corporal Douglas Gilland, who was hit in both legs and his left hand from the exploding grenade, also went down. Corporal Kyle Mastropasqua suffered shrapnel wounds to both legs and feet and his right arm from the flying shrapnel.

"Knospler fell straight back and six other Marines were also hit by the shrapnel," said Lieutenant Eckert. While Knospler was blown to the floor, the enemy fighter tossed down a second grenade on the scrambling Marines.

Knospler said, "I picked myself up and stumbled out of the building." Two Marines rushed over to the shaken and wounded Knospler and assisted him to a track.

The enemy grenades had decimated almost an entire squad of 1st Platoon. As the Marines assisted Corporal Knospler from the house, they were all screaming, 'No! No!'

"We had seven Marines down inside the house and only three or four Marines that had not been hit. The unwounded Marines began quickly dragging the casualties from the house. We got them out fast," Lieutenant Eckert recalled. "The corpsman outside the house began assessing the casualties, while Staff Sergeant Brown called for a Medevac. Corporal Knospler is a great Marine and was a phenomenal squad leader."

Sergeant Sam Williams remembered, "I saw Lance Corporal Hughes from Tennessee carry three wounded Marines and himself out of the building."

From the glare of the white lights strapped on the fallen Marine weapons that were now scattered about on the first floor, Lance Corporal

Hughes could see to grab at the wounded Marines, hoist them up and carry them from the house of horrors.

"I started working on Mastropasqua and when he came to, he told me, 'Don't cut my gear!'" Sergeant Williams recalled.

Mastropasqua recalls coming to outside the house, "They had cut my cammies and boots to check my wounds and I didn't want them to cut my other gear. When I saw them bring Knospler from the house with his face bleeding real bad, I wasn't worried about myself anymore. I thought about my fire team, but then I saw them all wounded and being loaded in the track with me."

Assaultman Squad Leader Corporal Nick Criddle remembered, "Billiot and I grabbed Corporal Douglas Gilland and began patching him up. But Gilland was worried about Knospler."

"Don't lose him! His wife just had a baby girl. Don't lose him!" Gilland shouted to his fellow Marines.

"Gilland had shrapnel wounds to both legs and his left hand but he wasn't worried about himself. He just kept talking about saving Knospler," said Corporal Criddle.

Corpsman HM3 Jones was quickly on the scene giving aid to the wounded Marines. "The amtracs pulled up and I'm screaming that we have a guy bleeding all over the place with half his face missing. They finally carried him to the amtrac and I went along back to the aid station with him. We tried to intubate him with a tube because he was having a hard time breathing. He was losing a lot of blood, but I knew he was a real strong guy and he would make it. The amtrac was full of wounded when we got back to the aid station at the Government Center."

While all of the casualties were being medevaced out, 1st Platoon began to regroup to clear the house of the enemy fighters. At 0300, Omohundro ordered everyone to pull back from the house while the tanks brought their main guns to bear on the building. The tanks fired fifteen rounds into the second floor of the house turning it into a brick of Swiss cheese.

The amtrac carried the seven wounded Marines back to the forward aid station for further medical attention.

Eckert's 1st Platoon had suffered seven casualties in a matter of seconds in searching just one house. Along with the three casualties earlier that night, a third of the platoon was now out of action in Fallujah.

Eckert met with his dispirited platoon outside the house on the sidewalk under a moonless sky. In just a few hours he had lost most of his squad and team leaders. "I'm telling them, 'Look the house is cleared out! The tanks hit it so many times, and if anyone was still in there, they're dead! We're going to get back in and take that house and go upstairs and find the enemy's body!'"

Sergeant Williams recounted the attempted taking of the house next to the mosque. "Gunny Brown came over and told me to scrape together what's left of the platoon and help clear this house. We used flashlights as we began to clear and then the house caught fire. We were all ordered out."

Apparently a tank round had started the fire in the main downstairs room. From the front porch, Eckert told one of his Marines to put the fire out. As the Marine was trying to stomp the fire out First Sergeant Whittington yelled for everyone to exit the house. The Marines ran back out of the house while the fire quickly spread inside the structure.

Sergeant Williams recalled, "When we left the house Lance Corporal Dominguez apparently got left behind. We all went across the street to another house and set up there. When Dominguez realized that he was the only one still in the burning house he ran out, jumped up on the Marine tank and began yelling that he was a friendly. Lance Corporal William Miller went out to get Dominguez. While Miller was standing near the tank, it fired a round from the main gun. The concussion from the blast affected Miller's hearing. He then came back into the house with Dominguez. We didn't want to attract any attention from the enemy to the house we were in so we were trying not to make any noise. Gunny Brown and I walked over to Miller and asked him if he was okay. He yells out in a very loud voice, 'I CAN'T HEAR YOU, MY HEARING IS IMPARED!' We just smiled and walked away."

Eckert said, "We abandoned that house and went to the house next door and set up our support by fire position on the mosque directly across the street. Early in the morning, we moved across the street to a house adjacent to the mosque. The Iraqis, in taking the mosque, all went off without a hitch."

The Marines below in the streets of Fallujah still had their guardian angel high above them in the form of Basher, the AC-130, which was on station over Bravo Company destroying enemy targets.

Upstate New Yorker, Sergeant Shawn Gianforte, Weapons Platoon, FiST Team related the night's action with Basher on duty in the skies above the city. "We get in this house and set up on the rooftop. We started receiving fire immediately. The whole area around started to erupt with enemy fire. We began working with Basher. We were told to hold our fire and if Basher saw a muzzle flash, he was to kill it. He would report that he saw about fifteen insurgents and he would come back on the radio and say, 'I've got eight or so. All right I got three more. Oh, two just ran into a house, I'm switching to 105s.' They did a play by play description of their night's work for us. It was like listening to the Super Bowl. We couldn't see the plane above us, but we certainly could see the shot and the explosion when it hit. That's what made him so awesome up there, you couldn't see him, but he saw you. Everyone wanted Basher out with us at night. I remember that as being one of the FiST Team's busiest nights when we were helping 1st Platoon in the shit storm they had been caught in."

In the fog of urban warfare mistakes can happen. "At 0400, I had set up in a position with about fifteen Marines. I was up top when I got a radio call that I have enemy personnel occupying a rooftop across from my position with small arms. I crawled over to this small wall around the top of the roof," Captain Omohundro said. "I was looking over the top, trying to identify where the enemy was located. I couldn't see anyone. I got back on the radio and asked, 'Where are they? What's going on?' They told me that Basher said they are getting closer to you and orienting on your position. I looked over the wall again and I still didn't see anyone. I asked, 'Which rooftop are they on?' Then it dawns on me to put on an infrared strobe light. Then the radio came on with, 'The enemy had acquired one of your strobes.' I hollered into the radio 'No! It's me! You were trying to target my position!'"

Omohundro shook his head in amazement after being targeted by Basher. He had seen what Basher could do to an enemy force that they had targeted. He was relieved that it hadn't fired on his company.

Lance Corporal Maldonado, 1st Squad, 2nd Platoon recalls the first time he was put into a 'him or me' position in the depths of Fallujah. "I shot the first man I ever shot that night. I was on watch on the rooftop second deck balcony with my new Team Leader Corporal Dat Ngo who had taken over Silva's position, who took over the squad after Wells died. Ngo and I were looking across an open field at a couple of houses. I went up to wake up the next shift and when I got back, Corporal Ngo told me that he thought he saw somebody. I looked through the scope and saw two guys moving. I said, 'I see them' I put the night vision scope on my SAW. Corporal Silva came up and I told him what we had seen. He said he had seen them too. He told me to open fire and as he looked through NVGs that you put on your helmet, he guided me to where to fire the shots. I fired and hit one of the insurgents and he went down while the other ran away," Maldonado said.

Floridian, Lance Corporal Xavier Forester, attached to 2nd Platoon said, "We bunkered down in this house for the night at about 0300. We set up security with some guys on the rooftop. Corporal Riggle, Lance Corporal Landis and myself were in this room and I said I would take first watch. I was on the first floor looking out a window. We're suppose to do one hour shifts, but I couldn't sleep for any length of time so I just stayed on watch. We put some desks and furniture to block the window, which left us just a peephole to look outside. After an hour, these guys were still sleeping so I stayed on watch. At around 0500, it was just starting to get a little lighter outside when I saw a squad of six men walking up the street. They were to my left and about a block away. We had the Iraqi troops fighting with us, so we had to identify what we would shoot at. Their weapons were on their shoulders and they were talking Arabic with each other, laughing and smiling. I told myself that, *These guys have to be Iraqi National Guard the way they were acting like they own the place*."

As the heavily armed fighters moved closer to the sleepy Lance Corporal Forester, he noticed that they were wearing tattered looking clothes and not military uniforms. Now Forester squinted and took a better look at the men moving casually up the street ever closer to his position. They were just ten meters away from his window when he finally realized they were fully armed insurgents. They were too close now and he couldn't risk calling to the sleeping Landis and Riggle. He was afraid that if he woke them up, they might make a noise and be heard by the armed insurgents, giving their position away. Forester tensed up as he tightened his grip on his M16. He silently switched the safety off. They were so close now he could see their faces. Forester felt he could almost reach out and touch them. He let the first three move past the barricaded window as he took notice of their weapons. The insurgents were armed with three AK-47s, a Dragunov sniper rifle, an RPG, and the last one had an RPK with RPG rounds strapped to his back. Forester concentrated on the man with the weapon that would do the most damage if fired, the sixth man walking with the RPG.

"I watched as the first three walked past, and then I flipped my rifle into three round bursts. I let loose on the fourth guy. I hit him but he ran behind a wall. I hit the fifth guy with a burst and he also made it behind the wall. The sixth guy started running toward the wall when my last burst caught him in the back hitting the rockets. The rockets caught on fire as he followed the others behind the wall, screaming and flailing at the flames. All I could hear was one big explosion. KABANG!" remembered Lance Corporal Forester.

The two sleeping Marines, Riggle and Landis, jumped up when they heard the first discharge and quickly grabbed their rifles and joined in the firing. The Marines posted on the building's rooftop had gotten into the act as they began laying down fire on the fleeing insurgents from above.

"Later that morning, we went out to check the enemy we had fired on and there were parts everywhere because of the exploding rockets on the one insurgent's back," Xavier Forester recalled.

Captain Omohundro's men sat around waiting for the Iraqi Security Force to be brought up in amtracs to attack the mosque. They finally arrived at the Attack Position with Bravo Company at 0530.

"One of my company objectives was that small mosque. At this point I have sixty Iraqi Security Forces attached to me," Omohundro said. "Their job, once I gained a foothold and provided over-watch, was to secure the mosque. We set up and they cleared the mosque a half-hour later at 0600." The Iraqi forces met no resistance when they took the mosque, and later were sent back to the ING compound.

After the mosque was cleared, Omohundro moved his company into the building and established a firm base. Bravo Company was continually harassed by heavy enemy sniper fire during its stay at the mosque. In fact, at 0900 the over-watch position was displaced from outside to the inside and the relative safety of the mosque.

From an Army family, M249 SAW gunner, Lance Corporal James Maxey, 22, Fayetteville, North Carolina, a member of 3rd Platoon, 2nd Squad recalls going to the mosque in the darkness, "As we were running across the street in the dark I fell in a hole and busted up my knee. My good friend Lance Corporal David Houck ran over and helped me up and then dragged me by my jacket and arm into the mosque. We were receiving fire from a nearby four-story hotel. Then they took me back to Camp Fallujah to have my knee worked on."

"As we got in the mosque, we heard reports of enemy moving up the street and all around us. We ended up getting into a twelve-hour firefight, surrounded at this mosque. They were coming from all directions. We were calling in artillery and mortars, as well as firing our own company mortars," said Omohundro. "Later, when I was talking to a Marine who told me I had some great quotes on the radio that day so I asked him which one? He said, 'That day when you were surrounded in the mosque and they wanted you to push south. And you said, 'Hell, I don't have to push south, I have the enemy right where I want them!'"

The enemy fighters were stepping out from doorways and alleys before firing at the Marines from the hip then sprinting back to the safety of a wall or courtyard. Other insurgents were snapping off rounds from the windows and rooftops of the surrounding buildings.

Corporal Brad Watson's sniper team was kept busy on the rooftop of the mosque. Corporal James Mendenhall recalled a kill by Corporal Kirk Bosselmann. "A man carrying a Draganov rifle was running across the street a couple hundred yards away while Corporal Bosselmann was on post. He picked up his rifle and without using the scope just fired and brought the enemy sniper down. Two more enemy fighters then ran out and a Marine with an M-240G opened up and dropped them. I had 20 confirmed kills and Bosselmann had 12 in the city. Kirk was an incredible shot," Watson said.

"Corporal Brad Watson and 'Ski' were taking out some targets from the roof when an enemy fighter fired and the round impacted the wall right beside me," Sniper Staff Sergeant Alicea said. "I asked Mendenhall if he saw where it had come from. He said he couldn't tell. For the next two hours the enemy sniper kept me pinned down. It eventually started to rain and I finally crawled away from that position. I saw some people across the street and Bosselmann, resting his rifle on the wall, lit one of them up. A round hit the building again and Bosselmann rolled off the wall for cover but left his rifle. He kept trying to reach up and get his rifle but every time he did the enemy fired at him. Finally Kirk reached up and got hold of his weapon and pulled it down with him. We all broke out laughing."

Scout Sniper Corporal Kirk Bosselmann, 21, had just become a citizen of the U.S. a few months before entering Fallujah. His family had moved from Canada to the countryside near Washington D.C. when he was seven-years-old. From Fallujah, three days before Thanksgiving, he had called home and reached his mother, Beverley. He had sounded very tired as he told his mom he couldn't wait to get home. (We hear and read a lot about the 20,000 Americans who went to Canada to avoid the draft during the Vietnam War. But we seldom read about the 40,000 Canadians who came south to join the U.S. Armed Forces and fight against communism during that period of time. 113 Canadians died fighting for the U.S. in Vietnam.)

Before leaving home to go to Iraq, Kirk had a conversation with his mother. He had taken her aside and told her he wasn't going to be coming back. He had also shared his feelings with his sister and several friends. Kirk made his mom promise that she would scatter his ashes on an island in the Potomac River where he and his best friend loved to spend time, also on Sugarloaf Mountain, where he spent many happy hours riding his horse, riding his mountain bike or hiking the trails. Kirk's family home has a lovely view of that mountain. His mother had asked her son to take care of himself and he promised her he would but he told her the safety of his comrades would always come first.

Marine artillery was called on to support Bravo Company while at the mosque. When the 105mm rounds came screaming in, the exploding impacts were ear splitting and bone jarring to the hunkered down Bravo Company Marines. When the Marines trained with 105s at CAX, deep in the California desert, they were never closer than 1,000 meters. In Fallujah, the Marines were as close as 500 meters to the exploding 105mm rounds. Eventually, the remaining insurgents faded south, deeper into the city. During the break in the fighting with the enemy snipers around the mosque, Bravo Company managed to squeeze in some time to re-fit, re-organize and rest. The Marines had had a long night of moving and fighting behind them.

During this time, the Iraqi Forces were again moved back to the mosque from the ING compound and incorporated into the overall defense of the building. While deploying to their positions, the Iraqis took sniper fire and incurred two casualties and the Marine liaison with them was also wounded. All three were quickly medevaced out.

"The Iraqi forces that fought along side of us had no food and water and we gave them what we could. In fact, when we where at the ING compound, there was a room full of uniforms, packs and other equipment and I told their commander to take what they needed," Captain Omohundro remembers.

At 1700, Bravo Company stepped out from the mosque and began pushing south again, reaching Phase Line White at approximately 2300 to the accompaniment of sporadic sniper fire. Captain Omohundro's men didn't have time to rest, for they were promptly ordered to continue on south to Phase Line Isabel. The move was to begin before daybreak. In the push, Bravo Company would have the help of AAVs in a supporting role.

As the Marines moved through the streets, they began witnessing horrific scenes of dead, bloated, rotting bodies scattered about, many with dogs gnawing at them. Many of the buildings had been turned to rubble in this part of the city. Dozens of electric and telephone lines lay dangling from the poles and into the streets. Abandoned cars and trucks lay scattered about along with garbage and human waste, which gave off an overwhelming odor; an odor the Marines who experienced it would never forget.

November 13, the Iraqi government declared the city secured, but the battle wasn't over yet and neither was the killing or the dying.

At 0600, Captain Omohundro ordered 2nd and 3rd Platoons to move south, and to occupy firm bases on the southern edge of Phase Line Isabel. First Lieutenant Chris Wilkens' 3rd Platoon mounted up in the AAVs which moved them down to Phase Line Isabel to establish an over-watch position for the rest of the company. The AAVs then raced back to bring up Second Lieutenant Steven Berch's 2nd Platoon. Once these two platoons where in place, they began to clear houses. Several caches were discovered, along with four detainees that they ended up apprehending.

2nd Platoon attacked south and detained another four insurgents while clearing a house they wanted to use as a firm base. The two platoons met very little resistance in this clearing operation. At 1600, Bravo's headquarters and Eckert's 1st Platoon received the order to displace and move south to the southern side of an open field and set up for the next day's attack.

Six tanks were brought in to fire across the open field at several buildings and houses from which Bravo Company had received sniper fire. The tanks took turns firing their main guns at the suspicious houses, tearing them apart.

"We had four young Iraqi men come up to us at this point and give themselves up, claiming that the majority of the enemy fighters were down farther south where they had weapon caches set up. They were claiming they had nothing to do with the insurrection, they were told if they didn't fight that bad things were going to happen to them and their families. We pushed across the open field to enter some buildings and surprisingly, we didn't receive much fire. I think they had pulled back. Once we got into the buildings we began receiving fire," Omohundro explained.

The night of November 13 was a relative quiet one for Omohundro's Marines of Bravo Company. There was little or no activity in their Area of Operation. The tired, sweaty and mud covered Marines tried to get some rest before the attack south shortly after daybreak.

When Corporal Knospler reached the FAS, Doc Jadick knew he had to get him back out of the city to the LSA for further medical care, and fast. Jadick rode alongside the badly wounded Knospler holding the wounded Marine's head in his lap. The lower part of Knospler's chin was gone from the exploding grenade. Jadick did all he could to soothe the Marine and to prevent him from dying by choking on his own blood. Jadick assured Knospler that everything would be all right. That he would live.

As the Marines moved through Fallujah, some units had Arabic translators attached to them. One message was intercepted and translated by the Marines in the city. An insurgent was overheard reporting to his commander on a cell phone, their only form of modern communication, "We are fighting, but the Marines keep coming. We are shooting, but the Marines won't stop!"

Alpha Company Mixes it up in the Push South

Lieutenant Colonel Brandl decided to mix things up for the insurgents in the coming days to attempt to keep them off-balance. He talked with Captain Cunningham, telling him to rest up his company for a night attack the following evening. Brandl hoped to catch the insurgents still in their safe houses with a quick night strike south. The movement was set for 0300. In the early morning hours, under the cloak of darkness, Alpha Company attacked south by quickly occupying several buildings, one of which contained a terrorist torture chamber. Eventually in Fallujah, three of these houses were found that had been used by the terrorists to torture and kill hostages. All three houses had walls and floors splattered with the dried blood of their victims. The walls displayed banners and flags typically used as backdrops in hostage videos released to the world media. At one building, searching Iraqi Security Forces found four videos of hostages being beheaded. One hostage was eventually rescued alive in one of the city's terrorist controlled house of horrors.

Day after day the Marines of Alpha Company pushed south through street after street, searching houses and fighting insurgents when and where they found them. Some company commanders rely on artillery for support while others choose mortars. Captain Cunningham relied on mortars and explained why. "The 81s were incredible. I would call in 81s closer than I was supposed to because the bad guys tried to get in close to us to negate our advantage of firepower. If you had a house between you and the mortar round impacts, you would be protected. Alpha Company's 81mm mortarmen fired over 700 rounds in support of the company in its attack south," Cunningham recalled.

Platoon tank commander, Second Lieutenant Jeffery Lee, 34, a native of Spartanburg, South Carolina and a graduate of the University of Louisville, attached to Alpha Company, remembered the sleepless nights in Fallujah. "I would eat some MREs, swig it with some water, and keep on going. We were going to push at nighttime because they were easier to do, but we were told we needed to push in the daytime too. The tanks would not allow the resistance to continue. We would push up, and if we received RPG shots, we would level that building. As we (tanks) pushed forward it would allow Alpha Company to push up as well," said Lee.

"We never had a lack of supplies and ammunition because we could push back with our amtracs and re-supply pretty quick," Captain Cunningham explained. "As for casualties, by the time it took me to do a proper Medevac report, they were all ready back there in the amtrac. Literally, from the time they were hit with a bullet or shrapnel, within minutes, they were back to the battalion surgeon."

The tanks supported Alpha Company very closely in their fight through the city. Captain Cunningham remembers, "I could just reach out and touch them, that's how close they worked with us in Fallujah."

"I had Lieutenant Lee to the west, and I had my Executive Officer Lieutenant Markley leading in his tank. Markley chose the terrain and pushed through with Lieutenant Ackerman following him, and Lieutenant Barnes following Lieutenant Lee's tanks," Tank Commander, Captain Meyers remembered. "Lee was loading his .50 cal and was shot in the bicep. He refused Medevac and stayed in the fight. Markley was engaging the ground, and my tank was engaging the enemy on the rooftops. We were fighting with the enemy down all the alleys in that part of the city. We led the whole way down."

As the Marines drove deeper into the city, they tried not to go too deep with their thoughts of home. They had to stay focused on the battle to stay alive. Captain Aaron Cunningham said, "I had pride in my young Marines who would sit out in the road with rounds and RPGs snapping around them and calmly put a rocket through a door or window. I saw that every day in Fallujah. I was proud to be among them. I remember telling my wife, Jennifer. 'Honey, I didn't think about family, home or you, nothing, but tanks, artillery, and my Marines for the first seven days in Fallujah.' I was focused on what was going on. I tried not to go down a path of thinking about other things, so I just never thought about them. This was my world, right there. I didn't go outside of it in Fallujah."

Lance Corporal James Thomas Bullen, 20, from Richlands, Kentucky, lugged his heavy SAW down the streets of Fallujah. He was a member of Lieutenant Ackerman's 1st Platoon and belonged to 3rd Squad's 1st Fire Team. Other members in the fire team were Corporal Hays, Team Leader; point man Corporal Pratt, and Lance Corporal Collins was the A gunner. Bullen recalled making a wise choice that most likely saved him, as well as the lives of the Marines in his fire team. "We got to this house that had a large weapons cache. They gave us a choice to either frag it with a grenade or go in with the SAW. I chose to breach with the SAW, and when we went into the house it was stacked from the floor to the ceiling with mortar shells. If we had fragged it with a grenade, we would have been blown up. We searched the house and found time fuses, detonators, RPG rounds, AKs, RPGs, PKMs, and we found the building had living quarters and had been bunkered."

Second Lieutenant Elliot Ackerman's 1st Platoon continued to search houses in the southern part of the city. The Marines cleared a house they wanted to use as the CO. Staff Sergeant Ricardo Sebastian, who had recently been assigned to Ackerman's hard hit 1st Platoon a few days before on November 12, and Sergeant Menard moved with a group of Marines up to the rooftop of the two-story house.

From the vantage of the roof Menard looked toward the rooftop of a house a few doors away. He saw an insurgent in a shed stairwell structure that was located on the roof. The Marines fired on the shed, while Sebastian ran downstairs and told Corporal Costa, Corporal Bessant, and four other Marines that they were going to clear the enemy held house. The platoon was so low on men that Sebastian said he would be point man and lead the assault on the house.

"I'll frag every room as we clear," Sebastian told his Marines.

Bessant disagreed, "They'll be too much smoke if you use frags."

"It will be better if we frag every room. I would rather have less visibility than take casualties," Sebastian answered.

The seven Marines ran in a dogtrot toward a building two doors down. They reached the front gate of the house's courtyard that held the enemy. They pressed their bodies against the outside wall for protection before entering. Sebastian checked the iron gate and decided they would push on to a second entrance to get into the courtyard. Sebastian, carrying his M16A4, picked one of the nine hand grenades he was carrying and leaned out from the ten-foot high wall to get a view of the house. He could see into the courtyard at a window and door of the house about ten feet away.

"I decided I would step out from the wall and throw the first grenade at the front door," said Sebastian.

Stepping out from the shadow of the wall and into the sunlight, Sebastian set up like a baseball pitcher with the grenade drawn back and was ready to throw. Suddenly the front door of the house burst open. Blocking the doorway was an insurgent with an AK-47. The enemy fighter and Sebastian stared at one another for only a split second before the insurgent began firing his weapon from the hip.

"I felt something hit my arm," Sebastian explained. Not feeling it at the time, he had also taken a round to his leg from the AK.

Sebastian was falling to the ground of the courtyard when he managed to toss the grenade at the enemy fighter in the doorway. Sebastian hit the ground and immediately rolled over on to his back. He didn't hear the sound of the exploding grenade as it shredded the insurgent. He looked up to see Corporal Bessant standing away from the wall and staring at him. The enemy fighter ran from the doorway into the courtyard with smoke pouring from his body and clothes.

"We took cover. We didn't know how many insurgents were in the house," Lance Corporal Bullen said. "We didn't know where Sebastian was. We were screaming and hollering to one another, 'Has anyone seen him?' I told my A gunner, Lance Corporal Collins, to cover me while I ran back across to see if Sebastian was still lying in the yard. Before running across, I stopped at a corner to make sure it was safe to go back in. The insurgent, who Staff Sergeant Sebastian had fragged, came running out of the house. He was still smoking from the explosion of the grenade. I fired a burst and put him on the ground. I was looking through the side gate. Someone yelled, 'Staff Sergeant Sebastian is running back from the house!' We all regrouped in the house we had taken cover in and began reloading our weapons before going back to clear that house. The insurgent who had been in there had burned his prayer mat and all kinds of stuff before leaving."

Sebastian limped from the courtyard to the safety of the street and continued limping back to the house two doors down. Once there he got on the radio and called for a Medevac. "They asked, 'For who?' I yelled, 'Me!'" Sebastian recalled.

Ackerman had heard the firing and came running. Assessing the situation, he decided he couldn't call for the use of tanks because of the angle of fire. The insurgents inside the house and the Marines around it began exchanging small arms fire. Ackerman and Sebastian's handpicked Marines moved back to the house to finish off the enemy fighters.

Ackerman regrouped his Marines before the final attack on the enemy-held structure. As they pushed back into the yard and then on into the house, the fighting had degenerated into single combat at point blank range. Firing his pistol, Ackerman and his handful of Marines finally cleared the enemy held house. Five dead insurgents were found inside.

Captain Cunningham described the fight put up by his Marines. "Staff Sergeant Sebastian and Lieutenant Ackerman got in an alley fight in a courtyard with grenades going back and forth. The house had five insurgents in it and the Marines assaulted the building. The two sides were only eight to ten feet apart. It became a pistol, grenade fight. Staff Sergeant Recardo Sebastian threw a grenade into the house. A terrorist ran out and put one through Sebastian's ankle, and then another round through his elbow. As Sebastian was falling down he managed to get the grenade off. When it exploded it ripped into the insurgent. After being shot twice he gets the grenade off and kills the bad guy. Then Lieutenant Ackerman pretty well forced his way into the house with grenades and pistol," Cunningham remembered.

Lance Corporal Bullen, along with other Marines, pushed to the house next door to the enemy held one. When they came closer to the structure, something just didn't seem right to them. Posted at the corner of the house with Corporal Perry and facing down the street, Bullen heard rounds going off and someone yelling, "Landslide!" which, in Marine lingo, means the building is ready to be blown by the enemy. He watched as Marines began piling out of the house. Lance Corporal David Landgrebe had been clearing a room when Bullen witnessed rounds hitting Landgrebe's right leg.

"Landgrebe said as calm as day, 'I'm hit!' I was screaming for someone to get Landgrebe out," Bullen recalled. "My Team Leader, Corporal Hays, ran up and began to drag Landgrebe out the door. We were waiting for the amtracs to come up and evac him out, and when it finally pulled up an insurgent threw a grenade from the roof at the amtrac. It bounced off and exploded next to it. Everyone was running for cover. Corporal Perry and I ran out in the open and started to lay down fire at the enemy fighters on the rooftop so everyone could get to cover."

Captain Cunningham was located in the education building standing over a prone Marine sniper who was engaging targets. A rocket hit the wall right near where Cunningham was standing and literally lifted him off his feet and catapulted him through the air before slamming him face down on the hard floor of the room. "I didn't know which end was up. I knew I had been hit with something, but I didn't feel any pain from being slammed to the ground. I looked through the smoke over to one of my lance corporals who was just standing there laughing. He said, 'That was the funniest thing I had ever seen.' So in the midst of all this combat, I'm thrown over in a somersault and he's laughing. He asked, 'You okay sir?' Then I started chuckling at myself. Our moods were always upbeat in the city. Marines were always giving the thumbs up. We were kicking their ass," Cunningham recalled.

One of the greatest weapons that American Soldiers and Marines possess is their innate sense of humor. They tend to find humor in almost everything, even war, even while in the inner bowels of Fallujah.

"We heard the battalion commander, battalion sergeant major, and the battalion gunner were all going to be coming to our position," Lance Corporal Bullen said. "We were going to go out and see if those houses we had fought over the previous day were secured. We began clearing out the house right next door to where Sergeant Sebastian had been hit. Corporal Pratt and Corporal Hays went in the house, which left me in the front. Some Marines behind me and I were in shock as a guy just came walking out of the house, like he was going to work or something. He was carrying two RPGs, one in each hand. Nervously, I raised my SAW. I had never been face to face with a guy who wanted to kill me before. I tried to pull the trigger, but my safety was on. I flipped my weapon off safety and I fired as he ran back into the house. I think I wounded him before he entered the door."

Bullen and the other Marines in his platoon pulled back into the house they had been staying in and set up a watch on the house the enemy fighters had run back into. Just then, Lieutenant Colonel Brandl, Sergeant Major Hope, and Battalion Gunny Athey showed up at 2nd Platoon's position. Lance Corporal Bullen remembered the visit deep in the city. "We had changed post and I was now watching the house the insurgent had run into. The battalion gunner walked up to us and asked me, 'What are you looking at Devil Dog?' I said, 'Well sir, we encountered an RPG gunner who had come out on the street and fired and then ran back inside.' The gunner told me to 'Keep an eye out.' As I'm sitting up on post, I see him walking back to the Humvee he had just come in on. He grabbed his rifle and calmly walked across the street and through the front gate of the house that held the insurgents. I started yelling, 'Someone get on the gunner!' All these guys in the Humvees, maybe twenty Marines, all started to pile out. Battalion gunner entered the house and the Marines came running after him," Bullen said.

Mounted up in the battalion gunner's turret in the Humvee sat Sergeant Kelley Starling from Headquarters Company, and part of Brandl's Hunter Mobile force. "They said there were insurgents inside the house. I watched as Gunner Athey jogged back across the street and walked up to the passenger door of our Humvee, opened the door and grabbed his M4 carbine." Starling was stunned to see the gunner calmly stroll back across the street and enter the enemy held house. "I ordered two riflemen and a SAW gunner to follow the gunner. I yelled to them, 'Go! Go!' A few minutes later I saw a Marine come out of the house and yell, 'the house is clear!'"

Lance Corporal Bullen, watching from his post, was just as flabbergasted as Gunner Athey began clearing the house alone. "Gunner Athey later exited the house and informed us that the house was clear," Bullen recalled.

Lance Corporal Drew Martin said, "November 15 was probably the hardest day for 2nd Platoon. We were leading off the company's final push to the edge of the city. They told us that in the last few blocks of the city we would find the real hard-core fighters. We were pushing with the tanks to our front, while they were doing recon by fire. The tanks would randomly fire on buildings hoping to attract enemy fire. The last block we got to, we had reached a vacant lot and began receiving fire over our heads. We got off the street and went into a three-story house to get out of the line of fire. Marines went to the roof to see who was firing at us when we began receiving fire from our tanks. We had to get the hell out of there, so we rushed out of the house and pushed west about a block. We were taking cover behind a house against an outside wall. There was still a lot of firing coming at us from the rooftops. Our Staff Sergeant, Richard Pillsbury, ordered 1st Squad to clear a three-story home across the street, while 2nd and 3rd Squads gave covering fire. 1st Squad was in the building for only twenty seconds when all kind of firing went off, and then I heard a grenade explode. 1st Squad began running out of the house and started yelling, 'Corpsman up!' as they pulled back to our position."

Lance Corporal Travis Desiato, 19, had walked down a hallway and started to enter one of the back rooms of the house when six insurgents opened fire with AKs, killing him instantly. Desiato didn't have a chance to fire back before going down. He had received several gunshot wounds to the upper part of his body and was still lying in the building. Then, the insurgents began throwing grenades at the remaining Marines inside the building. In the chaos of exploding grenades, the rest of the Marines managed to escape from the building. Earlier, at the Government Center, the Bedford, Massachusetts native, Lance Corporal Travis Desiato had been knocked unconscious by the concussion of a 500-pound bomb, and had refused to be evacuated from the city. Now he was down in the house.

Across the street, the Marines regrouped as Corporal Conners, the squad leader, quickly went through his options. Conners and four other senior Marines in the platoon, Corporal Eubaldo Lovato, Corporal

Camilio Aragon, Corporal Bradford Donaghy, and Corporal Lonny Longnecker went back across the street to try and get Desiato out of the house. The Marines would try flooding the house. Leaving Desiato in the house, among the enemy who had killed him wasn't an option these Marines would accept. He was a Marine, he was a brother, he was one of them, and they would bring him out, even if it meant putting their own lives at risk. Staff Sergeant Pillsbury took the remainder of 2nd Platoon to the safety of a house some thirty feet away.

The Marines would be moving into the enemy's set defenses. The advantage was with the insurgents. After entering the one-story sand colored house for a second time, they came under intense fire from a back bedroom. Everytime they came close to the hallway that held Desiato's body, the enemy fire drove them back. A SMAW rocket was fired at the side of the building to create a breach for the Marines to use as another entrance.

The Marines went back in a third time to retrieve Desiato. In another fierce exchange of grenades, the insurgents forced the Marines back out into the courtyard again. The noise of the firing inside the house had become deafening. The acrid smell of so many weapons firing caused the house to reek of gunpowder.

Staff Sergeant Richard Pillsbury, who had taken command of the platoon from the wounded and evaced Lieutenant Hunt, realized that he could easily lose more members of his command if they continued to advance into the enemy held house. He decided to utilize a tank's main gun to help eliminate the insurgents. He got a tank to rumble up and fire two main gun rounds into the house, which created two more breach holes in which to enter. The rounds threw up a dust storm that swirled throughout the house. The tank also raked the house with hundreds of .50 caliber rounds, chipping mortar from the exterior and interior walls.

And for the fourth time, the five Marines of Pillsbury's platoon attempted to get to Desiato. They had to withdraw quickly because they couldn't see once they got inside due to the heavy smoke from the tank's main gun. They regrouped outside and waited a short time before making a fifth insertion into the house. This time they entered through the two breaches and the door simultaneously. The smoke had cleared somewhat, which allowed the Marines to finally carry their comrade, Lance Corporal Travis Desiato, from the building. It had been a fierce 90-minute fight and if the enemy fighters had preplanned escape routes from the house, it didn't work. Six enemy bodies were counted, all located in the small back room.

"Lance Corporal Desiato was a good friend of mine. I watched as they brought an amtrac in and took his body out," Lance Corporal Drew Martin remembered.

Nearby, Lance Corporal Carmine Castelli and the squad he was in had been breaching doors and clearing houses all day. Castelli's squad was down to only four men, and one of them was a replacement from the company mortars. The Marines were getting tired when they reached a section where the houses formed an open area in the middle of the development.

Castelli recalled, "I tried kicking the gate in, and then I tried running into it without any luck. My Team Leader, Corporal Stephen Copenhaver, told us to go out back and try. When we got there, I tried to mule kick the door open when a grenade went off behind a wall. BOOM! We had no idea where it came from. Copenhaver told us, 'Keep your eyes open!' I was told to provide security out front while they went in. I heard Sergeant Stoy and Corporal Copenhaver talking through a window and I thought I heard them call my name. Just as I was starting to enter the house I heard a PLUNK outside. When I was inside they asked me, 'What's wrong?'" Stoy and Copenhaver never got an answer from Castelli as a grenade exploded outside. "I was petrified. I said, 'Oh shit!' I was standing right there, only seconds before," Castelli said.

The Marines ran from the house and discovered that the grenade thrower was located on the roof of the house next door. The insurgent had been tossing the grenades haphazardly from the roof at the Marines below. They brought a Javelin Team from Weapons Company up and launched one into the house.

"I said, 'F***, why don't they bring the house down?' After the round had been fired, my squad leader tossed a grenade in the house. We breached the door in the courtyard and started walking to the outside kitchen door," Castelli said. Just eight feet from the door, the bold grenade-throwing insurgent met the advancing Marines. But now he was manhandling an RPK machine gun at the kitchen window and began firing at them. Castelli and the other Marines found themselves in a low ceiling courtyard with enemy rounds flying just over their heads. Castelli said, "We shifted to a wall. I pushed a Marine out of the doorway just as the insurgent ran from the building right at us. My Team Leader, Copenhaver, pumped rounds into the insurgent bringing him down. We began to all pump rounds in the guy lying on the ground."

The insurgent still had one grenade on him and a Marine round ignited it. The grenade exploded with a blinding flash scattering deadly shrapnel at the standing Marines. "Copenhaver went down and I felt some shrapnel tear into my leg. My Team Leader had only been knocked down from the concussion of the blast," Lance Corporal Castelli recalled.

Corporal Copenhaver's team was now down to three uninjured Marines, only two of which were a part of his original team when they entered Fallujah a little over two weeks before. Lance Corporal Carmine Castelli was medevaced from the city.

"We set up in a house and later we started receiving RPG fire. That night we saw movement out in the field to our front through our NVGs. Marines were shooting off M-240Gs and M16s trying to hit those targets. The RPGs stopped, so we felt we had won," SAW gunner Lance Corporal James Bullen remembered. "Around three or four o'clock in the morning, Corporal Pratt, Lance Corporal Collins, and I were on post. I was using a thermal scope and I spotted something moving to our front, it looked like a dog. I asked Pratt to take a look. When he looked, he saw someone jump up and take off running. It was the insurgents they had been firing at earlier. We began firing using an infra-red laser sight and laced the enemy target. The next morning we went out to the position we had been shooting up. That was the first time I had been that close to dead Iraqis. One had powder burns on his body, another had a round impact right through his forehead. That was thanks to Sergeant Battles and his snipers. I saw another insurgent who had been blown to bits. We felt they had been trying to get to our amtracs."

Lance Corporal Landgrebe was taken back to the FAS and Chaplain Cox was there when they brought the wounded Marine in. "He was turning gray, the color that dead men have when there is no blood left. The corpsmen were double bagging Landgrebe. That is when they insert an IV in each arm. They were squeezing the bags to make the solution go in to his veins faster. I was holding his crushed leg while Jadick wrapped the leg to stem the heavy flow of blood," Cox said. "His leg was shattered and I thought they might have to amputate. When they loaded him on the track to take him out of the city, I said to him 'Landgrebe you better meet me when I get off that plane in Lejeune. I don't care if you're on crutches, in a wheel chair or in a bed. You had better meet me there.' I found out later that he didn't die. The whole platoon came back to the house they were staying in for the night. They brought some of Desiato's possessions like his spare barrel, sapi plate and his kevlar and used those items to set up a make shift alter in the corner of the courtyard to pay their respects to their friend."

In the push south, Cunningham's Marines had captured over twenty foreign fighters. They included Egyptians, Saudis and Syrians. "After November 15, we had taken the city and we began to back clear the houses," Lance Corporal Drew Martin remembered.

Bravo Company Fights to the Southern Edge of Fallujah (88 northing)

On November 12, Lieutenant Colonel Brandl contacted regiment to have them coordinate with RCT-1 in allowing the Marines of Battalion 3/1 on their flank to come south and link up with his Battalion 1/8. With the three companies from the two battalions on line, they would then push south, squeezing the insurgents to the edge of the city. Beyond the southern most houses in the city, only open terrain greeted the enemy fighters. This plan would also seal up the corridors that had been left open on the flanks of the battalions. These open spaces had been set up to help alleviate friendly fire, but had been used as safe zones by the enemy fighters. By advancing shoulder to shoulder in the push south these zones would be sealed off and wiped clean. RCT–1 agreed with Brandl on the final push to 88 northing, the edge of the city.

"We found out that when we pushed south the enemy would pull to the west, taking advantage of the seam between the two battalions. I talked to Lieutenant Colonel Willie Buhl of Battalion 3/1. He pushed a mechanized company and linked up with my Alpha Company. Now we would have Bravo pushing, Alpha pushing, and the Battalion 3/1 mechanized company all pushing south," Brandl recalled.

At 0630 November 14, Captain Omohundro called a commanders meeting to review the plan for the day's attack south to Phase Line Jenna. Attending the meeting were his platoon commanders, Tank Platoon Commander First Lieutenant Klingensmith, the Iraqi force's commander, and other members of Omohundro's command element. Bravo's officers dubbed this meeting, the "Ka-Bar meeting." When a Marine combat photographer snapped a picture during the planning meeting, it depicted Captain Read Omohnudro with his Marine Ka-Bar knife out and using it as a pointer for the map of Fallujah.

At the meeting, Bravo Company's officers were told that their Area of Operation was split in half with 3rd Platoon moving south along the boundary with Alpha Company to their west. 2nd Platoon was to push south, while keeping Phase Line Ethan to their east. Bravo Company was tasked with conducting a thorough sweep of their sector for insurgents and weapon caches. Six Marines from Eckert's 1st Platoon were detached and placed with Headquarters Platoon in order to establish a CCP and a re-supply point for the entire company. The attack was set for 0800 that morning. 1st Platoon's remaining Marines would travel along with the sniper teams to provide extra security for them.

The Ka-Bar meeting ended with everyone knowing his job for the final push to the southern edge of the city. The tired and foot weary officers left the meeting and returned to their equally tired Marines. Bravo Company had been on foot the entire time they had been fighting through the city.

The focus was now on the most southern section of the city, which held the poorest neighborhoods. This low area of Fallujah had a problem at times with flooding from the Euphrates River. Most of the roads weren't paved, and the houses, some unfinished, lay haphazardly scattered about the area, which provided excellent cover for the insurgents.

"Units from the Army's 2/2 came in with their Bradleys and tanks and set up behind us. Then during darkness, they rolled through the area that we were going to push through shooting everything up," Omohundro said.

The Army's 2/2 went through the southern area of the city in less than two hours time. The 2/2 was a mechanized unit that fought mainly from their tanks and APCs. They didn't have much in the way of dismounted infantry to thoroughly check out the houses as they punched through that zone. The insurgents basically went to ground until the massive mechanized Army unit had gone past them and then they just popped back out. They waited for the next unit to push through on foot, the weary Marines of Bravo Company.

"The Army's 2/2 took out as much as they could, and that gave me an opportunity to refit and rearm Alpha and Bravo Companies," said Brandl.

There were rumors among the Marines that experienced battle hardened Chechen snipers had joined the insurgency in Fallujah. These fighters had tested their mettle against the Russians in Chechnya, Soviet Union, and now had joined the jihad against the Americans in the city.

Getting set to follow the Army's attack through the southern sector, Bravo Company began setting up for the final push. The attack was held up as problems coordinating with the Army's 2/2 developed. They were eventually ironed out, and the attack pushed south at 1030. Multiple weapon caches were found in the quick sweep to Phase Line Jenna.

"We didn't even make it to the second group of buildings before we were pulling out thousands and thousands of artillery shells, AK-47s, sniper rifles, RPGs, and SAS missiles. It was all there. One house had 500 anti-tank mines inside. The area we were in was the main area of the insurgency. They even had a bunker center," Omohundro recalls.

Corporal James Mendenhall said, "Our sniper team oriented to the left and 'Ski's' team took our place on the roof of the building. We were getting set to advance into a neighborhood of the city known as Zarqawi's neighborhood."

Sergeant Major Hope had linked up with Bravo Company on their attack south. "We were up on the rooftop with Ziolkowski when they busted the concrete at the ledge of the roof for firing holes. Corporal Bosselmann was up there popping them at about three hundred meters away. Our snipers were shooting them as they tried running across the open street," Sergeant Major Hope recalled.

Bravo Company arrived at Phase Line Jenna at 1800 and went firm for the night after getting re-supplied.

"That night I remember as being really cold and I didn't have a coat on," Sergeant Major Hope said. "We were laying on the rooftop when about 0100 in the morning I rolled over on my elbows trying to stay warm. First Sergeant Whittington and Captain Omohundro were cold and we didn't have anything to cover us up. So I remember First Sergeant Whittington getting up, and I thought he was just making a head call. Well, a little later he came walking back with a big, big blanket and spread it over the captain, him and me. We snuggled up in the blanket trying to stay warm that night."

The next morning, Lieutenant Wilkens' told Staff Sergeant Alicea that his 3rd Platoon would be pushing into buildings to their front so his sniper team could find new positions of support. Alicea met with his snipers to talk about shifting down a block. Ziolkowski and Lance Corporal McAnally went across the street to see if they liked the angle of fire from the new position. They yelled back over to Alicea that their position had good angles and good lanes of fire and they would stay there.

A little later Alicea's team of snipers was waiting to move out when he heard a round being fired. Then the ominous yell of 'corpsman up!'

"The hair on my neck stood up when I heard the call for the corpsman," Alicea remembers. "I ran across the street and went up to the second floor rooftop and saw 'Ski' lying there. I asked McAnally 'Where did the shot come from?' He pointed to a man carrying an RPK."

Scout Sniper Corporal Nick Ziolkowski, 22, was raised in Baltimore, Maryland. He loved surfing the beaches off the Carolina coast near Camp Lejeune and had promised fellow sniper and good friend Kirk Bosselmann, also a resident of Maryland, that he would teach him how to surf. They had talked about going to California and working the beaches there after returning from Iraq. He hoped to eventually open a surfing shop in Cancun, Mexico. Ziolkowski was a popular, fun-loving, tall, good-looking Marine. Nicknamed Ski, he knew how to handle his M-40 bolt-action sniper rifle that he had gone to the rooftop to set up. He spent hours looking for insurgents through the scope and had brought down several targets before the Marines themselves came under heavy sniper fire. Two enemy snipers had begun working over the Marines on the rooftop. One was hidden in a large hotel building. The Marine sniper began to do battle when Ziolkowski was hit through a loophole he was manning. Because the scope on his rifle was wide, he sometimes took his helmet off to get a better view of his target. It was at that moment, with his kevlar off, that a sniper's bullet hit Ziolkowski in the head.

"I was on the rooftop with our snipers watching muzzle flashes from a building across the road when sniper Nick Ziolkowski said, 'Hey, look, I see something!' Next thing I know I saw a round hit him just as he stood up. It knocked him backwards and then he fell down. I low crawled over and tried to patch him up. He was still alive," said Corpsman HM3 Jones.

Located in a building directly across the alley, Omohundro recalled, "I was right across the street when he was hit. I was basically watching him shoot, and then I noticed he wasn't shooting anymore. The enemy put him in an uncompromising situation. One sniper team kept him occupied so the other sniper team could zero in on his position on the rooftop. When he pulled up to orient on the sniper team firing at him, the second enemy team hit him."

Sergeant Major Hope remembered that chilly Iraqi morning when he heard a statement every Marine loathes to hear, "Someone yelled, 'Marine down!' First Sergeant Whittington and I ran off the rooftop, down three flights of stairs, across the alleyway, and right back up to the roof of the next building. By the time we arrived, they already had 'Ski' on a stretcher. First Sergeant Whittington was yelling, 'Get him down! Get him down!' Everyone felt he was gone, but First Sergeant Whittington wouldn't hear it. He wanted him back to the aid station as fast a possible."

On an adjacent building was fellow sniper, Corporal Mendenhall. "I heard them yell for a corpsman and then we heard it was 'Ski' that had been hit. The infantry had their thing going and we had our thing. It was as though there were two battles going on at times."

The snipers were a tight, close knit group of Marines and they took the loss of three of their own in Iraq very hard. "'Ski' was one of my best friends," said fellow sniper Corporal Brad Watson.

"They got him on the amtracs and took him back to the forward aid station," said HM3 Jones.

Back at the forward aid station, HM2 Shawn Johns was told about his friend Corporal Ziolkowski's death. "The room we picked wasn't large but it was big enough for what we needed to do. I remember Zimmerman came up to me and said, 'I hate to be the one to tell you this but your buddy 'Ski' is dead.' I told him, 'That wasn't a funny thing to joke about.' He said, 'I'm being serious. He's dead!' Everyone loved 'Ski.' Everyone wanted to be like 'Ski.' He had this way about him that everyone loved. He just got along with everyone."

Ziolkowski's commander of snipers, Captain Mike Pretus said, "I heard 'Ski' had had a close call a day or two before he was killed. The day he died I was out checking on several of my teams attached to Charlie Company when I received a call to go back to the COC. A few other Marines including CWO Rich Robinson went back with me. We had to yell, 'friendlies coming in!' so as not to get shot. We crested this berm that had been erected by the engineers and went over to the Forward Aid Station where I saw a body bag, Doc Jadick, and an Army Ambulance parked. A Soldier, Lieutenant Wilson, walked up to me and said, 'Ski.' I immediately walked away to a private area and released some of my emotions before I went over and met with Stout's sniper team."

Sergeant Dustin Stout's Sniper Team had just arrived back at the Government Center from a mission when he heard that his captain was looking for him.

"We had been on a mission to check on this weapon cache located in this small building to the north of the Government Center. After passing through that area and not checking all the houses on the push south, we knew there were more insurgents to deal with," Stout said. "We had set up at the site for a second day. We didn't go to the roof of the building but took a position on the bottom floor in the kitchen. A curtain in the kitchen window shielded us from view. We killed two armed insurgents before moving back to the center. When we arrived, I heard that Captain Pretus was looking for us so I went to a small office in the center where he was located. He told me about 'Ski' being killed. 'Ski' was a good friend and I had urged him to get into snipers."

Out where Ziolkowski was killed Bravo Marines shut down one of the enemy snipers hidden in the hotel building but not before another casualty was suffered. Spotter, Staff Sergeant Ben Alicea was hit in his right elbow, left thigh and left shoulder by shrapnel. He had been positioned on the adjacent roof from where Ziolkowski had been hit.

Captain Pretus borrowed Chaplain Cox's phone and called home to his wife, Jessica to dictate a letter he had written to Ziolkowski's parents. He asked his wife to send it off to his sniper's parents.

At 0600 November 15, Captain Omohundro called another meeting with his platoon commanders and section heads in order to coordinate the day's attack south to the limit of Fallujah city (the 88 northing). From where Bravo Company was positioned they could now see the southern limits of Fallujah, three or four blocks south.

Order of movement for the final push by the battalion to the southern limits of the city of Fallujah was for 3rd Platoon to attack from the west, 2nd Platoon to the east, followed by the headquarters element. FiST on AAVs and 1st Platoon were to move last to help with security for any caches found during the sweep.

At 0800 Bravo Company stepped off on the attack. Almost immediately, only 300 meters south of the Line of Departure, at 0900 First Lieutenant Wilkens' 3rd Platoon came under heavy fire and suffered a casualty. Moving forward with his squad, Lance Corporal Bradley Parker, 19, carrying his SAW, was hit by shrapnel from an exploding IED which killed him instantly. The Marine who wanted to teach history, was in the midst of making history. Lance Corporal Michael Rodriguez was only three yards from his good friend Parker. "I was knocked on my ass from the concussion. Parker was one of my best friends. We had gone through SOI (School Of Infantry) together. It really bothered me when he was killed," Rodriguez said.

Bradley Parker, the young man who had wanted to be a Marine since he was six-years-old, joined when he was seventeen. He hailed from

Mannington, West Virginia and had loved going to the Carolina beaches near Camp Lejeune. Parker had already completed 17 college credits toward becoming a history teacher. Parker's body was medevaced out while 3rd Platoon regrouped and continued their movement south toward another mosque.

2nd Platoon Marine, Lance Corporal Benjamin Voorhees, 24, from Sarasota, Florida remembered when his friend Bradley Parker was killed. "Seeing a dead Haji was not a big deal for me because they deserved what they got. But I remember the day Lance Corporal Parker died. When he died, I walked outside, got on a knee and cried. I don't think I had ever cried like that before, or since. Parker and I use to hang out at Myrtle Beach together," Voorhees recalled.

"There was a school where the insurgents were firing on us from. They kept moving back and forth on a two-meter wall. We tried to blow open a double steel gate so we could better see them. This Marine had never fired an AT-4 before, so I coached him on how to do it. He makes the shot and hits the gate on the first try. The AT-4 is a one shot weapons system too," Omohundro said.

Bravo Company finally reached the 88 northing with little or no opposition, and established a company firm base in the vicinity of the boundary between their company and Alpha Company.

"We went as far as you could go in the city and beyond that there was nothing but open desert until you reached the river. We set up a firm base in a schoolhouse with Alpha Company to our south. We received some small arms fire that was quickly suppressed by our Marine snipers, tanks, and air strikes," Captain Omohundro explained. "There was a water tower near us that had two snipers on it. We killed the snipers, but in the process punched bullet holes in the side of the tower, and water was constantly leaking out."

New Smyrna Beach, Florida native Lance Corporal Matthew Forester, 20, 2nd Platoon, 1st Squad recalled when the insurgents tried to turn the tables by clearing the Marines from a house. "We had been moving all night when we got to this mosque. Our squad had to go and supply over-watch security for the tanks attached to us. We moved about three to four houses down from a mosque. As we walked down the street, we saw dirt fly up as bullets hit the ground in front of us." It reminded Forester of a dirt sprinkler as the rounds kicked up the sand about them. "We went around the block and came back to this house and set up security inside. We had five Marines on the roof, and everyone else was on the bottom providing security. We had been in the house for two hours and then I hear Marines yelling on the roof, 'Get down!' Then I heard a grenade go off. A loud BANG! An insurgent on the adjacent roof had snuck up and tossed a grenade on the roof of our building. Lance Corporal Phillip Green called it out and everyone on the roof dove behind one metal trash can, which fortunately absorbed all the shrapnel from the grenade. Then everyone came running down the stairs. Lance Corporal Lamond was supplying security on the front door downstairs as we put three rifles in every opening in the house. No one was firing because we still didn't have any visible targets yet. We were still talking over and trying to figure out the whole story of what had happened. Our Corpsman, Doc Lucas Jushinski, was standing by a window when he heard a couple guys outside talking in Arabic. He silently got our attention. These insurgents were preparing to clear the house we were in. One insurgent tossed a grenade into the outer room, but we had the door closed. The grenade bounced off and exploded," Forester said.

The insurgents then moved into the house. "My Team Leader, Corporal Nick Spencer, opened the door of the room, fired a few rounds and shot him. Spencer also grabbed a grenade and threw it into the room. The insurgent was pretty well done after that. I opened the door and fired about eight rounds into his head to make sure he was dead," Forester recalled.

There is a saying among infantrymen: *Anything worth shooting is worth shooting twice; Ammo is cheap, life is expensive.*

Lance Corporal Matthew Forester continued, "We then went back into the main part of the house where I saw this guy run across this open area outside the house. I sprayed about ten rounds into this guy and saw him fall down."

Lance Corporal Forester and the other twelve Marines in the house decided it was time to leave. They got on the inter-squad radio and contacted the Marines at the mosque and asked them to: "Get us the hell out of here!" Just like ordering up a cab, within five minutes an amtrac pulled up at the front door to evacuate the besieged Marines.

Lance Corporal Matthew Forester said, "When the amtrac pulled up we were all ready to go. We ran out, but the back door of the amtrac was still closed. We weren't receiving any fire at the time so we stood there for a few minutes while my Team Leader, Corporal Spencer, began banging on the front door of the amtrac. Finally the door opened and we loaded up. Everyone was just piling in as fast they could. People were getting trampled but no one got hurt. It was a wonder no one was injured during that fight."

At 1530 two reporters were brought into a nearby minaret to photograph a dead insurgent to prove that insurgents were using protected sites for caches and fighting positions against the Marines. Before taking the reporters inside, Eckert's 1st Platoon was tasked to re-clear the mosque for the photo op not knowing a live sniper, with an AK-47, was positioned up in the minaret patiently waiting to ambush the hard hit platoon.

A young twenty-one-year-old Team Leader, Corporal James Mulak from Buffalo, New York recalled the mission. "We were tasked to go back to the minaret to photograph the dead insurgent inside. The insurgent had been shot earlier by our 3rd Platoon. Lance Corporal Miller was point as we moved back north from our base. Sergeant Sam Williams called me over after we reached the minaret to assist him in clearing a bathroom area near the mosque."

Lance Corporal William Miller, 22, from Pearland, Texas, point man, cut the lock and was followed in by Corporal Michael O'Brien. They entered the minaret and began winding their way up the darkened stairwell. Tanks had earlier punched several holes in the structure, which allowed some sunlight to stream in to the tall tower. As the stack of Marines moved slowly up the stairs they were met by a sudden burst of gunfire from the insurgent situated in the top of the tower.

"I heard a burst of gunfire coming from the minaret," Corporal Mulak said.

The first Marine in, Lance Corporal Miller, had advanced 30 steps up the tower when he was hit in the face by a six round burst of gunfire from upstairs. Miller fell mortally wounded on the stairwell. The stack of Marines directly behind him quickly backed down the minaret while Miller lay silently on the stairwell.

Sergeant Sam Williams remembered, "There was one burst and Miller went down. The Marines ran back out and regrouped and started back in when the insurgent threw some rubble down on them."

Second Lieutenant Andy Eckert watched as his Marines again hurriedly scrambled back out of the minaret. "The Marines came out coughing with soot and ash all over their faces," Eckert recalled. "Sergeant Williams, who was now one of my squad leaders, and I conferred. I asked him if Miller was hit. He said, 'I think so sir.' I said, 'Let's get him!' I sent up another stack with Williams leading them. As they entered, the enemy began pushing ash again down on their faces."

The Marines pulled back out of the minaret to brush the soot and ash from their faces and catch their breath before preparing to push back in.

The Marines outside called out their fallen comrades name, "Miller? Miller?" But to no avail. There was no answer.

Sergeant Williams yelled that he needed someone with an automatic to come over and support them as they went up the third time to reach Miller.

Before entering again, they peppered the outside of the minaret with grenades. "O'Brien and I began firing out M203 grenade launchers at the outside of the minaret to try and shake up and stun the insurgent or insurgents inside," Mulak said.

The 1st platoon Marines surrounded the minaret and out of anger began firing up at the structure. A couple of M203 grenade rounds were fired at the solid minaret. One bounced off the structure and wounded three more Marines. Corporal Michael O'Brien was hit in the neck and Lance Corporal Demarkus Brown was grazed on the lip with a piece of Marine shrapnel and Lance Corporal Gentry took shrapnel below one eye.

Mulak said, "Brown came over to me with blood pouring from his mouth. I checked him out and noticed he had lost a tooth from the shrapnel. I calmed him down by telling him he was going to be okay."

Then Corporal Mulak, Lance Corporal Kam from Henrietta, New York, Sergeant Williams and Lance Corporal Goggin from Boston, with his SAW would make a fourth trip up the winding stairs.

The Marines had tried three times to retrieve Miller's body from the stairwell. The fourth time, Mulak and Kam, along with Goggin, finally emerged from the deadly minaret with Miller's lifeless body.

Williams recalled, "That last time Goggin fired as we went up the steps, I had my M16 resting on his shoulder. When I tapped him he would fire three rounds off up the steps at the sniper. We used our flashlights to see and we all grabbed Miller and pulled him down the steps. As we pulled him out, we all fell backwards."

One of the Marines that helped get Miller's body out, Lance Corporal Michael Goggin, 19, later told an embedded reporter, "I was trying to be careful, but I was trying to get him out."

"Sergeant Williams and Lance Corporal Goggin went up and pulled him out. Miller was dead when they put him on the amtrac to take him out," said HM3 Milton Jones who was attached to 1st Platoon as a corpsman.

"The wounded O'Brien was told to take the track back to the aid station with the other casualties," Williams recounted. "When we were leaving I looked back and saw O'Brien get off the track and run back to join us. He had his weapon in one hand and his other hand held gauze on his neck wound."

Mulak, who had lost Miller from his team, said, "I was real mad and upset by the loss of Miller."

As 1st Platoon pulled back south to their firm base, the sniper in the minaret rubbed salt into their wounds by firing a few rounds at them.

Air strikes were called in to destroy the minaret once and for all. At 1545 an air strike took both the mosque and the enemy sniper out.

The Marines of hard hit Bravo Company conducted a re-supply and bedded down early for the night. High above them, Basher was on station throughout the night keeping a watchful eye on the enemy.

The shaken Marines took the death of Lance Corporal William Miller to heart. Lance Corporal David Houck began honoring the dead Marines from Bravo Company by putting their names on the camouflage cover of his kevlar helmet. Miller's name was added next to Anderson, Wells, Jimenez, and Ziolkowski's names. When Captain Omohundro found out he was concerned that the enemy would use a long-range camera to take a picture of Houck's helmet and then use it for propaganda purposes. Or that one of the photographers with the battalion could take a picture of the helmet and the photo might make its way into hometown newspapers before the families of the Marines had been properly notified. Listening to his captain, Houck covered his kevlar helmet with duct tape but, being the resourceful person that he was, found another way to honor his fallen comrades. Finding a discarded sandbag, he affectionately and painstakingly inscribed the ten names of his fallen buddies on the fabric of the sandbag, which flew at half-mast on the flagpole of an abandoned schoolyard in the heart of Fallujah.

"We took it hard that night, everyone was crying, no one said anything, it was just quiet," Corpsman Jones remembered.

Sergeant Sam Williams said, "When we were back at our firm base, I was bitching about our platoon doing the dirty stuff and Gunny Brown came over and put his hand on my shoulder and told me to 'calm down!' He kept us focused in the city."

"The next morning we were riding up north in amtracs to occupy a firm base in the center of the city when we stopped by the mosque and the minaret which had held the sniper. Our Doc had left his medical bag there the day before," said Eckert. "On top of the pile of rubble from the minaret, lay a dead body, the sniper."

That day, Tank Platoon Commander First Lieutenant David Klingensmith, received a radio call from Bravo Company near Phase Line Isabelle. "They said they needed us so we headed back down and got in the alleyway where they were. I saw three Marines on the ground with a corpsman working on them. I moved my tank around them and just as I did, two or three insurgents came out of the alleyway shooting from the hip. We fired killing some of those guys, and also an AC-130 came in and killed a bunch of them. Bravo wanted to push down near a clearing where I had been ambushed earlier that day. I recommended, and he agreed, that we not take that route. Instead, they pushed back down Phase Line Ethan. I had one tank facing south and one facing into a house they wanted to enter. Both of our tanks immediately started to take fire. As Bravo Company Marines entered the house they met insurgents. The Marines came pouring out yelling, 'Avalanche!' meaning the enemy was ready to explode it. I destroyed that house and fire finished it off as it burned from secondary explosions," Klingensmith explained.

The Marines had reached the southern rim of the city and from this point there was nothing but desert until you reached the river. Reaching the edge of the city didn't mean they could declare victory. Not yet. Now the Marines had to root out the enemy that had gone to ground to the north when the battalion passed through.

Bravo Company was one of two companies in all of Fallujah, Marine or Army, who walked the entire way through the city. Maybe put more appropriately, fought their way on foot, all the way through the city.

"When we reached the southern reaches of the city and there were no more houses for the enemy to hide and fight from, the initial assault was over," Omohundro said.

Bravo Company Begins to Clear by Sectors

Brandl knew his Marines were wearing down from the strain of the constant fighting and from being in a hot combat zone for so long. "I went down there to eyeball the Marines and I knew they were tired. Not that they couldn't continue, but they needed to get a little rest and re-supply for that last final push," Lieutenant Colonel Brandl explained. "Although tired and exhausted, their feeling was, 'Let's get the job done.'"

The Marines of 1/8 would have to internalize the grief of losing buddies in the bitter street fighting, for the job of clearing the city would require clear heads and nerves of steel.

On November 18, after ten days of continuos fighting, Bravo Company Marines rotated out of the city to take showers. The one day of rest and showers would end too soon for the battle-weary Marines. Upon their return to Fallujah, Omohundro's platoons began to prepare for the clearing of sectors within their zone. They would be trying to dig out the die-hard remnants of the insurgency that still wanted to play cat and mouse. That day of showers was one of the quieter days Bravo Company had spent in the city.

Things would change dramatically the following day, November 19. 1st Platoon was tasked to clear sector 848 at 0800. Meanwhile 2nd

Platoon was standing internal security for the company and Chris Wilkens 3rd Platoon became the QRF (Quick Reaction Force) for the company.

Second Lieutenant Eckert's 1st Platoon began clearing the area when they saw several unarmed males walking around with white flags. They made note of the men, but could do nothing since the curfew in the city was 0800 to 1200 each day. These men were within curfew, so they waved and let them go.

About two hours had passed and 1st Platoon continued their clearing movement down the rubble-strewn streets. "We were clearing block after block," said Eckert.

Outside a house the Marines of 1st Platoon spotted a man who was just standing there waving a white flag and smiling at them as they passed slowly by. The Marines checked him out before cautiously moving off down the street. A few Marines suspiciously glanced over their shoulders at the friendly man still seen waving at them. As soon as the Marines began turning a corner the man dropped the white flag, jumped over a fence, and grabbed a hidden weapon.

After moving a short distance the Marines began receiving small arms fire from a building in the northeastern corner of sector 848. Eckert quickly moved his platoon to isolate the building and cordon off the area. Then the Marines moved forward to make entry into the building to clear it out.

An enemy fighter hidden inside the building was ready for the Marines as they entered the front door. The insurgent had waited patiently for the patrolling Marines before springing his deadly trap. Corporal Mulak's team, consisting of Brown and Gavriel, entered the house. Mulak went left into one room and Brown and Gavriel went right. As Brown and Gavriel attempted to enter a room off the foyer, the enemy fighter fired his AK-47 through a crack in the door. Inside the house the noise from the AK-47 was unbelievably loud.

"I heard the loud gunfire and turned to see Gavriel get knocked up off his feet and get blown back. He went down. Brown was also hit. I could see muzzle flashes coming from the crack in the door. After firing, the insurgent then slammed the door shut. I tried to fire but my gun jammed. I reached for a grenade but I had used them all," Mulak said.

Lance Corporal Demarkus Brown, 22, from Martinsville, Virginia, took a piece of shrapnel to his left shoulder that traveled into his chest. Wounded, Brown quickly stumbled from the house into the safety of the street.

"When Brown came running out of the house he was yelling, 'I'm blind! I can't see!' Doc Nadermann and Doc Jones began working on him," Sergeant Sam Williams recalled. "When Doc Jones saw the extent of Brown's wound he said, 'Oh shit!' He knew it was bad."

Corporal Mulak was the only member of his team not wounded and he was now isolated in a room in the house with his weapon jammed. Clearing it would draw attention from the insurgents. "I looked over at Gavriel and saw him roll over and give me the thumbs up sign that he was still alive and then he rolled back over," Mulak remembers.

Finally Mulak, with his weapon still jammed, sprinted from the house. "I was yelling, 'friendly coming out! As I exited the house. I told Gunny Brown where Gavriel was located in the common area of the house and that he was okay but pinned down and which room the insurgent was fighting from. I checked Brown out before posting security at the back of the house. He keep saying, 'I don't want to die.' I kept telling him he was going to be all right. They were trying to stabilize him but he looked as though he was fading fast," Mulak said.

Lieutenant Eckert made his way to the rear of the house, climbed a wall, and jumped to the roof. He yelled for other Marines to follow him to the rooftop. A few minutes went by as Marines climbed and clawed there way up to the roof of the house to join Eckert. Because they were loaded down with heavy equipment, a few Marines fell backwards from the wall while trying to climb. Eckert was going to have his Marines reverse the usual assault pattern of a stack by attacking from the roof down. They would secure the rooftop, then the inside top deck, followed by each individual lower level to the bottom deck. Eckert already had the courtyard secured.

"I sent a stack down a stairwell from the roof," Eckert said. "I went to the front gate of the house. When the stack reached the first floor they were in a position where the insurgents couldn't see them from the back room. The enemy threw a grenade out into the hallway and it exploded."

The grenade took down three more Marines from 1st Platoon, Lance Corporal Christian Hussong suffered shrapnel wounds to his leg, foot and arm and Eckert's radioman, PFC Manuel Sanabria, was hit in the left arm and right shoulder. Sanabria, who had earlier hurt is ankle on entering Fallujah, had followed Eckert almost every foot of the way through the volatile city. Lance Corporal Dimitrios Gavriel, 29, the former Wall Street broker from New York already wounded and down in the house, was hit with more shrapnel this time from the grenade blast. Sergeant Brandon Croll, Weapons Company, took shrapnel wounds to his left shoulder. The company's friendly Iraqi interpreter, Moo, who had rushed into the house expecting to talk to the residents, was mortally wounded from three rounds from an AK-47. He would later die from the wound among the men who shared his beliefs of serving and honoring his country.

One of the only original squad leaders that had entered the city with Eckert's platoon that had not become a casualty yet, Corporal Scott Nolin, took shrapnel wounds to his face, right leg and left arm.

"Sergeant Samuel Williams, Corporal Eric Goss, and Sergeant McDade in the house, began throwing grenades around the corner into the room containing the insurgents," Eckert said. The concussion of the exploding grenade rocked the house.

Williams remembered, "I went into the house with McDade and Goss. The insurgent was only three or four feet away from us in the next room. We would throw a grenade in and after the explosion we could hear them talking so we would throw another in. After five or six grenades we saw the gunmen's hand drop out the doorway. Goss went in to make sure he was dead."

Eckert remembers, "I was talking to the Marines through an open window from the porch as they fired on the insurgent. When they pushed into the room they found the guy riddled with shrapnel and a round to the head. When I went in I recognized him as the man who earlier had waved and smiled at us." Eckert stared at the dead man and shook his head before getting back into the fight.

A Medevac and the Quick Response Force Platoon rushed to the area to assist 1st Platoon at 1030. The Marines return fire had killed one insurgent and wounded two others in the fierce firefight that had flared around the house.

"We were waiting for the casualties to come in," Corpsman HM3 Jones said. "They brought in one of my closest friends, Lance Corporal Demarkus Brown. He loved football and martial arts. I asked him, 'Are you ready to come home? When we get back we'll go see your girlfriend.' Because, before we came to Fallujah he had been talking about getting married. He said, 'I'm hit bad!' and told me he wanted to go home. I patched him up and waited for the amtracs to come up and get him back to the forward aid station. Tears were rolling from my eyes."

HM3 Jones helped carry his good friend, Lance Corporal Demarkus Brown, on a stretcher to the waiting amtrac. His fellow Marines also assisted Lance Corporal Dimitrios Gavriel's body into the back of the amtrac. Gavriel had been wounded earlier on November 11 and had opted to rejoin his fellow Marines in the fight. But this time he had succumbed to his wounds while the battle raged in the enemy held house.

Sergeant Major Hope recalled Lance Corporal Demarkus Brown when he had first received a minor wound, and then later arriving at the forward aid station with the fatal wound. "I was standing outside the aid station and Brown was standing there with a bandage on his lip where a grenade had fragged him. His First Sergeant Daniels and I went over to talk to him. I said, 'Hey Devil Dog, keep your head down! You already have that Purple Heart. You be careful when you go back out there.' He got on the amtrac and went back out and the next day we had WIAs coming in pretty regularly. When the amtrac pulled up, someone said it was Brown. I was standing there waiting to see the results of it. They were working on Brown and I could see Gavriel was already gone. I kept standing there waiting. About ten minutes later they came out and said he didn't make it. I think of all the Marines we lost, that bothered me the most. Everytime you saw him he always had a smile on his face. You could tell he was a good young man. After this happened, I knew I had to be out with my Marines. After that we all went out to Bravo Company, who had suffered a lot of casualties. I went everywhere the Colonel went, but when we were with Bravo Company I told the Colonel, 'Sir I'm going to stay out here with them.' I needed to be with the Marines. He agreed," Hope said.

A few hours later, HM3 Jones remembered the call that every Marine dreads receiving, that a friend has died. "They radioed back from the forward aid station a few hours later and told me that Lance Corporal Brown didn't make it," Jones remembered.

Corporal James Mulak had earlier lost Lance Corporal William Miller at the minaret and now both Gavriel and Brown in one house. He was the only member of his team left standing.

Bravo Company ran patrols over the next few days looking for the elusive enemy and their caches of weapons still hidden deep in the city.

Since entering the city twelve days before, infantrymen had not been able to write home. Over the next few days the Marines would dash off a letter to anxious love ones waiting at home. On November 20, Lance Corporal David Houck, Bravo Company, finally found time to jot down a few quick lines to his family to ease their fears:

> Dear Dad & Mom,
> Well, as you can probably tell by now, I'm sitting smack in the middle of Fallujah, Iraq. I've collected a couple of new scratches from broken glass, but otherwise I'm unharmed. There has been a couple of reporters following us around throughout the main portion of the fighting, so you might find some pictures of us in the New York Times between 09 Nov. through 18 Nov. The fighting has been fairly bloody so far but the insurgents seem to have switched tactics to a more hit and run approach. There is still no word of relief, but at least I

can write letters now. Just remember that I am really
good at what I do and try not to worry.
Love,
David

This would be the last letter Lance Corporal David Houck would ever write.

On November 23, Lance Corporal Jeffery Holmes, Bravo Company had time to write a short letter home to his family describing the fighting:

Dear Mom, Dad, & Cory,

How is everything? I am doing well. We are probably going to be in Fallujah for awhile. It's been pretty scary. We have lost a lot of Marines. It seems like the bad guys are everywhere. We are killing them though. We've found lots and lots of RPG and AKs, Mortars, and ammo. Hopefully it helps out in the end. A lot of them are starting to turn themselves in. They know they have no chance against us. We have blown them up everywhere they go. If they try to hide in a house we blow that up too. It's pretty cool. We use everything we can to kill them. It's still scary but I put everything behind me for now to focus on the mission. You have probably seen and heard us on the news. Its kind of weird always watching the news growing up and now knowing your on it in something so big that everyone will see. Supposedly this is supposed to be a big one for the Marine Corps history. They said this city has never been taken a long time in the past. We are the first and it feels pretty good knowing I was here to take part in it. There is a lot of death here too. You see on TV and movies and think it's cool but there's nothing pretty about it. We joke around about the enemy though. They deserve every bullet we put in them. They are all cowards....

Love, your son Jeff

On November 23, Corporal Gentian Marku, 22, who had been born in Piraj, Albania and was now an infantryman in Bravo Company, also managed to write home to his worried family. He told them he was all right but that he had already lost a lot of good friends in the fighting in the city, one of which was Lance Corporal Bradley Parker. The young Marine from Albania was thankful and proud for the chance to serve his new adopted country. He loved his job and enjoyed the camaraderie of his fellow Marines in 1/8. He was optimistic about his return and told his younger sister Joana, 16, that he would teach her to drive when he returned home from Iraq.

Captain Kahn, Weapons Company CO, at the fire support center in the Government Center, remembered receiving a call for a fire mission from Lieutenant Collins of Bravo Company. Collins was located in the southern part of the city.

"He said the target, a group of guys trying to set up a mortar, was about a thousand meters away from him. The fire mission was approved. A few minutes later Collins shifts his firing position," Kahn said.

After the fourth shift mission the perplexed Kahn asked him, "What's going on?"

Collins answered, "Well, these guys keep setting up this mortar tube and we keep shooting them and they're dying and the rest run. Then they come back and try to set it up again."

Kahn said, "We had one of the unmanned UAVs over the site with a video camera trained on the insurgents. We could see everything on a small video monitor at the Government Center. We saw a couple of dead guys and then another pile of dead guys and then another pile of dead guys. On the monitor we could see these guys coming back out, dragging the mortar tube. Then we saw them run back into the house. We approved the dropping of the house." The use of the Dragon Eye and the fire mission put an end to the cat and mouse game being played by that insurgent mortar team.

Another instance of the effective use of this UAV occurred even before the push through Fallujah began, wrote 1st Lieutenant Chris Wilkens:

> *In August, I was asked to send one of my best Marines in the platoon to a class to learn how to fly an Unmanned Aerial Vehicle called the Dragon Eye that was to be used for aerial surveillance during our company-level operations. David (Houck) immediately came to mind. David's proficiency flying the surveillance plane was quickly recognized by the highest ranks in our battalion and was used on numerous occasions including the operation leading into Fallujah.*

Thanksgiving Day with Bravo Company

While family and friends in the States were trying to enjoy their turkey dinners and watch football teams battle one another on television, thousands of miles away in Fallujah, the Marines of Battalion 1/8 were involved in a real battle, one that meant life or death to them.

The next few days fighting would be hard on Bravo Company; the casualties they suffered would bear this out. Bravo Company's decimated 1st Platoon began clearing sector 854 while 3rd Platoon started clearing zones 851 and 852. The tedious task of knocking in doors and searching for the elusive enemy became an extremely dangerous job for the Marines.

At 0730, November 25, First Lieutenant Chris Wilkens' 3rd Platoon began its movement north with the assistance of AAVs that had been attached for additional fire support and to provide immediate Medevac of casualties if needed. Captain Read Omohundro had the use of four tanks and the use of a D-9 bulldozer during the clearing operation.

At 0800, Second Lieutenant Andy Eckert's 1st Platoon reported back to Omohundro about a lot of suspicious civilian traffic in the vicinity of a nearby mosque. Eckert questioned the civilians and found out that regiment was running a food and water distribution point near the mosque and water tower, without Bravo Company's prior knowledge. This was later confirmed by radio with the battalion.

Chaplain Cox recalled, "Captain Matthew Nodine with JAG, and First Lieutenant Palmer Jones, Assistant Operations Officer, had been ordered to set up a food distribution for the civilians who had on their own accord stayed in the city. They did a great job in Fallujah."

Attaching themselves with Eckert's platoon on patrol, Chaplain Cox and his Protector Corporal Zeno who was armed with his M16, walked along with the Marines. The forty-one-year-old Cox had talked his way into going out with the decimated 1st Platoon. "I just wanted to let these young men know that if I go with them, God is with us. The Marines at this time in the fight were still highly motivated. They were awesome. When they were told to move by their officers, they quickly got up and moved. They didn't hesitate," Cox said.

Omohundro said, "We occupied positions along Phase Line Henry orienting to the south to a building center where we started to receive enemy fire. We had questioned a family, an elderly man, two sons, a woman, and two children, that lived there to find out what was going on." Not getting any useful information from the Iraqi family, Omohundro had them released.

Phase Line Henry, where Bravo Company now found themselves, was a wide six-lane wide highway that had a built up grass median.

Corporal Silva, 3rd Platoon, 1st Squad recalled, "We started finding weapon caches with RPKs, RPGs, Molotov cocktails, you name it, everything was in that room. I couldn't reach Lieutenant Wilkens on the radio until I moved up on top of the roof. He had Pennock's squad move over to our Area of Operation, and told us to take them back to the firm base for EOD (Explosive Ordnance Disposal). I said, 'Sir why can't EOD come over here with trucks?' I didn't want to take our squad through a neighborhood we hadn't cleared yet. He said, 'No, go back to the firm base and get EOD.'"

First Lieutenant Wilkens had earlier requested that the EOD walk to them, but he in turn was ordered to send a squad back and escort the two EOD Sailors through the volatile streets of Fallujah.

Silva said, "I took my squad with SMAW gunner Lance Corporal Llerena. A good friend of mine, Corporal Marku, from Warren, Michigan, whose father had been a captain in the Albanian police force, came over to me as we were pushing out. I told him, 'I'll be right back bro.' When we left I heard a lot of firing behind us and when I got back to the firm base, I immediately got on the radio to find out what was going on."

Around 1000 Corporal Jason Pennock's 3rd Squad, 3rd Platoon came up to relieve 1st Squad at the large weapons cache in zone 851. He kept one team at the cache site, and sent his second team over to an adjacent building to clear it. After entry the 3rd Squad came under small arms fire from within the house.

First Lieutenant Wilkens immediately called in the AAVs and a MAP section to help eliminate that growing threat. Now under steady fire, 3rd Platoon began to take casualties. Tank support was quickly called in to assist the beleaguered Marines. First Lieutenant Wilkens' platoon pushed the insurgents back to a nearby building and began to cordon off the entire area. The insurgents had prepared the house as an ambush site, as well as a fallback position from which to make a last stand. The enemy fighters in the house weren't going to run away. They were going to die fighting and try to take as many Marines as they could with them.

The house the insurgents had taken refuge in looked a mirror image of thousands of others in Fallujah. It was a one-story structure, which had a courtyard that was surrounded by a high brick wall. Only this house had an RPK aimed directly at the front door where the Marines would be entering.

Team Leader Corporal Gentian Marku led the Marine stack to the front entrance of the building and proceeded to kick in the door. Two of the Marines in the stack, Lance Corporal Rodriguez and Lance Corporal Holmes had both been wounded in action just days before. Holmes had taken shrapnel to his neck and had been treated. First Lieutenant Wilkens had wanted to have the pair medevaced out at that time but both Marines had refused and chose to stay with their fellow infantrymen in Fallujah.

As soon as the door was kicked open the RPK immediately opened up on the exposed Marines standing about the front entrance. Instantly Marku was hit but managed to make his way around a corner and out of view of the enemy fighters. As long as he braced himself upright, against the wall, the wounded Marku would stay out of the enemy fire zone. He found himself propped against the wall at the east-end of the house near the front door. Growing steadily weaker from the loss of blood, Marku slowly slid to the ground becoming visible to the insurgents. He was hit once more by enemy fire. But to attest to his will to live and to his stamina, he once again pushed himself back up against the wall and out of the enemy fire zone.

The 3rd Platoon Marines were now under intense enemy fire in the courtyard and began suffering more casualties from exploding enemy grenades. Texan Lance Corporal Thomas Hodges was hit with multiple shrapnel wounds to the neck, right shoulder, right hip, and his right foot.

A young Marine who loved football, Lance Corporal Jeffery Holmes, 20, from the small New England town of White River Junction, Vermont was killed by the blazing enemy fire coming from within the house. Holmes' body lay in the doorway to the kitchen at the far end of the wall. Lance Corporal Michael Rodriguez was also hit and went down.

Engineer Lance Corporal Blake Benson, a good friend of Marku, who also hailed from Michigan, took painful shards of shrapnel to his head, right foot, right thigh, and knee. Although wounded Benson continued to supply suppressing fire on the enemy while other Marines moved to whatever cover they could find.

Sheer chaos now enveloped the courtyard as Lance Corporal Benson tried to rescue his Team Leader Marku. During the rescue attempt Benson took a round to the head. This round almost destroyed his right ear and also broke his jaw. Now badly wounded, Lance Corporal Benson continued to fire his weapon at the enemy until more support arrived.

Also badly wounded and bleeding profusely, Lance Corporal Michael Rodriguez managed to get to his feet and work his way over to the protection of a brick wall in the courtyard where he to began returning fire with his M16. "I fired a magazine through the open window and then dropped to the ground. When I hit the ground I dislocated my shoulder. I could hear about eight insurgents talking to each other in the house. They outgunned us," Rodriguez remembered.

None of the Marines of Marku's stack had made it into the house and still found themselves pinned down under heavy accurate enemy fire in the open courtyard.

An insurgent ran to an open window in the front of the house and started spraying RPK machine gun rounds at those Marines pinned down in the open quadrant. Impacting bullets were chipping pieces of mortar off the courtyard wall and kicking up gravel and dirt. The noise from the M16s, machine guns, and exploding grenades was ear shattering to the Marines pinned down in the courtyard.

Staff Sergeant Ben Alicea who was positioned near the fighting describes the chaos. "I heard Hodges yell to us, 'Stop throwing grenades!' I then saw an insurgent run out of the house and throw a grenade that didn't explode. He ran back in the house. The fighting went on for a long time," recalled Alicea.

Feigning death and lying under the window near the badly wounded Hodges, Rodriguez heard the unmistakable thud of an enemy grenade hit the ground near him. He rolled over Hodges body to escape the blast. "I thought Hodges was dead and he would shield me from the blast. When the grenade exploded it caused a lot of smoke so I jumped up and made my way to the courtyard wall. Lance Corporal Blake Benson, a combat engineer, had his bag with C-4 plastic explosives in it catch on fire. He tossed it but the C-4 began popping off and a piece of it landed on my leg. I started freaking out. I used a tool and tried to break through the courtyard wall to the rest of the platoon in the street," Rodriguez said.

Nearby, a Marine tank with the name Rommel painted in black on its barrel trained the main gun on the house but had to withhold fire for the sake of their fellow Marines still trapped in the courtyard and still under intense fire from within the house.

Corporal Vela, manning an M-240G, was positioned to the rear of the building where he could isolate the enemy fighters who tried to escape out the back door through a shed that was covered with a corrugated roof. As the enemy fighters gathered in the shed a FiST Marine, Lance Corporal Burton, tossed cement cinder blocks down on the roof to open a breach wide enough to get a grenade into it. After a second cinder block opened a huge hole in the roof, the Marines began to throw grenades into the shed filled with the insurgents.

Back in the courtyard, Corporal Gentian Marku's strength finally gave out and he slowly slid to the ground of the courtyard where he died.

The insurgents in the house had either run out of room to maneuver or were just tired of running from the Marines. Either way, now, they were going to stand and die fighting in that house. It continued to be a vicious fight for the Marines.

Meanwhile other Marines attempted to enter the courtyard and rescue those still pinned down. They continually engaged the enemy in close combat. One Marine sniper's actions would cause his superiors to submit him for a Navy Cross for rescuing fellow Marines. Lance Corporal David Houck, along with Corporal Vela, Lance Corporal Coppick, Corporal Hoogsteden, Corporal Straub and that Marine sniper were all occupying a nearby roof and were under heavy enemy machine gun fire. From their vantage point they continued to direct fire on one of the enemy fighters driving him deeper into the building and allowing the Marines to start rescuing the wounded. The noise around the house was so deafening that it was hard for the Marines to communicate with one another.

The Marine sniper quickly moved to an overwatch position and spotted the wounded Marines down in the courtyard. He courageously low-crawled close to the enemy stronghold to gain intelligence and then ran along the rooftops under intense enemy fire to relay the intelligence to First Lieutenant Wilkens. The sniper returned and threw a grenade silencing one of the enemy's machine guns. He low-crawled again to another area and dropped a grenade through a hole in the roof, eliminating several more enemy personnel and silencing another machine gun. Lance Corporal Houck then rushed down from the rooftop and along with the Marine sniper went back into the courtyard under heavy enemy fire to help rescue the badly wounded Hodges.

First Lieutenant Chris Wilkens described this heroic act by his Marines. Wilkens wrote:

> *Immediately after the tank knocked a part of the wall down, a sniper attached to 3rd Platoon ran into the intense gunfire and pulled Lance Corporal Blake Benson to safety. HM3 Ruizpupo immediately began administering first aid to Benson. The Marines in 3rd Platoon watched in awe as a Marine sniper ran into the courtyard again. This time he was joined by Lance Corporal Houck. The two Marines grabbed and pulled Corporal Hodges who had severe bleeding from the neck. As Houck stopped the bleeding on Hodges, the tank commander threw a Marine sniper a fire extinguisher, and he extinguished the fire on Corporal Marku's head. After he extinguished the fire, he carried Marku's body to safety. Houck and the Marine sniper both did these acts under extreme, accurate and close enemy fire. It was a miracle that neither one of them was hit doing such heroic deeds. There were so many enemy guns in such a small area, we made several attempts to enter that courtyard, and as soon as we peeked over a wall or tried to go through a gate, we were met with immediate gunfire that was too close for comfort. Houck and the Marine sniper both knew, and unhesitatingly ran into the courtyard.*

Now safely outside the courtyard, Houck held his hand on Hodges wounded throat to prevent him from bleeding to death until the Navy corpsman could get to him. Blood oozed from between Houck's fingers but he managed to keep Hodges alive on the streets of Fallujah. For his actions on this day Houck would be submitted for a Navy Commendation Medal with a Combat "V" for Valor. Later that evening, Houck grieved over not being able to also rescue his good friend, Corporal Gentian Marku.

Sergeant Allen Hayden, 21, a married Marine from Immokalee, Florida, 2nd Squad Leader, 3rd Platoon, was located one street over when the Marines were fired on at that house. He describes the fight on that Thanksgiving Day. "I heard the firing and we quickly began to cordon off the building behind the house where 3rd Squad had taken fire from. I sent one team to the outside of the house to a hole in the wall.

They were covering the hole to stop any escape from the building. Then we got the call that they needed support. We helped the Guardian Angel's mortar section to the top of the building and then I moved my squad to link up with Lieutenant Wilkens at a building adjacent to the enemy occupied house. The insurgents had an RPK machine gun firing from a front window. Lieutenant Wilkens told the tank to knock down the courtyard wall so my squad could go through the breach to get our wounded out. The tank was still positioned in front of the breach and my seven Marines moved around the back of the tank for cover to get to the other side. We went back to the wall and jumped over into the courtyard. Now there were six of us in the courtyard. Three of us began laying down suppressive fire on the window while the other three Marines started to drag out casualties through an open gate," Hayden said.

Corporal Pennock got on his "grunt phone" and told the tank which courtyard wall to knock down but he informed the tank commander that "there were friendlies on the other side of the wall." The Marines nearby felt the hot breath of the tank's exhaust on their faces, as it maneuvered in the street in support of the downed infantry.

"I saw one Marine still alive in the courtyard; Lance Corporal Michael Rodriguez. Although wounded, he was still standing and returning fire near a wall. He was firing at the outside window the insurgent was using. The enemy machine gunner then pulled back from the window Rodriguez was firing into," Sergeant Hayden recounted. "Rodriguez, with his accurate firing, had driven the enemy machine gunner back into the house. Marku was lying on the ground. Near him and also lying on the ground was one of our engineers, Lance Corporal Benson. I told Lance Corporal Charles Neely to lay down covering fire for Corporal Wayne Bowman, Corporal Pennock, and Staff Sergeant Scott Parry so they could go in and recover Rodriguez."

Staff Sergeant Parry ordered an AAV to punch a hole in the west side of the courtyard wall. Corporal Pennock then went through the hole punched by the AAV and began retrieving the wounded Rodriguez. Then Corporal Bowman and Staff Sergeant Parry followed through the hole less than two minutes after Pennock had entered the courtyard. The enemy fire was so intense that they decided not to take a chance of exposing Rodriguez by taking him back out the hole in the wall. Instead they would lift him over the wall of the courtyard.

Sergeant Hayden remembers, "They ran in and pulled him to the side of the building out of the direct fire and started to give him first aid. Rodriguez was still in the courtyard but out of the line of fire. At this time two other Marines and I moved to the next courtyard over and tried to knock a hole in the wall to help get Rodriguez out of the courtyard so he wouldn't have to exit through the gate which was under fire. The wall was too hard and thick so we hoisted him over the wall and took him to an AAV."

"Finally Corporal Bowman and Corporal Pennock patched me up and tossed me over the wall. They got me on a track," a grateful Rodriguez recalls.

Staff Sergeant Parry, Corporal Bowman, Corporal Pennock and Corporal Billiot all entered the house and saw a canister tossed toward them and pulled back out the front door. The Marines were trying as quickly as humanly possible to get their brother Marines from the deadly courtyard.

At last, all the wounded and dead Marines were taken from the kill zone of the courtyard. All of the injured Marines were medevaced out of the fire zone by 1230.

The Marines continued to engage the enemy in a fierce firefight for at least another hour. Now the Marines pushed back into the house a second time to clear it of insurgents. Inside the house the Leathernecks repeatedly went back outside to reload and then return to the fight.

"After entering (again), they heard POPS, which they assumed were grenades going off and pulled back out the front door into the courtyard. The grenades were CS grenades (chemical smoke), so they went back and pulled Holmes from near the doorway of the building," Hayden said.

Once all the Marines were out of the area, a GBU (Guided Bomb Unit) bomb was dropped on the enemy held house. Another bomb took out a second structure to the immediate south where some movement by the enemy had been spotted earlier.

"After everyone was out of the courtyard and heading back to the firm base, they called in an air strike on the house. We heard the explosions which destroyed the house," Sergeant Hayden recalled.

In just a matter of seconds, 3rd Platoon had suffered six casualties in the fight. Four wounded, including Corporal Straub who was hit in the face, and two killed, in one clearing operation.

Corporal Silva, 22, said, "I found out over the radio about the casualties and I was pissed. I threw my helmet and began kicking over water bottles and just started bawling. If we hadn't found that weapons cache and gone back to the firm base that day, that would have been my squad and me in that house. Marku wanted to become a police officer when he left the Corps. He first came to the United States when he was fifteen. He was a wheeler-dealer. He could get you anything. He was loved by everybody."

Chaplain Cox remembered hearing about the death of Marku, "He was just a nice kid. Earlier when Gavriel died, Marku had turned to me and said, 'I don't know why' and I answered 'I don't know either.' And we both hugged and cried."

3rd Platoon's only corpsman Luis Ruizpupo from Elizabeth, New Jersey, remembered, "The experiences and emotions you feel out there don't compare to anything else. One time we were under heavy machine gun fire and from across the street I saw what looked like a Marine get shot in the face. Really it was a piece of concrete that ejected from the wall and made a hole in his nose, but at the time, with all the blood, I thought he was shot. When I ran over to provide medical assistance, he just looked up at me and asked, 'Am I still pretty?' It was then when I realized that to survive in combat you have to have a little bit of humor. I saw myself as one of them. I took part in the battles, I did everything they did, but I had some medical knowledge and could bandage them up."

2nd Platoon, Weapons Company Marine, Lance Corporal Sven Mozdiez, who spent the first week or two in Fallujah sleeping in his Humvee at night, recalled assisting a line company in a fight, "The company we were supporting had discovered a tunnel system between two houses. A firefight developed in the street with two Marines trapped inside. One was hit with a Molotov cocktail and the other was strafed with an RPK. Gunnery Sergeant Cayee, Corporal Ray and I dismounted our truck and ran up to aid the line company. We helped get both Marines out of the house. We put them up on our Humvee and took them to the BAS."

Every Marine is a rifleman first. Tank Commander Chris Meyers found those words to be true even for tankers in the southern part of the city as he and some of his Marines became infantrymen in the clearing of a house. Meyers said, "One afternoon there was a firefight along the boundary between the Iraqi forces and Bravo Company and two of the friendly Iraqi forces got shot and we ended up going in. I took my Executive Officer Markley, my loader Lance Corporal Martinez, and the XO's loader, Corporal Alexander. The D-9 dozer had gotten stuck in a nearby building that we believed harbored some enemy. We had already shot twenty main gun rounds into the house. Finally the five of us dismounted our tanks, and armed with shotguns and M16s we ended up clearing this entire three-story house." The rifle has been and remains the backbone of the Marine Corps.

At 1500 the battalion commander, Lieutenant Colonel Brandl and the Regimental Commander, Colonel Tucker, visited with Bravo Company. While there, Brandl issued orders to Captain Omohundro for the clear in zone to be executed on the following day, November 26.

That night Bravo Company officers talked over the day's action as they prepared to conduct the sweep in zone the following morning. As things quieted down, the company eventually bedded down for the night, but not before having access to a late-night Thanksgiving dinner.

November 25, Thanksgiving Day, Fallujah. A Charlie Company Marine, Lance Corporal Giusti, 21, remembered Thanksgiving in Fallujah, "It was the best meal we had had since coming to the city. We had been living on MREs the whole time until we got the turkey. We got to relax and tell our stories to each other. Basically, we just relaxed that evening. But right after eating we had to go back on post."

It was a bittersweet Thanksgiving for members of Bravo Company after taking several casualties on that day. Chaplain Cox said, "I was asked to say a blessing for that Thanksgiving meal. It was right after Marku and Holmes were killed and I thought, *what could I possibly give thanks for?* I said in the prayer, 'We are thankful for the honor and privilege of knowing great men like Holmes and Marku.'"

"I talked to Holmes' team leader and a fellow squad member who had been in the fight. One had been wounded in the nose but had refused treatment until later. I spent time letting them talk and process what had happened. The wounded Marine was so animated during our discussion that he was splattering blood on me when he talked," Chaplain Cox said.

Cox tried not to pay attention to the Marine's wound. He didn't want to make the Marine feel self conscious about it. A Chaplain has Marines coming to him to confide in, someone to tell about what is bothering them, but the chaplain has no one to confide in but God.

AVV Marine Lance Corporal Jonathan Olexa got to call his parents' home in Connecticut. It was the first time he had reached and talked to them since November 1, before entering the city. At home his family couldn't bring themselves to feast on a large Thanksgiving meal while their son was in Fallujah. Instead the Olexa family broke open MREs. The same rations their son and his fellow Marines had been eating for weeks along the smelly, dirty streets and alleyways of Fallujah.

Operation Deer Drive With Alpha Company

Brandl had Captain Bethea's Charlie Company and the Iraqi Security Forces under his command set up blocking positions in the eastern part of the battalion's zone of operations. He would then have Bravo Company and Alpha Company clear all of the houses in their zones. "I would have three companies moving from west to east," said Brandl. "There were a good chunk of holdouts still in that area. The enemy was used to seeing us on routes running north to south, so we turned things around on them and we attacked west to east. It threw the enemy off guard."

"My two tanks led the Iraqi forces, Klingensmith's tanks led Bravo Company, and Lee's tanks led Alpha Company during Operation Deer Drive," explained Captain Meyers.

November 26; "As we went farther south the insurgents had no where to go but to fight and I saw more of the fanatical fighters. We fought them on the streets, alleyways and courtyards, and in the homes, in bedrooms and kitchens. We had several bad engagements where we pushed the enemy into the blocking force. We found a lot more caches as we went house to house. Because of casualties, one of my mortar sections became a rifle squad in the city," said Captain Cunningham.

"Those young Marines were true heroes. My lieutenants didn't get to the company until a month before we were deployed to Iraq and they did great. They were tremendous leaders. Our staff NCOs did great," Captain Cunningham remembered.

Without hesitation the Marines pushed through the city's dangerous streets. Covered in sweat and sometimes with hunger gnawing at them, they pressed on without complaint to get the mission done. As they moved they would scan the buildings up and down the streets and alleys. The search went street by street, house by house and then room by room. "Contact right!" or "Contact left!" would be shouted out. The young Marines would then clear the downstairs and proceed up deck by deck until the house or building was cleansed of the threat from the enemy fighters.

One of the young Marines in Cunningham's company, Corporal Michael Ergo, 1st Team Leader, 2nd Squad, 3rd Platoon remembers advancing to a suspicious looking two-story house with a courtyard in the back. The Marine from California who loved snowboarding, hiking and weight lifting also had time for his girlfriend, Sarah Hendrey. Receiving letters from her would make him smile, despite the fear and anxiety he felt while in Fallujah. Ergo said, "We had already pushed all the way to the south and set up a firm base and we were clearing sectors house by house. We cleared out this one house that had been barricaded. Because of the barricade we were suspicious that it had been a place where they had, or were, holed up. It was pretty well fortified with weapons. A couple of the insurgents had jumped over the wall to come back to the house, not knowing that we're now there. Lance Corporal Cushings saw one of these guys jump back over the wall. I took a few of my Marines and we chased them house to house until we had cleared about four houses. One of the insurgents threw a grenade at me that failed to go off. My team caught up to me and we continued to chase the bad guys. We reached a house that had two Marine squads on the other side, so I knew the insurgents had to be in there."

Ergo's team quickly kicked open the door of the house and began clearing it, fully expecting to find the insurgents behind the next door they entered. On television there is a game show where they try to identify what's behind the door and win a prize. But in Fallujah, the Marines played the game for keeps, and the best prize behind the door was when no armed insurgents were waiting to kill you.

The house that Ergo and the other Marines entered still had its furniture and must have looked exactly as the occupants had left it weeks before. After conducting what they thought had been a complete search of the house, Ergo and his team were surprised that the insurgents they had been chasing were not there. The perplexed Marines went up on the roof and searched and still no terrorists. On top of the roof Ergo told his team that maybe the insurgents were hiding in the back courtyard in the bushes, so they hurried back down the stairs. There was a small bathroom located at the foot of the stairs on the first floor. No one in Ergo's team had given it much thought since it was felt to be too small to hold the group of terrorists they were searching for.

"I was getting ready to go out the back door, which is right by the bathroom, when I told Lance Corporal Rayburn to kick the bathroom door in and check it out. He kicked it in and I heard him yell. He was pretty surprised that there were two guys in the room. After Rayburn had retreated from the room, the insurgents quickly closed the door again. I went to the doorway of the bathroom and Rayburn and I are now shoulder to shoulder firing through the door," Corporal Ergo said. He remembered the fear and chaos inside the house as the noise from their weapons echoed loudly off the plastered walls. "The insurgents began shooting through the door at us. We felt bullets go by both of our faces. They were yelling and chanting 'Allah Akbar!' We weren't sure if our fire was hitting them or not. We knew that at least one of the insurgents was still alive. We could still hear him yelling. We tried to kick the door in again but one of the insurgents had wedged his foot or body up against it."

The reverberation of gunfire and explosions created chaos within the small house. The noise bouncing off of the concrete walls was so loud at times that the Marines couldn't hear the shouts of one another. Communication in these vicious close quarter room-to-room fights was almost non-existent. Even screaming in a fellow Marine's ear sometimes couldn't be heard.

To Ergo and Rayburn's amazement the door they had been trying to force open, suddenly swung wide and out popped a grenade from the small bathroom. The grenade exploded in the hallway scattering pieces of jagged metal against the walls. Ergo and Rayburn quickly checked themselves and realized that neither of them had been hit by any of the flying shrapnel. The Marines quickly retaliated by throwing their own grenade into the hallway in front of the bathroom door to try and keep the insurgents pinned up in the tiny bathroom. After the grenade exploded, both Ergo and Rayburn lurched forward into the hallway and then proceeded to kick open the bathroom door. The insurgents were caught by surprise at the sudden move and Ergo, with his M16 at the ready, burst into the room.

"I shot this guy about ten times in the chest before he finally dropped. Rayburn apparently had hit the other guy and he was lying on the floor," Ergo said.

The die-hard insurgent wasn't done yet. He reached for a grenade and tossed it toward the Marines in the small room. "Another grenade was dropped by one of the insurgents and we quickly backed out of the room. The grenade, only a few feet away from us, failed to explode," Corporal Ergo recalled. "We couldn't tell how many bad guys were in that room because of all the smoke and haze. It was like the clowns in the small car trick. They just kept popping out. I threw another grenade in the hallway and when it exploded I ran back in and kicked open the door again. There was smoke everywhere. I shot the guy who I had originally dropped, in the head, to make sure he was dead. I looked at the other guy and see something flopping around. His leg had been blown to the ceiling and his foot was hanging down from the door, still twitching. He lifted his head up a little and I tapped two to his face."

Just down the street from Ergo's fight, Lance Corporal Dale Lett and the rest of his squad ran two hundred yards over rough terrain to get to the protection of a large mansion. While running, Lett and the other Marines could see rounds pursuing them as bullets kicked up dirt on impact. After running into the building, Lett positioned himself downstairs. "We received several RPGs while at the mansion. I heard one of the rockets explode and heard, 'corpsman up!' Fox had been hit and Sergeant Billy Leo took shrapnel from the same RPG round. Gomez said he saw a guy in a nearby house. I unloaded an entire 200 round drum into the house with my SAW. I was guarding the door when Captain Cunningham and First Sergeant Fry came in," Lett said.

SAW gunner Lance Corporal Joshua Bush, 19, a native of Evergreen, Alabama recalled the same house. "We were in a big mansion that was still in pretty good shape. Lance Corporal Faircloth and I were on the second floor sitting on a Haji bed looking through a window together, when we heard a loud HISSING sound. It sounded like bullets coming through the window behind us. The glass shattered. We thought it was an RPG. It looked like a red flash and it kept spinning around. We hauled ass out of the room and jumped behind a wall waiting for the RPG to go off. After a minute or so nothing happened so we peaked around the corner and whatever it was, it wasn't on fire anymore and we couldn't see it. We walked back in the room looking for an RPG. We didn't see anything until Lance Corporal Faircloth kicked around the edge of the bed and we found a good-sized tracer round. We felt a little silly at the time. A little later that day my squad leader, Corporal Fox, was hit in the shoulder by RPG shrapnel while on the mansion rooftop."

Lance Corporal Brett Dayton, 20, 2nd Platoon said, "We had set up a firm base at the edge of the city and began cleaning out houses. Every house we went into was empty and we were taking it easy until we reached this one house. Lance Corporal Swenson was the first one in, then me, then Lance Corporal Martinez, followed by Corporal Madden. When we entered I noticed that there was a stairwell to the right with open space beneath them. When we all got in, Lance Corporal Madden was facing to his left. Lance Corporal Swenson, Lance Corporal Martinez and I passed by the stairwell and we start to turn toward Madden, when all of the sudden we see there are three guys hiding under the stairwell. We started firing at each other at point blank range. Swenson tripped over a kerosene drum on the floor and fired as he landed on the floor. Martinez, Madden and I pulled out of the house and left Lance Corporal Swenson there alone. A few seconds later Swenson came bursting out of the house. He said he had killed one of them, and that he had hit the other two pretty bad. The two wounded ones were taken in for questioning by Staff Sergeant Holcomb."

"By this time we all had beards. We hadn't shaved or bathed for fifteen straight days. But if you look at the pictures of us in Fallujah we had the thousand mile stare at that time, but you also see a lot of smiling, which is amazing for what we were going through, to see a lot of smiles. Everyone grew up a little bit in that city," Captain Cunningham said.

"I remember a time when we were under heavy fire in the city and had pushed to the walls of a house for security," Lance Corporal Dayton said. "My friend Lance Corporal Joshua Blevins was against the wall and out of nowhere he starts hopping across the ground on his butt yelling, 'I got hit! I got hit!' I asked, 'Where?' He yelled, 'In my legs!' So we hurriedly pulled his pants off and he had a small bullet wound to his right leg that didn't go deep enough to bleed. We all started laughing and even Blevins laughed too."

Lance Corporal Chandraka Roopnarine, 24, "Roop" to his friends, was a native of Hyattsville, Maryland and carried an M-240G in Fallujah. He was a member of Weapons Platoon, attached to 1st Platoon, Alpha Company. Roopnarine said, "I was standing post with a team of eleven and a sniper team on a rooftop. I was on my machine gun and we had been taking fire from every direction that day. When the fire began to slow down we became suspicious. I was using my machine gun to suppress the enemy when I saw an RPG round coming right at me. It exploded a couple feet below me on the wall of the building I was in. I was lucky not to take any shrapnel or concrete from the blast." The concussion from the blast blew Roopnarine back from his machine gun. Marines from his team rushed over to pick him up and get him out of the line of fire. "They took me down stairs to check me out. I was shaken by the concussion. After an hour downstairs I went back up on the roof. Lieutenant Ackerman was calling in air support on a grid of nearby houses. They took the houses down. I never found out if they took the fighter who had fired the RPG at me."

Second Lieutenant Elliot Ackerman who had fought in the candy store, down Haji Alley, on countless rooftops and through countless houses without being wounded had the law of averages catch up to him when he was hit with shrapnel to his lower back on November 18.

Lance Corporal Bradley Faircloth was well liked by the Marines in Alpha Company and had been given the nickname of "Barbarian" by his Marine friends. On patrol or pushing through the cluttered streets and destroyed houses, Faircloth always wanted to be the point man in his squad.

Lance Corporal Joshua Bush, 3rd Platoon remembered the day when his best friend and fellow Alabama native, Lance Corporal Bradley Faircloth was killed. "We were on patrol clearing sectors and we were set to spend the night out there when we finished our sector. We had come to the last group of houses that we had to clear that day. Our squad split up and I was in the house across the street from the one Faircloth had gone in. I had just stepped back out of the building when I heard gunfire across the street and a lot of Marines hollering. I could hear people yelling that someone was in the house. I heard Lieutenant Barnes hollering for assistance, so I ran down to the corner. He told me where he had seen insurgents running from a house. The rest of my team came running up to the corner where we were standing and we all began firing through the gate where the insurgents had been seen. Marines began to call, 'corpsman up!' That was the first we had heard someone had been hit in the house. I heard someone say that it was Faircloth that didn't make it out. We had both written death letters before we had gone to Fallujah and promised that if anything happened to one, the other would send the letter home to their family. A few weeks later I sent the letter to Faircloth's mother," Bush recalled. Lance Corporal Bradley Faircloth had been an only child.

The day before, thousands of miles away in suburban Mobile, Alabama, Bradley Faircloth's family had set a place for him at their Thanksgiving dinner table.

Sergeant Major Hope recounted meeting the fellow Marine from his home state of Alabama, Lance Corporal Bradley Faircloth, a few days before his death, "It was the first time we had talked, and we mostly reminisced about Alabama. The next day I went back to the Government Center and Lance Corporal Faircloth was killed the following day."

Lance Corporal Scott Green, 21, a native of Holliston, Massachusetts, was a vehicle commander in one of the trucks in 1st Platoon. He had been in his second year at Bryant College when he felt the calling to join the Marines. "I asked myself, why should someone fight for me when I'm perfectly capable and able to fight for myself," Green said. His grandfather and great-grandfather had both served in the Marines, so it was a "gimme" that he would also join the Corps.

November 26 will be a day Corporal Green remembers for the rest of his life. "We were in the south of the city supporting Alpha Company, and Lance Corporal Bradley Faircloth, 20, made entry into a house that held a couple of insurgents with RPKs. As soon as he went in they opened up on him. He was hit several times and he ended up dying. They called us and my truck pulled in right when they were dragging his body around the other side of the building. I remember pulling up and seeing his body. I kinda looked at him and I checked with the other Marines to get an idea where the fire was coming from and where these guys were located. I just started to see blood, I was so pissed off. I wasn't thinking about anything, my family, or myself. I was just thinking about the Marines around me and killing these guys who had just taken one of my brothers away. Our Lieutenant Lee went up to talk to the point of contact on the scene to find out what was going on. They isolated the house with the six insurgents in it and began firing. We swung around the right side of the house with our vehicles into a hundred-square-foot-field. I was up with the Mk19 and our other truck in 2nd Section with the .50 cal pulled up beside us. Lieutenant Lee called in the 1st Section to join us in the field. We opened up on the house, coordinating fire between the Mk19 and the .50 cal. We would roll out and they would fire a TOW into the building, and then we would roll back in and keep shooting. In three or four minutes I must have fired eight cans of Mk19s," Green explained.

While shooting at the house, Lance Corporal Green saw one of the insurgents run out an open doorway and into the sunlight. Green was traversing his fire from left to right across the house when bricks scattered by the impacting rounds brought down one of the insurgents. "It was a good feeling as I lowered my weapon and put a ten-round burst into him right where he fell. He had an AK-47 on him and a good amount of ammo strapped on. We saw some horrible things over there. Dogs eating bodies and even now back in the states, I will smell something that brings back the smells of Fallujah, like rotting flesh," Green said. Green and the other Marines eventually went in and found four or five additional bodies lying about in the rubble.

In urban fighting it is imperative to have qualified engineers to assist the infantry by breaching any doors or obstacles in their way. One of those important cogs in the fight for Fallujah was Combat Engineer, Corporal Michael R. Emans, 22, assigned to Lieutenant Barnes 3rd Platoon, Alpha Company. He used just about every trick of the trade to open stubborn doors, rusty gates, and breach holes in walls during an all out assault on the insurgents hiding in Fallujah.

Corporal Randy L. Bernard, a Marine reporter, talked to Engineer Corporal Emans, a native of Bowling Green, Ohio who described his experiences in Fallujah. "I used to like blowing up ordinance, which is explosive already, and we just stack more explosives on top of it and blow it. I like it a lot better out here, running up to a door under fire, throwing a stick of C-4 on the door, yelling 'smoke' and the time on the fuse and then waiting for the explosion. You get to be so much closer and you can feel the explosion. Destruction is very gratifying."

Emans joined the Marines three-and-one-half-years before Fallujah to become a combat engineer. His father had also been a combat engineer in the Marines. He described himself as a grunt with explosives.

Lance Corporal Thomas J. Brennan, 19, an assaultman with 3rd Platoon, Alpha Company said, "His job made it great because he could set up a charge and blow a door so that we could all just flood in the building. Plus it has a great shock effect on the enemy."

Explosives were just one way for the Marine engineers to open breaches and doors. They also used sledgehammers, bolt-cutters, and a crowbar-like device called a hooligan tool.

Corporal Emans told Marine reporter Corporal Bernard, that, "Ninety percent of the time when we were fighting house to house, we blew everything because we were in a hurry and we were under fire."

In Fallujah, Emans alone used seventy pounds of C-4 and more than one-thousand-feet of detonation cord to clear the way for the infantrymen in Alpha Company.

Emans remembered a close call in Fallujah, "I was blowing a cache with three rocket propelled grenades and a launcher, but I only had a twenty second fuse, so I had to do a mad dash for cover."

Lance Corporal Brennan, a native of Randolph, Massachusetts recalled overdoing one breach, "We put a charge on a big reinforced door with four locks. We both had to run out of the house, and when it exploded the door went flying two houses down the street."

Bravo's Bloody November 26

Bravo Company was up early on the morning of November 26, as reveille sounded at 0600. Captain Omohundro's Bravo Company along with other units began *Operation Deer Drive*. They began to prepare for the sweep of their Area of Operation. This was their eighteenth day of fighting in Fallujah and the Marines of Bravo Company, as the Marines in Alpha Company, had the thousand-mile stare as they assembled before sunrise. Captain Read Omohundro called a commander's meeting at 0700 in order to review the scheme of maneuver for the day's operation. The meeting lasted a half-hour as Omohundro made sure everyone was on the same page for Operation Deer Drive. 1st Platoon from Charlie Company was attached to Bravo Company for the duration of the operation in order to replenish the diminished ranks due to combat injuries suffered the last few days. One of Charlie Company's squads from 1st Platoon was attached to Eckert's 1st Platoon Bravo Company, and the other two squads were tasked to defend Bravo Company's firm base.

"The fight in the city was a challenge in that the battlefield was three-dimensional," Omohundro explained. "We had to look to our front, back, above, and even below, subterranean."

At 0900, Bravo Company pushed across the line of attack, and in the first few hours of the sweep uncovered sizeable weapon caches, SA-7 missile systems, mortar systems, IED making devices, and all types of chemicals for making explosive items.

At 1230, First Lieutenant Chris Wilkens' 3rd Platoon, which had been hard hit the previous day, ran into the enemy to their immediate front in sector 875.

North Carolina native, Lance Corporal James Maxey 22, had been outside the city at the hospital at Camp Fallujah for about ten days recuperating from an injury when he talked the doctors into letting him come back into Fallujah and rejoin his buddies in 3rd Platoon. "I had to show the doctor I could bend and walk around on the knee and then they said, 'okay let's get you back into the city.' I came back in on an AAV ammunition re-supply. A few days later we were out on a routine patrol checking on a weapon cache when we were tasked to clear a house. My good friend Lance Corporal David Houck kicked the door down and then threw in a frag. After the frag exploded Houck entered first with his M16."

In a letter Lance Corporal Alex Saxby wrote:

> *We had been on a search mission since about 0500 and found a shop that had working .50 cals under a bunch of dates. EOD was going to blow the ammo, so we went about three houses down the street. While we were setting up security, Dave found a Dragonov sniper rifle in an abandoned car. Just before the blast, our squad took refuge in the third house. After the blast, me and Dave found a bird wounded by shrapnel. It was hurt pretty bad, so we put it out of its misery. Sergeant Hayden then got a call on the radio that first squad found a weapons cache. Me and Dave were talking about the bird, and how men could drag the rest of the world into hell with it as we walked down the street. Our squad continued to search for more weapons down an adjoining street. We searched two houses with nothing to be found. In the third house, we walked in ranger file into the living room – it was Dave, Bowman, LaForce, Landers, then myself. As we walked into the room – you came in from the back right corner – there was a blue couch directly on the left. Another matching blue couch was directly in front. The kitchen door was opposite the couch on the left. Dave noticed a towel wedged under the kitchen door, which seemed mighty strange to all of us. Dave motioned for all of us to silently pile our packs on the couches in case we needed to get out in hurry. When Dave turned around and said, 'You*

ready?' the insurgents ambushed us. Dave died instantly from small arms fire right through the door. We were pinned down for almost 45 minutes in that room as bullets seared through the walls.

Corporal Jeremy LaForce also remembers, "I almost went through that kitchen door which swung back to the left, but 'Hawk' fell backward, wedging himself between the couch and the door which kept the insurgents at bay. I started calling out names and everyone answered 'cept 'Hawk.' Later I thought *if 'Hawk' had not fallen the way he did, the insurgents could've opened that door, tossed in grenades and none of us would have made it out alive.* They knew we were coming in; they were even waiting on the roof to toss grenades on anyone who was outside."

Florida native, Sergeant Allen Hayden, 21, with wife April and a son at home, led his 2nd Squad down the streets. He also described the deadly action. "We were clearing houses along the street. As we moved to this one house which had the gate and door wide open, my 1st Team entered. While I was clearing outside, they hollered that the first room was clear. My point man, Lance Corporal David Houck, noticed that there was a towel wedged under an inside door that went to an interior room. Houck told his Team Leader he was going to enter the house and check it out. Then all hell broke loose and Houck's team leader, Corporal Jeremy LaForce, radioed to me that Houck was down. As soon as Houck touched the doorknob, the enemy shot through the door with an AK-47 striking him in the head and killing him instantly. Corporal Jeremy LaForce radioed to me that Houck was down. At that time Lance Corporal Michael Fonda and I were right outside the door. I left Fonda outside as I entered the house. After I got in, I checked to see where my men were and where the firing was coming from. It felt like seconds after entering that I heard an explosion from outside. Fonda yelled, 'I've been hit and I'm bleeding!' I radioed the Lieutenant and told him what was going on and about the wound to Fonda. Corporal Wayne Bowman low-crawled over and pulled Houck over to his position near the inside door. Then Staff Sergeant Scott Parry entered the house to find out what was going on. Shrapnel from a grenade had hit Fonda in the neck. When Parry got in, we laid suppressive fire on the door that the insurgent had fired through. This allowed Parry to go over to Bowman's position in the room. Parry then dragged Houck over to me. We weren't receiving steady fire but it was sporadic and the insurgents were chanting something," Hayden explained.

"Grenades were going off and everyone was yelling and firing," Maxey said. "I fired two 200 round drums at that house. Someone yelled

'Let's take the bastards out!' 'Get in the room!' We went back in and it was so tight that Marines were squeezing behind small objects in the room for any kind of cover. The firing was intense and deafening. Then someone shouted, 'Pull the guys out of the house!'"

Hayden said, "Parry told me to drag Houck away from the building. I pulled Houck by his arm to a safe position in the courtyard. One of the engineers then helped me get him to one of the AAVs. I ran back inside and began laying suppressive fire on the door. Inside along with me, it was Parry, Lance Corporal Alex Saxby, Corporal Robby Landers, Lance Corporal Frank Gravano, and Corporal Wayne Bowman. I yelled to my guys that when I shoot at the door, exit the building. When I started firing everyone bounded out. Then I ran from the house while Corporal Jeremy LaForce was firing his M16 into a kitchen window. Lance Corporal Charles Neely took his place firing while LaForce ran out the gate. Then I followed Neely out the gate."

"I could hear the insurgents chanting inside and then a few of them came out and we mowed them down. Macanaly and I saw a guy pop out and jump back behind a corner of the building, then peek out. We fired, killing him. A grenade hit a wall near us and I dove to avoid it. I didn't even hear it explode, but I was hit with some of the flying shrapnel. It was just minor cuts to my elbow," Staff Sergeant Alicea said.

The Marines were using the stack tactics to take a house in reverse. "We cordoned off the building while a Marine fired a SMAW rocket into the structure. Part of the second deck collapsed, but the Marines positioned in the rear of the building could still see enemy movement from within. They called up the D-9, which bulldozed the building to rubble, collapsing the roof of the building on the insurgents. One insurgent tried to escape by running out the back door and was shot. After they leveled the building, we went in and pulled eleven enemy bodies from the rubble. It really hurt when Dave Houck was killed. He was a good friend," Sergeant Hayden recalled.

The die-hard insurgent fighters in the southern part of the city were trying to hold onto what little terrain they held. These fighters would have to be dug out by the Marine infantrymen, and if they couldn't dislodge them, then the D-9 bulldozer would be brought in to totally destroy the houses with the remaining enemy still inside.

A Marine who loves baseball and mountain biking, Lance Corporal Daniel Bystricky, 24, from Massapequa, New York remembered the clearing operation of 2nd Platoon. "November 26 had to be one of the two worst days I had in Fallujah. It was a real rough mission, Operation Deer Drive. We were moving along clearing out our sector, going house to house finding weapon caches. We had come up to this one house where my buddy Lance Corporal Alexander Lamond and I had this eerie feeling. We were looking at it and didn't notice anything out of the ordinary, but something just didn't feel right. The house smelled like urine and we figured someone had been around there recently."

Carrying his weapon at the ready, Bystricky, Lamond, and the other Marines cleared house after house working their way to the suspicious looking structure. They cleared the one next door to the foul smelling house. Then the Marines targeted the foul smelling, strange looking house. Still in the building next door, Bystricky began working his way to the outer perimeter when a sudden burst of gunfire broke the silence. It had come from the eerie looking house right next door. Two well-armed insurgents had been waiting for the Marines to enter.

Corporal Hamilton's team was the first one to enter the foul smelling house. When they walked in, all hell broke loose. Lance Corporal David Ojeda recounted the swirling action, as everything seemed to slow down to microseconds of pure horror. "My team was to go next door and clear this one house out. A big iron gate outside the house was locked. We couldn't get in there so we sent Lance Corporal Philip Green and Lance Corporal Jacob Hassell over the wall to unlock the gate while we maintained security out in the street by the house. They unlocked the gate and all of us were setting up to go into the house. I was the number three man in the stack. Lance Corporal Green led, Engineer Palacios was second, and I was third. As soon as we broke through the door an insurgent popped his AK-47 around the corner and sprayed the whole room with rounds. I thought, *What's going on?* But we continued pushing forward into the fire. I looked to my right and watched as Lance Corporal Green fell to the ground. As lead man he had taken the brunt of everything. I thought, *Holy crap what am I going to do?* I was still moving forward looking at Green when it felt like someone had taken a baseball bat and whacked me in the shoulder with it. I dove to a corner of the room behind a stove where Lance Corporal Palacios was supporting by fire. I landed right next to him and I immediately checked my arm for blood. I didn't see any blood on my shoulder and I found out I could still move it. We were both carrying SAWs. We looked over to Lance Corporal Green staring at us asking for help, 'Get me out of here. Help me.' The insurgent was shooting right over our heads so we couldn't do anything about it. If we had moved we would have been killed. Finally I told myself I wasn't just going to sit here and let him kill me. I ask Palacios to put fire down on the insurgent. We began putting rounds back at the guy firing at us from the hallway. The insurgent stopped to reload after dumping several magazines in the room at us. I told Palacios you cover me, I'm going to make a run to get out and then I'll cover for you.

I got up and ran from the house when I heard more firing from within the building. I turned to re-enter when my Team Leader, Corporal Jeremy Hamilton, who had been grazed on the cheek from one of the rounds, told me not to go back in, Ojeda recalled.

Out in the street, Lance Corporal David Ojeda helped hold security as his wounded shoulder began to throb with pain. He had felt the blow to his shoulder in the house but didn't realize a round had caused it. Finally he took the time to look at his shoulder out in the sunlight and saw that his whole right sleeve was saturated with his own blood. He turned to his Team Leader, Corporal Hamilton, and told him that Green and Palacios where still under fire and pinned down in the house. The Marines outside moved over to the house next door for cover. Palacios and Green, both wounded, finally made it from the enemy held house.

"When I looked over, there was a Humvee parked right outside the house with a .50 caliber machine gun mounted on top firing into the house that held the insurgents. The corpsman was patching us up and I kept checking on Green who was shot up pretty bad. I found out it's a helpless feeling when you can't help out your fellow Marine when he's lying on the ground wounded," Lance Corporal Ojeda said.

Team Leader Corporal Hamilton had taken shrapnel from a ricochet to his left cheek. Ohio native Lance Corporal Philip Green was hit multiple times in his arm, lower abdomen, and his back. Lance Corporal David Ojeda was shot in the right shoulder. One of the engineers, Lance Corporal Matthew Palacios, was hit with shrapnel to his hip, shoulder, lower abdomen and both shins before he went down. The two insurgents were quickly dispatched with fire from the .50 caliber mounted on the Humvee.

"Corporal Hamilton's First Fire Team had entered the house and drew the enemy fire. They shot up my buddy Lance Corporal Green who took about thirteen rounds. We brought them back over in the yard where we had been. He looked worse for wear at the time. Doc Jushinski and I began to patch him up. Right there at that time, I thought I was going to break out in tears seeing him. He was a young kid with a baby face who looked about thirteen-years-old just shot up like that. He was telling me how much it hurt. He kept asking Doc to give him some morphine to ease the pain. Doc didn't want to give him any there, but wanted to get him on the AAVs and get him out of there. No one was killed, thank God, but basically the whole First Team had been decimated in one house. That was pretty rough, knowing how fast your numbers could be depleted like that. 1st and 2nd Squads were combined after that because of all the losses," Lance Corporal Bystricky recalled.

After another deadly day in Fallujah, Captain Omohundro gave his Marines some much-needed rest that night. They were re-supplied while the company gunny, Kristian Ekholm, moved to their firm base to re-stock ammunition and chow for the coming day's fight.

"When we got back to the Firm Base Camp for the night they began yelling names out to see who was there," Lance Corporal James Maxey said. "When they called Houck's name out and no one answered, it dawned on us that he was really dead. He was gone. We broke down and there were tears everywhere that night." The Marines in Bravo Company added Houck's name to his sandbag flag that night.

Lieutenant Colonel Brandl said, "At this stage of the game the Marines were seasoned veterans. Everything you ever read or saw pictures of our Marines, that's exactly how they looked and what they were, veterans. I was awed at the transformation of these young Marines." The colorful Brandl provided another sound bite to a BBC news film crew. Commenting on the insurgency in Fallujah, Brandl said, "We're crushing his back, one vertebra at a time."

While visiting his Marines fighting in the southern part of the city, Brandl's Humvee column pulled up in an alley near a house which held some civilians. Brandl went inside where his men were questioning an old man and some young teenage boys. He stayed a short time before exiting the house with a few of his Marines. They walked back down the alley to get to their parked vehicles. They passed by an open window at the back of the house they had just left. Later, the Marines found several insurgents hiding in that same house. With one quick RPK burst through the open window the insurgents could have taken out the commander of the battalion. In this kind of urban fighting the commander is just as vulnerable as his men are.

At home, wives, sweethearts, and family members of 1/8 were reading every bit of information they could find. Wives would share with each other any information they came across on the fighting in Fallujah. Nicky Omohundro read an article in the *New York Times* by Dexter Filkens that mentioned her husband, Captain Read Omohundro:

> *"...For hours, they succeeded, pinning down perhaps 150 marines led by Capt. Read Omohundro, a strapping graduate of Texas A & M who has a habit of walking around upright during bursts of mortar and grenade fire while everyone else is hugging an outcropping of concrete..."*

Reading the article, thousands of miles away, Nicky Omohundro was thinking, *'Damn, get down and hug some concrete!'*

November 27, Operation Deer Drive, With More of the Same for Bravo Company

Up early before the sun, at 0530, Captain Omohundro and Gunnery Sergeant Ekholm moved to the intersection of Phase Line Henry and Phase Line Grace to link up with the rest of the company to begin the days clearing operations. The company gunny, Gunnery Sergeant Kristian Ekholm, moved closer to First Lieutenant Wilkens' 3rd Platoon's Area of Operation to be available for support in CASEVACS. First Lieutenant Chris Wilkens' Marines were tasked to clear sectors 872, 876, and 877. Second Lieutenant Steven Berch's 2nd Platoon would maneuver north of Phase Line Heather in order to help clear sectors 849 and 850 due to reported enemy activity. Second Lieutenant Andy Eckert's 1st Platoon was tasked in clearing the rest of sectors 853, 854, and 855.

The sectors were just numbers on a map, but those numbered areas still contained some fanatical die-hard enemy fighters and the Marines would have to pry them out.

Clearing operations began at 0600. Eckert's 1st Platoon moved swiftly and safely through their assigned sectors. They breathed a sigh of relief as they met with no enemy activity, while the nearby 2nd Platoon immediately encountered several military-aged personnel moving about.

As is the policy, Berch's Marines gave them a gunpowder test to ascertain whether they had recently fired a weapon. The individuals failed the gunpowder residue test and also had inconsistencies in their stories. They, along with another three individuals, were detained while Marines searched a house next to another weapons site. Two of the three males did not look Iraqi, and the third male had a fresh bullet wound to his left leg. Also all the men detained that morning by 2nd Platoon were living in houses adjacent to sites where Marines had found a weapons cache. At 0900 Berch had the detained men taken to Bravo Company's firm base for further questioning.

"We picked up early that morning and moved down our sector," Lance Corporal Bystricky said. "It was strange, after going through most of the city we hadn't run into civilians, but now, right down this street, it seemed like every house had someone living in them. We came up on one house built from corrugated metal. I had a weird feeling about it. I just didn't like the looks of it. Two older men and three younger guys, one hobbling on crutches obviously from a recent wound, came out. I remember he had a smirk on his face and I just wanted to go down to him and butt-stroke him in the face to knock that smirk off. We took them to the EPW collection point." Bystricky had already lost several friends in the bitter fighting for Fallujah.

Floridian, Lance Corporal Benjamin Voorhees carried an M16A4 with a scope mounted on his weapon in Fallujah. He was in the 2nd Fire Team, 2nd Squad of 2nd Platoon. Besides his weapon, pack and ammo he also carried a spare radio. It had broken down on his second day in the city, but Voorhees still had to carry it. "Lance Corporal Agustin Garcia and I switched off point because we felt that was the most dangerous job entering the houses. It was constant house clearing every single day. It was exhausting. The hardest part about it was, you cleared a hundred houses in one day and all it took was one house to lose people. That was the hardest part about it, keeping yourself sharp for the next house. It became harder and harder each day. We didn't get much sleep at all. The junior guys had to do most of the watches, which cut down on needed sleep. As we moved to a schoolhouse that we were going to use as a Firm Base, I had so much stuff in my pack the bottom fell out. I had to stuff everything in and bear hug it for about five hours. I had never been so tired in all my life. I was exhausted and scared," Voorhees said.

The Marines in 2nd Platoon continued searching their sectors for the few remaining elusive enemy fighters. At 0930, as a team entered a courtyard of a house adjacent to where the three foreign males had been detained earlier, they received fire. The Marines pushed forward and quickly cleared the house. This is how it went day after day in Fallujah.

"As we pushed through the streets we started taking shots from here and there from enemy snipers," Weapons Company Marine, Lance Corporal Llerena recalled. Even in bad situations the call of nature sometimes intervenes and something as mundane as relieving ones self became stressful and dangerous for the Marines in Fallujah. "We kept ducking in and out of houses searching for the snipers. We took fire from an area where we saw this one Iraqi. He surrendered to us. We searched his house and began to take fire again. We started punching holes in walls and putting charges against the walls to create firing holes. I had to go to the bathroom, so I put my pack down and went into a dark small room. I sat down and started to do my thing when I heard glass breaking and voices from outside the building." He felt exposed and defenseless. "I can't reach my rifle and my pants are down. I tried whispering back to the Marines in the next room. I finally got their attention, and two Marines went out the front door and around back. They threw a grenade over the wall into the courtyard and the voices stopped." Lance Corporal Llerena got back to his unfinished business with some peace and quiet.

An embedded reporter for the New York Times, Dexter Filkins, traveled the streets of Fallujah with Bravo Company. He gained immense respect for those Marines walking beside him. He wrote:

> "Despite their youth, the Marines seemed to tower over their peers outside the military in maturity and guts. Many of Bravo Company's best Marines, its most proficient killers, were 19 and 20 years old; some directed their comrades in maneuvers and assaults. Bravo Company's three lieutenants, each responsible for the lives of about 50 men, were 23 and 24 years old.
>
> They are a strangely anonymous bunch. The men who fight America's wars seem invariably to come from little towns and medium-size cities far away from the nation's arteries along the coast. Line up a group of Marines and ask them where they are from, and they will give you a list of places like Pearland, Tex.; Lodi, Ohio; Osawatomie, Kan."

The Marines cautiously moved through the streets littered with debris, rubble, all types of trash, dead dogs, downed electric and phone lines. As they walked down the alleyways and streets any open window or rooftop could be harboring an insurgent with an AK-47 or a snipers rifle pointing directly at them. Some of the houses and buildings they entered harbored

316

machine guns in bunkered and even tunnel positions. But the insurgent's favorite fighting positions were still on the rooftops and balconies of the houses. What the Marines called the second and third decks.

Lance Corporal David Graham, New York, who loved playing baseball and football, moved along with his 1st Squad in Second Lieutenant Berch's, 2nd Platoon on the dangerous killing streets of Fallujah. Graham said, "It was around 1000 in the morning and like the movies show it, everything just happened in slow motion. I looked over and saw a barrel of a weapon sticking out from a window, and then everything just started opening up. I looked up and saw two insurgents up on a roof throwing grenades down. A round hit me in the leg and I stumbled forward and caught myself before I fell to the ground. The bullet felt like a little fist punching me when it impacted. The adrenaline was just going through me and I just kept running. I didn't get a chance to fire back, I was running so fast."

Lance Corporal Graham quickly jumped over a wall to get out of the accurate line of fire. From the initial burst of fire he had suffered a bullet wound to his left calf and Lance Corporal Michael Ray had received shrapnel wounds from a grenade to his left arm and thumb. Graham, with blood staining his pant leg from his calf wound, continued giving directions on the whereabouts of the enemy.

"We were keeping over-watch on the house from the rooftop. In the house there was a big wall with a gate in front to a small courtyard that led to the house. It was Corporal Gonzales' team that went in to the courtyard. They got maybe three paces in when automatic fire opened up on them," Lance Corporal Voorhees remembered. "As soon as I heard firing, everyone jumped up trying to figure out what was going on. Corporal Charlie Gonzales screamed, 'Oh f***!'"

A twenty-year-old Marine from Charleston, South Carolina, Lance Corporal Jacob Hassell who was a member of 1st Squad in Berch's 2nd Platoon remembered the action. "I was walking point when we came up to a house that looked unoccupied. When I entered the courtyard I saw a woman just standing in the doorway of the house. I yelled 'someone here!' I then told the woman to 'Get down! Get down!' She just looked at me crazy like and didn't move," Hassell recounted.

Clutching his M16, Hassell stared at the woman just as another Marine pushed forward and pulled the startled woman from the open doorway. As point, Hassell was the first one to push into the house and was surprised to see three men just sitting meekly on the floor.

"Get down!" Hassell yelled as the Iraqi men quickly obeyed. "Part of our team watched the three men as the rest of us cleared the house. Lance Corporal Lamond had taken Arabic and he asked the three men if there was anyone else there and they answered 'no.' We then pushed to the next house and Lucero had to use Dep Cord to breech an opening for us. The explosion blew the front gate back. Lance Corporal Lucero, Lance Corporal Graham, Lance Corporal Ray and I rushed through the gate just when shots rang out. Graham got hit in the leg and Lucero was grazed on the shoulder blade by the sudden eruption of enemy rounds."

Finding themselves under fire, the shaken Marines of 1st Squad quickly ran from the enemy fire zone in the courtyard back out into the open street. They positioned their weapons on the six-foot courtyard wall that surrounded the house and began returning fire. Lance Corporal Ray raked his SAW across the openings of the door and windows.

Hassell said, "Two SMAW rockets were fired into the house and then the D-9 came up and leveled that house and then all the houses on the street. Voorhees saw some movement in a house behind where we were positioned. An AAV came over and fired grenades into the house for about five or ten minutes and then things quieted down.

The Marines fighting in the city seemed to inspire one another. Voorhees said, "I saw Lance Corporal Graham running and limping at the same time. He had been shot and he was still able to stand up and run from the house. It was one of the most amazing things I'd ever seen. Graham was standing out in the open telling people to go different places although he had been wounded. He was eventually taken out. We blew the hell out of the house for a few minutes. I was shooting as many rounds as I could at the muzzle flashes coming from the windows."

Immediately after contact, tanks were pushed up to cordon off the house while the D-9 dozer was quickly brought in to rubble the house. The tank reported seeing a wounded insurgent on one of the upper decks of the house. Bravo Company's Executive Officer, Lieutenant Mark Mendez, moved forward with the attached AAVs and grabbed the wounded enemy fighter and pulled him from the deck. They had him transferred over to Bethea's Charlie Company for further questioning and for medical treatment.

"Machine guns had opened up on the Marines entering the courtyard," Lance Corporal Bystricky said. "It became a pretty big firefight. We had two squads shooting at this house, trying to get whoever was in there."

Lance Corporal Agustin Garcia, 19, 2nd Platoon, from Passaic, New Jersey recalled the fierce firefight, "I was on a rooftop across the street with six other Marines when a grenade was thrown at the Marines entering the house. I heard the explosion and then they began firing an AK-47 at our position from an open aperture in the roof. The wounded Marines were quickly evacuated from the house. We began firing at the insurgents for about twenty minutes without any luck, when Lance

Corporal Forester hollered for me to bring him a SMAW rocket. He was located on the rooftop next to us. I low crawled over to an opening on my roof and I hollered down for someone to get a rocket brought up to the rooftop. Lance Corporal Hardeman brought one up and handed it to me. I got up and ran across and jumped four-feet over an alleyway to the other house. I was scared, but I had a lot of adrenaline to help me do it. Lance Corporal Matthew Forester fired the rocket and helped cave the house in. Then a D-9 came up to finish the job. The D-9 had worked on the house for about ten minutes when an insurgent ran out through an opening from the side. We fired and he fell in the open area."

Lance Corporal Voorhees also made it up on the roof carrying a SMAW rocket with his fellow point man, Garcia. "Garcia and I didn't have time to come down off the roof before they fired the SMAW rocket. They told us to get down next to the wall, hug each other and get in a ball to protect ourselves from the blast. We curled up as Forester took the house apart with one rocket. A rock came flying up from the impact of the blast and hit Garcia in the knee. He wasn't seriously hurt, but he was screaming and cussing. Everyone started cheering while Forester did a touchdown dance. It was pretty funny," said Lance Corporal Benjamin Voorhees, 2nd Platoon, 2nd Squad, 2nd Fire Team.

For almost an hour 2nd Platoon Marines exchanged fire with the enemy insurgents hidden in the house while the D-9 made rubble of the building. Nearby tanks waited like lions for their prey to try an escape their lair. The bulldozer eventually dropped the roof on the insurgents in the house but several enemy fighters managed at the last second to run from the debris, only to be cut down in the open alleyway by several .50 caliber machine guns mounted on the waiting tanks.

Lance Corporal Graham, "We were then taken over to Doc Jushinski to be patched up. Sergeant Ramirez and Staff Sergeant Torres ran over to see how I was doing. They put me on an AAV and took me back to camp. Lance Corporal Joshua Lucero took my spot on the 1st Team."

"On our push through the city we found another weapons cache in a big house," remembered Puerto Rico native, Lance Corporal Maldonado, 21, 1st Squad, 3rd Platoon. "That's when Marines from 2nd Platoon ended up with all those bad guys in the house. I heard the shots and I went out to the front of the house. Lieutenant Wilkens was to my front when I saw insurgents on the roof of a house across the street. I wanted to bring my weapon to bear on them but the lieutenant was in the line of fire. I hollered, 'Get down!' He dropped right there and I opened fire and the insurgent dropped down. Two minutes later I saw another guy pop up. I turned to the left and fired at the target but I missed. I asked Corporal Silva if I could go to the roof for a better shot. He shouted,

'Go!' I went up and got behind a wall. I kept up a steady fire to keep their heads down so the guys in the house could get out."

"The Marines had made it out of the house and Corporal Johnson, the gunner and I were told to go to the house directly behind the one we were on. Llerena had taken down one level of the house already with his SAW. We had them trapped in the house and I could hear the Iraqis screaming and chanting," Maldonado recounted. "We were waiting for the D-9 dozer to come up and put it down. I saw a guy run down the alleyway in back of the house and everyone was shooting, but they didn't hit him. He ran to a house on the corner. I was watching as the D-9 began to take that last corner house down. That's when the guy peeked out. He didn't know I could see him from up on the roof." Maldonado rested his SAW on the ledge and slowly squeezed the trigger. The insurgent was cut down in the alleyway.

"After the D-9 finished, they began pulling enemy bodies out of the rubble. I think they pulled nine bodies out," Maldonado said.

"We picked up a Marine casualty from Bravo Company," Ohio native Lance Corporal Lew, Weapons Company, remembered. "He had been in a house and when they brought him out they had to put him on a bed because they had no stretcher. He lived only a short time, and we had to put him on top of one of Lance Corporal Schmitz's trucks and take him to Charlie Company's firm base. That was the hardest and most upsetting scene I had to witness in Fallujah."

Those images of their fellow Marines who died in combat in Fallujah would be etched in their young minds forever.

Several other nearby houses were identified as harboring enemy fighters, and the D-9 quickly turned its vengeance on those structures, pulverizing them into a pile of rubble where a house once stood. Nearby, out popped several more enemy fighters attempting to flee from one of the houses the D-9 was working over. The D-9 bulldozer quickly crushed the insurgents.

At 1100 Berch had his Marines push across the street to secure a building just south of their position.

Lance Corporal Jacob Hassell said, "We moved to a nearby house and Lucero and I were on the first floor keeping watch out a window. We were just talking about home and he was telling me that he planned to marry his fiancée when he got back to the states."

Another Marine interrupted the conversation of Lucero and Hassell. Hassell was told to move to the rooftop and provide security. Hassell lugged his M16 up the stairs and set up near a wall on the open roof that had a small hole where he could look out on the scene below. His thoughts turned to a friend, Lance Corporal Philip Green, who had been wounded a few days before in the fighting. He wondered how he was doing.

Squinting out the hole looking for roaming insurgents, his mind began to wander. *"Everyone around me was getting hurt in the city. I knew it was only a matter of time until I got hit,"* Hassell thought to himself. "We were there about ninety minutes when Lance Corporal Hamilton came up on the roof and yelled, 'We're Moving! Let's go!' We were going to the house where Voorhees had earlier seen someone moving. The same one the AAVs had worked over. We formed in a stack with Lance Corporal Kevin Miller (attached from Alpha Company) at point, followed by me, Lucero and Lance Corporal Ray."

The Marines warily moved toward the two-story tan looking house. They had to climb up onto a four-foot ledge to get even with the first floor of the house.

Lance Corporal Hassell recalled, "I looked over to Lance Corporal Miller as we moved and said, 'there's something wrong here. Lance Corporal Voorhees answered that 'the shades had been moved since the last time we saw it.'"

The four Marines passed by a cartridge belt filled with ammo hanging from a hook, attached to a wall, slowly twisting in the light breeze right outside the main door of the house. It was a bad omen for the advancing Marines. They pushed the already blown front door out of the way and began pushing into the house. Immediately after entering, they stopped and waited for their eyes to adjust to the light inside. From near the doorway the four Marines stared down a long hallway into the inner depths of the house.

"Miller cleared a bathroom to our right. For a toilet it just had a hole in the floor. I took three or four steps down the hall and entered a room to the left," Hassell remembered.

Sunlight was streaming through an outside window as Hassell double-checked the storage room with his M16 at the ready before moving on. He had just turned to walk back out into the hallway, when out of the corner of his eye he saw Lance Corporal Lucero move past the doorway to join Miller already moving down the hall.

Hassell said, "As soon as I turned around a guy had popped out of a door at the end of the long hallway and began firing. Miller got hit in the shoulder and ran for cover in the small bathroom. Lucero was hit and fell back into me and we both tumbled backwards. Lucero died instantly. I felt a bullet graze my head and shoulder. The wound to my head was bleeding all over me. After I hit the ground everything quieted down. While I was lying there I pulled a grenade and was ready to pull the pin. I wasn't going to let them take me like that." The thought of taking his own life quickly passed as he put the grenade back. *"I'm not going to do this,"* he told himself as he quickly got back into the fight. Bleeding profusely from his wounds, Hassell picked up his weapon, "I got up and leaned out of the room and aimed down the hallway. While I was standing there an enemy grenade slowly rolled down the hallway straight at me."

Everything went into to slow motion mode as Hassell reacted and kicked the storage door closed with his left foot to give himself some protection from the direct blast of the grenade. The explosion from the grenade was loud and kicked up a lot of dust and smoke in the hallway of the house. It also blasted the storage door back on Hassell. It only took a few seconds for the smoke to clear before Hassell, still bleeding from his wounds, peered out from the room. He came face to face with an insurgent crawling down the hallway with an AK-47 trying to take the fallen Lucero's weapon.

"He looked up and it felt like a lifetime passed before I unloaded a magazine at him," Hassell recalled. "I heard Voorhees and Morel yelling from outside the front doorway of the house. 'Hassell is dead!' They had mistaken the fallen Lucero for me. I yelled, 'no I'm not! I'm here! Lucero's dead!'"

Lance Corporal Voorhees said, "Lieutenant Berch leaned out and saw Lucero's legs in the doorway. He started yelling, 'We have a dead body! We have a dead Marine in the doorway!' One insurgent tried to get over to Lucero's body to take his weapon. He didn't see that Hassell was still alive in a room to the insurgent's left. So as the insurgent knelt to take his gear, Hassell shot him about ten times. I ran downstairs to try and get our guys out. As we made our way up to the house with the down Marines, I ran up behind Lance Corporal Anthony Morel and grabbed Lucero by the back of his collar and pulled him out. Corporal Hobbs came flying up because he saw it was one of his engineers."

Voorhees continued, "We yelled in the house to Hassell that we had security and he could come out, it was safe. He darted out quicker than I'd ever seen anyone run. We began throwing frags in the house. I was never so pissed. I was holding security when Bystricky threw the last frag. The insurgents started to open fire from the top window where I had been earlier. Lance Corporal Bystricky and I hit the ground behind this little ledge. I looked up and I could see the bullets making a line across the wall where we had just been. It was scary. I fired as Bystricky pulled back. Then I heard another M16 firing behind me. I looked over to see Lance Corporal Forester firing in support. We pulled back to another house. The hardest part for me was knowing a Marine for a year and then seeing them dead. It was hard. All the Marines we lost over there were great guys. Lucero always had a smile on his face. He was one of the guys who made the time there easier."

Corporal Daniel Bystricky described the deadly ambush. "When we pushed on, 1st and 2nd Squads that had been combined, made entry into a house, then we heard gunfire blowing out in the there. We didn't know what was going on after that due to the fog of war. We were located in an alley and I was holding security on a door when my buddy, Lance Corporal Kevin Miller, came running out screaming, 'Friendly!' at the top of his lungs," Bystricky said. "My heart skipped a couple beats as Miller flew out the back door. He had been hit in the biceps with shrapnel. He ran right on to the amtrac. I heard them shout that Lance Corporal Lucero was still in the building, and we didn't know what his situation was. We kept asking people, 'Is he still alive?' They said, 'We can't tell. He's down in a hallway.' We began working on trying to get him the hell out of there. Some of my friends and I just grabbed our balls and ran in to get him out."

Hassell remembered, "They yelled 'come on out and we'll cover you!' I looked back down the hallway and didn't see anybody so I ran out of the house and didn't stop until I got over the ledge in the yard. Then Voorhees and Morel pulled Lucero from the house and I helped get him over the ledge. Miller had also gotten out of the house. 'Doc Ski' came over and looked at my wounds and told me 'you're getting out of here.'" Hassell credited Lance Corporal Joshua Lucero with saving his life. "If it wasn't for Josh I wouldn't be here today."

Lance Corporal Agustin Garcia remembered the deadly firefight. He was located in a house just south of where the Marines had been ambushed. "We moved into a house and everything was quiet, but then a loud explosion rocked us coming from the house to the south of us. We knew one of our teams had just entered that house. We were screaming, 'What the hell is going on?' A Marine from our rooftop spotted one of our men lying in front of the door of the house next door. He was screaming, 'Man down in the doorway!' We tried talking to the downed Marine but we got no response. From within the house we heard Lance Corporal Hassell who was screaming, 'I'm in here!' Then Lance Corporal Morel, Lance Corporal Bystricky, and Lance Corporal Voorhees risked their lives under fire to run back and pull the prone Marine from the doorway. The Marine was Lance Corporal Joshua Lucero, a combat engineer. Doc Goodman and I checked him out. He was dead. Bystricky, Voorhees and Morel provided cover fire as Hassell ran safely from the house."

The gunfight lasted no more than five or ten minutes of pure hell and terror for the Marines of 2nd Platoon. Lucero had absorbed most of the grenade saving the lives of the two other Marines that had also been pinned down inside the house.

Engineer, Lance Corporal Joshua Lucero, nineteen-years of age demonstrated exceptional knowledge and bravery by breaching entryways to reduce booby-traps for his fellow Marines in Fallujah. He was always volunteering to be one of the first Marines during entry by assault in the city. He had cleared over fifty structures with the breach team, many while receiving enemy fire. Only one and a half-hour earlier Lucero had been shot in the shoulder while helping to clear another enemy stronghold. He was rated a medical evacuation out of the city at that time, which he had refused to take and instead chose to stay on the battlefield with his fellow Marines.

A few days before Lance Corporal Joshua Lucero, engineer, from Tucson, Arizona had a chance to call home to his parents. In the conversation he apologized for not calling before. He asked about his one-year-old son, Joey, and said he was looking forward to returning to the states and marrying his fiancée. He said his son's presence was with him. He told his parents he was tired, dirty and hungry but that he was all right and not to worry. Lucero asked his parents to pray for him before hanging up the phone.

Participating in this operation in the southern part of the city was Corporal Kirk Bosselmann, 21, an active sports minded young man from the state of Maryland who belonged to the Scout Sniper Platoon. He was attached to Bravo Company and was positioned on a rooftop two houses over from where Lance Corporal Lucero had been killed. Days earlier an enemy sniper had killed his friend and fellow sniper, Corporal Nick Ziolkowski. Now Bosselmann found himself being stalked from a distance by an unseen enemy sniper.

"When we got on the rooftop we could hear the enemy below us in the building whispering and moving about. I had Corporal Ochman secure the stairwell that led up to our rooftop," Corporal Watson recalled. "We would go over to the stairwell and toss a grenade down on the enemy to keep them off balance until a clearing team secured the house. The insurgents were using the street as an avenue of approach against us. There were eight bodies in the road and I don't know how many in the courtyards around us. I was called up to the third floor roof. The Marines told me there was a guy sticking his head out every so often. I was waiting for him to stick his head out when I heard a single shot."

Corporal Mendenhall said, "We had secured this building and moved to the second deck on the rooftop of an adjacent three story structure. I was banging a hole in the wall with a sledgehammer from which to fire from. Bosselmann was on post. I heard a single shot and I looked over just as Bosselmann fell. His gun hit the roof. At first I thought he had just slipped."

"Mendenhall was calling for me," Watson said. "I yelled for a corpsman when I was moving from roof to roof when a round hit near my ass. I was told that the corpsman was coming up. I went back down to the second deck with my team. We couldn't move because the enemy below us hadn't been cleared out yet. We waited about two hours then we wrapped Bosselmann in a poncho and carried him up the stairs onto the third deck of another house and then made our way down the stairs."

The enemy sniper, situated between two houses, had shot a round that hit Bosselmann in the head. Corporal Kirk Bosselmann died instantly from the gunshot wound.

Bosselmann's commander of snipers, Captain Mike Pretus, was outside the city at Camp Fallujah when Bosselmann was killed. He had heard on the radio that they had suffered another casualty. "I tried to get a casualty report when they finally gave the name in code on the radio. When I heard the letter 'B' I knew it was Bosselmann. Lieutenant Paul Steketee and I went over to see Kirk when his body came in. In Iraq our Sniper Platoon suffered three killed and one listed wounded."

Staff Sergeant Choquette, whose father had also been a Marine, recounted. "We were attached to Bravo Company as they began sweeping the city. We got to the point where my trucks would go through the front gates of houses firing .50 cals through front windows before the infantry would make entry. Lieutenant Wilkens and Staff Sergeant Parry's platoon got into a situation where some of their Marines had gone through the front door of a house and been hit. Marines were still stuck in the house as we fired .50 cals over their heads. We did everything we could to get them out. I ended up launching three TOW missiles and I had my Marines drop five or six cans of Mk19 rounds at the house, and we still couldn't kill the insurgents. I fired tracers to direct my Marines fire. One of my Marines killed an insurgent on the roof with small arms fire. Some of those houses had walls over a foot thick. Lance Corporal Brandon Smith was firing an Mk19 about 15 meters from the door of the house. He was blowing rounds through the door and windows, and the insurgents inside were throwing grenades back out at us. One of our rounds hit the wall and bounced back exploding. I saw Lance Corporal Smith's head snap back, and he fell down into the turret. I thought he had been killed. I jumped into the turret and grabbed his machine gun and kept firing at the house. Staff Sergeant Parry looked up at me and told me, 'Your boy is hurt bad!' There was blood all down the side of the truck. I told the driver, 'Go!' When we went around the corner I reached down and grabbed Smith's face. He had a hole about the size of a half-dollar under his eye. He was unconscious. I touched him and he twitched and then came to. I put gauze in his wound and held it until we arrived at the Government Center."

The main guns of the tanks were now brought to bear on the house. The tanks swiveled their guns but were quickly engaged by the enemy from a nearby house that they had turned to rubble. Small arms fire and grenades began hitting and exploding around the tanks to no effect. Apparently four to six enemy had survived the demolition of the building, or crept back into the rubble to set up and attack the Marines. The tanks fired their main guns and their machine guns and finally killed the attacking enemy fighters. With the insurgents destroyed in the rubble of the nearby house, the D-9 lumbered up and began dismantling the house harboring the enemy that had ambushed the Marines.

"There were still some insurgents in the house and the D-9 was trying to level the building the same time Captain Omohundro was calling in an air strike to destroy it. The D-9 didn't have a radio," Tank commander Captain Chris Meyers recalled. "I said I would go and tell the guys so I jumped down off the tank and ran up to the D-9."

As Captain Meyers stood by the D-9 trying to get the attention of the driver in the large bulldozer an insurgent hidden in a nearby tree was taking a bead on him. The insurgent fired at Meyers as he turned to jog back down the street to his waiting tank. The sniper's first shot missed the tanker, but the enemy fighter continued to fire hitting Meyers in the left arm with a round that penetrated his bicep. When the wounded Meyers reached his tank he directed Sergeant Ducasse to move his tank forward and machine gun the sniper in the tree.

"Lieutenant Lee, who had been hit earlier in the bicep, got off his tank and was laughing his ass off at me. We began joking around about it while Lee cut off my sleeve and wrapped it for me. We stayed a few more hours in that area," Meyers said.

"They brought up the D-9s and the engineers. The house was eliminated. After I don't know how many hours of firing, it finally quieted down. The saddest part was when I was on the rooftop holding security and I just kind of glimpsed back and I saw them taking Lance Corporal Lucero's body covered with a poncho on the back of an amtrac. That was one of the worst two days I had in Fallujah," admitted Lance Corporal Daniel Bystricky.

At 1300, after the house was destroyed and its occupants killed, the Marines of 2nd Platoon pushed into the rubble and began counting the enemy dead. The Marines removed fourteen dead enemy fighters and laid them out on the ground.

Later, the members of Bravo Company added two more names to Houck's sandbag flag, those of Corporal Kirk Bosselmann and Lance Corporal Josh Lucero. Corporal Dan Vela would now carry the sandbag flag inscribed with the fallen Marines of Bravo Company with him.

Berch's 2nd Platoon continued its clearing operation but with one major difference, the tanks were now accompanying them. While the platoon entered houses in their sector, Basher, flying above the city, located enemy movement to their south going to a large structure. Basher quickly targeted and destroyed the building.

Lieutenant Mark Mendez, Executive Officer of the company, along with two AAVs, pushed down an alleyway to collect enemy weapons and ordnance. Several of the dead insurgents were still lying about in the rubble. The Marines noticed that one of the insurgents was still moving. They quickly checked out the bodies and found that three of the insurgents were pretending to be dead. Mendez apprehended them, and the captured insurgents joined others at Charlie Company's firm base for exploitation and interrogation.

Amtracker, Lance Corporal Jonathan Olexa remembered his time in Fallujah. "We hardly ever left our vehicles. I wore the same socks, shirt and drawers for three weeks," Olexa said.

Sergeant Gianforte recalled, "FiST had about thirty to thirty-five calls to use artillery, firing about 1,000 to 1,200 rounds in support of Bravo Company in Fallujah. The entire battalion only used 1,300 to 1,500 rounds of artillery. We exploited artillery to our advantage in the fight for the city."

Tanks and Wolverine 2 (Weapons Company) launched an attack north to south along sector 850 in order to finish off the remainder of the insurgent forces in the area. They received reports of movement in a schoolhouse and brought it under intense fire, quickly destroying the structure.

"We could tell when there were dead insurgents in the houses just by the smell. In Fallujah I considered that our Marines (Weapons Platoon) were the right hand punch for the infantry. When they came under real trouble we came in with the big guns," remembers Staff Sergeant Richard Choquette, Weapons Platoon.

Marines fighting in Fallujah would always remember the smell of human waste, which became part of the fabric of the rotting city. In some areas, sewers drained right out onto the street, walks or yards of the houses. The residents burned everything and there was always a sickly smoke smell hovering over the city.

At 1900, the executive officer, Mendez and Gunnery Sergeant Ekholm moved to the company's firm base to re-supply the company for the next day's clearing operations.

Over the next few days the Marines patrolled repetitively on foot through the almost deserted city. On patrol all they would hear were the sound of their boots softly crunching on sand and the debris still lying in the streets. Occasionally the Marines would hear a plane or chopper flying above them. A hungry dog would sometimes attach itself to the Marines as they cautiously moved along. The Marines favorite tactic of jokes and pranks on one another sometimes relieved the tedium of the continuous foot patrols in Fallujah.

Captain Omohundro explained, "I remember one house we were in where the interior walls had been damaged from the effects of war. I took a moment to look around and then I started laughing. The men around me thought their CO had lost his mind. I explained to them that some people at home would pay my wife a lot of money to have her create this distressed look on their walls when all they really needed were Marines with M16s, SAWs and grenades to do the job."

Corporal Brad Watson's sniper team, which accounted for over 40 confirmed enemy kills in Fallujah, got caught up in their own private war with the enemy snipers. Sniper Corporal James Mendenhall said, "One day we were on a second floor rooftop and we were taking fire from two or three of the enemy located on the first floor of an adjacent house. Corporal Watson said, 'I'm going to throw a grenade through that window.' This window was small and had iron bars crisscrossing on it. I laughed and said, 'No way you can get a grenade in that small opening.' He threw the frag anyway and it went right through the bars and into the house. I said, 'Holy shit!' And just as I said that it went off. It was just like in the Hollywood movies." Watson and Mendenhall looked at one another after the success with the grenade and then did a high five.

"The Marines of 2nd Platoon we're like my brothers in Fallujah, a second family," Watson remembers. "Captain Pretus was the best officer we could have had for the job we had to do. He cared deeply about his unit."

When Battalion 1/8 left the City of Fallujah on December 8, 2004, Second Lieutenant Andrew Eckert had only thirty of his original forty-six men.

Captain Omohundro's Bravo Company had paid a stiff price in the city, twenty-nine wounded and ten killed from the company and three KIA's from Marines attached to them, in the action. "My Marines were true warriors. They remained focused on the mission during our time in Fallujah," Captain Omohundro stated.

Fallujah's End Game

According to estimates, two thousand Iraqi insurgents and foreign fighters were killed in the battle for Fallujah. Hundreds more were wounded in the bitter fighting, and hundreds of others were captured. The headquarters, base-operating areas, storehouses, weapon caches, ammunition dumps and bomb factories that had fed the insurgency in Iraq, were seized by the Marines and Soldiers. More importantly than the casualties and weapon caches, the Marines and Soldiers triumphed over the dire predictions of urban warfare for American forces.

The cost in American lives, while heart-rending, was far less than the media had predicted in the taking of the urban city. The insurgents had had months to prepare for the coming battle. The Pentagon reported that seventy-one American Marines and Soldiers were killed in the fight for Fallujah, and approximately 450 were wounded. Sixteen Marines of Battalion 1/8 had lost their lives and one attached Marine. Some 198 were casualties in the fierce battle. Eleven of those killed in action suffered gunshot wounds, and five died from shrapnel. Sixty-percent of those that were wounded returned to duty shortly after the battle. Of the total casualties suffered in Battalion 1/8, seventy-three were grenade and shrapnel wounds, and forty-five were from gunshots. Eighty of the Marines suffered an assortment of non-hostile wounds such as heat stroke, sprained ankles and other injuries.

Fallujah had been the biggest urban battle since the Marines took Hue City from the Viet Cong and North Vietnamese forces during the Tet Offensive in 1968. The battle for Hue took an entire month and cost the lives of almost five hundred American and South Vietnamese troops. Fallujah had been taken in a third of the time and at less than one-fifth the casualties.

What the American forces found in Fallujah proved that it had been a legitimate military target. Weapons found in Fallujah could arm a battalion or two of insurgents. They discovered 1,000 anti-tank and anti-personnel mines, 800 mortar rounds, hundreds of grenades, 86 anti-tank guided missiles, 6,000 artillery and mortar fuses, 87 122mm and 107mm rockets, 328 rounds for recoilless artillery pieces, and uncounted numbers of Kalashnikov automatic rifles and other assorted arms.

Al Zarqawi and the rest of his insurgency leadership had escaped before the fighting had begun. Upwards of 3,000 of his fighters had remained behind to fight to the death in a city that a Marine from Bravo Company, Battalion 1/8, was overheard to remark, "Fallujah may not have been Hell, but it was in the same Zip Code."

The Marines and Army had broken the back of the insurgency within Fallujah, but would the coalition be able to keep control of the city?

At the conclusion of the Battle for Fallujah, Lieutenant Colonel Gary Brandl sent this e-mail to his wife, Mona Rae, who forwarded it on to the family members of Battalion 1/8. He also issued copies to his company commanders to be posted and read to the members of the battalion:

> "The senior leadership says that Battalion 1/8 (Task Force Hunter) will go down in the history books for our contribution to the battle fought in Fallujah. I don't dwell on that, there is still a lot to do. I made a comment to one reporter that **uncommon valor is still a common virtue in our Corps**. I don't think it ever made the press but I'm firmly convinced of it. I saw enough acts of valor, bravery, and guts to last a couple of lifetimes, and it has had a profound impact on all who were there.
>
> We cut into and crushed the heart of the enemy defense of the city and destroyed a lot of them in the process. By my conservative estimate Battalion 1/8 killed over 600 evil die-hards, out of an estimated 2000+ (we left some for the other battalions.) It was tough, close up urban fight, at times 360 degrees, against fanatical Jihads, many of them foreign fighters with a one way ticket to Allah.

We are still uncovering and destroying huge stockpiles of weapons and ammunition as well as hunting down pockets of resistance and preparing for the civil affairs effort that will rebuild the city. I said that Satan has a face and it's in Fallujah – we found torture chambers, chemical labs and terrorist training facilities. This operation (Phantom Fury) had to take place. Fallujah was the recruiting, training and resource center for terrorism and insurgency throughout Iraq and beyond. Our Marines and Sailors took part in a very noble endeavor in which they can forever take pride. They directly contributed to a safer world and carved out a piece of history in the process.

I'm grateful that our battalion was given the opportunity to contribute. I mourn for our fallen brothers and their families. And am humbled to be in the company of such brave men."

Aftermath

When Sergeant Major Anthony Hope, a white Marine from Alabama, returned home from Iraq, he felt he had to go see black Marine Lance Corporal Demarkus Brown's mother who lived in Virginia near the North Carolina border. He felt he had to pay his respects to the Marine who always had a smile on his face. "I took leave and was going to Alabama but first I wanted to stop and see Brown's mother. On a Sunday I arrived at around 1000 in the morning and went to the address I had. There was no one there. I asked a neighbor and she took me to the church to meet Brown's mom. The neighbor went in to bring his mom out and when we saw each other I couldn't open my mouth for five minutes. I was crying like a two-year-old."

A memorial fund has been established for Lance Corporal Demarkus D. Brown. This fund is used to help a church member with college expenses. As Mark's mother, Chynita Belcher, puts it, "I would love to let the world know that Mark's memory lives on in another young person." Divine Faith Holiness Church, P.O. Box 3024, Martinsville, VA 24115, Attention: Elder Marshall Wells, Jr.

Lieutenant Colonel Brandl said, "I was blessed to lead Battalion 1/8 in Fallujah." In June 2005, Colonel Gareth Brandl was reassigned to Joint Forces Command located in Norfolk, Virginia.

Captain Theodore C. Bethea II, returned to the states from Iraq, and in September, after Hurricane Katrina hit the Gulf Coast, he went with Battalion 1/8 to the Gulf Coast to help in the recovery. He eventually made it into New Orleans and viewed the destruction of his beloved city. Both his parents and his grandmother's homes were unlivable. He said he witnessed more destruction in New Orleans than he had in Fallujah.

While helping out in the Gulf Coast, Corporal Robert Day, Alpha Company suggested a detour to the home of one of their fallen, Lance Corporal Bradley Faircloth's home in Mobile, Alabama. Eight Marines from 1/8 were given thirty hours to go and assist Kathleen Faircloth, Bradley's mother, in repairing damage suffered during the storm. The Marines repaired the roof, the shutters and did yard work. "I may have lost a son, but I gained a brotherhood," Kathleen Faircloth said. "I have children all over the country. The Marine Corps really is a family." Brad's wish was carried out in April 2006 when Murphy High School's Panther statue was erected on campus.

Captain Omohundro fought with his company through Fallujah without receiving a scratch, only to return home to Jacksonville, North Carolina where he had a motorcycle accident, which broke his leg in several places. He later wrote, "For those of us that were there, only we can comprehend the ravages of war."

First Lieutenant Dan Malcom was presented with a Presidential Citation and the Bronze Star Medal (with combat distinguishing device) posthumously on November 22, 2005. His sister Dana Killebrew accepted the awards. Dan Malcom was buried in Arlington National Cemetery. A Marine Officer's sword and a scholarship have been endowed through The Citadel Foundation in Malcom's memory. First Lieutenant Malcom was a 2001Graduate of The Citadel, The Military College of South Carolina.

Lance Corporal Carmine Castelli was scheduled to receive a medical discharge from the Marines due to the severe leg wound he suffered in Fallujah and planned to return to his hometown of Brooklyn, New York.

The Marine his staff sergeant called an RPG magnate, Corporal Rob Sarka, received the Navy-Marine Corps Achievement Medal with a Combat "V" and a Purple Heart for his wound from the exploding RPG round in Fallujah. Like other Marines, after leaving the city, he would immediately call his family to inform them he was all right.

Corporal Jacob Knospler would not get to meet his newborn daughter until December 21, 2004. He also met President Bush while convalescing in Bethesda Naval Hospital and received the Purple Heart from the Commander-in-Chief himself. Upon his return home, the married Marine was made a sergeant. He underwent countless operations to repair the damage from that exploding grenade.

Captain Aaron Cunningham was made a major on his return to Camp Lejeune in North Carolina.

Each May the family of Sergeant Richard Lord is invited to come to their local courthouse in Florida to participate in the Memorial Day program that honors fallen veterans from their area. A monument on the court house lawn bears Ricky's name.

The family of Corporal Todd Godwin remembers that Todd brought fun and laughter wherever he went. Perhaps this is one of the reasons a Marine friend of Todd's, Corporal Benjamin Czap wrote to the family and told them:

> *Todd was the light and life of his family and friends...The Battalions' deployment to Iraq in 2004 was VERY difficult. We lost so many GREAT MEN. There is not a day that goes by that I don't see all their faces and hear all of their voices. We were a brethren, we had love for each other that is of non-comparison. When Todd was taken, it changed us. It made us live EVERY second, stop and breathe every breath.*

The Corporal Todd Godwin Memorial Fund furthers the cause of the Christian Gospel at home and abroad and also assists in getting the hope of the Gospel to our troops. Corporal Todd Godwin Memorial Fund, c/o Newark Bible Church, 35 Gainor Avenue, Newark, OH 43055.

Lance Corporal Joshua Lucero received the Combat Distinguishing Device posthumously for his heroic actions in Fallujah. Michael and Tina, parents of Lance Corporal Joshua Lucero, have five other children. Antoinette serves with the Marines. Her twin brother Anthony serves with the Army, Jasmine is in college and plans to become a doctor so she can work with injured veterans, Samuel and Robert are both high school students and will enter Marine boot camp upon their graduation. Parents, Michael and Tina, are very active with Support the Troops rallies and other efforts to make sure U.S. military men and women know that American citizens love and support them.

Lance Corporal Jeffery Walker, who wanted to become a Marine officer and had been turned down twice in his attempt to enter Annapolis, was admitted to the academy in February 2005.

Gunnery Sergeant Ryan P. Shane received the Bronze Star Medal for bravery displayed during the fighting near the Cultural Center in Fallujah.

On January 19, 2007, Sergeant Aubrey McDade received the Navy Cross for his actions in rescuing several wounded Marines in an alley in Fallujah.

Captain Mike Pretus returned home and continues to stay in contact with the men in his sniper unit. On his desk he keeps pictures of three of his fallen men, Corporal Todd Godwin, Corporal Nick Ziolkowski, and Corporal Kirk Bosselmann.

Two scholarship funds have been established to honor Corporal Nicholas Ziolkowski. The Nicholas Ziolkowski Scholarship that aids people coming out of the military and going back to school at Towson University. The Nicholas Ziolkowski Scholarship, c/o Towson University Foundation, Towson University, 8000 York Road, Towson, MD 21252 and The Boys' Latin School of Maryland, 822 W. Lake Ave., Baltimore, MD 21210.

The Women's Auxiliary of the Veterans of Foreign Wars in Belington, WV has set up a memorial fund in honor of Sergeant Romulo J. Jimenez. Contributions can be sent to the R. J. Jimenez Memorial Fund, Freedom Bank, Belington, WV 26250. Contributions are used to support the local Toys for Tots Program. The Barbour County Commission has named a portion of a West Virginia highway, U.S. Route 250 from the Barbour/Randolph county line to the intersection West Virginia State Route 92 in Belington, West Virginia as the "Sgt. R. J. Jimenez Highway. A monument honoring Sergeant Romulo J. Jimenez has been placed outside Talbott's Funeral Home in Belington, WV. The monument is dedicated to all veterans and was placed in memory of Sergeant Jimenez. His family later received notice that he was granted promotion to Sergeant, effective November 10, 2004, the day he died.

Corporal Gentian Marku was born in Priaj, Albania. His family took his body back to his homeland where he rests among his ancestors. A school that he attended, and a street, both in Piraj, have been named in his honor. Corporal Marku was named a National Martyr of Albania and received the Golden Eagle, a very significant honor that assures he will be remembered as a part of Albanian history. Members of the Albanian Army and the United States Marine Corps escorted Corporal Marku's casket as he returned to his homeland.

On a warm sunny day in April 2005, back on Camp Lejeune, Chaplain Denis Cox was working at his desk in his office when he heard a knock on the door. When Cox turned around he saw Lance Corporal David Landgrebe standing in the doorway on crutches and a broad smile on his face. Landgrebe said, "I'm fulfilling my vow sir." Cox jumped up and hugged the lance corporal that had indeed fulfilled his promise to him.

On March 4, 2006, Lance Corporal David Houck's parents, Bob and Beth Houck, from Millbridge, North Carolina, received the Navy Commendation Medal with a Combat "V" device for valor posthumously that their son had earned for rescuing several Marines on November 25, 2004. David was buried in section 60 of Arlington National Cemetery in the same row as other fallen heroes from 1st Battalion 8th Marines – Dimitrios Gavriel, Nicholas Ziolkowski and Daniel Malcom. In lieu of flowers, the Houck family requested that all memorial gifts be given to his former church youth group in Salisbury, North Carolina. Instead of using the gifts for themselves, the teens of the youth group opted to give the entire amount to a missionary family working with displaced Iraqis and their children living in Jordan. Following is the letter of thanks they received:

> Oct. 1, 2005
> Dear Houck Family,
> On behalf of the Iraqi Grace School in Amman, Jordan, we want to send our deep thanks for the generous gift given in your son's memory. We share your sorrow in this great loss. But what a precious way to honor his life –by sharing the Word of Life with others who have not had it in their hands before! May it comfort you to know that his memory is touching the lives of Iraqi children in Jordan. The school serves refugee children who cannot go to public school here. We have over 350 children in the school this year. Most are from non-Christian backgrounds. Many have seen or experienced traumatic situations in Iraq – family members killed or kidnapped, being kidnapped themselves, living through war, etc. We desire to give them hope and healing through showing Christ's love.
> We have a daily Bible class for all ages. With your gift, we have purchased 150 Arabic bibles which will be used by the older students. They will use them in Bible class, and then be able to keep them as their personal copy. The remainder of your gift will be used to turn a newly rented workshop into more classroom space so we can allow more Iraqi children in Jordan to go to school.
> Please e-mail a photo of your son. We plan to share with the students how these Bibles came into their hands – because someone gave his life for them and their country. We think it will also be a great bridge to

compare to the One who gave His life for their eternal well-being.
Thank you again, and may the God of all Comfort give you His comfort in these days.

Corporal Dan Vela, Bravo Company would carry Houck's sandbag memorial flag that honored the fallen from the company, home with him.

On March 4, 2006, Lance Corporal Bradley Parker's mother, Carla, met with President Bush at his request in Wheeling, West Virginia. Friends and family said Parker would be remembered for his infectious smile through good times and bad.

Lance Corporal Cesar Machado-Olmos and his family moved to the United States from Mexico when Cesar was a child. He received his U.S. citizenship posthumously.

Lance Corporal Michael Halal had planned to pursue a career in law enforcement.

On January 12, 2007, Elliott Ackerman, then a First Lieutenant in Alpha Company, was awarded the Silver Star for his actions in Fallujah. The citation read, his actions took him through a "gauntlet of deadly enemy fire."

Marines don't forget their fallen comrades. When Corporal Jeremy LaForce returned home from Iraq, he and his wife agreed to name their first son after his point man and good friend, David Houck. He would be called David Hawk LaForce.

Corporal Anthony Silva and his wife have added a third child to their family. They named their son Mark, in honor and remembrance of Tony's good friend Corporal Gentian Marku.

The funeral for Lance Corporal William Miller took place on his 23rd birthday, November 24, 2004. The Texas State Senate passed a resolution, no. 354, in memory of William Lewis Miller on February 28, 2007. Memorials in honor and memory of Lance Corporal William L. Miller can be sent to: Injured Marine Semper Fi Fund, 825 College Blvd, Suite 102, PMB 609, Oceanside, CA 92057.

Staff Sergeant Jose Torres and his wife welcomed a new son into their family on June 28, 2006. Their son's name is Romulo Jose-Jimenez Torres. Their child is of course named in honor of Jose's good friend, Romulo J. Jimenez, whose birth date was June 28, 1983.

Upon returning to Lejeune, Corporal Jason Huyghe named his newborn son Nathan in honor of his good friend Corporal Nathan Anderson who died in the fighting in Fallujah. Included among the honors and memorials given for Corporal Nathan R. Anderson were some very special gifts from the children of the East Knox Elementary

School in Blandensburg, Ohio. The children planted a tree in Nate's honor and placed books in their school library given in memory of Nate.

The state of Vermont named a bridge in West Hartford, Vermont the Patriot's Bridge in honor of three of their fallen sons, Tom Stone, Bryon Lane and 1/8's Jeffery Holmes. The Jeffery Scott Holmes Memorial Fund has been established at Hartford High School. A graduating senior who most resembles Jeff in character receives an engraved plaque and a monetary award: "To recognize a senior male or female furthering his/her education, not necessarily at the top of his/her class, who demonstrated good work ethics, a sense of humor, dedication to his/her duties and responsibilities, and who is honest, friendly, and has compassion for others." Every year every senior entering the military also receives an engraved plaque and a monetary award. Anyone wishing to contribute can mail a check to Mascoma Savings Bank, Attn: Suzanne Berry, P.O. Box 1274, White River Junction, Vermont 05001.

Lance Corporal Jonathan Olexa, amtracker who fought along side the Marines of 1/8, returned home with his father's U.S. flag that had gone into battle with him in Fallujah. In January 2007 he left the Marines and decided to enter college to become a teacher of history. He wears a KIA bracelet remembering his former grenade course instructor Sergeant Lonny D. Wells.

Sergeant Lonny D. Wells' brother and his wife became new parents on November 15, 2006. Larry Wells, Jr. and his wife named their new son DyLonn Ryan Shane Wells. DyLonn honors his late uncle, Lonny D. and Ryan Shane honors Gunnery Sergeant Ryan Shane who sacrificed so much in his efforts to save the life of his friend, Sergeant Lonny D. Wells. Sergeant Wells' mother Yvonne Lynn wishes to share this message: *"Gunny Shane is one of the many Marine heroes we have, we thank them all for being there for my son and doing what Marines do – they leave no one behind. Thank you all and Semper Fi."*

In November 2006, Staff Sergeant Richard Pillsbury received the Silver Star for his gallant actions in leading a platoon in Fallujah.

In the summer of 2006, Christina Gavriel, the sister of Lance Corporal Dimitrios Gavriel, who lost his life in Fallujah, joined the Marine Corps. Scholarship funds have been established to honor the memory of Lance Corporal Dimitrios Gavriel. Brown University, Gift Accounting and Biographical Records, Box 1908, Providence, RI 02912 and Timberlane Regional High School, 36 Greenough Road, Plaistown, NH 03865.

The Lance Corporal Travis R. Desiato Memorial Scholarship, Bedford High School, Bedford, Massachusetts is awarded to a college freshman each year. This scholarship is privately funded. Bedford High School also provides a football non-monetary award in Travis' honor and name to the player who exhibits leadership, academic excellence and team play.

LCDR Rich Jadick returned to his family in South Carolina. In January 2006 he received the Bronze Star with a Combat "V" for Valor for saving wounded Marines lives while under direct enemy fire in the streets of Fallujah. He would write a book on his experiences in Fallujah, *On Call in Hell, A Doctor's Iraq War Story.*

Corporal Jonathan Brown had 17 surgeries in only an eight month period on his shredded arm.

Hospital Corpsman Luis Ruizpupo received the Navy and Marine Corps Commendation Medal with Combat Distinguishing Device on June 21, 2006.

Sergeant Eubaldo Lovato received the Bronze Star.

Corporal Timothy Conners received the Silver Star.

Staff Sergeant Robert C. McMillen received the Bronze Star with Combat "V."

Staff Sergeant Dennis Nash received the Bronze Star with Combat "V."

Gunnery Sergeant John E. Collins received the Navy and Marine Corps Commendation with Combat "V."

Gunny Sergeant Gordon R. Hill Jr., Platoon Sergeant of the Mobile Assault Platoon, Weapons Company, received the Bronze Star with Combat "V."

Lance Corporal Blake Benson, engineer, received the Bronze Star with Combat "V."

Staff Sergeant Stephen J. Davis would receive the Silver Star for his decisive and bold action in helping to save PFC Paul Volpe's life in the deadly streets of Fallujah.

The Marine Davis helped save, PFC Paul Volpe, met the president on a visit to Bethesda Naval Hospital.

The Indian Prairie Educational Foundation in Illinois now presents the "Sergeant David Mitchell Caruso USMC Freedom Award" scholarship to one graduating senior from the Waubonsie Valley or Neuqua Valley High Schools on an annual basis. The recipient of this scholarship is judged by his or her characteristics that most resemble David's Leadership Qualities; Service to Community; Drive for Achievement. They also submit an essay entitled, What Freedom Means to Me. "David M. Caruso Memorial Park: A park in our neighborhood, has been dedicated to David at the request of our Homeowners Association. A sign was installed by the township and a bench was built by the Cub Scouts (the same Cub Scout pack to which David belonged as a child). Landscape designs have been donated and discussion is currently underway for landscaping to begin in the spring. Bridge Dedication: The bridge that David built as his Eagle Scout project has been dedicated to him by the Forest Preserve District of DuPage County. Also, the trail on which the bridge is built has been named the Caruso Trail. This trail is used on school field trips to help children learn to identify trees and leaves. A man whose brother served as a Marine in Vietnam also created a scholarship in Dave's memory. The scholarship benefits St. Agnes of Bohemia, a Catholic elementary school in the inner city Chicago. A plaque in Dave's memory was placed at the flagpole of Dave's elementary school. Memorial bricks have been place in a park in downtown Naperville for all the servicemen who have been killed from our city. At this time we have lost six servicemen. Work in progress - A memorial and web site is being created for ALL servicemen and women from Naperville who have served in the military. This is to cover the time period from the time Naperville first began, 175 years ago," wrote Joe and Gloria Caruso.

On March 4, 2005 the battalion held a memorial service on Camp Lejeune's Field House organized by Chaplain Denis Cox who had been sent back early to plan the event. There were over 1,500 people in attendance. Every next of kin family attended except for two.

Kirk Bosselmann's mother, Beverley, kept her promise to her son. The family spread Kirk's ashes on his beloved island in the Potomac and on nearby Sugarloaf Mountain. "Our home has a lovely view of that little mountain so whenever I look at it, Kirk is with me. An unconditional love for one another is a trait that is common to all those who shared Kirk's fate. They are an extraordinary breed of men and we are all blessed to have had them in our lives. They leave us, who remain behind, with an outstanding example of the integrity of the human spirit," Beverley Bosselmann said. "In our sorrow and grief our family wanted to honor, and say thank you, to the valiant men and women who have committed to serve this country. A friend suggested that Kyla (Kirk's sister) and I run the Marine Corps Marathon, a fitting tribute to our Kirk. In conversations with friends, we spoke of Kirk's devotion to helping others and many began to express their desire to join us in honoring his memory. With a common goal to raise funds for the families of those Marines who did not come home, a team was formed to complete the 26.2 miles of the Marine Corps Marathon on October 30, 2005. All twenty-one members of "Team Kirk" running for the families of fallen heroes completed the marathon raising donations for the Navy-Marine Corps Relief Fund in excess of $35,000. Donations to the Navy-Marine Corps Relief Society can be sent to 875 North Randolph Street, Suite 225, Arlington, VA 22203-1977.

In mid July 2006, Battalion 1/8, as a part of 24th MEU, was called on again to return to Beirut, Lebanon. This time to help in the evacuation of Americans from that war torn country. Twenty-four years had passed since 1/8 had been in Beirut.

Three Marines who were part of the Fallujah fighting have died since returning home. Corporal Gary A. Koehler lost his life during the 1/8 deployment in 2006. He was killed by an IED in Haditha, Iraq, November 1, 2006. He was from Ypsilanti, Michigan. Lance Corporal Joseph A. Naranjo, who fought with 1/8 in Fallujah, lost his life in an automobile accident outside Camp Lejeune in 2005. He was 21 and hailed from New Jersey. One of the fine young Marines I interviewed for this book, Lance Corporal James Thomas Bullen, accidentally drowned while swimming off North Topsail Beach, North Carolina in May 2007.

The Marine Corps has a way of stirring the pot when units return from operations overseas. Some of the Marines I talked to and about, have left the Corps for a variety of reasons including combat related injuries, while others have been transferred to other units. Wherever they are, the Marines who fought in Fallujah have a bond. They won't ever forget those that fell in Fallujah. Many will never see one another again, but they will always have that bond. Nothing can ever take away the bond they have with their fellow Marines because they fought in *Fallujah, With Honor*.

Sources

Newspapers and Internet:
BBC News
Global Security.Org
SFGate.com
Talkingproud.us
The New York Times

Personal Interviews and accounts:
Second Lieutenant Elliot Ackerman
Staff Sergeant Ben Alicea
HA Ernesto Argueta
Captain Theodore C. Bethea II
Lieutenant Colonel Gareth Brandl
Lance Corporal Andrew Braunschweig
Corporal Jonathan Brown
Lance Corporal James Thomas Bullen
Lance Corporal Joshua Bush
Lance Corporal Daniel C. Bystricky
Lance Corporal Mark Cabang
PFC Ross Caputi
Staff Sergeant Richard W. Choquette III
Lance Corporal Jason R. Carpenter
Lance Corporal Carmine Castelli
Corporal Nick Criddle
Navy Lieutenant Denis Cox
Captain Aaron M. Cunningham
Lance Corporal Brett Dayton
Lance Corporal Dante Di Pasqua
Lance Corporal Keith Dyment
Second Lieutenant Andrew Eckert
Corporal Michael Ergo
Lance Corporal Matthew Forester
Lance Corporal Xavier Forester

Sergeant Robert Edward Frederick
Lance Corporal Agustin Garcia
Sergeant Shawn Gianforte
Lance Corporal Dominick Vincent Giusti
Lance Corporal David C. Graham
Lance Corporal Scott B. Green
Lance Corporal Jacob Hassell
Sergeant Allen Hayden
Lance Corporal Thomas Hodges
Sergeant Major Anthony R. Hope
Second Lieutenant Ryan Hunt
Captain Jacob A. Jenkins
HM2 Shawn J. Johns
PFC Michael Johnson
HM3 Milton L. Jones, Jr.
Captain Stephen P. Kahn
First Lieutenant David L. Klingensmith
Corporal Jacob Knospler
Lance Corporal Brian M. Koskey
Second Lieutenant Jeffery T. Lee
Lance Corporal Christopher Dale Lett
Lance Corporal Adam Alan Lew
Lance Corporal Andres Llerena
Staff Sergeant Corey J. Lohr
Lance Corporal Edwin R. Maldonado
Corporal Kyle Mastropasqua
Lance Corporal Drew Martin
Lance Corporal Benny Mathew
Lance Corporal James Maxey
Lance Corporal Zachary McWilliams
Corporal James Mendenhall
Captain Christopher V. Meyers
Sergeant John Megahan
Lance Corporal Sven T. Mozdiez
Corporal James Mulak
Lance Corporal Danny Myers
Lance Corporal Greg F. Nichols
Lance Corporal David A. Ojeda
Lance Corporal Jonathan William Olexa
Captain Read M. Omohundro
Lance Corporal Stephen Ross O'Rourke
Lance Corporal Rafael A. Peguero

Lance Corporal Michael Rodriguez
Lance Corporal Chandraka Roopnarine
Lance Corporal Chad Ryan Patterson
Captain Mike Pretus
Corporal Robert Sarka
Staff Sergeant Ricardo Sebastian
Staff Sergeant Christopher Shaw
Corporal Anthony Silva III
Sergeant Kelley Starling
Lance Corporal Steven J. St.Clair, Jr.
First Lieutenant Paul W. Steketee
Sergeant Dustin Stout
Sergeant Daniel Stoy
Lance Corporal Joshua Thompson
Lance Corporal Thomas James Tribou
Second Lieutenant Brandon Hal Turner
PFC Paul J. Volpe
Lance Corporal Benjamin Voorhees
Lance Corporal Jeffery Walker
Corporal Brad Watson
Sergeant Samuel Williams
Lance Corporal Chris Willson
Major Mark Winn
Lance Corporal Craig R. Wintrow

Written Accounts, Diaries and Journals:
After battle statement from Lt Col Brandl
Bravo and Charlie Company's after battle reports
Personal letter from SSgt Corey Lohr to his wife
Alpha Company Award Citations
Alpha Company and Bravo Company rosters and Award Citations
Letters of the deceased Marines and accounts from family members
Letters to the Houck family from First Lieutenant Chris Wilkens